Books by Nick Lyons

FISHERMAN'S BOUNTY (ed.)

THE SEASONABLE ANGLER

JONES VERY: SELECTED POEMS (ed.)

FISHING WIDOWS

LOCKED JAWS

BRIGHT RIVERS

THE SONY VISION

TROUT RIVER (text to photographs by Larry Madison)

FISHERMAN'S BOUNTY

A TREASURY OF FASCINATING LORE
AND THE FINEST STORIES
FROM THE WORLD OF ANGLING

EDITED BY

NICK LYONS

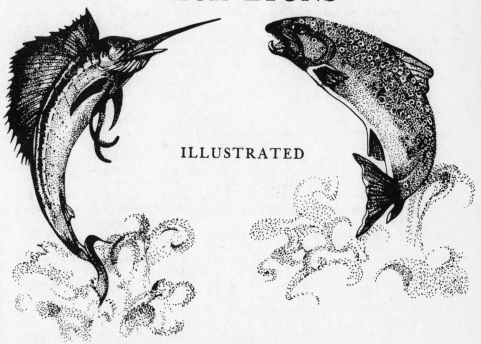

ILLUSTRATED

A FIRESIDE BOOK
PUBLISHED BY SIMON & SCHUSTER INC.
NEW YORK   LONDON   TORONTO   SYDNEY   TOKYO

10   9   8   7   6   5   4   3   2   1 Pbk.

Library of Congress Cataloging in Publication Data

Fisherman's bounty.: a treasury of fascinating lore and the finest stories from the world of angling/
edited by Nick Lyons.—1st Fireside ed.
p.   cm.
"A Fireside Book."
Reprint. Originally published: New York: Crown, c1970.
Includes index.
ISBN 0-671-65745-3 Pbk.
1. Fishing.   2. Fishing stories.   I. Lyons, Nick.
SH441.F499 1988   88-11371
810'.8'0355—dc19   CIP

ACKNOWLEDGMENTS

FOR HELPFUL SUGGESTIONS and other aid in the preparation of this anthology my warm thanks go to J. Michael Migel, Frank Mele, William Humphrey, George Goodspeed, and a grand legendary gentleman who with characteristic modesty has chosen to remain unnamed—but will not go unremembered.

For permission to reprint the following copyrighted material, I am grateful to the authors, their agents, and the publishers indicated:

"The River God" by Roland Pertwee. Copyright Roland Pertwee. Reproduced by permission of Curtis Brown Ltd, London.

"Memories of Michigan" by Ernest Schwiebert. Copyright © 1970 by Ernest Schwiebert. Used by permission of the author from his book *Remembrances of Rivers Past*.

"When All the World Is Young" by Howard T. Walden 2d. From *Big Stony*, copyright 1940, © 1968 by Howard T. Walden 2d. Reprinted by permission of the estate of Howard T. Walden 2d.

"One of the Schultz Boys Fishing" by Millen Brand. Copyright © 1970 by Millen Brand. From *Local Lives*, Clarkson N. Potter, Inc. Used by permission of Crown Publishers, Inc.

"Dame Juliana Berners" and "Theodore Gordon" by John McDonald. Copyright © 1965 by John McDonald. Reprinted by permission of Harold Matson Co., Inc. Originally appeared in *McClane's Standard Fishing Encyclopedia*.

"The Selectivity of Trout" by Art Flick. From *Art Flick's New Streamside Guide to Naturals and Their Imitations*. Copyright © 1969 by Arthur B. Flick. Used by permission of Nick Lyons Books, Inc.

"The Hidden Hatch" by Vincent C. Marinaro. From *In the Ring of the Rise*. Copyright © 1974 by Vincent C. Marinaro. Used by permisison of Nick Lyons Books, Inc.

"The Carp" by Leslie P. Thompson. From *Fishing in New England* by Leslie P. Thompson. Copyright © 1955 by The Chiswick Press. Used by permission of Eyre & Spottiswoode, Ltd.

"Excalibur: The Steelhead" by Paul O'Neil. Reprinted courtesy of *Sports Illustrated* from the March 11, 1957 issue. Copyright © 1957 by Time Inc. All rights reserved.

"Salmon in Connemara and in Devon" by Arnold Gingrich. Copyright © 1965 by Arnold Gingrich.

Reprinted from *The Well-Tempered Angler* by Arnold Gingrich, by permission of Alfred A. Knopf, Inc.

"Marlin Off the Morro" by Ernest Hemingway. From *By-line: Ernest Hemingway*, edited by William White. Copyright 1933 Ernest Hemingway; copyright renewed © 1961 Mary Hemingway. Reprinted with the permission of Charles Scribner's Sons, an imprint of Macmillan Publishing Co.

"Mr. Theodore Castwell" by G. E. M. Skues. Copyright Seely Service & Co., Ltd. The material taken from *Sidelines, Sidelights, and Reflections* by G. E. M. Skues. Copyright 1947 by G. E.M. Skues. Used by permission of Penguin-Viking, London.

"The Culprit" by Anton Chekhov. From *The Portable Chekhov*, edited by Avrahm Yarmolinsky. Copyright 1947 by The Viking Press, Inc. Copyright © 1968 by The Viking Press, Inc. Copyright renewed © 1975 by Avrahm Yarmolinsky. All rights reserved. Reprinted by permisison of Viking Penguin Inc.

"Murder" by Sparse Grey Hackle. From *Fishless Days, Angling Nights*. Copyright © 1954 by Alfred W. Miller. Copyright renewed © 1971 by Alfred W. Miller. Used by permisison of Nick Lyons Books, Inc.

"A Wedding Gift" by John Taintor Foote. Copyright 1924 by D. Appleton and Company. Renewal © 1952 by Jessie Florence Foote. Used by permission of the estate of John Taintor Foote.

"Tomorrow's the Day" by Corey Ford. Reprinted from the April, 1952 issue of *Field and Stream* magazine by permission of Harold Ober Associates Incorporated. Copyright 1952 by Henry Holt & Company, Inc.

"Gourmet Salmon, Trout, and Bass" by Col. Henry A. Siegel. Copyright © 1970 by Col. Henry A. Siegel. Used by permission.

"Fishing's Just Luck" by Elmer Ransom. From *Fishing's Just Luck* by Elmer Ransom. Copyright © 1945 by Mrs. Elmer Ransom. Used by permission of Crown Publishers, Inc.

"The One-Eyed Poacher's Legal Salmon" by Edmund Ware Smith. Copyright © 1947 by Edmund Ware Smith. Used by permission of Crown Publishers, Inc.

"A Day's Fishing, 1948" by Ed Zern. Copyright © 1965 by Edward Zern. Reprinted by permission of the author.

"The Intruder" by Robert Traver. From *Trout Madness*. Copyright © 1960 by Robert Traver. Used by permission of Peregrine Smith Books.

"Once on a Sunday" by Philip Wylie. From *Fish and Tin Fish*. Reprinted by permission of Harold Ober Associates Incorporated. Copyright © 1943 by Philip Wylie.

"Striped Bass and Southern Solitude" by Ellington White. Reprinted from the October 10, 1966 issue of *Sports Illustrated*. Copyright © 1966 by Ellington White. Reprinted with permission of the author.

"Fish Are Such Liars!" by Roland Pertwee. Copyright Roland Pertwee. Reproduced by permission of Curtis Brown Ltd., London.

"Song of the Angler" by A. J. McClane. Copyright © 1967 by Holt, Rinehart & Winston Co. Reprinted from the October 1967 issue of *Field & Stream* magazine by permission of A. J. McClane.

"The Fish" by Elizabeth Bishop. From *The Complete Poems 1927–1979* by Elizabeth Bishop. Copyright 1940, copyright renewed © 1968 by Elizabeth Bishop. Reprinted by permission of Farrar, Straus & Giroux, Inc.

"The Fisherman" by W. B. Yeats. Reprinted with permission of Macmillan Publishing Company from *The Collected Poems of W. B. Yeats*. Copyright 1919 by Macmillan Publishing Company, renewed 1947 by Bertha Georgie Yeats.

"Blue Dun" by Frank Mele. Copyright © 1970 by Frank Mele. Used by permission of the author.

"To Know a River . . ." by Roderick L. Haig-Brown. From *A River Never Sleeps* by Roderick L. Haig-Brown. © 1944, 1946 by Roderick L. Haig-Brown. Copyright renewed © 1974 by Roderick L. Haig-Brown. Reprinted by permission of Nick Lyons Books, Inc.

*This edition is dedicated
to my friend
William Humphrey*

CONTENTS

3

A FIERCE AND GENTLE PASSION

4

A SEPARATE AND VARIED BREED

5
MORE THAN TO FISH

PREFACE TO THE 1988 EDITION

IT IS A GREAT PLEASURE for me to see *Fisherman's Bounty* reprinted nearly twenty years after I first compiled it. Rereading it, the excitement I felt when I first read many of the stories and articles has returned. Mike Migel introduced me to John Taintor Foote's delicious "A Wedding Gift" and Sparse Grey Hackle told me about Roland Pertwee's two stories, "The River God" and "Fish Are Such Liars," along with several others; I also remember the day Sparse told me I could use "Murder," and how happy I was to be able to include it. He was my "grand legendary gentleman" and would accept no public thanks then.

Since 1970, Sparse has died and so has my great fishing pal Mike, and so have Arnold Gingrich, Roderick Haig-Brown, Miller Brand, and Howard Walden, whom I admired so much both on the page and off.

One great disappointment when I first edited *Fisherman's Bounty* was the loss of William Humphrey's hilarious "The Spawning Run." Bill, an old and close friend and my former English teacher, had never written a story about fishing. I cajoled him into writing that one—the first of a small but remarkable group of sporting essays—and was pleased that *Esquire* wanted to publish it before I did. But the story won a flush of praise. Bill's editor at Knopf decided to publish it as a separate little book and tried to muscle me into postponing publication of my volume for a full season. This I wouldn't do—and perhaps the biggest fish got away.

I was tempted to include "The Spawning Run" in this edition but reluctantly decided not to do so for two reasons: first, it would have meant dropping one or more of the original selections, and, second, Bill's great story is currently in print in his fine treasury of sporting pieces, *Open Season*.

Since *Fisherman's Bounty* was published I've discovered four or five pieces I should have included; and a number of truly fine writers have come into their maturity and graced the literature of angling with some superb stories and essays. I'm delighted to see important writers of fiction and nonfiction taking the sport—especially the fly fishing end of it —so seriously; they will fill all the new anthologies, as they should.

As for me, this is the only one I intend to compile. It is limited and fallible, as all anthologies must be, but most of the selections still seem worthwhile and it still seems to me a full and rewarding treasury, representing a broad range of different perspectives from the diverse world of angling.

I hope new readers will agree.

NICK LYONS
JANUARY 1988

INTRODUCTION

THE WORLD OF ANGLING is richly diverse. Carp fishing with dough balls in the Charles River is no less within its realm than the pursuit of giant marlin off the Morro. Purists and one-eyed poachers, theorists and pragmatists, poets and even a brand of murderer find their way into its ranks. It elicits some of the sweetest and deepest qualities in man—and, occasionally, some of the worst. It can be coolly dispassionate, lyrical, or maddeningly intense. It can be filled with robust camaraderie, or the solitude of a lonely southern beach on a still evening when time is suspended and the only sounds are those of the waves and the gulls, and that of a scuttling line when a bull striper is on. It has also produced an impressive body of lore, poetry, and fiction that both implies and records its inherent values and diversity.

FISHERMAN'S BOUNTY is an attempt to gather together some of the finest writing about this world, in a variety of its modes and stances. Some, like Father Walton's *Compleat Angler* and the marvelously abrupt *Barker's Delight,* have entertained and instructed anglers for centuries. Others, like the encyclopedia entries on Dame Juliana Berners and Theodore Gordon—those two pivotal innovators in England and America—by the angling scholar John McDonald, show the persistence and importance of angling tradition; hopefully they will serve as introductions to Mr. McDonald's two important books, *The Origins of Angling* and his superb edition of Theodore Gordon's letters, *The Complete Fly Fisherman.*

"Angling is somewhat like poetry, men are to be born so," says Walton. Frank Mele suggests this in the opening passages of his delicate and elusive "Blue Dun"; it is implicit in R. D. Blackmore's "Crocker's Hole," often called the finest of angling stories, and in that master entomologist Ernest Schwiebert's quietly nostalgic account of his first trout, taken on grasshoppers on a Michigan stream. Roland Pertwee's "The River God" shows how a young angler's heroes will be towering fishermen; it is a superb story, and Pertwee, too long overlooked, more than warrants the two selections in this anthology. And angling somehow figures centrally in the early lives of such born anglers; Howard T. Walden 2d's warm and moving "When All the World Is Young" shows a boy on the brink of manhood: a day angling becomes the turning point.

The more one fishes, the more one learns how much incisive lore is required of the fisherman; the simple means of the young angler give way to the unending complexities of a mature sport as inexhaustible as "the Mathematics." Though this will vary radically for each different brand of angling, general evidence of the care, thoughtfulness, and patient observation required of the angler may be found in Art Flick's solid and sensible "The Selectivity of Trout" and Vincent C. Marinaro's detailed examination of how to fish, with the finest of tackle, for trout feeding on microscopic insects—the most delicate and demanding form of angling. No less knowledge of the feeding habits and life patterns of one's quarry is required of the big-game angler, as Ernest Hemingway shows in his "Marlin Off the Morro," and Charles Holder in his spritely piece on the early days (1903) of tuna fishing, "King of the Mackerel." "Excalibur: The Steelhead" by Paul O'Neil is an affectionate and full portrait of a great western game fish; and Arnold Gingrich brings sophistication, wit, and an intimate knowledge of tradition to his pursuit of salmon in Connemara and Devon. "The Carp" by Let Thompson raises the status of that lowly sport to that of the dry-fly purist; it's also marvelously funny.

Perhaps the most interesting phenomenon of angling is the notorious passion its practitioners bring to it. G. E. M. Skues saw the Hell that fishing can become in his remarkably Dantean "Mr. Theodore Castwell"; and the redoubtable Sparse Grey Hackle, whose few superb pieces will remain always among the very finest and most discerning angling memoirs, registers his sure knowledge of how, to the exclusion of all else, fishing can become mere escape, even mere murder. John Taintor Foote, in his delicious "A Wedding Gift," portrays one of the most extreme cases of such angling passion—though Andrew Lang's "The Lady or the Salmon" demonstrates that not only a wife but also one's life may be forfeited in the unbridled pursuit of salmon or trout.

Chekhov's "The Culprit" shows the extraordinary lengths to which a simple peasant-fisherman will go to fulfill his angling needs—even to taking the nuts from railroad-track bolts because they make the best sinkers: it is incomprehensible to him that the judge who incarcerates him cannot understand this. And De Maupassant's brilliant—if surely mordant—"A Fishing Excursion" is another classic study in the blissful abstractedness of anglers oblivious to their fate until they are summarily shot and fed to the fishes they had lately fished for, after which their own catch is neatly dispatched by the icy Prussians. It can be a tragic compulsion, indeed.

But angling literature is leavened by its perennial wit and often ribald humor. Corey Ford's rendering of the Opening-Day syndrome, Elmer Ransom's treatment of "luck," more antics by Edmund Ware Smith's one-eyed poacher, and Rudyard

Kipling's hilarious treatise "On Dry-Cow Fishing as a Fine Art" are the most obvious examples here of this type of writing. But the evidence, in fishing literature, is everywhere: for most fishermen delight in angling's attendant comedy.

Since anglers are perhaps a separate and varied breed, there will be unique and recurrent themes in the world of angling. One is that secret spot—that private pool or cove or jetty whose whereabouts the avid fisherman dreads he may uncover in a moment of giddiness or weakness or braggadocio. Robert Traver's fine story, "The Intruder," treats such a private pool with warmth and deep insight. Another classic theme is that of the passionate angler's relationship to members of his family: the irony in Henry van Dyke's "A Fatal Success" should be instructive. And angling skill often has other uses; the clergyman in Philip Wylie's "Once on a Sunday" has learned to turn his success with fish into a more successful role as a fisher of men. One splendidly knowledgeable and humorous story, "Fish Are Such Liars," shows angling from the fish's point of view; for myself, I have no doubt that rainbow trout are quite so sophisticated as Roland Pertwee fashions them. Ed Zern's gentle piece, "A Day's Fishing," may surprise some of the many ardent readers of his more baldly humorous stories; he is a man of many modes—a fierce conservationist and, here, a solitary angler attuned to the simplicity of a quiet stream and to the richness of a laconic old man's character.

Several distinguished poets and novelists, otherwise not anglers, have written a piece or two that crystallizes some aspect of angling, or qualities it evokes; they remind us, as is their province, of the very highest values. I can remember hearing for the first time, as a benediction by the poet Theodore Weiss over the largest brown trout I had then ever taken—a huge old soak with a mangled hook of a lower jaw—Elizabeth Bishop's moving poem "The Fish," with its haunting denouement:

> . . . until everything
> was rainbow, rainbow, rainbow!
> And I let the fish go.

I had not. And I had been perhaps too proud of my haul, and have only since learned to welcome her counterpoint and her impeccable eye for detail. Like Thoreau, she teaches us to see and to feel. I have heard their echoes a hundred times while fishing and they have enriched me. I have heard echoes from Melville's stark chapter in *Moby Dick,* too; one may well argue that "Stubb Kills a Whale" is not sportfishing and that whales are not even fish. Agreed. But in the indifferent corpse-making there is an image some fishermen might fruitfully study.

Like philosophy, angling also has the power to elevate. Yeats's sun-freckled angler "in grey Connemara clothes," rising "at dawn to cast his flies," is spiritually pure, "wise and simple" in his solitary and intent life—while everywhere there is a mindlessness afoot in the world, working its crude mischief:

> The witty man and his joke
> Aimed at the commonest ear,

>   The clever man who cries
>   The catch-cries of the clown,
>   The beating down of the wise
>   And great Art beaten down.

In Mele's "Blue Dun," angling is also a kind of balm and salvation, and the elusive and changing colors of that rare Blue Dun hackle contain mysteries that penetrate the heart.

I am moved by A. J. McClane's enduring passion for angling, which says something about the inexhaustibility of the sport as well as the fullness of the man; for he is of a new breed of fisherman: the expert, the professional, the man whose vocation is angling. His excellent technical work is well known; his excursions to the ends of the world, to fish for giant rainbows, sailfish, and the golden dorado are the envy of everyone who casts a line. He could have become cold and indifferent. Yet he can still say, in "Song of the Angler":

> The music of angling is more compelling to me than anything contrived in the greatest symphony hall. What could be more thrilling than the ghostly basso note of a channel buoy over a grumbling surf as the herring gulls screech at a school of stripers on a foggy summer morning? Or an organ chorus of red howler monkeys swinging over a jungle stream as the tarpon roll and splash in counterpoint? I have heard them all—the youthful voice of the little Beaverkill, the growling of the Colorado as it leaps from its den, the kettledrum pounding of the Rogue, the hiss of the Yellowstone's riffles, the sad sound of the Orinoco, as mournful as a G chord on a guitar.

And I have ended with that resonant ending from Roderick Haig-Brown's *A River Never Sleeps,* with its paean to the rewarding knowledge a river yields.

> I still don't know why I fish or why other men fish, except that we like it and it makes us think and feel. But I do know that if it were not for the strong, quick life of rivers, for their sparkle in the sunshine, for the cold grayness of them under rain and the feel of them about my legs as I set my feet hard down on rocks or sand or gravel, I should fish less often. A river is never quite silent; it can never, of its very nature, be quite still; it is never quite the same from one day to the next. It has its own life and its own beauty, and the creatures it nourishes are alive and beautiful also. Perhaps fishing is, for me, only an excuse to be near rivers.

Yes. Surely one of the richest bounties of angling is to grow deeply intimate with the inner life of the world of nature, and in so doing to come closer to your deepest self. In a world that increasingly threatens to urbanize us with its steel and concrete, to chisel us down with its cheap and gaudy gimmickry, I can only think that the fresh ponds and streams, shorelines and oceans—none of them inexhaustible—are still forces to make us more moral and human. Henry van Dyke spoke of the spare time and pastime that fishing provided as an integral part of "the good life: too often ignored by our fierce reformers and perverted by our frivolous amusement salesmen." Yes.

Another bounty, surely, is the congenial company one often meets while fishing. Some old favorites will not be here, and there are many more fine ones in the literature of angling, but I hope you will find and secure a few new life-long friends among this diverse company of anglers.

NICK LYONS

THE GREEN YEARS

"Angling is somewhat like poetry, men are to be born so . . ."
—IZAAK WALTON

THE RIVER GOD

Roland Pertwee

WHEN I WAS A LITTLE BOY I had a friend who was a colonel. He was not the kind of colonel you meet nowadays, who manages a motor showroom in the West End of London and wears crocodile shoes and a small mustache and who calls you "old man" and slaps your back, independent of the fact that you may have been no more than a private in the war. My colonel was of the older order that takes a third of a century and a lot of Indian sun and Madras curry in the making. A veteran of the Mutiny he was, and wore side whiskers to prove it. Once he came upon a number of Sepoys conspiring mischief in a byre with a barrel of gunpowder. So he put the butt of his cheroot into the barrel and presently they all went to hell. That was the kind of man he was in the way of business.

In the way of pleasure he was very different. In the way of pleasure he wore an old Norfolk coat that smelt of heather and brine, and which had no elbows to speak of. And he wore a Sherlock Holmesy kind of cap with a swarm of salmon flies upon it, that to my boyish fancy was more splendid than a crown. I cannot remember his legs, because they were nearly always under water, hidden in great canvas waders. But once he sent me a photograph of himself riding on a tricycle, so I expect he had some knickerbockers, too, which would have been that tight kind, with box cloth under the knees. Boys don't take much stock of clothes. His head occupied my imagination. A big, brave, white-haired head with cherry-red rugose cheeks and honest, laughing, puckered eyes, with gunpowder marks in their corners.

People at the little Welsh fishing inn where we met said he was a bore; but I knew him to be a god and shall prove it.

I was ten years old and his best friend.

He was seventy something and my hero.

Properly I should not have mentioned my hero so soon in this narrative. He belongs to a later epoch, but sometimes it is forgivable to start with a boast, and now that I have committed myself I lack the courage to call upon my colonel to fall back two paces to the rear, quick march, and wait until he is wanted.

The real beginning takes place, as I remember, somewhere in Hampshire on the Grayshott Road, among sandy banks, sentinel firs and plum-colored wastes of heather. Summer-holiday time it was, and I was among folks whose names have since vanished like lizards under the stones of forgetfulness. Perhaps it was a picnic walk; perhaps I carried a basket and was told not to swing it for fear of bursting its cargo of ginger beer. In those days ginger beer had big bulgy corks held down with a string. In a hot sun or under stress of too much agitation the string would break and the corks fly. Then there would be a merry foaming fountain and someone would get reproached.

One of our company had a fishing rod. He was a young man who, one day, was to be an uncle of mine. But that didn't concern me. What concerned me was the fishing rod and presently—perhaps because he felt he must keep in with the family—he let me carry it. To the fisherman born there is nothing so pro-voking of curiosity as a fishing rod in a case.

Surreptitiously I opened the flap, which contained a small grass spear in a wee pocket, and, pulling down the case a little, I admired the beauties of the cork butt, with its gun-metal ferrule and reel rings and the exquisite frail slenderness of the two top joints.

"It's got two top joints—two!" I exclaimed ecstatically.

"Of course," said he. "All good trout rods have two."

I marveled in silence at what seemed to me then a combination of extravagance and excellent precaution.

There must have been something inherently understanding and noble about that young man who would one day be my uncle, for, taking me by the arm, he sat me down on a tuft of heather and took the pieces of rod from the case and fitted them together. The rest of the company moved on and left me in Paradise.

It is thirty-five years ago since that moment and not one detail of it is forgotten. There sounds in my ears today as clearly as then, the faint, clear pop made by the little cork stoppers with their boxwood tops as they were withdrawn. I re-member how, before fitting the pieces together, he rubbed the ferrules against the side of his nose to prevent them sticking. I remember looking up the length of it through a tunnel of sneck rings to the eyelet at the end. Not until he had fixed a reel and passed a line through the rings did he put the lovely thing into my hand. So light it was, so firm, so persuasive; such a thing alive—a scepter. I could do no more than say "Oo!" and again, "Oo!"

"A thrill, ain't it?" said he.

I had no need to answer that. In my new-found rapture was only one sorrow—the knowledge that such happiness would not endure and that, all too soon, a blank and rodless future awaited me.

"They must be awfully—awfully 'spensive," I said.

"Couple of guineas," he replied offhandedly.

A couple of guineas! And we were poor folk and the future was more rodless than ever.

"Then I shall save and save and save," I said.

And my imagination started to add up twopence a week into guineas. Two hundred and forty pennies to the pound, multiplied by two—four hundred and eighty—and then another twenty-four pennies—five hundred and four. Why, it would take a lifetime, and no sweets, no elastic for catapults, no penny novelty boxes or air-gun bullets or ices or anything. Tragedy must have been writ large upon my face, for he said suddenly, "When's your birthday?"

I was almost ashamed to tell him how soon it was. Perhaps he, too, was a little taken aback by its proximity, for that future uncle of mine was not so rich as uncles should be.

"We must see about it."

"But it wouldn't—it couldn't be one like that," I said.

I must have touched his pride, for he answered loftily, "Certainly it will."

In the fortnight that followed I walked on air and told everybody I had as good as got a couple-of-guineas rod.

No one can deceive a child, save the child himself, and when my birthday came and with it a long brown paper parcel, I knew, even before I had removed the wrappers, that this two-guinea rod was not worth the money. There was a brown linen case, it is true, but it was not a case with a neat compartment for each joint, nor was there a spear in the flap. There was only one top instead of two, and there were no popping little stoppers to protect the ferrules from dust and injury. The lower joint boasted no elegant cork hand piece, but was a tapered affair coarsely made and rudely varnished. When I fitted the pieces together, what I balanced in my hand was tough and stodgy, rather than limber. The reel, which had come in a different parcel, was of wood. It had neither check nor brake, the line overran and backwound itself with distressing frequency.

I had not read and reread Gamages' price list without knowing something of rods, and I did not need to look long at this rod before realizing that it was no match to the one I had handled on the Grayshott Road.

I believe at first a great sadness possessed me, but very presently imagination came to the rescue. For I told myself that I had only to think that this was the rod of all other rods that I desired most and it would be so. And it was so.

Furthermore, I told myself that, in this great wide ignorant world, but few people existed with such expert knowledge of rods as I possessed. That I had but to say, "Here is the final word in good rods," and they would accept it as such.

Very confidently I tried the experiment on my mother, with inevitable success. From the depths of her affection and her ignorance on all such matters, she produced:

"It's a magnificent rod."

I went my way, knowing full well that she knew not what she said, but that she was kind.

With rather less confidence I approached my father, saying, "Look, father! It cost two guineas. It's absolutely the best sort you can get."

And he, after waggling it a few moments in silence, quoted cryptically:

"There is nothing either good or bad but thinking makes it so."

Young as I was, I had some curiosity about words, and on any other occasion I would have called on him to explain. But this I did not do, but left hurriedly, for fear that he should explain.

In the two years that followed I fished every day in the slip of a back garden of our tiny London house. And, having regard to the fact that this rod was never fashioned to throw a fly, I acquired a pretty knack in the fullness of time and performed some glib casting at the nasturtiums and marigolds that flourished by the back wall.

My parents' fortunes must have been in the ascendant, I suppose, for I call to mind an unforgettable breakfast when my mother told me that father had decided we should spend our summer holiday at a Welsh hotel on the river Lledr. The place was called Pont-y-pant, and she showed me a picture of the hotel with a great knock-me-down river creaming past the front of it.

Although in my dreams I had heard fast water often enough, I had never seen it, and the knowledge that in a month's time I should wake with the music of a cataract in my ears was almost more than patience could endure.

In that exquisite, intolerable period of suspense I suffered as only childish longing and enthusiasm can suffer. Even the hank of gut that I bought and bent into innumerable casts failed to alleviate that suffering. I would walk for miles for a moment's delight captured in gluing my nose to the windows of tackleists' shops in the West End. I learned from my grandmother—a wise and calm old lady—how to make nets and, having mastered the art, I made myself a landing net. This I set up on a frame fashioned from a penny schoolmaster's cane bound to an old walking stick. It would be pleasant to record that this was a good and serviceable net, but it was not. It flopped over in a very distressing fashion when called upon to lift the lightest weight. I had to confess to myself that I had more enthusiasm than skill in the manufacture of such articles.

At school there was a boy who had a fishing creel, which he swapped with me for a Swedish knife, a copy of *Rogues of the Fiery Cross,* and an Easter egg which I had kept on account of its rare beauty. He had forced a hard bargain and was sure he had the best of it, but I knew otherwise.

At last the great day dawned, and after infinite travel by train we reached our destination as the glow of sunset was graying into dark. The river was in spate, and as we crossed a tall stone bridge on our way to the hotel I heard it below me, barking and grumbling among great rocks. I was pretty far gone in tiredness, for I remember little else that night but a rod rack in the hall—a dozen rods of different sorts and sizes, with gaudy salmon flies, some nets, a gaff and an oak coffer upon which lay a freshly caught salmon on a blue ashet. Then supper by candlelight, bed, a glitter of stars through the open window, and the ceaseless drumming of water.

By six o'clock next morning I was on the river bank, fitting my rod together and watching in awe the great brown ribbon of water go fleetly by.

Among my most treasured possessions were half a dozen flies, and two of these I attached to the cast with exquisite care. While so engaged, a shadow fell on the grass beside me and, looking up, I beheld a lank, shabby individual with a walrus mustache and an unhealthy face who, the night before, had helped with our luggage at the station.

"Water's too heavy for flies," said he, with an uptilting inflection. "This evening, yes; now, no—none whateffer. Better try with a worrum in the burrun."

He pointed at a busy little brook which tumbled down the steep hillside and joined the main stream at the garden end.

"C-couldn't I fish with a fly in the—the burrun?" I asked, for although I wanted to catch a fish very badly, for honor's sake I would fain take it on a fly.

"Indeed, no," he replied, slanting the tone of his voice skyward. "You cootn't. Neffer. And that isn't a fly rod whateffer."

"It is," I replied hotly. "Yes, it is."

But he only shook his head and repeated, "No," and took the rod from my hand and illustrated its awkwardness and handed it back with a wretched laugh.

If he had pitched me into the river I should have been happier.

"It is a fly rod and it cost two guineas," I said, and my lower lip trembled.

"Neffer," he repeated. "Five shillings would be too much."

Even a small boy is entitled to some dignity.

Picking up my basket, I turned without another word and made for the hotel. Perhaps my eyes were blinded with tears, for I was about to plunge into the dark hall when a great, rough, kindly voice arrested me with:

"Easy does it."

At the thick end of an immense salmon rod there strode out into the sunlight the noblest figure I had ever seen.

There is no real need to describe my colonel again—I have done so already—but the temptation is too great. Standing in the doorway, the sixteen-foot rod in hand, the deer-stalker hat, besprent with flies, crowning his shaggy head, the waders, like seven-league boots, braced up to his armpits, the creel across his shoulder, a gaff across his back, he looked what he was—a god. His eyes met mine with that kind of smile one good man keeps for another.

"An early start," he said. "Any luck, old fellar?"

I told him I hadn't started—not yet.

"Wise chap," said he. "Water's a bit heavy for trouting. It'll soon run down, though. Let's vet those flies of yours."

He took my rod and whipped it expertly.

"A nice piece—new, eh?"

"N-not quite," I stammered; "but I haven't used it yet, sir, in water."

That god read men's minds.

"I know—garden practice; capital; nothing like it."

Releasing my cast, he frowned critically over the flies—a Blue Dun and a March Brown.

"Think so?" he queried. "You don't think it's a shade late in the season for these fancies?" I said I thought perhaps it was. "Yes, I think you're right," said he. "I believe in this big water you'd do better with a livelier pattern. Teal and Red, Cock-y-bundy, Greenwell's Glory."

I said nothing, but nodded gravely at these brave names.

Once more he read my thoughts and saw through the wicker sides of my creel a great emptiness.

"I expect you've fished most in southern rivers. These Welsh trout have a fancy for a spot of color."

He rummaged in the pocket of his Norfolk jacket and produced a round tin which once had held saddle soap.

"Collar on to that," said he; "there's a proper pickle of flies and casts in that tin that, as a keen fisherman, you won't mind sorting out. Still, they may come in useful."

"But, I say, you don't mean—" I began.

"Yes, go in; stick to it. All fishermen are members of the same club and I'm giving the trout a rest for a bit." His eyes ranged the hills and trees opposite. "I must be getting on with it before the sun's too high."

Waving his free hand, he strode away and presently was lost to view at a bend in the road.

I think my mother was a little piqued by my abstraction during breakfast. My eyes never, for an instant, deserted the round tin box which lay open beside my plate. Within it were a paradise and a hundred miracles all tangled together in the pleasantest disorder. My mother said something about a lovely walk over the hills, but I had other plans, which included a very glorious hour which should be spent untangling and wrapping up in neat squares of paper my new treasures.

"I suppose he knows best what he wants to do," she said.

So it came about that I was left alone and betook myself to a sheltered spot behind a rock where all the delicious disorder was remedied and I could take stock of what was mine.

I am sure there were at least six casts all set up with flies, and ever so many loose flies and one great stout, tapered cast, with a salmon fly upon it, that was so rich in splendor that I doubted if my benefactor could really have known that it was there.

I felt almost guilty at owning so much, and not until I had done full justice to everything did I fasten a new cast to my line and go a-fishing.

There is a lot said and written about beginners' luck, but none of it came my way. Indeed, I spent most of the morning extricating my line from the most fearsome tangles. I had no skill in throwing a cast with two droppers upon it and I found it was an art not to be learned in a minute. Then, from overeagerness, I was too snappy with my back cast, whereby, before many minutes had gone, I heard that warning crack behind me that betokens the loss of a tail fly. I must have spent half an hour searching the meadow for that lost fly and finding it not. Which is not strange, for I wonder has any fisherman ever found that lost fly. The reeds, the buttercups, and the little people with many legs who run in the wet grass conspire together to keep the secret of its hiding place. I gave up at last, and with a feeling of shame that was only proper, I invested a new fly on the point of my cast and set to work again, but more warily.

In that hard racing water a good strain was put upon my rod, and before the morning was out it was creaking at the joints in a way that kept my heart continually in my mouth. It is the duty of a rod to work with a single smooth action and by no means to divide its performance into three sections of activity. It is a hard task for any angler to persuade his line austerely if his rod behaves thus.

When, at last, my father strolled up the river bank, walking, to his shame, much nearer the water than a good fisherman should, my nerves were jumpy from apprehension.

"Come along. Food's ready. Done any good?" said he.

Again it was to his discredit that he put food before sport, but I told him I had had a wonderful morning, and he was glad.

"What do you want to do this afternoon, old man?" he asked.

"Fish," I said.

"But you can't always fish," he said.

I told him I could, and I was right and have proved it for thirty years and more.

"Well, well," he said, "please yourself, but isn't it dull not catching anything?"

And I said, as I've said a thousand times since, "As if it could be."

So that afternoon I went downstream instead of up, and found myself in difficult country where the river boiled between the narrows of two hills. Stunted oaks overhung the water and great boulders opposed its flow. Presently I came to a sort of natural flight of steps—a pool and a cascade three times repeated—and there, watching the maniac fury of the waters in awe and wonderment, I saw the most stirring sight in my young life. I saw a silver salmon leap superbly from the caldron below into the pool above. And I saw another and another salmon do likewise. And I wonder the eyes of me did not fall out of my head.

I cannot say how long I stayed watching that gallant pageant of leaping fish—in ecstasy there is no measurement of time—but at last it came upon me that all the salmon in the sea were careering past me and that if I were to realize my soul's desire I must hasten to the pool below before the last of them had gone by.

It was a mad adventure, for until I had discovered that stout cast, with the gaudy fly attached in the tin box, I had given no thought to such noble quarry. My recent possessions had put ideas into my head above my station and beyond my powers. Failure, however, means little to the young and, walking fast, yet gingerly, for fear of breaking my rod top against a tree, I followed the path downstream until I came to a great basin of water into which, through a narrow throat, the river thundered like a storm.

At the head of the pool was a plate of rock scored by the nails of fishermen's boots, and here I sat me down to wait while the salmon cast, removed from its wrapper, was allowed to soak and soften in a puddle left by the rain.

And while I waited a salmon rolled not ten yards from where I sat. Head and tail, up and down he went, a great monster of a fish, sporting and deriding me.

With that performance so near at hand, I have often wondered how I was able to control my fingers well enough to tie a figure-eight knot between the line and the cast. But I did, and I'm proud to be able to record it. Your true-born angler does not go blindly to work until he has first satisfied his conscience. There is a pride, in knots, of which the laity knows nothing, and if, through neglect to tie them rightly, failure and loss should result, pride may not be restored nor conscience salved by the plea of eagerness. With my trembling fingers I bent the knot and, with a pummeling heart, launched the line into the broken water at the throat of the pool.

At first the mere tug of the water against that large fly was so thrilling to me that it was hard to believe that I had not hooked a whale. The trembling line swung round in a wide arc into a calm eddy below where I stood. Before casting afresh I shot a glance over my shoulder to assure myself there was no limb of a tree behind me to foul the fly. And this was a gallant cast, true and straight, with a couple of yards more length than its predecessor, and a wider radius. Instinctively I knew, as if the surface had been marked with an X where the salmon had risen, that my fly must pass right over the spot. As it swung by, my nerves were strained like piano wires. I think I knew something tremendous, impossible, terrifying, was going to happen. The sense, the certitude was so strong in me that I half opened my mouth to shout a warning to the monster, not to.

I must have felt very, very young in that moment. I, who that same day had been talked to as a man by a man among men. The years were stripped from me and I was what I was—ten years old and appalled. And then, with the suddenness of a rocket, it happened. The water was cut into a swath. I remember a silver loop bearing downward—a bright, shining, vanishing thing like the bobbin of my mother's sewing machine—and a tug. I shall never forget the viciousness of that tug. I had my fingers tight upon the line, so I got the full force of it. To counteract a tendency to go headfirst into the spinning water below, I threw myself backward and sat down on the hard rock with a jar that shut my teeth on my tongue—like the jaws of a trap.

Luckily I had let the rod go out straight with the line, else it must have snapped in the first frenzy of the downstream rush. Little ass that I was, I tried to check the speeding line with my forefinger, with the result that it cut and burnt me to the bone. There wasn't above twenty yards of line in the reel, and the wretched contrivance was trying to be rid of the line even faster than the fish was wrenching it out. Heaven knows why it didn't snarl, for great loops and whorls were whirling, like Catherine wheels, under my wrist. An instant's glance revealed the terrifying fact that there was not more than half a dozen yards left on the reel and the fish showed no sign of abating his rush. With the realization of impending and inevitable catastrophe upon me, I launched a yell for help, which, rising above the roar of the waters, went echoing down the gorge.

And then, to add to my terrors, the salmon leaped—a winging leap like a silver arch appearing and instantly disappearing upon the broken surface. So mighty, so all-powerful he seemed in that sublime moment that I lost all sense of reason and raised the rod, with a sudden jerk, above my head.

I have often wondered, had the rod actually been the two-guinea rod my imagination claimed for it, whether it could have withstood the strain thus violently and unreasonably imposed upon it. The wretched thing that I held so grimly never even put up a fight. It snapped at the ferrule of the lower joint and plunged like a toboggan down the slanting line, to vanish into the black depths of the water.

My horror at this calamity was so profound that I was lost even to the consciousness that the last of my line had run out. A couple of vicious tugs advised me of this awful truth. Then, snap! The line parted at the reel, flickered out through the rings and was gone. I was left with nothing but the butt of a broken rod in my hand and an agony of mind that even now I cannot recall without emotion.

I am not ashamed to confess that I cried. I lay down on the rock, with my cheek in the puddle where I had soaked the cast, and plenished it with my tears. For what had the future left for me but a cut and burning finger, a badly bumped behind, the single joint of a broken rod and no faith in uncles? How long I lay there weeping I do not know. Ages, perhaps, or minutes, or seconds.

I was roused by a rough hand on my shoulder and a kindly voice demanding, "Hurt yourself, Ike Walton?"

Blinking away my tears, I pointed at my broken rod with a bleeding forefinger.

"Come! This is bad luck," said my colonel, his face grave as a stone. "How did it happen?"

"I c-caught a s-salmon."

"You what?" said he.

"I d-did," I said.

He looked at me long and earnestly; then, taking my injured hand, he looked at that and nodded.

"The poor groundlings who can find no better use for a river than something to put a bridge over think all fishermen are liars," said he. "But we know better, eh? By the bumps and breaks and cuts I'd say you made a plucky fight against heavy odds. Let's hear all about it."

So, with his arm round my shoulders and his great shaggy head near to mine, I told him all about it.

At the end he gave me a mighty and comforting squeeze, and he said, "The loss of one's first big fish is the heaviest loss I know. One feels, whatever happens, one'll never—" He stopped and pointed dramatically. "There it goes—see! Down there at the tail of the pool!"

In the broken water where the pool emptied itself into the shallows beyond, I saw the top joints of my rod dancing on the surface.

"Come on!" he shouted, and gripping my hand, jerked me to my feet. "Scatter your legs! There's just a chance!"

Dragging me after him, we raced along by the river path to the end of the pool, where, on a narrow promontory of grass, his enormous salmon rod was lying.

"Now," he said, picking it up and making the line whistle to and fro in the air with sublime authority, "keep your eyes skinned on those shallows for another glimpse of it."

A second later I was shouting, "There! There!"

He must have seen the rod point at the same moment, for his line flowed out and the big fly hit the water with a plop not a couple of feet from the spot.

He let it ride on the current, playing it with a sensitive touch like the brushwork of an artist.

"Half a jiffy!" he exclaimed at last. "Wait! Yes, I think so. Cut down to that rock and see if I haven't fished up the line."

I needed no second invitation, and presently was yelling, "Yes—yes, you have!"

"Stretch yourself out then and collar hold of it."

With the most exquisite care he navigated the line to where I lay stretched upon the rock. Then:

"Right you are! Good lad! I'm coming down."

Considering his age, he leaped the rocks like a chamois.

"Now," he said, and took the wet line delicately between his forefinger and thumb. One end trailed limply downstream, but the other end seemed anchored in the big pool where I had had my unequal and disastrous contest.

Looking into his face, I saw a sudden light of excitement dancing in his eyes.

"Odd," he muttered, "but not impossible."

"What isn't?" I asked breathlessly.

"Well, it looks to me as if the joints of that rod of yours have gone downstream."

Gingerly he pulled up the line, and presently an end with a broken knot appeared.

"The reel knot, eh?" I nodded gloomily. "Then we lose the rod," said he. That wasn't very heartening news. "On the other hand, it's just possible the fish is still on—sulking."

"Oo!" I exclaimed.

"Now, steady does it," he warned, "and give me my rod."

Taking a pair of clippers from his pocket, he cut his own line just above the cast.

"Can you tie a knot?" he asked.

"Yes," I nodded.

"Come on, then; bend your line onto mine. Quick as lightning."

Under his critical eye, I joined the two lines with a blood knot. "I guessed you were a fisherman," he said, nodded approvingly and clipped off the ends. "And now to know the best or the worst."

I shall never forget the music of that check reel or the suspense with which I watched as, with the butt of the rod bearing against the hollow of his thigh, he steadily wound up the wet slack line. Every instant I expected it to come drifting downstream, but it didn't. Presently it rose in a tight slant from the pool above.

"Snagged, I'm afraid," he said, and worked the rod with an easy straining motion to and fro. "Yes, I'm afraid—no, by Lord Bobs, he's on!"

I think it was only right and proper that I should have launched a yell of triumph as, with the spoken word, the point at which the line cut the water shifted magically from the left side of the pool to the right.

"And a fish too," said he.

In the fifteen minutes that followed, I must have experienced every known form of terror and delight.

"Youngster," said he, "you should be doing this, by rights, but I'm afraid the rod's a bit above your weight."

"Oh, go on and catch him," I pleaded.

"And so I will," he promised; "unship the gaff, young un, and stand by to use it, and if you break the cast we'll never speak to each other again, and that's a bet."

But I didn't break the cast. The noble, courageous, indomitable example of my river god had lent me skill and precision beyond my years. When at long last a weary, beaten, silver monster rolled within reach of my arm into a shallow eddy, the steel gaff shot out fair and true, and sank home.

And then I was lying on the grass, with my arms round a salmon that weighed twenty-two pounds on the scale and contained every sort of happiness known to a boy.

And best of all, my river god shook hands with me and called me "partner."

That evening the salmon was placed upon the blue ashet in the hall, bearing a little card with its weight and my name upon it.

And I am afraid I sat on a chair facing it, for ever so long, so that I could hear what the other anglers had to say as they passed by. I was sitting there when my colonel put his head out of his private sitting room and beckoned me to come in.

"A true fisherman lives in the future, not the past, old man," said he; "though, for this once, it 'ud be a shame to reproach you."

I suppose I colored guiltily—at any rate, I hope so.

"We got the fish," said he, "but we lost the rod, and a future without a rod doesn't bear thinking of. Now"—and he pointed at a long wooden box on the floor, that overflowed with rods of different sorts and sizes—"rummage among those. Take your time and see if you can find anything to suit you."

"But do you mean—can I—"

"We're partners, aren't we? And p'r'aps as such you'd rather we went through our stock together."

"Oo, sir," I said.

"Here, quit that," he ordered gruffly. "By Lord Bobs, if a show like this after-

noon's don't deserve a medal, what does? Now, here's a handy piece by Hardy—
a light and useful tool—or if you fancy greenheart in preference to split bamboo—"

I have the rod to this day, and I count it among my dearest treasures. And to
this day I have a flick of the wrist that was his legacy. I have, too, some small
skill in dressing flies, the elements of which were learned in his company by
candlelight after the day's work was over. And I have countless memories of that
month-long, month-short friendship—the closest and most perfect friendship,
perhaps, of all my life.

He came to the station and saw me off. How I vividly remember his shaggy
head at the window, with the whiskered cheeks and the gunpowder marks at the
corners of his eyes! I didn't cry, although I wanted to awfully. We were partners
and shook hands. I never saw him again, although on my birthdays I would
have colored cards from him, with Irish, Scotch, Norwegian postmarks. Very brief
they were: "Water very low." "Took a good fish last Thursday." "Been prawning,
but don't like it."

Sometimes at Christmas I had gifts—a reel, a tapered line, a fly book. But I
never saw him again.

Came at last no more cards or gifts, but in the *Fishing Gazette,* of which I was
a religious reader, was an obituary telling how one of the last of the Mutiny
veterans had joined the great majority. It seems he had been fishing half an hour
before he died. He had taken his rod down and passed out. They had buried
him at Totnes, overlooking the River Dart.

So he was no more—my river god—and what was left of him they had put into
a box and buried it in the earth.

But that isn't true; nor is it true that I never saw him again. For I seldom go
a-fishing but that I meet him on the river banks.

The banks of a river are frequented by a strange company and are full of
mysterious and murmurous sounds—the cluck and laughter of water, the piping
of birds, the hum of insects, and the whispering of wind in the willows. What
should prevent a man in such a place having a word and speech with another
who is not there? So much of fishing lies in imagination, and mine needs little
stretching to give my river god a living form.

"With this ripple," says he, "you should do well."

"And what's it to be," say I—"Blue Upright, Red Spinner? What's your fancy,
sir?"

Spirits never grow old. He has begun to take an interest in dry-fly methods—
that river god of mine, with his seven-league boots, his shaggy head, and the gaff
across his back.

MEMORIES OF MICHIGAN

Ernest Schwiebert

AUGUST MORNINGS WERE BRIGHT ON the wind-riffled surface of the bay, and beyond the shallow inlet, there were whitecaps on the darker water of the lake. Its surf rolled and broke on the beaches. Ore boats moved slowly south along the horizon. They steamed toward the mills at Chicago or traveled lazily back, empty and riding high in the water, bound for the ironfields of Lake Superior.

The town was almost forgotten. There were only five or six houses to remind its oldtimers of the lumber port that had once boasted five hundred buildings. The logging drives had stopped. Brook trout were coming back in the little river, although the delicate grayling were gone, and its gentle currents had slowly filled the harbor with sand and silt.

The piers and jetties were gone, and only the ebony skeletons of their pilings remained where the summer people fished for perch. Outside the inlet channel to the harbor, the rolling waves pounded and flowed through the pilings that remained to mark the breakwater. The pale beach reached for miles, marred only by the weathered bones of a schooner lost in a winter squall a century before, its broken timbers like the ribcage of some ancient whale imprisoned in the sand.

The post office and general store had a high false front, and a single gasoline pump stood in the dusty street. There was a tiny clapboard church and its weed-filled cemetery. The broken windows of the Grange Hall had stared at the jack-pine landscape since farms were abandoned in the thirties, and the school was the only building that had been painted in years. The saloons and rooming houses and sawmills were gone. There were few echoes of a thriving past except in the skeletal pilings of the harbor and cellars long forgotten in the weeds.

There were several cottages on the lake in those boyhood years. It was often too cold for swimming, but its unspoiled beaches were empty. Sand dunes rose hundreds of feet above the lake, pale with beach grass and dark with trees. Those Michigan summers were peaceful times when my father fished and worked at his research, or prepared his lectures for the coming term.

My fishing began with perch and pumpkinseeds. Many summers have passed

33

since that long-ago summer when I was introduced to trout. After the foolish
perch and pumpkinseed shallows below the cottage, trout were a revelation, and
since that first morning they have obsessed me with a passion that has paled other
fish to unimportance. Only salmon have ever distracted me from my single-
minded odyssey in the years that followed.

Those first hours are still fresh in my mind.

Long before daylight I was awake. The week of hot weather ended in a squall
off the lake, and I listened to the wind and rain on the roof. It was still dark
when we finished breakfast, but the sudden storm front had passed.

Getting the grasshoppers for bait was sport in itself, and we gathered them in
the wet grass. They were sluggish in the cold just after daylight, and we searched
the meadows with our fruit jars, picking grasshoppers like berries.

My classroom was on the headwaters of the river. Its meadows were willow
bordered, its origins deep in the springs of a cedar swamp.

It was dark with conifers above the meadows. Some places it flowed through
quivering bogs of sand and marl, and it reached the sunlight in a logging pond.
The shallows were filled with stumps and deadfalls. There was a beaver house
below the inlet. Its occupants once frightened me into jettisoning a rod just before midnight. They discovered me during a night fishing session and their
warning tail-slaps were a series of explosions in the darkness.

Courage failed and I ran. Fifty yards down the logging road I stopped. My
mouth was dry and there was an ache in my side. Several minutes passed until
my breathing returned to normal, and I went back for the rod with my heart
still beating wildly.

The pond was less formidable in the morning. Brook trout were deep over the
emerald moss of its channel, cruising in nervous schools. They were bright with
color in these swampy waters, and they cruised beyond the range of boyhood
casting.

Below the pond was almost a mile of dark swamp-colored water we never
fished. It was densely grown with hemlocks and cedars. The mileage below was
a pleasant reach of meadow water, marked with a serpentine row of willows.
Halfway through the meadow, the stream was bridged with a simple tractor span
of planking and logs. There was a hill above the bottom of the meadow, with
an old cemetery in the jackpines.

My parents restricted me to the meadows, but the temptation of the pond was
strong. It caused a number of furtive expeditions. These attempts were fishless,
but nagging memories of fish prowling the mossy channel always brought me
back.

The meadow was easier. The first hole was below a sluice culvert, where the
current poured under the road. The deepest place was tight against the roots of
a giant elm. My equipment was a stiff fly-rod and a precious Leonard reel. The
agate guides and cane were intricately wrapped with silk. The rod was perfect
for grasshoppers.

It was cool the morning I caught my first trout. The wind was almost cold off

the lake, but it was warmer on the river. Our approach to the sluice-culvert hole went infantry style, lying flat in the roots of the elm. The grasshopper chosen for sacrifice was worked past the lid of my pickle jar, protesting with brown juices that stained my fingers.

It was lowered into the current tight against the roots. The action was instantaneous. There was a wild splash and the rod dipped, and I derricked the trout into the branches.

My father laughed and extricated it from the tree, and we sat in the grassy shade admiring its colors. Foot-long brook trout are still treasured in the adult world, and in boyhood it seemed like a salmon.

Later I became skilled at snaking fish high on the banks, but twice I hooked trout that broke off. The best of the summer was a plump fifteen-inch brown, and in trying to quiet its wild flopping, I fell into some nettles.

Most days were lucky. There were never any fishless days after that first session under the elms, and I often took fish to twelve inches.

My consistent luck was a source of amusement in the general store. Its freezer was filled with ice cream and trout. The locals kept their fish there and it was a kind of angling scoreboard. Daily catches were common knowledge.

That summer I fished every possible minute, while my father was usually busy with his writing. My packages of trout soon surpassed his and the general store regulars laughed.

"You be right nice to your boy." They winked at him each time we deposited our fish. "You buy him enough ice cream," they laughed, "and he might tell you how he caught them trout."

"You're right." My father smiled.

There was a swift run below the sluice culvert where cattle forded the stream. The current eddied and deepened above some tangled deadfalls. Bog willows sheltered the run. There were good fish in the deepest place, but the boggy ground trembled when we approached and they were skittish. They always bolted and disappeared under the deadfalls. It was a good lesson.

Willows covered the water downstream, except for a single swirling hole. It always held good fish. We crawled close through the grass and peeked at the water to fish. Crayfish burrows were clustered like swallow nests in the banks.

The fish held deep where the sun-filled current slipped back into its leafy tunnel, and sometimes we lost them in the willows.

There were several open runs between the willows in the half mile that followed. The hay-meadow bridge was below. The current was dark under its planks and timber cribbing. It boiled out from the willows where the debris of past spring freshets were tangled in the fence.

Big trout lived under the bridge. We sometimes watched between the planking, where the narrow patterns of sunlight reached the bottom. It was almost impossible to fish there because of the fences above and below the bridge. Its big browns were a challenge we failed to solve that summer.

The downstream meadows were filled with cattle. The fish hid under the banks. The cattle seldom frightened them, but it was difficult for us to approach.

We crawled the banks, staying well back from the current, and fished our grass-hoppers against the grass. These meadow trout ran smaller, and took our bait with eager splashes. There were bigger fish in one place where the foam eddied up into a soapsuds crescent against a fence.

It was still and deep, and once I hooked a fish there that easily snapped my leader when I tried to horse it on the bank. It had looked immense, and I repaired my leader with trembling hands.

The fishable water ended at the cemetery, and fishing there was a little frightening. The grass was thickly tangled in its cast-iron fences, and its headstones leaned at strange angles or lay flat in the weeds. Wind stirred through the jack-pines on most days, but when it was still, there was a faint odor of fading wreaths and flowers.

It was a logging-camp cemetery from the lumbering years in Michigan. There was no trace of the camp or its canvas-tent church. Those lumbering years have a colorful history, with more than their share of bacchanalia. There were killings and gambling tents and tenderloins and hanging trees. Cemetery hill had once been covered with tent camps when the valley was lumbered and the logging pond was built, and my boyhood imagination often explored those lumbering years.

There was no doubt in my mind that the cemetery was filled with sinful men and camp followers, or that its graves were an unhappy residue of a jackpine Sodom and Gomorrah.

Night fishing in those lower meadows below the cemetery was filled with delicious shivers of fear. There was swamp fire sometimes in the marl bogs downstream, and moonlight danced and gleamed on the polished headstones.

Later that summer, one of the local fishermen caught a six-pound brown in the marl bogs. It was taken with a night crawler. It seemed to prove what a man could accomplish if he would only brave the demons of Hell (boyhood imagination could conceive no other destination for the loggers and their girl friends) in the dark of the moon. The temptation of such fish was considerable, but my fear of the cemetery and the swamp prevailed. It was the mysterious swamp fire and the dead that tipped the scale toward caution.

The man who caught the big brown looked old enough to have been a logger. It was possible to imagine him topping timber and felling trees during the day, and wasting his wages in sinful revels (once I had seen him drunk on the courthouse lawn in Manistee) in the tenderloins all night. When I finally decided the old man was a lumberjack, his brave expeditions into the swamp seemed less impressive. No lumberjack would be afraid of a cemetery filled with friends.

The cemetery was too formidable for me. Except for my traumatic encounters with the beavers in the logging pond, my nights were properly passed in bed. Those hours were spent listening to the sullen rhythm of the lake, and the wind in the pines above our cottage. Thoughts of fishing filled my head until sleep finally came, as they sometimes do years later, and I fished back through success and failure.

Sometimes I tried to solve fishing problems in those moments of half sleep, and I often returned to the little river and its frustrations in my mind. Such nocturnal problem solving always seemed to return to the tractor bridge in the meadows.

It had been a raw windy morning the first time I discovered the big fish under the bridge. Gusts of wind tossed the willows and the sun glittered on the riffles. The slender leaves writhed in the wind, turning green and silver.

When I reached the bridge, several trout were working in its shadows. The wind rose and gusted across the meadows, and the trout began rising again. There were five of them.

The wind was blowing terrestrial insects into the stream. There was an obvious relationship between its rising gusts and a subsequent increase in activity among the fish. Four of them were deep in the shadows of the planking. The fifth was working tight against the cribbing. They were all browns. Excitement rose inside me when I looked down through the bridge floor. They ranged from about fifteen inches to a dark spotted fish of two pounds.

They looked huge. My fish averaged about nine inches that summer. The tractor bridge became my secret enigma, and I often dreamed of arriving in triumph at the store with such trophies.

Because of the fences at the bridge, there was no way to fish them. It was like a cage with a planking roof. The problem caused some restless nights. Its solution was devised in some moments just before sleep, and it seemed foolproof enough that I slept soundly.

The bridge planking would be shifted aside carefully, until I could lower a grasshopper directly to the fish.

The leader should be heavy, I thought, *and I can weight it with sinkers to hold it steady.*

There were no other fishermen the morning I tried it. The trout eagerly accepted several grasshoppers I threw into the current above the bridge.

Everything seemed perfect, and I coaxed my biggest grasshopper from his pickle-jar prison. The leader was tested and ready. The fish were right under me. It was now or never. The planking was heavy, but I moved it soundlessly until a bright streak of sunlight exploded across the bottom and the fish bolted wildly upstream.

Several years later I returned. It was a sentimental pilgrimage back into my boyhood, but that past was gone. The town had all the symptoms of mindless progress. There were ice-cream stands and a diner. The drive-in movie stood in the meadow where we had watched the deer on August evenings. There was a supermarket, and the automobile graveyard sprawled down from the shiny service station into the shallows where I had fished for perch.

The fishing was changed too.

Memories of those first grasshopper summers crowded my mind. The men who had helped me learn about trout were all gone, part of the timeless cycle of the seasons now, and without them something was missing on the Au Sable and the swift-flowing Pine and the dark teacolored currents of the Black.

The wind off the lake still smelled cool and clean. Clouds moved swiftly inland. The logging camp cemetery was still there, headstones askew and sprawled flat in the tangled weeds and grass. Two men were fishing the culvert under the road, and I stopped to talk.

"What are you using?" I called.

"Cheese," they answered.

The little river still wound lazily through its meadows and the wind moved in the willows. There were three new houses in the pasture upstream. The logging pond and its beaver house were gone, and there were no fish where the tractor bridge had been.

CROCKER'S HOLE

R. D. Blackmore

I

THE CULM, WHICH RISES IN Somersetshire, and hastening into a fairer land (as the border waters wisely do) falls into the Exe near Killerton, formerly was a lovely trout stream, such as perverts the Devonshire angler from due respect toward Father Thames and the other canals round London. In the Devonshire valleys it is sweet to see how soon a spring becomes a rill, and a rill runs on into a rivulet and a rivulet swells into a brook; and before one has time to say, "What are you at?"—before the first tree it ever spoke to is a dummy, or the first hill it ever ran down has turned blue, here we have all the airs and graces, demands and assertions of a full-grown river.

But what is the test of a river? Who shall say? "The power to drown a man," replies the river darkly. But rudeness is not argument. Rather shall we say that the power to work a good undershot wheel, without being dammed up all night in a pond, and leaving a tidy back stream to spare at the bottom of the orchard, is a fair certificate of riverhood. If so, many Devonshire streams attain that rank within five miles of their spring; aye, and rapidly add to it. At every turn they gather aid, from ash-clad dingle and aldered meadow, mossy rock and ferny wall, hedge-trough-roofed with bramble netting, where the baby water lurks, and lanes that coming down to ford bring suicidal tribute. Arrogant, all-

engrossing river, now it has claimed a great valley of its own; and whatever falls
within the hill scoop sooner or later belongs to itself. Even the crystal "shutt"
that crosses the farmyard by the woodrick, and glides down an aqueduct of last
year's bark for Mary to fill the kettle from; and even the tricklets that have no
organs for telling or knowing their business, but only get into unwary oozings in
and among the water grass, and there make moss and forget themselves among
it—one and all, they come to the same thing at last, and that is the river.

The Culm used to be a good river at Culmstock, tormented already by a factory, but not strangled as yet by a railroad. How it is now the present writer does
not know, and is afraid to ask, having heard of a vile "Culm Valley Line." But
Culmstock bridge was a very pretty place to stand and contemplate the ways of
trout; which is easier work than to catch them. When I was just big enough to
peep above the rim, or to lie upon it with one leg inside for fear of tumbling
over, what a mighty river it used to seem, for it takes a treat there and spreads
itself. Above the bridge the factory stream falls in again, having done its business, and washing its hands in the innocent half that has strayed down the meadows. Then under the arches they both rejoice and come to a slide of about two
feet, and make a short, wide pool below, and indulge themselves in perhaps two
islands, through which a little river always magnifies itself and maintains a
mysterious middle. But after that, all of it used to come together, and make off
in one body for the meadows, intent upon nurturing trout with rapid stickles,
and buttercuppy corners where fat flies may tumble in. And here you may find
in the very first meadow, or at any rate you might have found, forty years ago,
the celebrated "Crocker's Hole."

The story of Crocker is unknown to me, and interesting as it doubtless was,
I do not deal with him, but with his Hole. Tradition said that he was a baker's
boy who, during his basket rounds, fell in love with a maiden who received the
cottage loaf, or perhaps good "Households," for her master's use. No doubt she
was charming, as a girl should be, but whether she encouraged the youthful
baker and then betrayed him with false role, or whether she "consisted" throughout—as our cousins across the water express it—is known to their *manes* only.
Enough that she would not have the floury lad; and that he, after giving in his
books and money, sought an untimely grave among the trout. And this was the
first pool below the bread walk deep enough to drown a five-foot baker boy. Sad
it was; but such things must be, and bread must still be delivered daily.

A truce to such reflections—as our foremost writers always say, when they do
not see how to go on with them—but it is a serious thing to know what Crocker's
Hole was like; because at a time when (if he had only persevered, and married
the maid, and succeeded to the oven, and reared a large family of short-weight
bakers) he might have been leaning on his crutch beside the pool, and teaching
his grandson to swim by precept (that beautiful proxy for practice)—at such a
time, I say, there lived a remarkable fine trout in that hole. Anglers are notori-
ously truthful, especially as to what they catch, or even more frequently have not
caught. Though I may have written fiction, among many other sins—as a nice
old lady told me once—now I have to deal with facts; and foul scorn would I

count it ever to make believe that I caught that fish. My length at that time was not more than the butt of a four-jointed rod, and all I could catch was a minnow with a pin, which our cook Lydia would not cook, but used to say, "Oh, what a shame, Master Richard! They would have been trout in the summer, please God! if you would only a' let 'em grow on." She is living now and will bear me out in this.

But upon every great occasion there arises a great man; or to put it more accurately, in the present instance, a mighty and distinguished boy. My father, being the parson of the parish, and getting, need it be said, small pay, took sundry pupils, very pleasant fellows, about to adorn the universities. Among them was the original "Bude Light," as he was satirically called at Cambridge, for he came from Bude, and there was no light in him. Among them also was John Pike, a born Zebedee if ever there was one.

John Pike was a thickset younker, with a large and bushy head, keen blue eyes that could see through water, and the proper slouch of shoulder into which great anglers ripen; but greater still are born with it; and of these was Master John. It mattered little what the weather was, and scarcely more as to the time of year, John Pike must have his fishing every day, and on Sundays he read about it, and made flies. All the rest of the time he was thinking about it.

My father was coaching him in the fourth book of *The Aeneid* and all those wonderful speeches of Dido, where passion disdains construction; but the only line Pike cared for was of horsehair. "I fear, Mr. Pike, that you are not giving me your entire attention," my father used to say in his mild dry way; and once when Pike was more than usually abroad, his tutor begged to share his meditations. "Well, sir," said Pike, who was very truthful, "I can see a green drake by the strawberry tree, the first of the season, and your derivation of 'barbarous' put me in mind of my barberry dye." In those days it was a very nice point to get the right tint for the mallard's feather.

No sooner was lesson done than Pike, whose rod was ready upon the lawn, dashed away always for the river, rushing headlong down the hill, and away to the left through a private yard, where "No Thoroughfare" was put up and a big dog stationed to enforce it. But Cerberus himself could not have stopped John Pike; his conscience backed him up in trespass the most sinful when his heart was inditing of a trout upon the rise.

All this, however, is preliminary, as the boy said when he put his father's coat upon his grandfather's tenterhooks, with felonious intent upon his grandmother's apples; the main point to be understood is this, that nothing—neither brazen tower, hundred-eyed Argus, nor Cretan Minotaur—could stop John Pike from getting at a good stickle. But, even as the world knows nothing of its greatest men, its greatest men know nothing of the world beneath their very nose, till fortune sneezes dexter. For two years John Pike must have been whipping the water as hard as Xerxes, without having ever once dreamed of the glorious trout that lived in Crocker's Hole. But why, when he ought to have been at least on bowing terms with every fish as long as his middle finger, why had he failed to know this champion? The answer is simple—because of his short cuts. Flying as he did like an arrow from a bow, Pike used to hit his beloved river at an elbow, some furlong below Crocker's Hole, where a sweet little stickle sailed away down-stream, whereas for the length of a meadow upward the water lay smooth, clear, and shallow; therefore the youth, with so little time to spare, rushed into the downward joy.

And here it may be noted that the leading maxim of the present period, that man can discharge his duty only by going counter to the stream, was scarcely mooted in those days. My grandfather (who was a wonderful man, if he was ac-customed to fill a cart in two days of fly fishing on the Barle) regularly fished downstream; and what more than a cartload need anyone put into his basket?

And surely it is more genial and pleasant to behold our friend the river grow-ing and thriving as we go on, strengthening its voice and enlarging its bosom, and sparkling through each successive meadow with richer plenitude of silver, than to trace it against its own grain and good will toward weakness, and littleness, and immature conceptions.

However, you will say that if John Pike had fished upstream, he would have found this trout much sooner. And that is true; but still, as it was, the trout had more time to grow into such a prize. And the way in which John found him out was this. For some days he had been tormented with a very painful tooth, which even poisoned all the joys of fishing. Therefore he resolved to have it out and sturdily entered the shop of John Sweetland, the village blacksmith, and there paid his sixpence. Sweetland extracted the teeth of the village, whenever they required it, in the simplest and most effectual way. A piece of fine wire was fast-ened round the tooth, and the other end round the anvil's nose, then the sturdy blacksmith shut the lower half of his shop door, which was about breast-high, with the patient outside and the anvil within; a strong push of the foot upset the anvil, and the tooth flew out like a well-thrown fly.

When John Pike had suffered this very bravely, "Ah, Master Pike," said the blacksmith, with a grin, "I reckon you won't pull out thic there big vish"—the smithy commanded a view of the river—"clever as you be, quite so peart as thiccy."

"What big fish?" asked the boy, with deepest interest, though his mouth was bleeding fearfully.

"Why, that girt mortial of a vish as hath his hover in Crocker's Hole. Zum on 'em saith as a' must be a zammon."

Off went Pike with his handkerchief to his mouth, and after him ran Alec Bolt, one of his fellow pupils, who had come to the shop to enjoy the extraction.

"Oh, my!" was all that Pike could utter, when by craftily posting himself he had obtained a good view of this grand fish.

"I'll lay you a crown you don't catch him!" cried Bolt, an impatient youth, who scorned angling.

"How long will you give me?" asked the wary Pike, who never made rash wagers.

"Oh! till the holidays if you like; or, if that won't do, till Michaelmas."

Now the midsummer holidays were six weeks off—boys used not to talk of "vacations" then, still less of "recesses."

"I think I'll bet you," said Pike, in his slow way, bending forward carefully, with his keen eyes on this monster; "but it would not be fair to take till Michaelmas. I'll bet you a crown that I catch him before the holidays—at least, unless some other fellow does."

II

The day of that most momentous interview must have been the 14th day of May. Of the year I will not be so sure; for children take more note of days than of years, for which the latter have their full revenge thereafter. It must have been the 14th, because the morrow was our holiday, given upon the 15th of May, in honor of a birthday.

Now, John Pike was beyond his years wary as well as enterprising, calm as well as ardent, quite as rich in patience as in promptitude and vigor. But Alec Bolt was a headlong youth, volatile, hot, and hasty, fit only to fish the Maelstrom, or a torrent of new lava. And the moment he had laid that wager he expected his crown piece; though time, as the lawyers phrase it, was "expressly of the essence of the contract." And now he demanded that Pike should spend the holiday in trying to catch that trout.

"I shall not go near him," that lad replied, "until I have got a new collar." No piece of personal adornment was it, without which he would not act, but rather that which now is called the fly cast, or the gut cast, or the trace, or what it may be. "And another thing," continued Pike; "the bet is off if you go near him, either now or at any other time, without asking my leave first, and then only going as I tell you."

"What do I want with the great slimy beggar?" the arrogant Bolt made answer. "A good rat is worth fifty of him. No fear of my going near him, Pike. You shan't get out of it that way."

Pike showed his remarkable qualities that day, by fishing exactly as he would have fished without having heard of the great Crockerite. He was up and away upon the millstream before breakfast; and the forenoon he devoted to his favorite course—first down the Craddock stream, a very pretty confluent of the Culm, and from its junction, down the pleasant hams, where the river winds toward Uffculme. It was my privilege to accompany this hero, as his humble Sancho; while Bolt and the faster race went up the river ratting. We were back in time to have Pike's trout (which ranged between two ounces and one half pound) fried for the early dinner; and here it may be lawful to remark that the trout of the Culm are of the very purest excellence, by reason of the flinty bottom, at any rate in these the upper regions. For the valley is the western outlet of the Black Down range, with the Beacon hill upon the north, and Hackpen long ridge to the south; and beyond that again the Whetstone hill, upon whose western end wark portholes scarped with white grit mark the pits. But flint is the staple of the broad Culm Valley, under good, well-pastured loam; and here are chalcedonies and agate stones.

At dinner everybody had a brace of trout—large for the larger folk, little for the little ones, with coughing and some patting on the back for bones. What of equal purport could the fierce rat hunter show? Pike explained many points in the history of each fish, seeming to know them none the worse, and love them all the better, for being fried. We banqueted, neither a whit did soul get stinted of banquet impartial. Then the wielder of the magic rod very modestly sought leave of absence at the teatime.

"Fishing again, Mr. Pike, I suppose," my father answered pleasantly; "I used to be fond of it at your age; but never so entirely wrapped up in it as you are."

"No, sir; I am not going fishing again. I want to walk to Wellington, to get some things at Cherry's."

"Books, Mr. Pike? Ah! I am very glad of that. But I fear it can only be fly books."

"I want a little Horace for eighteenpence—the Cambridge one just published, to carry in my pocket—and a new hank of gut."

"Which of the two is more important? Put that into Latin, and answer it."

"*Utrum pluris facio? Flaccum flocci. Viscera magni.*" With this vast effort Pike turned as red as any trout spot.

"After that who could refuse you?" said my father. "You always tell the truth, my boy, in Latin or in English."

Although it was a long walk, some fourteen miles to Wellington and back, I got permission to go with Pike; and as we crossed the bridge and saw the tree that overhung Crocker's Hole, I begged him to show me that mighty fish.

"Not a bit of it," he replied. "It would bring the blackguards. If the blackguards once find him out, it is all over with him."

"The blackguards are all in factory now, and I am sure they cannot see us from the windows. They won't be out till five o'clock."

With the true liberality of young England, which abides even now as large and glorious as ever, we always called the free and enlightened operatives of the period by the courteous name above set down, and it must be acknowledged that some of them deserved it, although perhaps they poached with less of science than their sons. But the cowardly murder of fish by liming the water was already prevalent.

Yielding to my request and perhaps his own desire—manfully kept in check that morning—Pike very carefully approached that pool, commanding me to sit down while he reconnoitered from the meadow upon the right bank of the stream. And the place which had so sadly quenched the fire of the poor baker's love filled my childish heart with dread and deep wonder at the cruelty of women. But as for John Pike, all he thought of was the fish and the best way to get at him.

Very likely that hole is "holed out" now, as the Yankees well express it, or at any rate changed out of knowledge. Even in my time a very heavy flood entirely altered its character; but to the eager eye of Pike it seemed pretty much as follows, and possibly it may have come to such a form again:

The river, after passing through a hurdle fence at the head of the meadow, takes a little turn or two of bright and shallow indifference, then gathers itself into a good strong slide, as if going down a slope instead of steps. The right bank is high and beetles over with yellow loam and grassy fringe; but the other side is of flinty shingle, low and bare and washed by floods. At the end of this rapid, the stream turns sharply under an ancient alder tree into a large, deep, calm repose, cool, unruffled, and sheltered from the sun by branch and leaf—and that is the hole of poor Crocker.

At the head of the pool (where the hasty current rushes in so eagerly, with noisy excitement and much ado) the quieter waters from below, having rested and enlarged themselves, come lapping up round either curve, with some recollection of their past career, the hoary experience of foam. And sidling toward the new arrival of the impulsive column, where they meet it, things go on which no man can describe without his mouth being full of water. A V is formed, a fancy letter V, beyond any designer's tracery, and even beyond his imagination, a perpetually fluctuating limpid wedge, perpetually creneled and rippled into by little ups and downs that try to make an impress but can only glide away upon either side or sink in dimples under it. And here a gray bough of the ancient alder stretches across, like a thirsty giant's arm, and makes it a very ticklish place to throw a fly. Yet this was the very spot our John Pike must put his fly into, or lose his crown.

Because the great tenant of Crocker's Hole, who allowed no other fish to wag a fin there, and from strict monopoly had grown so fat, kept his victualing yard—if so low an expression can be used concerning him—without above a square yard of this spot. He had a sweet hover, both for rest and recreation, under the bank, in a placid antre, where the water made no noise, but tickled his belly in digestive ease. The loftier the character is of any being, the slower and more dignified his movements are. No true psychologist could have believed—as Sweetland the blacksmith did, and Mr. Pook the tinman—that this trout could ever be the embodiment of Crocker. For this was the last trout in the universal world to drown himself for love; if truly any trout has done so.

"You may come now, and try to look along my back," John Pike, with a reverential whisper, said to me. "Now, don't be in a hurry, young stupid; kneel down. He is not to be disturbed at his dinner, mind. You keep behind me, and look along my back; I never clapped eyes on such a whopper."

I had to kneel down in a tender reminiscence of pastureland and gaze carefully; and not having eyes like those of our Zebedee (who offered his spine for a camera, as he crawled on all fours in front of me), it took me a long time to descry an object most distinct to all who have that special gift of piercing with their eyes the water. See what is said upon this subject in that delicious book, *The Gamekeeper at Home.*

"You are no better than a muff," said Pike, and it was not in my power to deny it.

"If the sun would only leave off," I said. But the sun, who was having a very pleasant play with the sparkle of the water and the twinkle of the leaves, had no inclination to leave off yet, but kept the rippling crystal in a dance of flashing facets, and the quivering verdure in a steady flush of gold.

But suddenly a May fly, a luscious gray drake, richer and more delicate than canvasback or woodcock, with a dart and a leap and a merry zigzag, began to enjoy a little game above the stream. Rising and falling like a gnat, thrilling her gauzy wings, and arching her elegant pellucid frame, every now and then she almost dipped her three long tapering whisks into the dimples of the water.

"He sees her! He'll have her as sure as a gun!" cried Pike, with a gulp, as if he himself were "rising." "Now can you see him, stupid?"

"Crikey, crokums!" I exclaimed, with classic elegance; "I have seen that long thing for five minutes; but I took it for a tree."

"You little"—animal quite early in the alphabet—"now don't you stir a peg, or I'll dig my elbow into you."

The great trout was stationary almost as a stone, in the middle of the V above described. He was gently fanning with his large clear fins, but holding his own against the current mainly by the wagging of his broad-fluked tail. As soon as my slow eyes had once defined him, he grew upon them mightily, molding himself in the matrix of the water, as a thing put into jelly does. And I doubt whether even John Pike saw him more accurately than I did. His size was such, or seemed to be such, that I fear to say a word about it; not because language does not contain the word, but from dread of exaggeration. But his shape and color may be reasonably told without wounding the feeling of an age whose incredulity springs from self-knowledge.

His head was truly small, his shoulders vast; the spring of his back was like a rainbow when the sun is southing; the generous sweep of his deep elastic belly, nobly pulped out with rich nurture, showed what the power of his brain must be, and seemed to undulate, time for time, with the vibrant vigilance of his large wise eyes. His latter end was consistent also. An elegant taper run of counter, coming almost to a cylinder, as a mackerel does, boldly developed with a hugeous spread to a glorious amplitude of swallowtail. His color was all that can well be desired, but ill described by any poor word palette. Enough that he seemed to tone away from olive and umber, with carmine stars, to glowing gold and soft pure silver, mantled with a subtle flush of rose and fawn and opal.

Swoop came a swallow, as we gazed, and was gone with a flick, having missed the May fly. But the wind of his passage, or the skir of wing, struck the merry dancer down, so that he fluttered for one instant on the wave, and that instant was enough. Swift as the swallow, and more true of aim, the great trout made one dart, and a sound, deeper than a tinkle, but as silvery as a bell, rang the poor ephemerid's knell. The rapid water scarcely showed a break; but a bubble sailed down the pool, and the dark hollow echoed with the music of a rise.

"He knows how to take a fly," said Pike; "he has had too many to be tricked with mine. Have him I must; but how ever shall I do it?"

All the way to Wellington he uttered not a word, but shambled along with a mind full of care. When I ventured to look up now and then, to surmise what was going on beneath his hat, deeply set eyes and a wrinkled forehead, relieved at long intervals by a solid shake, proved that there are meditations deeper than those of philosopher or statesman.

III

Surely no trout could have been misled by the artificial May fly of that time, unless he were either a very young fish, quite new to entomology, or else one afflicted with a combination of myopy and bulimy. Even now there is room for plenty of improvement in our counterfeit presentment; but in those days the body was made with yellow mohair, ribbed with red silk and gold twist, and as thick as a fertile bumblebee. John Pike perceived that to offer such a thing to Crocker's trout would probably consign him—even if his great stamina should overget the horror—to an uneatable death, through just and natural indignation. On the other hand, while the May fly lasted, a trout so cultured, so highly refined, so full of light and sweetness, would never demean himself to low bait, or any coarse son of a maggot.

Meanwhile Alec Bolt allowed poor Pike no peaceful thought, no calm absorption of high mind into the world of flies, no placid period of cobbler's wax, floss silk, turned hackles, and dubbing. For in making of flies John Pike had his special moments of inspiration, times of clearer insight into the everlasting verities, times of brighter conception and more subtle execution, tails of more elastic grace and heads of a neater and nattier expression. As a poet labors at one immortal line, compressing worlds of wisdom into the music of ten syllables, so toiled the patient Pike about the fabric of a fly comprising all the excellence that ever sprang from maggot. Yet Bolt rejoiced to jerk his elbow at the moment of sublimest art. And a swarm of flies was blighted thus.

Peaceful, therefore, and long-suffering, and full of resignation as he was, John Pike came slowly to the sad perception that arts avail not without arms. The elbow, so often jerked, at last took a voluntary jerk from the shoulder, and Alex Bolt lay prostrate, with his right eye full of cobbler's wax. This put a desirable check upon his energies for a week or more, and by that time Pike had flown his fly.

When the honeymoon of spring and summer (which they are now too fashionable to celebrate in this country), the heyday of the whole year marked by the budding of the wild rose, the start of the wheat ear from its sheath, the feathering of the lesser plantain, and flowering of the meadowsweet, and, foremost for the angler's joy, the caracole of May flies—when these things are to be seen and felt (which has not happened at all this year), then rivers should be mild and bright, skies blue and white with fleecy cloud, the west wind blowing softly, and the trout in charming appetite.

On such a day came Pike to the bank of Culm, with a loudly beating heart. A fly there is, not ignominious, or of cowdab origin, neither gross and heavy-bodied, from cradlehood of slimy stones, nor yet of menacing aspect and suggesting deeds of poison, but elegant, bland, and of sunny nature, and obviously good to eat. Him or her—why quest we which?—the shepherd of the dale, contemptuous of gender, except in his own species, has called, and as long as they two coexist will call, the Yellow Sally. A fly that does not waste the day in giddy dances and the fervid waltz, but undergoes family incidents with decorum and discretion. He or she, as the case may be—for the natural history of the river-bank is a book to come hereafter, and of fifty men who make flies not one knows the name of the fly he is making—in the early morning of June, or else in the second quarter of the afternoon, this Yellow Sally fares abroad, with a nice well-ordered flutter.

Despairing of the May fly, as it still may be despaired of, Pike came down to the river with his masterpiece of portraiture. The artificial Yellow Sally is generally always—as they say in Cheshire—a mile or more too yellow. On the other hand, the Yellow Dun conveys no idea of any Sally. But Pike had made a very decent Sally, not perfect (for he was young as well as wise), but far above any counterfeit to be had in fishing-tackle shops. How he made it, he told nobody. But if he lives now, as I hope he does, any of my readers may ask him through the G. P. O. and hope to get an answer.

It fluttered beautifully on the breeze, and in such living form that a brother or sister Sally came up to see it, and went away sadder and wiser. Then Pike said: "Get away, you young wretch," to your humble servant who tells this tale; yet, being better than his words, allowed that pious follower to lie down upon his digestive organs and with deep attention watch. There must have been great things to see, but to see them so was difficult. And if I huddle up what happened, excitement also shares the blame.

Pike had fashioned well the time and manner of this overture. He knew that the giant Crockerite was satiate now with May flies, or began to find their flavor failing, as happens to us with asparagus, marrow-fat peas, or strawberries, when we have had a month of them. And he thought that the first Yellow Sally of the season, inferior though it were, might have the special charm of novelty. With the skill of a Zulu, he stole up through the branches over the lower pool till he came to a spot where a yard-wide opening gave just space for spring of rod. Then he saw his desirable friend at dinner, wagging his tail, as a hungry gentleman dining with the Lord Mayor agitates his coat. With one dexterous whirl, untaught by any of the many books upon the subject, John Pike laid his Yellow Sally (for he cast with one fly only) as lightly as gossamer upon the rapid, about a yard in front of the big trout's head. A moment's pause, and then too quick for words was the thing that happened.

A heavy plunge was followed by a fearful rush. Forgetful of the current the river was ridged, as if with a plow driven under it; the strong line, though given out as fast as might be, twanged like a harp string as it cut the wave, and then Pike stood up, like a ship dismasted, with the butt of his rod snapped below the ferrule. He had one of those foolish things, just invented, a hollow butt of hickory; and the finial ring of his spare top looked out, to ask what had happened to the rest of it. "Bad luck!" cried the fisherman; "but never mind, I shall have him next time, to a certainty."

When this great issue came to be considered, the cause of it was sadly obvious. The fish, being hooked, had made off with the rush of a shark for the bottom of the pool. A thicket of saplings below the alder tree had stopped the judicious hooker from all possibility of following; and when he strove to turn him by elastic pliance, his rod broke at the breach of pliability. "I have learned a sad lesson," said John Pike, looking sadly.

How many fellows would have given up this matter, and glorified themselves for having hooked so grand a fish, while explaining that they must have caught him, if they could have done it! But Pike only told me not to say a word about it, and began to make ready for another tug of war. He made himself a splice rod, short and handy, of well-seasoned ash, with a stout top of bamboo, tapered so discreetly, and so balanced in its spring, that verily it formed an arc, with any pressure on it, as perfect as a leafy poplar in a stormy summer. "Now break it if you can," he said, "by any amount of rushes; I'll hook you by your jacket collar; you cut away now, and I'll land you."

This was highly skillful, and he did it many times; and whenever I was landed well, I got a lollipop, so that I was careful not to break his tackle. Moreover he made him a landing net, with a kidney-bean stick, a ring of wire, and his own best nightcap of strong cotton net. Then he got the farmer's leave, and lopped obnoxious bushes; and now the chiefest question was: What bait, and when to offer it? In spite of his sad rebuff, the spirit of John Pike had been equable. The genuine angling mind is steadfast, large, and self-supported, and to the vapid, ignominious chaff, tossed by swine upon the idle wind, it pays as much heed as a big trout does to a dance of midges. People put their fingers to their noses and said: "Master Pike, have you caught him yet?" and Pike only answered: "Wait a bit." If ever this fortitude and perseverance is to be recovered as the English Brand (the one thing that has made us what we are, and may yet redeem us from niddering shame), a degenerate age should encourage the habit of fishing and never despairing. And the brightest sign yet for our future is the increasing demand for hooks and gut.

Pike fished in a manlier age, when nobody would dream of cowering from a savage because he was clever at skulking; and when, if a big fish broke the rod, a stronger rod was made for him, according to the usage of Great Britain. And though the young angler had been defeated, he did not sit down and have a good cry over it.

About the second week in June, when the May fly had danced its day and died —for the season was an early one—and Crocker's trout had recovered from the wound to his feelings and philanthropy, there came a night of gentle rain, of pleasant tinkling upon window ledges, and a soothing patter among young leaves, and the Culm was yellow in the morning. "I mean to do it this afternoon," Pike whispered to me, as he came back panting. "When the water clears there will be a splendid time."

The lover of the rose knows well a gay voluptuous beetle, whose pleasure is to lie embedded in a fount of beauty. Deep among the incurving petals of the blushing fragrance, he loses himself in his joys sometimes, till a breezy waft reveals him. And when the sunlight breaks upon his luscious dissipation, few would have the heart to oust him, such a gem from such a setting. All his back is emerald sparkles, all his front red Indian gold, and here and there he grows white spots to save the eye from aching. Pike put his finger in and fetched him out, and offered him a little change of joys, by putting a Limerick hook through his thorax, and bringing it out between his elytra. *Cetonia aurata* liked it not, but pawed the air very naturally, and fluttered with his wings attractively.

"I meant to have tried with a fern web," said the angler; "until I saw one of these beggars this morning. If he works like that upon the water, he will do. It was hopeless to try artificials again. What a lovely color the water is! Only three days now to the holidays. I have run it very close. You be ready, younker."

With these words he stepped upon a branch of the alder, for the tone of the waters allowed approach, being soft and sublustrous, without any mud. Also Master Pike's own tone was such as becomes the fisherman, calm, deliberate, free from nerve, but full of eye and muscle. He stepped upon the alder bough to get as near as might be to the fish, for he could not cast this beetle like a fly; it must be dropped gently and allowed to play. "You may come and look," he said to me; "when the water is so, they have no eyes in their tails."

The rose beetle trod upon the water prettily, under a lively vibration, and he looked quite as happy, and considerably more active, than when he had been cradled in the anthers of the rose. To the eye of a fish he was a strong individual, fighting courageously with the current, but sure to be beaten through lack of fins; and mercy suggested, as well as appetite, that the proper solution was to gulp him.

"Hooked him in the gullet. He can't get off!" cried John Pike, laboring to keep his nerves under. "Every inch of tackle is as strong as a bell pull. Now, if I don't land him, I will never fish again!"

Providence, which had constructed Pike, foremost of all things, for lofty angling—disdainful of worm and even minnow—Providence, I say, at this adjuration, pronounced that Pike must catch that trout. Not many anglers are heaven-born; and for one to drop off the hook halfway through his teens would be infinitely worse than to slay the champion trout. Pike felt the force of this, and rushing through the rushes, shouted: "I am sure to have him, Dick! Be ready with my nightcap."

Rod in a bow, like a springle riser; line on the hum, like the string of Paganini; winch on the gallop, like a harpoon wheel, Pike, the headcenter of everything, dashing through thick and thin, and once taken overhead—for he jumped into the hole, when he must have lost him else, but the fish too impetuously towed him out, and made off in passion for another pool, when, if he had only retired to his hover, the angler might have shared the baker's fate—all these things (I tell you, for they all come up again, as if the day were yesterday) so scared me of my never very steadfast wits, that I could only holloa! But one thing I did, I kept the nightcap ready.

WHEN ALL THE WORLD IS YOUNG

Howard T. Walden 2d

THE ROAD TO SCHOOL TOOK him past the things he loved to the things he hated. It took him, first, past the white house that had been the home of Lank Starbuck who had taught Chris how to fish for trout. Chris had been glad when old Lank's son, Thad, had left, and he hadn't wanted anyone else to move into the place. If it was empty he could go by it and think of old Lank, but if someone else moved in it wouldn't mean old Lank to him any more. A house wasn't just a house, it was who lived in it. If the man who lived in it was your friend the house was your friend, too. But when a stranger moved in, the house became a stranger and you had to get to know the house all over again, by another name. He hadn't liked it when Dr. Martin had moved in there, last summer. Dr. Martin, they had said, was needed here. There wasn't a really good doctor in Forks Township and the nearest help folks could get for a sick person was fifteen miles away. Maybe so, but he hadn't liked it.

But, thinking now about how he hadn't liked it at the time, he could see how foolish he had been. That was a kid thing—standing pat on what you have and seeing no good at all in something different. When he had begun to change was the day Dr. Martin had called on his Dad, early last fall, just after Dr. Martin had moved in. Chris had been scared, that time. He hadn't known what was the matter, but any time his Dad went to bed in the middle of the day it was scary. But after Dr. Martin had seen his Dad and had come downstairs and talked to him, he wasn't scared any more. He didn't remember what the Doctor had said. But he knew his Dad was going to get well and that everything, the whole world, was all right again.

After that he felt like looking again at the old Lank Starbuck house when he went by.

And he had even got to thinking of it, now, as the Martin house, thinking easily of it that way, not with homesickness, being glad to hook up the name Martin with it. The first day of school last September a yellow-haired girl had run out of the Martin door as he had gone by. "I'm Rosemary," she had said. "I'm going to your school. Can I go with you?"

The road took him, second, past the bridge over the Big Stony, the bridge just upstream from the March Brown Club water and just downstream from the junction of the Little Stony. He wasn't allowed to fish the water below the bridge, though his Dad owned it. That was a hard thing for Chris to under-stand—it was a grown-up thing—but he was beginning to get it, now. He had met two of the March Brown members and he liked them, and that made it easier for him to understand the rule and to respect it, which he had, now, for nearly a year. Those people paid a lot of money to fish his Dad's water. The idea of paying to fish was something he hadn't thought of until lately. You didn't pay to play ball or fly a kite though you paid for the ball and the kite cord. You bought a fishing rod but not the use of it. He had no money to pay for that and he knew he wouldn't pay for it if he had because he could fish the entire Little Stony for nothing. The fishing wasn't as good up there, but it was good enough, if you knew how to go after 'em. Trout were in there. So far this year he had taken twenty-eight, in ten tries, counting only keepers of course. And that, he knew darn well, was double the number Sticks Hooker had caught, in twice as many tries. Sticks lived up the Little Stony, on a back road, in one of the several houses Chris's father owned in Forks Township. Living right on the stream, Sticks had all the chance in the world to fish. Sticks didn't pay for his rod, even—he cut it in the woods. And he thought Chris a kind of a stuck-up dude for fishing with a bought rod. . . . Sticks was all right, though. Chris liked him in a way, but Sticks was just enough older and bigger to try to bully him a little—and he liked Rosemary a little too well. Chris wanted to be friends with Sticks, but something—he didn't know what—got between them like a wall. Maybe it was his fault, maybe Sticks would like to be friends with him, too.

It took him, finally, to school, to books with dreary words in them, and to windows with dingy red-brown shades under which his eyes would stray to the outside world of blossom and bird song and wind-filled trees, and, over there, beyond that hump of a pasture, the little valley where the dark stream ran. It took him to the smell of chalk dust and old paper and of children who do not get enough baths, the school smell, the smell of the Hooker kids. It took him to Miss Spencer, standing in her straight black dress at the blackboard with a long pointer hovering over long rows of figures and suddenly lighting on one like a fish hawk spotting a chub, or tap-tapping over States on a down-rolled map and coming to rest on a yellow one near the middle—Miss Spencer who would say much less than she thought but make you think she meant a lot more. "To what capital of what state am I pointing, Christopher, and what is its chief industry?" And he would answer, "Topeka, Illinois, and they make glassware there," and she would lay down her pointer slowly on the eraser shelf, as if giving up the whole thing in disgust, and say, "*Christopher Wintermute*." That's all she'd say. But she'd mean, "You, the son of the richest man in Forks Township, do not know that Topeka is the capital of Kansas and that they never heard of glassware in Topeka." And all the class would know that was what she meant.

*

He gave the whistle, that May morning, to Rosemary, as he went by. Their private signal had been decided on, sometime ago, after a good deal of deliberation. Rosemary knew the bobwhite call of the quail and had wanted to make it that. But Chris had overruled her—there were too many real bobwhites whistling in these fields in the spring and summer, and he didn't want any false alarms bringing Rosemary to her door. The whistle of the greater yellowlegs, the *whew-whew—whew-whew*—a one-note, two-syllable, once-repeated call, would be better. That was a sound heard from natural sources only in April and September around here, and not often then. It was easy and it carried, but it wasn't loud. It wouldn't stir up grown people or bring dogs running when you didn't want 'em. And besides, it was uncommon: it gave him a chance to explain to Rosemary what the greater and lesser yellowlegs were. . . . Bet Miss Spencer never heard of 'em and wouldn't know one if she saw it. Schoolteachers, who were supposed to know everything, didn't know important things like this at all.

The front door of the Martin house opened as if his whistle had made some secret contact with its lock. Rosemary took the porch steps in two strides and ran down the walk, her bright hair flying. She had on the white dress he liked, a high-waisted thing with ruffles and a sash the color of her hair.

"Want to run?" she said. "Look, I'll race you to the bridge."

"Aw, no. You couldn't keep up with me. No, I want to talk to you. Let's walk."

"You're 'fraid I can beat."

"All right, then. Give me your books so you can run free. On your mark—set—go!"

He let her draw away from him in the first fifty feet, then he spurted a little and kept an even distance between himself and the flying heels and the white dress and the streaming hair. She made the left turn onto the bridge road and gained a little on the down slope to the stream. For a girl, she could run. He hadn't expected her to hold the pace and now he had a momentary real fear that she would reach the bridge ahead of him. The heavy schoolbooks, a strapped bundle in each arm, handicapped him. But he put all he had into a final sprint and beat her to the log rail by a stride.

They sat on the lower rail, on the upstream side of the bridge, Rosemary flushed and panting, Chris trying to keep his breath even.

"You can run," he said.

"But boys always beat. I wish I was a boy."

"If you were—who'd you want to be?"

"Oh-h-h. How do I know?" She tried to make a circle in the roadside dust with the toe of her shoe. But her legs still had the running in them, they were trembling and unsure. "If I was Sticks Hooker I'd be tall and strong—the best ballplayer in school. If I was you I'd have a rich Dad, an' I could get things, nice clothes."

"Listen, my Dad isn't rich. He's got a lot of land so people think he's rich but he's land-poor. He's worried about taxes an' rents he can't collect—I heard him say so. But don't tell that—that's a secret, like our whistle."

"I won't."

"Anyway—"

"What?"

"Is that all you'd have?"

"Is *what* all I'd have?"

"If you were me. A rich Dad—if he *was* rich?"

"Oh." Rosemary erased the circle in the dust with her shoe. "You're nice, Chris. I like you."

"Better'n you like Sticks?"

"Maybe. . . . I like Sticks, too. He brought me a trout yesterday."

"One?"

"Um-h-m-m. That's all he promised."

"How big?"

"Eight inches. We measured him on my ruler. Gosh, he was good. Had him for breakfast this morning."

Chris got up from the lower rail and turned around and leaned against the upper one, up to his armpits, and looked for a long minute at the water flowing under the bridge, and his eyes followed it slowly upstream, as if studying each foot of its dark fast surface, to the point where the Little Stony comes in from the north. Rosemary stood up, too, and looked from Chris's face to the water and back to Chris's face, and kept silent, respecting something she felt to be going on in his mind.

"Look, Rosemary," he said, finally, "I'll get you five trout, none under eight inches, maybe some bigger." He looked straight at her blue eyes. "Five. Maybe one will be twelve inches."

"Five? Altogether—at once? From Little Stony?"

"Sure, from Little Stony. Why?"

"Sticks said you fished the Club water sometimes because your Dad owns it—an' that's why you catch more than he does."

Chris pondered that for a moment. It was why, maybe, Sticks didn't like him. Then he looked squarely at Rosemary again. "I *have* fished down there—two or three times—last year. But each time I had to sneak it, past the guard. I'm not allowed to fish there. When I fish there I'm poaching, and Sticks can do the same thing any time he wants to try it. An' I'll tell him so. . . . Today," he added, "I'll fish Little Stony only. Word of honor. . . . Believe me?"

"Yes," she said.

"The water's right, Rosemary. I can get 'em from Little Stony."

"How do you know? Is that what you were looking at, so long—to see if the water's right?"

"Yes."

"How does it tell you?"

"I don't know. Right pitch, right color. An' the day's right—cloudy but it won't rain an' it'll stay warm. . . . It all smiles at me when it's right—it looks friendly, like you look when you smile at me." He had heard old Lank Starbuck say that, years ago, and he had never forgotten it.

"But maybe, by the time school's out, it won't be right any more."

"It's an all-day job, Rosemary. I won't go to school."

"Oh-h-h. But you can't do that. That's hooky."

"Sure, hooky." He said it casually, with an offhand assurance that puzzled her, made her think he had done it before.

"But you can't," she persisted, to draw him out. "Where's your fish pole—and what do you do with your schoolbooks? An' if you go home to get your pole, now, an' your Dad sees you, what'll he do?"

"He'd do plenty. He'd look sad an' he'd *be* sad. No one else could see he was sad but *I* can. An' he'd be calm. He wouldn't rant at me—he'd talk easy. An' then he'd whale me. Gosh, you don't know how he can hurt. . . . But he won't see me. 'Cause I won't go home. . . . You know what a cache is—I told you."

"Um-h-m-m. I remember—the time you left the muskrat skin for my fur collar by our back fence."

"That's right. Miss Spencer wouldn't tell you, 'cause she wouldn't know. Well, my rod—don't call it a pole, it's a rod—my rod is cached up along Little Stony. I leave the books there, pick up the rod, leave the rod there when I get through fishing and pick up the books an' take 'em home."

Rosemary looked at him, admiringly. There was enough deviltry in that technique to appeal to her. She wanted a part in it—but she was only a girl.

"I won't tell," she said, finally, with satisfaction. That gave her a definite role, however small, in the plot. She elaborated it: "Look. If Miss Spencer asks me where you are I'll tell her you started out with me but you got all out of breath at the bridge and decided you didn't feel like coming to school today. Is that some kind of a lie—a white lie?"

"Nope. It's true—except I didn't get *all* out of breath. I can run farther than that. I ran all the way to school once. . . . But that's good—you tell her that, before class, hear? Then maybe I won't need an excuse from Dad."

"All right. . . . But hooky. That's wrong."

"Why?"

"I don't know. It just is—like stealing."

"No it isn't. I'll tell you sometime. . . . 'By, Rose."

He headed into the woods along the north bank of the stream. When he was up to the confluence of the Little Stony he stopped and looked back to the bridge. She had gone. The road north of the bridge was not visible through the trees except for one short stretch where it topped a rise two hundred yards away. He laid his sight on this spot like a barrage, and presently the white dress and the yellow sash and the yellow hair crossed it, walking fast.

He wondered, now, why he hadn't kissed her good-bye. He had wanted to. It had been the moment, when he had left her—she had been "right" then, like the stream was right for fishing. No good, now, to call to her to stop and to run to her. The moment was past; he had lost it. . . . He could take the stream for fishing, always, when it offered itself, as he was taking it now, even at a good deal of risk—for he knew the chances to be better than even that his truancy would be found out and punished. But he couldn't take her who presented no risk at all. If his conscience had called it wrong he could understand. His conscience called plenty of things he did wrong and kept him awake at night thinking of them. But his conscience approved this and still he was afraid of it. It bothered him, like a buzzing fly that he couldn't swat.

Well, he'd swat it tonight, once and for all, and clear the air of the thing. When the time came for him to leave her this evening, after giving her the trout, he'd claim his reward. It would be another right moment, on her front porch, with the dusk drawing in, and this time he would grab it.

There was a narrow path that led him along the northeast bank of the Little Stony, upstream. A fisherman's path, it was never far from the water in its gradual climb up the valley. About a quarter-mile above the bridge Chris turned off it to the right and entered a little swale grown thicky with birches and witch hazel. A woodcock whistled up out of it, a native bird, fat with the spring worms. An ancient oak stood in the middle of this small area. Chris stooped and reached into an opening at the base of the great hollow trunk and drew out a cloth-cased steel rod and a willow creel. He opened the lid of the creel to see that all his gear was intact—his double-action reel with the enameled line on it, the packet of leaders, the cork full of eyed hooks and the tobacco can for worms.

A flat brown Geography, a blunt green Practical English Grammar, a stout red Elements of United States History and a thin black Graded City Speller, well strapped with a double loop of webbing, took up the occupancy of the old trunk where the rod and creel left off.

A good trade, he thought.

Occasional hooky was not against his conscience either, any more. It had been, once. His father had talked to him of the duties and responsibilities of men and of what men owed to their society and to the world at large. A duty was something that was unpleasant now, but that paid you some sort of reward later on. You got an actual reward—money, perhaps, or maybe only a better character—at some future time by doing something unpleasant now. God paid you, in some way, for the duties you did. Education was one of those rewards and going to school the duty that got it for you. It had sounded right, even brave, the way his father had put it. But thinking about it later, in the dark of his room, when the ring of his father's words had died out of his ears, he thought he could see something selfish in the pursuit of duty. If you were after a reward anyway perhaps you could take your reward now—have fun now instead of later. It all came to the same thing in the end, God paid it anyway, now or afterward. That hadn't decided him, though. That wasn't strong enough—it was only his little kid idea against the ancient wisdom of his father which had proved itself too many times to be doubted. That had been one of the times he had wanted a mother's opinion, too. He had felt that a mother's judgment would have some nameless tenderness, be less severe and easier to live with. But he didn't even remember his mother, who had died when he was two years old. His father had to do.

But one day last summer when he was poaching on the Club water, sneaking around a big rock at the head of the Pasture Pool, he had met face to face, head on, a princess. His first instinct had been to run, for anyone met on the private water was probably his enemy. But he had looked into her face, met her eyes, and known at once that there was no need to run from her. She was grown up but not old, and not a real princess of course, but she looked like the princess in the fairy-tale book he had at home. She had asked him his name and given him hers, Priscilla, and told him to call her that. He had thought of "Princess Priscilla" and the words had seemed to fit, to swim together. She was the daughter, she had said, of a real Army Colonel who had fought in the war and who was a member of the March Browns. She had asked him to sit down on the rock and talk with her a while. The Pasture Pool was an open spot where the guard could see him easily if he went by, but that would be all right, she had said, she'd take care of that. The talk had turned to poaching and had gotten around, as he had known it would, to the question of whether it was his duty not to poach. "What do *you* think?" she had asked. And you had to answer her straight, you couldn't just answer the way a nice boy was supposed to. That was the way you answered Miss Spencer at school, but not her. She had a face and a voice you couldn't lie to. So he had turned the thing over in his mind for a couple of minutes before replying, trying to line it all up with what his father had told him of duty.

"In a way," he had said, finally, "it's my duty to poach."

"How?" she had asked.

"Well, it takes a little nerve to poach here—I have to be a little brave about trying it. That's hard. And being careful not to get caught—sneaking—that's hard, too, if you do it all day. But sometimes God pays me with a big trout, bigger'n I'd get upstream."

She had seemed to think about that for a long while. Then she had said: "I like that, Chris. I like you for saying it."

They had talked for an hour or more, there on the rock. She hadn't advised him to keep off the stream nor to go on it again, but had left that for him to decide. "Another duty is having fun," she had said, and it had sounded like his father's words in reverse, "so long as it doesn't spoil other people's fun." She had told him to have all the fun he could while he was a boy and to keep on having it when he was grown, fun in his mind when his body got too old for it. "The great men are simple men," she had said. "They never quite get over being kids."

Since that day he had never again fished the Club water.

But playing hooky was his own affair. That didn't spoil the fun of a single soul on earth.

He took the steel rod out of its cloth case and stowed the case in the hollow oak with the schoolbooks. He collected enough worms by kicking over some grass hummocks on the far side of the swale, put them in the tobacco can and headed upstream again.

The Hooker house was three hundred yards above here, well back from the other bank and partly visible through the trees. Just opposite the Hooker house his path would come out high above the stream overlooking one of the best runs of trout water on the whole of the Little Stony, a place where he had taken more than one good fish. If this were a Saturday he would give it a look but on a school day the smart thing was to leave the path before he came in sight of the house, make a wide detour through the woods and return to the path at a point well above. For if one of the younger Hooker kids saw him he would tell Sticks afterward, and Sticks might tell the teacher.

He heard their voices, across stream, as he worked his way past through the woods. Regaining the path above, he proceeded almost a mile before he stopped and assembled his gear. This was his favorite place to start. A little riffle spilled into deep fast water between two boulders below which a dark pool arched down to a flat undercut rock at its lower end. With luck he could take two fish here, one in the fast run and one from under the rock below.

Crouching well back from the bank and well above the head of the run Chris let the worm go into the dark water, deep, with a little slack to keep it down. For a second he could see its course in the riffle, then he lost it. The current straightened his slack—the worm should be between the rocks now. He held his breath for the strike and it came. He hit back, felt the strong resistance of the trout, guided the fish up through the fast water, lifted him clear and swung him to the bank. A deep ten-inch native and a good start on his day. He bent back the trout's head, gathered some ferns and laid the fat fish on them in the creel.

Another try in the same water was part of the technique he had inherited from Lank Starbuck. He went through with it, gave it plenty of time, but nothing happened. The slow center of the pool, sometimes good for a fish, yielded nothing either. He crossed the stream, wading nearly to his knees, for it was necessary to fish the undercut rock at the pool's tail from the other side. He backed away from the bank, crouched low, waited a minute, two minutes, up to the limit of his patience. Then he put on a fresh worm and swung it gently into the slow current upstream from the rock. It was out of his sight below the rock's edge, drifting deep in the black water, just the way he had wanted it to go. In a moment the drift of his line halted though the current all around it kept on. He knew what it was: there was nothing to snag him on that smooth bottom. His line, the part of it he could see, started upstream then, gaining speed. He struck and felt at once that he was into a bigger fish than he had dreamed of hooking up here. The trout raced for the head of the pool, taking line from the reel, then turned and bored downstream. The lip of the pool was a shallow curving wash over a flat rock bottom, only inches deep. The trout thrashed into it, exposing its great proportions, seemed to roll once or twice and slid back into deep water again as Chris's line went suddenly slack.

A curious and empty quiet was all through the woods and over the water. If any birds had been singing they were still now. The little pool had lapsed to its former expressionless calm. It might never have held a trout, and this one, just lost, might have been only imagined or dreamed. That vacant sense of stillness was inside Chris, too, in the region of his heart. He had known it before, many times. It was pure loss. No word nor act could, at the moment, answer its thrust. Only time could put it behind—an hour's fishing, with its new problems, new hopes and perhaps new success.

He reeled in. His hook and half his leader were gone. He cut the frayed end of the leader cleanly off and tied on a new length of gut and a new hook. By noon he had regained complete control of his day and he could look back, now, on the loss of the big one and see it as a definite part of the sport of fishing. Three trout were now on the ferns in his creel, an eight-inch native and a nine-inch brown added to the first one. He needed two more to keep his promise to Rosemary.

And he'd get 'em. He'd get one extra, six in all, so he could keep one for himself. They were coming, and when they were coming he could take six if he was very careful. This was the day, perhaps the best he'd see this year. The high tide —it came once in every season, and he had spotted it. It was worth the risk he was taking, worth being caught and all that that would entail.

A wood thrush sang into the noon stillness. A gray squirrel sat on a windfall ahead of him, jerked its tail twice like a mechanical toy and raced down the log at his approach. In a wide backwater which he had to cross on his way downstream a muskrat ploughed straight as a tugboat, towing a leafed branch. He was happy in the way a trout fisherman can be happy when all the world is young and the day is right and confidence is with him. He had that rare fishing happiness which can forget for a while mere keenness for the chase and indulge itself with the quiet asides of angling. He sat down on an old stump and spent half an hour watching the water and the woods on the far bank, and thought about the little unseen lives that lived and died there, year by year, while boys went to school and men worried over taxes and their duty to a society which worried as much as they.

Then he went back to it, fishing carefully, approaching with great caution each likely run and pool on his way downstream. Another native and another brown, ten inches each, were in his creel before three o'clock. His promise of five trout to Rosemary was kept. . . . Wait till Sticks hears about this.

But he needed another one and he wanted it to be big. He had mentioned a twelve-incher to Rosemary. The one he had lost had been well over that but he couldn't say much about the "big one that got away." Even Rosemary, who knew nothing about fishing, had heard that tale too many times to be impressed. She would laugh at it and the effect of the five good trout would be lost in her scorn.

The big one, if he got it, would be for Rosemary, and that would free one of his ten-inchers for his own dinner tonight. Bringing home a trout would need no explaining: it could have been caught after school as some of his others had been this year. . . . His stomach, without food since breakfast, was beginning to talk to him, to nag at him, interrupting his fishing now and then with its assertions. He began to think too much of the dinner that he would have. Trout or no trout, it would be a good one, as it always was. Old Sarah, his Dad's cook, could turn it out. There would be a fat ham and baked potatoes and peas—or maybe a great smoking stew, with dumplings—and a huge tumbler of milk, filled twice, and all the fresh bread and butter he could eat, and an apple pie. And he could feel how sleepy he would be after it and how good his bed would feel as he would lie in the cool sheets just before sleep caught him, looking up at the ceiling at the angular shadow cast from the dim hall light by his half-open bedroom door, and feeling the spring night fanning his cheek . . .

The Hooker house was just below him now, on the opposite bank. He had come up to the point at which he had rejoined the trail this morning, after his detour around the danger zone, and if he were to retrace his steps he should leave the trail here. He stood still in the path, to ponder the question a moment and to listen. The vicinity of the Hooker house was still a no-man's-land, so far as he was concerned. It was not yet time for school to be out and his presence here on the stream would give him away now as surely as it would have this morning. Sticks wouldn't be home for half an hour at least. The other Hooker kids were making no sound. They were in the house or far off in the woods, for when they were nearby you could always hear them. He might—he might just possibly—get away with trying that good run of water directly opposite the house. It was a desperate chance—it made him feel as poaching on the Big Stony used to make him feel—but today his reward might be there.

The path from here on climbed gradually above the stream bed; just opposite the Hooker house it emerged from the trees into an open slashing, a badly exposed position for anyone sneaking it as he was. But it held an advantage: its altitude above the water gave him a penetrating view, when the sun was high, of that sand-bottomed run. There was something about that run which he never had been able to understand. Its straight fifty-foot stretch was totally devoid of windfalls, rocks or overhanging banks. It had no trout cover worthy of the name, and certainly it could offer little in the shape of underwater food. Yet it was a place where large trout loved to lie. The small fish, he knew, were afraid of its bright exposure. . . . If a fish was in sight he would maneuver down to it; if not, he would leave the trail at once and go home.

He studied the house—as much as he could see of it from the shelter of the woods—before he dared the open trail ahead. A blue column of wood smoke stood up straight out of the chimney. But no sound came from it and no one was in sight. If the Hooker kids would stay indoors while he did what he wanted to do, he might yet get by with it.

Once beyond the cover of the trees there was no need to crouch for if someone looked toward him out here he would be seen, crouching or standing, and crouching would make him look more suspicious. So he walked erect along the high open trail to the vantage point where he could scan the bright water below.

He had to look sharp: there were a few vague shadows on the bottom, and a waterlogged stick or two. For a minute he saw no sign of a fish; then, as if his straining eyesight had created it, a large trout was there, directly below him, its tail fanning almost imperceptibly in the gentle current. He wondered that he hadn't seen it before, it was so distinct now. A rainbow—all of sixteen inches long. He could see its pink stripe and its myriad tiny spots. A great trout, strayed up from the Club water, probably—the biggest trout he had ever seen in the Little Stony.

He faded back up the path to the woods, walking backward, his eyes on the fish. Then he sneaked rapidly down the wooded bank to the stream and baited his hook with the worm he had been saving for just this chance.

Well upstream from his fish, Chris put the worm in with a short gentle flick and let the easy current take it down, drawing out the slack between his reel and first guide. Though he would do his best to keep the worm drifting as long as possible he knew it would sink and come to rest on the bottom fifteen or twenty feet above the trout. It would be better to work it a little nearer but he dared neither a long cast nor a closer approach. Alternately feeding slack to the current and raising his rod tip to keep the worm up, Chris could feel it along the line when at last the worm settled into the sand. His line, soaked with the day's fishing, submerged itself gradually upstream until only a few inches of it were visible between his rod tip and the surface.

There was nothing to do now but crouch and wait—and control himself, if he could. He was a little ashamed of his agony of expectation and the way his heart and his hands were affected by it. Even this fish—the biggest trout he had ever deliberately angled for—shouldn't make his heart pound like that nor cause his hands to tremble so that he couldn't hold his rod steady. He tried to be cool and thoughtful, to figure the chances of that rainbow seeing his worm, and coming upstream to take it if he did see it, and the possibility of his leader escaping notice. To lose his terrific excitement he tried to discourage himself. But it was no good: despite all his reasoning there was still an outside chance of that giant taking hold, and it was this nearness to such success as he had never known that might prove too much for him to bear.

His rod had caught the trembling infection from his hands. That little length of visible line between his rod tip and the water jerked back and forth in the slow current. He watched it steadily as if trying by the very intensity of his gaze to make it still, and as he watched he discerned a movement in it which even his trembling hands could not have caused. The visible short stretch lengthened a little, downstream, came five or six clear inches out of the water, straightening itself in a widening angle from the rod. It lapsed back, almost to its former position, then straightened again swiftly, six feet of dripping line knifing out of the surface below his rod. Chris Wintermute stood up and struck . . .

He tried to recall that battle afterward; once, when she was in a mood to be still and listen, he tried to give Rosemary the details out of the long view which retrospect should have made clear. But he could never quite track it down. His memory of it remained a confused picture of a surface shattered like glass, a surface erupting all over at once with a great trout bursting from each eruption, a memory of spray and the noise of breaking water, a memory of a frenzied dream, of something that couldn't happen in real life, and a slow awakening from it as the fish tired, a gradual return, after an incredible time, to the familiar world on which he could plant his feet and feel safe. . . . And of his happiness at the end, when he eased that huge exhausted trout up the slope of a little sand beach at the lower end of the run—but there were no words for that and he had never even tried to give that part to Rosemary or to anyone else. That was for himself, only, to know—for himself only, that happiness, to think about sometimes when he was alone . . .

Just then, at that moment when the fish came up on the sand, he didn't believe it. He had known that there were rainbow trout in the world as big as this one, but that one so big should be his own, caught by himself, he didn't believe.

Neither did the two Hooker kids who had materialized from nowhere, on the opposite bank, in time to see Chris beach his fish.

"Sucker, ain't it, Chris?" one called across. "Big sucker—I seen one in here."

"Sucker, my eye." Chris was looking around for a short stout club, for this fish was too large to kill by the usual method. "He's a trout—a rainbow."

The arrival of the Hooker kids on the scene annoyed him. Up to that moment his adventure had been a complete success. To have taken this trout quickly and gotten away unseen would have made his day perfect. But now he was discovered. The Hooker kids had broken in on his secret. They didn't know what playing hooky was but they would tell Sticks they had seen him, and Sticks would know. And tomorrow it would be all over school, and tomorrow night his father would have it.

"Aw, trout ain't that big. Sticks said they ain't."

"Because he can't get 'em that big." Chris was beginning to get mad.

"He could so—if they grew that big." The youngest Hooker boy was loyal to his big brother. The other one, the next younger to Sticks, seemed to hold certain doubts. "Shut up," he said quietly. "Maybe Sticks can't. Sticks ain't so good at fishin'. . . . Let's go see it."

Chris found the right club and killed the trout with two blows on top of its head. The Hooker kids, barefooted, rolled up their faded blue overalls to their thin thighs and waded in. They had legs like those which had given Sticks his nickname. All the Hooker kids could be called "Sticks," he was thinking.

"You ought to have sneakers on, or somethin'," Chris said. "Some o' those rocks are sharp."

"Aw, we ain't got shoes," the larger one replied, thrashing across, heedless of where he put his feet. "None of th' kids in our house got shoes but Sticks. Sticks needs 'em 'cause he goes t' school."

Chris looked at them, coming across. The thought of their being without shoes, having nothing at all to wear on their feet, hurt him deeply like an insult, as if someone had called him a darned fool for ever thinking the world was beautiful. The thought, he knew, was never going to be far from him. It would come back to him again and again; in the nights, in the alone moments when he got out the thoughts he had loved, this thing would come breaking in on them and leering at them and chasing them away.

He held up the big fish before their devouring eyes. "Is it a trout?" he said.

They stood looking in silence, trying to make their minds believe the story their eyes had to tell.

"Right in our own front yard, too," the smaller one said, finally. "Betcha Sticks would have got 'im if *you* hadn't come by."

"Like ta have 'im for my supper t'night," said the other one. "Boy, would he taste good!"

"Um-m-m. Better'n ol' corn mush."

"I like corn meal mush all right," Chris said. "I have that for breakfast, sometimes. You don't have it for supper, do you?"

"Sure. Supper—breakfast too. All meals."

"Gosh. You must like it better'n anything."

The two Hooker kids looked at each other and smiled in a little superior way, a mutual acknowledgment of a bit of information not known to Chris.

"We hate it," the larger one said. "Wouldn't be so bad 'f you could have a lotta milk on it. 'Thout milk it's dry—gets in your teeth."

"But—if you don't like it—why, why do you eat it so much?"

They exchanged the same look a second time and the larger one spoke again: " 'Cause there ain't much else in our house t' eat. Mom planted some beans an' pertaters but they ain't up yet. She gets dandylions an' wood herbs. But they don't fill ya—ya can't eat much of 'em. Fried dough fills ya—we have that, some."

"Once in a while Sticks gets a fish," the smaller one put in. "We try to but we don't get none. Been tryin' all mornin' to snare some suckers. No luck. . . . Fried dough fills ya *too* much," he added, quietly, as if talking to himself. "Made me puke, las' night."

"You make too much noise," said Chris. "That's why you don't get any fish. I heard you this morning, on the way up." He uttered those words but he wasn't thinking them. It was as if someone else, over whom he had no control, had put them in his mouth merely to keep up the talk while he thought about something else—about corn meal mush, day after day—and about why Sticks's legs and his brothers' legs were so thin—and about having no shoes—

"Get any others, Chris?"

—and about fried dough and dandelions, and Mom who had planted beans and potatoes but they weren't up yet—Mom, whom he had never seen but whom, he thought oddly, he could love—

"What does your Dad do?" he asked suddenly, seizing on a forlorn shape that had come up out of the gloom in his brain.

"Pop? He ain't home," the small one said.

"I mean—doesn't he work? Doesn't he make any money to buy food?"

"He was workin'," the older one said. "He worked in Post's garage, over at th' Forks. But he don't, now. He lost his job. Get any other fish, Chris?"

A faint complaining cry drifted down to them from the house across the stream.

"What's that?" Chris asked.

"The baby. She's sick."

The forlorn shape receded back into the murk of the corn meal mush, the fried dough and the shoeless feet, like something that slowly heaves up and goes down again in roiled water.

"Did you—did you get any others?"

"Five others," he said.

"O-o-o-h. Can we see 'em?"

Chris opened his creel and they crowded up to it, and their eyes seemed to crowd into the trout- and fern-filled cavity, staring and eager and hungry. The smaller one touched some of the trout with his finger tips, daintily, as if to be sure they were real. "Gosh," he muttered, after a minute, "you're a good fisherman."

"You roll 'em in corn meal or flour," Chris said. "An' fry 'em—till they're brown on both sides. Put salt an' pepper on while they're fryin'—"

A visible trickle drooled out of the mouth of the smaller Hooker.

"Tell your Mom that," Chris added. "She might not know."

"Aw—she can cook a trout. But we don't have any. Did you think we had any?"

"You've got these," he said. "I'm giving 'em to you." . . . It was out, now; and no more thinking about his promise to Rosemary would put the words back in his mouth nor keep the trout in his creel.

Their eyes wrenched away from the trout and up to Chris's face, unbelieving, then sought each other's for some confirmation, some assurance that it was true.

"All of 'em?"

"Sure. Look, I've got to get home, fast. Can I see your Mom a minute, right away?"

"Sure. . . . Gee—six trout for supper. Come on, we'll give 'em to her. She can cook 'em. Yay! Boy—oh—boy!"

They went into the stream again, shouting, "Mom! Mom! We got six trout. Mom! Chris Wintermute gave us six trout!"

Chris followed, picking his way carefully through the knee-deep water of the lower run.

The uproar from the kids had brought Mrs. Hooker to the door. While the noise attending the display of the trout was going on Chris stood a little apart, looking closely, for the first time in his life, at this house which he had always avoided on his trips upstream. It was going to collapse. Its roof sagged in the middle and a lot of shingles were gone from the roof. Those places had been patched with scraps of tar paper and pieces of tin fashioned out of flattened oil cans. If its old boards had ever had any paint they had long since lost it; they were gray and naked to the weather. In the four front windows several panes of glass were out, replaced by squares of cardboard or brown paper. The entire structure seemed to lean as if tottering with its own creaking weight. There was not a straight line nor a right angle: the vertical and horizontal planes all slanted in ways that looked dangerous . . .

Sticks, living in this place, came into his mind and suddenly he found himself admiring Sticks in a way that was new and strange to him. Sticks had been able to come every day from this house, which was dying, to school and go back to this house at night and come to school again and play the best baseball of any kid there, and get good marks, and fish with a pole he had cut in the woods and give a trout to Rosemary when he was starving for it himself. . . . Sticks had guts.

But when the kids had gone inside with the trout and quiet had come again over the little square of clean-swept dirt which was the front yard, and Mrs. Hooker stood there in the leaning doorway, in a little area of sunlight, as if framed by the old house behind and above her—Chris knew that the house was *not* going to collapse, after all. Mrs. Hooker held it up and always would hold it up. Mom . . . Mom was where Sticks got his guts. He didn't go to school from a dying house—he went from Mom and he took something of Mom with him to make him good at baseball and to get him good marks.

No one could call *her* "Sticks." She was tall and broad in her blue gingham apron and her hair was a gold-gray, neatly drawn back from her high proud forehead. She stood straight and clean, a brave and kind figure, looking at him. Her mouth was straight across, as if set in a fighting position against something that battled her from inside, but her blue eyes had sunlight in them and they were smiling at him.

And suddenly he knew that he could not say what he had come to say. She was too proud, too strong, to take it from a kid. No. . . . He would have to tell his father, later. And that would mean confessing that he had been fishing up here today. And tomorrow, when Miss Spencer asked his father for an excuse for his absence, the two things would hook up, fit together. . . . But he couldn't tell Mom. She would talk him out of it and he didn't want to be—he couldn't be—talked out of it. If he were talked out of *that* he'd want to take his trout back. It would be the end, the complete and final ruin of a day that had suddenly cracked up on him anyway.

He returned her smile and tipped his cap to her. She took a step toward him but as she did so the baby cried again from somewhere in the old house. Chris saw her step halt and retrace itself. He saw a little wincing look, as if from a sharp pain, cloud the sun and the smile that had been in her eyes. She turned from him, and her fine straight back disappeared into the gloom of the leaning and rotten doorway.

He walked away, down the path. He crossed the stream again, hurried back to his hollow oak trunk, stowed his rod and creel, took up his books and started home.

There was no fishing left in his mind, now—none of the high hope of the morning. That moment, only six or seven hours ago, when he had left Rosemary at the bridge, seemed to him now an age away, back in his early childhood. Something bigger than fishing had taken up all the space in his brain and his heart, a thing he had gotten hold of and couldn't drop, a tremendous thing that was heavy, perhaps too heavy for him to handle. A man's thing. It didn't make him sad except in a small way, in its revelation of a certain loss to himself. He could not define that loss, but he knew what it was. It was the loss of his pure kid's joy in fishing and in life. For it *was* lost now, beyond recall. He would fish again, and do other things again, and get fun out of them, but behind them always would be this thing he had seen today, which was poverty and famine, something he had thought of vaguely and heard of from his father, but had never really believed until this afternoon. It was not particularly the Hookers on the

Little Stony but the Hookers who—he knew now—were all over the world, the Hooker way of life multiplied a million times.

That thing had made him older. It was perhaps that boundary line in his life about which he had so often wondered. There was a line somewhere, he had told himself, that a kid came up to and stepped over, and when he stepped over it he was a man. This was it, then, and he had stepped over it.

The day had done that for him, at least. In all other ways it had licked him. His promise to Rosemary was broken. His truancy was going to be found out and surely punished. And Rosemary was involved in that, too, since she had given an excuse for him to the teacher. He was going to be in bad with Rosemary, his father, the school, everyone. But along with all that mess of failure, the day had given him—suddenly and when he least expected it—a man's job to do. And he had begun on that job and would finish it when he got home. . . . And maybe those ways he had been licked were kid ways, and the way he had won was a man's. He didn't know. . . . He wondered, as he walked up the long drive to his house, how his father now, and Rosemary later, would take his separate confessions, and whether he could bear up, proud, in the way that Sticks was proud, in the way that took guts, if they should condemn him for what he had done.

His father was nowhere around, outside. Perhaps he was in his little office off the sitting room, at his ledgers, as he often was at this time of day. Chris opened the door, tossed his cap on the rack in the long hall and looked into the adjoining sitting room and his father's office beyond it. Both were empty. He called upstairs, "Dad."

Sarah labored heavily in, on her flat pads, from the kitchen, and the early nebulous fragrance of a dinner's beginnings followed her through the opened door.

"Yo' Dad ain' home, Christ'pher. He an' Harry Stack taken ol' Korn over t' Long Holler t' wait on some cow."

"Oh. Did he say when he'd be back?"

"Dinnah tahm, reckon. He said not much befo' then."

Chris went upstairs to his room, took off his wet shoes and stockings and lay down on his bed looking up at the pattern of the ceiling paper. He wanted his father to be home, right now, while his mind was made up to tell him what he had to tell. Time was against him. It was almost four o'clock and if he had to wait until dinner time to see his father he might find reasons, in those long hours, to go back on his plan. For if he didn't tell his father he might still get away with it, so far as his playing hooky was concerned. The chances were pretty good. The excuse he had told Rosemary to give Miss Spencer wasn't so bad, after all. It might hold, and if it should then Rosemary was not mixed up either. . . . Perhaps it were better, that way. Let the other thing wait a week, until his absence from school should be well forgotten. But that would give Mom Hooker a week longer to worry. She looked as if she could stand it, but because she looked that way he didn't want her to have to . . .

No. As soon as his Dad came in he'd tell him.

He got up after a while, put on dry stockings and shoes, unstrapped his school-books and tried for half an hour to master the six pages of his Practical English Grammar which, he guessed, would be the lesson for tomorrow. He liked it—alone among all his studies at school—and ordinarily he would have had it cold in fifteen minutes. . . . He left it at last and went to his window and looked out on the fading unpeopled afternoon. And as he stood there his father's big truck purred up the road, turned in between the gate posts and crunched up the gravel drive. Harry Stack was driving and the big Holstein bull, Sir Piebe Korndyke Segis Colantha—affectionately known to the household as "Old Korn"—rode with majestic dignity in the rear, home from another seeding in a far country.

Chris heard the truck stop and then go on again as Harry Stack drove it back to the barn. He heard his father come in at the front door and walk through the sitting room to his office. He stood there at the window a few seconds more, looking out, then turned and went downstairs.

As Chris entered the office his father looked up from an entry he was making in a little ledger marked "Bull Services." He turned his craggy, inflexible counte-nance up to his son. It was a large face of promontories and furrowed cliffs, with eyes of a color hard to define, so deeply shadowed were they under the great eaves of its brows.

"Well Chris," he said, "how'd it go at school?"

"I wasn't at school today, Dad."

"Eh?" That rigid and chiseled face showed little if any change: the emotions worked deep underneath it but only a terrific upheaval could disturb its surface rock.

Chris sat down in the odd chair at the side of his father's big roll-top desk. "I played hooky, Dad."

Christopher Wintermute, Sr., looked at his son studiously for a moment and returned to his entry on the ruled page. "I'm sorry, Chris," he said. "I've felt good today and I don't like it to end up like this. You know what my stand is on hooky."

"I know. I felt good this morning, too. The stream looked right—it was a peach of a day—and I knew I could take 'em. I promised Rosemary five and I got six."

"Of course." His father blotted the entry, closed the book and regarded his son keenly. "That was the temptation. This afternoon I could have charged old Amos Kinsey thirty dollars for a service and he'd have paid me. That might have been a temptation, too. But I charged him twenty. . . . We have been all over that, before. It seems that a father's words have no weight in this day. . . . Well."

He sighed and got up from his chair, closed the door and the single window. From a corner of the little room which the door had concealed while it stood open he procured a short thin cane. There was no woodshed formality about the elder Wintermute's administrations of justice. "My stand on hooky is the same as it was last time," he said. "Hooky is hooky, even when you confess it like a man. . . . Loosen your belt, Chris, and take 'em down."

His father had never shown him anger. He could call him Chris, the affectionate nickname, even when he was about to flog him. The whippings were as impersonal as a lightning bolt except for the expressions of wounded and betrayed trust which always preceded them and the deep forgiveness which came afterward, in the dark. That would follow, tonight, after Chris had gone to bed. His father would come upstairs, enter Chris's room, take Chris in his arms and kiss him. He would speak but a few words and they would be shaky, and the dim hall gas jet would make a blended pattern of light and shadow on the uplands and valleys of the great face, like moonlight over a landscape.

Chris stood before his father, small and white and naked from his waist to his knees, his embarrassment gone in the deeper tide of his apprehension of pain. He had steeled himself for the sting of that lash, the increasing agony as the repeated blows would seem to cut into flesh made tender and raw from the first one. The last time he had not cried out until the ninth, with only one more to go. There were always ten, never more nor less.

"I'm ready," he said. "But before you start can I tell you something—something awful important that I found out today?" He felt a little ashamed of himself, as if he were begging for mercy, as his father stood looking at him in a faint surprise.

"Well?"

"Dad, you own that old house on Little Stony, the one the Hookers live in?"

"I do. Why?" The elder Wintermute was impatient as if he, too, had steeled his will to the task his conscience had imposed and dreaded, now, lest time take the fine edge from his decision. "Make it quick," he said, "and let's get this over with."

"How much rent do you charge 'em—if you don't mind telling me?"

"Ten dollars a month. . . . What is this, Chris?"

He felt the warm nudge of confidence, sensing that his first sally had scored. He followed it up: "Do they pay it?"

"Every cent—promptly when due. What is your interest in the Hooker house?"

"Would you—do you need that ten dollars a month?"

"It is business. I have a right to it and they need the house. But—"

"They need a decent house. That thing—you wouldn't keep your cows in it. Listen, it's—"

"The lease stipulates no repairs, at that rental. And anyway, what—"

"Have you seen it lately?"

"No."

"Well I did, today, when I was up there fishing. Dad, it's falling down. It's rotten—the paint's gone—the shingles are off—windows busted and patched up with cardboard."

His father took this in silence. . . . What had been faint and far off was with him, now, and full grown, the knowledge that he was going to win. Beating or no beating, he had his man on the run. . . .

"It's falling in on 'em, I tell you. Four kids in there—and the littlest one sick. An' the old man—Mr. Hooker—lost his job. They haven't any money. I mean *no* money—not a cent—'cept what they might be givin' toward your rent. The kids have no shoes to wear—only Sticks has shoes, the big one, 'cause he has to go to school. An' not a thing to eat but corn meal mush an' fried dough an' dandy-lions an' wood herbs that Mom—Mrs. Hooker—picks. She's got potatoes an' beans planted, but they're not up yet—"

"Before you go any further, Chris—pull your pants up. A man can't talk with his pants down, and I can't talk to him." Wintermute's expression hadn't changed in the slightest except that under his great brows the shadow was perhaps deeper. "It's stuffy in here," he said. He moved to the window and opened it. He sat down in his desk chair again, facing the gathering twilight beyond the window. "I didn't know it was that bad up at the Hooker place," he mused. "I've been meaning to get up there, but I've been busy." Then he wheeled suddenly toward his son. "Well, what are you leading up to?"

"Your taxes are heavy, you told me—"

"Well?"

"An' you said it's a hard job making a living at farming."

"It is."

"But we're so much better off than they are. . . . Dad—would you—would you fix that house up for Mom—Mrs. Hooker—an' the kids—an' maybe let 'em have it rent free, at least for a while? I thought you would an' I was going to tell Mrs. Hooker—but when I saw her I couldn't. She's proud, Dad. She wouldn't take that from a kid. . . . But she would from you. Look, I'll chip in my allowance."

Wintermute looked for a long moment into the eyes of his son. They met his own steadily and all he could see there was a flaming eagerness.

"God," he said, at length. "I didn't know they were that poor." His eyes turned from Chris to some papers on the desk before him. "Yes," he said, wearily. "Yes, of course. What else can a Christian do? . . . I'll go up there tomorrow. Listen," he turned again to Chris and his great face was coming alive as the beginnings of a smile trickled into all its furrows like a spring rain on parched ground, "suppose we put up a dinner for them tonight? Sarah's got a big ham on—"

"Don't have to—tonight. I gave 'em my six trout—and one of 'em was—well, that long."

"Eh? You gave 'em the fish you promised to your girl?"

"Would *you* have?"

His father didn't answer. He got up from his chair again, stepped to the door and opened it. He put the cane back in its old place in the corner behind the door; then he took it up again suddenly, broke it in half across his knee, tossed the two pieces into the waste basket beside his desk and sat down again.

"You have grown, Chris," he said. "Hooky is a kid's game and a licking is a kid's punishment. Still, hooky is hooky. . . . I'll take your rod and tackle for the rest of the season. . . . No. That's a kid's punishment, too. You may have them—and fish when your conscience, as a man, tells you it's all right. . . . I think we can swing this Hooker matter, financially, without the aid of your allowance. And perhaps new shoes for the kids." His voice trailed off until it was scarcely audible, but Chris heard him say: "and perhaps a job for the father. We'll see."

The big knocker on the front door banged three times.

"Go see who it is, Chris, while I—liquidate this matter of the hooky." Wintermute took out his pen and drew a letter head from the dark recesses of his desk. "There is still your excuse to write to your teacher."

At the door stood Rosemary Martin, looking worried. Beyond her, at the end of the stone walk, stood Dr. Martin's black coupé, with Dr. Martin in it.

"I brought my Dad to plead for you—if it's not too late." Rosemary spoke nervously, in a half whisper. "He said *your* Dad would do anything for him."

"You told him I played hooky?"

"Yes." She looked at him sharply, as if annoyed that he should question her. "Is it too late?"

"Yes—no—I mean, I told Dad myself. An' it's all right."

"Oh. . . . Wait." She ran down the walk and said something to Dr. Martin. He nodded and backed out of the drive and drove off down the road. Rosemary ran back to Chris and he could see that the anxiousness was out of her face. But she asked him, immediately and in a stern whisper, "Where are my trout?"

"If I had kept 'em I'd have brought 'em to you."

"If you'd kept them! Do you mean to say you caught them, and—well, where are they?"

"I caught six—one that big. I was going to bring you five an' keep one for myself." He didn't feel that he could explain everything to her now. Tomorrow he could, but just now he was tired explaining to others all that was so clear to himself. But he began, weakly: "Did you ever see the Hooker house—how they live?—"

The solemn and slightly hurt look left her face. She stepped to his side and surprisingly took his hand in hers. "Never saw it till this afternoon," she said.

"This afternoon?"

"Yes. I went up there—with Sticks. He knows you played hooky an' he's goin' to tell it all over. . . . Look, let's go out to your summerhouse. It's nice there— we can talk." She led him down the steps and back toward the little rustic and morning-gloryed structure.

When they were seated on the old gray boards of the bench she said: "I'm being mean to you, Chris. I know all about the trout. I went up there with Sticks *and* Dad. Sticks came down to our house this afternoon—he ran all the way—to get Dad. His baby sister is sick. Poor kid."

"I heard her cry. She sounded awful sick."

"She won't die, Dad said. Listen, I saw that house—I even went inside. It makes me cry to think of it—of Sticks living there—"

"Dad said he'd fix it up. He owns it. An' get 'em some shoes, maybe."

"Oh, I'm awfully glad." Then she added, "I saw your trout, too."

"What did Sticks think of those fish?"

"He said you were the best fisherman and best feller he knew in the world— an' he wished you liked him. Honest."

"Aw—did Sticks say that, honest?"

"Honest an' truly. And he's not the only one who thinks so."

"Who else?"

"*I* do—there."

They were silent, pondering the import of that confession. The dusk in the summer house deepened. The broad lawn spread away, and beyond it the maples stood breathless in the quiet evening.

"You gave up something you wanted, and that's brave. And you told your Dad you'd played hooky. That was the best way. That was brave, too."

"Look, did you give Miss Spencer that excuse, this morning?"

"No. It takes nerve to do something you know is wrong. An' I'm not brave—like you. But afterwards I wished I had. That's why I brought Dad along, soon's I could, to help you. But this morning it seemed too much like a lie. . . . And besides, I was mad at you then."

"Why?"

"Because you left me so quick—at the bridge—after I'd promised to help you. You didn't kiss me good-bye, even."

He thought, vaguely, that he would never, never know anything about girls, as long as he lived.

"Can I make that up to you, now?" he asked, after a moment.

"If you don't, I might still be mad."

ONE OF THE SCHULTZ BOYS FISHING

Millen Brand

Consider how strong a person's hand is, sometimes,
at ninety, and the memory too.
Both may be slow
but a moment of backward-going thought
takes the half-smiling mind by the hand
and leads it to childhood:
"There were locks above the sawmill
and the water ran out to the 'swamps'
below the hill, but on the swamp we cut hay.
In the creek
We often went fishing with a coal-oil light
with a fish spear and a large net.
We stood so, and in the stagnant water

it was plentiful with eels and catfish.
We had to have our hands full of sand
to hold them and kill them.
We had a spear with four prongs.
The lamp had a large hood to it
that threw the light on the water.
The light, I think, blinded them.
The catfish are good eating.
By moonshine
we went sometimes without a light,
set the net in
and splashed, splashed and drove the fish down
into the net—whitefish, catfish, carp, silverfish.
Sometimes the net was heavy with fish."
He draws yet on the net
of his Douglas Township childhood,
his face lit with vanished moonlight.
"Yes, the West Branch Creek
of the Perkiomen we fished.
The *hecht*—pike—he was a still sitter,
and we had a red wire loop,
and we moved it sloooowly
so he didn't see it
till it was over his head,
then we pulled and caught him.
In the fall there was eels especially.
They had a notion and were made that way
to go down a stream and I know
that we put—made a catch for the eels.
We put a lock across the stream
that's below the sawmill,
say about ten feet long—
little slats, little laths.
When the eels dropped in there,
they couldn't get out any more,
weren't like a copperhead
that could crawl up—"
A boy with boots to his thighs
walking with his brothers and father
as water cools and dimples and descends
in the creek of his mind, his eyes
focused on the mirror at his feet.
"We were many to eat,
and the fish helped. Yes,
it was an addition to the fields."

2

TRADITION AND LORE

*"Angling may be said to be so like the
mathematics that it can never fully be learnt . . ."*
—IZAAK WALTON

THE COMPLEAT ANGLER

Izaak Walton and Charles Cotton
(Selections)

NOW FOR THE ART of catching fish, that is to say, how to make a man that was none to be an angler by a book, he that undertakes it shall undertake a harder task than Mr. Hales, a most valiant and excellent fencer, who in a printed book called "A Private School of Defence" undertook by it to teach that art or science, and was laughed at for his labor. Not but that many useful things might be learnt by that book, but he was laughed at because that art was not to be taught by words, but practice: and so must angling. And in this discourse I do not undertake to say all that is known or may be said of it, but I undertake to acquaint the reader with many things that are not usually known to every angler; and I shall leave gleanings and observations enough to be made out of the experience of all that love and practise this recreation, to which I shall encourage them. For angling may be said to be so like the mathematics that it can never be fully learnt; at least not so fully but that there will still be more new experiments left for the trial of other men that succeed us.

But I think all that love this game may here learn something that may be worth their money, if they be not poor and needy men: and in case they be, I then wish them to forbear to buy it; for I write not to get money, but for pleasure, and this discourse boasts of no more; for I hate to promise much, and deceive the reader.

And however it proves to him, yet I am sure I have found a high content in the search and conference of what is here offered to the reader's view and censure. I wish him as much in the perusal of it. And so I might here take my leave, but will stay a little and tell him that whereas it is said by many that in fly-fishing for a trout, the angler must observe his twelve several flies for the twelve months of the year; I say he that follows that rule shall be as sure to catch fish and be as wise as he that makes hay by the fair days in an almanac, and no surer; for those very flies that use to appear about and on the water in one month of the year may the following year come almost a month sooner or later, as the same year proves

The Compleat Angler or the Contemplative man's Recreation.

Being a Discourse of

FISH and FISHING,

Not unworthy the perusal of most *Anglers.*

Simon Peter *said,* I go á fishing : *and they said,* We also wil go with thee. John 21.3.

London, Printed by *T. Maxey* for Rich. Marriot, in S. Dunstans Churchyard Fleetstreet, 1653.

doubtleß he had done so, if
death had not prevented
him ; the remembrance of
which hath often made me
sorry ; for, if he had lived to
do it, then the unlearned
Angler (of which I am one)
had seen some Treatise of
this Art worthy his perusal,
which (though some have
undertaken it) I could never yet see in English.

But mine may be thought
as weak and as unworthy
of common view: and I do
here freely confeß, that I

A 4　　should

colder or hotter; and yet in the following discourse I have set down the twelve flies that are in reputation with many anglers, and they may serve to give him some light concerning them. And he may note that there are in Wales and other countries peculiar flies, proper to the particular place or country; and doubtless, unless a man makes a fly to counterfeit that very fly in that place, he is like to lose his labor, or much of it; but for the generality, three or four flies neat and rightly made, and not too big, serve for a trout in most rivers all the summer. And for winter fly-fishing it is as useful as an almanac out of date. And of these (because as no man is born an artist, so no man is born an angler) I thought fit to give thee this notice.

*

And for you that have heard many grave, serious men pity anglers; let me tell you, Sir, there be many men that are by others taken to be serious and grave men which we condemn and pity. Men that are taken to be grave, because nature hath made them of a sour complexion, money-getting men, men that spend all their time first in getting, and next in anxious care to keep it, men that are condemned to be rich, and then always busy or discontented. For these poor-rich-men, we anglers pity them perfectly, and stand in no need to borrow their thoughts to think ourselves happy. No, no, Sir, we enjoy a contentedness above the reach of such dispositions, and as the learned and ingenuous Montaigne says, like himself freely, "When my cat and I entertain each other with mutual apish tricks, as playing with a garter, who knows but that I make my cat more sport than she makes me? Shall I conclude her to be simple, that has her time to begin or refuse sportiveness as freely as I myself have? Nay, who knows but that it is a defect of my not understanding her language (for doubtless cats talk and reason with one another) that we agree no better? and who knows but that she pities me for being no wiser, and laughs and censures my folly for making sport for her when we two play together?"

Thus freely speaks Montaigne concerning cats, and I hope I may take as great a liberty to blame any man, and laugh at him too, let him be never so serious, that hath not heard what anglers can say in the justification of their art and recreation. Which I may again tell you is so full of pleasure that we need not borrow their thoughts to think ourselves happy.

*

PISCATOR. O, Sir, doubt not but that angling is an art! Is it not an art to deceive a trout with an artificial fly? a trout! that is more sharp-sighted than any hawk you have named and more watchful and timorous than your high-mettled merlin is bold! And yet I doubt not to catch a brace or two tomorrow for a friend's breakfast. Doubt not therefore, Sir, but that angling is an art and an art worth your learning. The question is rather whether you be capable of learning it! for angling is somewhat like poetry, men are to be born so. I mean, with inclinations to it, though both may be heightened by practice and experience; but he that hopes to be a good angler must not only bring an inquiring, searching, observing wit, but he must bring a large measure of hope and patience and a love and propensity to the art itself; but having once got and practised it, then doubt not but angling will prove to be so pleasant that it will prove, like virtue, a reward to itself.

VENATOR. Sir, I am now become so full of expectation that I long much to have you proceed and in the order that you propose.

PISCATOR. Then first, for the antiquity of angling, of which I shall not say much but only this: some say it is as ancient as Deucalion's Flood; others, that Belus, who was the first inventor of the godly and virtuous recreations, was the first inventor of angling; and some others say, for former times have had their disquisitions about the antiquity of it, that Seth, one of the sons of Adam, taught it to his sons, and that by them it was derived to posterity; others say that he left it engraven on those pillars which he erected and trusted to preserve the knowledge of the mathematics, music, and the rest of that precious knowledge and those useful arts, which by God's appointment or allowance and his noble industry were thereby preserved from perishing in Noah's Flood.

These, Sir, have been the opinions of several men, that have possibly endeavored to make angling more ancient than is needful or may well be warranted; but for my part, I shall content myself in telling you that angling is much more ancient than the incarnation of our Savior; for in the Prophet Amos mention is made of fish-hooks; and in the Book of Job—which was long before the days of Amos, for that book is said to be writ by Moses—mention is made also of fish-hooks, which must imply anglers in those times.

But, my worthy friend, as I would rather prove myself a gentleman by being learned and humble, valiant and inoffensive, virtuous and communicable, than by any fond ostentation of riches, or wanting those virtues myself, boast that these were in my ancestors—and yet I grant that where a noble and ancient descent and such merit meet in any man it is a double dignification of that person—so if this antiquity of angling—which for my part I have not forced—shall, like an ancient family, be either an honor or an ornament to this virtuous art which I profess to love and practise, I shall be the gladder that I made an accidental mention of the antiquity of it; of which I shall say no more but proceed to that just commendation which I think it deserves.

And for that I shall tell you that in ancient times a debate hath risen—and it remains yet unresolved—whether the happiness of man in this world doth consist more in contemplation or action.

Concerning which some have endeavored to maintain their opinion of the first by saying, "that the nearer we mortals come to God by way of imitation the more happy we are." And they say, "that God enjoys himself only by a contemplation of his own infiniteness, eternity, power, and goodness," and the like. And upon this ground many cloisteral men of great learning and devotion prefer contemplation before action. And many of the fathers seem to approve this opinion, as may appear in their commentaries upon the words of our Savior to Martha, Luke 10:41, 42.

And on the contrary there want not men of equal authority and credit that prefer action to be the more excellent, as namely "experiments in physic and the application of it, both for the ease and prolongation of man's life"; by which each man is enabled to act and do good to others, either to serve his country or do good to particular persons; any they say also "that action is doctrinal and teaches both art and virtue and is a maintainer of human society"; and for these and other like reasons to be preferred before contemplation.

Concerning which two opinions I shall forbear to add a third by declaring my own, and rest myself contented in telling you, my very worthy friend, that both these meet together and do most properly belong to the most honest, ingenuous, quiet, and harmless art of angling.

And first, I shall tell you what some have observed, and I have found to be a real truth, that the very sitting by the river's side is not only the quietest and fittest place for contemplation but will invite an angler to it. And this seems to be maintained by the learned Pet. du Moulin, who, in his discourse of the Fulfilling of Prophecies, observes that when God intended to reveal any future event or high notions to his prophets, he then carried them either to the deserts or the sea-shore, that having so separated them from amidst the press of people and business and the cares of the world he might settle their mind in a quiet repose and make them fit for revelation.

*

And for the lawfulness of fishing, it may very well be maintained by our Savior's bidding St. Peter cast his hook into the water and catch a fish for money to pay tribute to Caesar. And let me tell you that angling is of high esteem and of much use in other nations. He that reads the voyages of Ferdinand Mendez Pinto shall find that there he declares to have found a king and several priests a-fishing.

And he that reads Plutarch shall find that angling was not contemptible in the days of Mark Antony and Cleopatra and that they in the midst of their wonderful glory used angling as a principal recreation. And let me tell you that in the Scripture angling is always taken in the best sense and that though hunting may be sometimes so taken, yet it is but seldom to be so understood. And let me add this more. He that views the ancient ecclesiastical canons shall find hunting to be forbidden to churchmen, as being a toilsome, perplexing recreation; and shall find angling allowed to clergymen, as being a harmless recreation, a recreation that invites them to contemplation and quietness.

*

My next and last example shall be that undervaluer of money, the late Provost of Eton College, Sir Henry Wotton, a man with whom I have often fished and conversed, a man whose foreign employments in the service of this nation and whose experience, learning, wit, and cheerfulness made his company to be esteemed one of the delights of mankind. This man, whose very approbation of angling were sufficient to convince any modest censurer of it, this man was also a most dear lover and a frequent practiser of the art of angling; of which he would say, " 'Twas an employment for his idle time, which was then not idly spent"; for angling was, after tedious study, "a rest to his mind, a cheerer of his spirits, a diverter of sadness, a calmer of unquiet thoughts, a moderator of passions, a procurer of contentedness; and that it begot habits of peace and patience in those that professed and practised it." Indeed, my friend, you will find angling to be like the virtue of humility, which has a calmness of spirit and a world of other blessings attending upon it.

Sir, this was the saying of that learned man, and I do easily believe, that peace and patience and a calm content did cohabit in the cheerful heart of Sir Henry Wotton, because I know that when he was beyond seventy years of age, he made this description of a part of the present pleasure that possessed him, as he sat quietly in a summer's evening on a bank a-fishing; it is a description of the spring, which, because it glides as soft and sweetly from his pen as that river does at this time, by which it was then made, I shall repeat it unto you:

> This day Dame Nature seemed in love;
> The lusty sap began to move;
> Fresh juice did stir th' embracing vines;
> And birds had drawn their valentines.
>
> The jealous trout, that low did lie,
> Rose at a well-dissembled fly;
> There stood my friend with patient skill
> Attending of his trembling quill.
>
> Already were the eaves possessed
> With the swift pilgrim's daubed nest;
> The groves already did rejoice,
> In Philomel's triumphing voice;
>
> The showers were short, the weather mild,
> The morning fresh, the evening smiled.
> Joan takes her neat-rubbed pail, and now
> She trips to milk the sand-red cow;
>
> Where for some sturdy foot-ball swain
> Joan strokes a syllabub or twain;
> The fields and gardens were beset
> With tulips, crocus, violet;
>
> And now, though late, the modest rose
> Did more than half a blush disclose.
> Thus all looks gay and full of cheer
> To welcome the new-liveried year.

These were the thoughts that then possessed the undisturbed mind of Sir Henry Wotton. Will you hear the wish of another angler and the commendation of his happy life, which he also sings in verse, *viz.* Jo. Davors, Esq.?

82

IZAAK WALTON AND CHARLES COTTON

Let me live harmlessly and near the brink
  Of Trent or Avon have a dwelling-place,
Where I may see my quill or cork down sink
  With eager bite of perch, or bleak, or dace;
And on the world and my Creator think;
  Whilst some men strive ill-gotten goods t'embrace,
And others spend their time in base excess
Of wine or worse, in war and wantonness.

Let them that list these pastimes still pursue,
  And on such pleasing fancies feed their fill,
So I the fields and meadows green may view
  And daily by fresh rivers walk at will
Among the daisies and the violets blue,
  Red hyacinth, and yellow daffodil,
Purple Narcissus like the morning rays,
Pale gander-grass, and azure culver-keys.

I count it higher pleasure to behold
  The stately compass of the lofty sky,
And in the midst thereof, like burning gold,
  The flaming chariot of the world's great eye,
The watery clouds that in the air up-rolled
  With sundry kinds of painted colors fly;
And fair Aurora, lifting up her head,
Still blushing rise from old Tithonus' bed.

The hills and mountains raisèd from the plains,
  The plains extended level with the ground,
The grounds divided into sundry veins,
  The veins enclosed with rivers running round;
These rivers making way through nature's chains
  With headlong course into the sea profound;
The raging sea, beneath the valleys low,
Where lakes and rills and rivulets do flow.

The lofty woods, the forests wide and long,
  Adorned with leaves and branches fresh and green,
In whose cool bowers the birds with many a song
  Do welcome with their quire the summer's queen;
The meadows fair where Flora's gifts among
  Are intermixed with verdant grass between;
The silver-scalèd fish that softly swim
Within the sweet brook's crystal watery stream.

All these, and many more of his creation
    That made the heavens, the angler oft doth see,
Taking therein no little delectation,
    To think how strange, how wonderful they be,
Framing thereof an inward contemplation
    To set his heart from other fancies free;
And whilst he looks on these with joyful eye,
His mind is rapt above the starry sky.

*

PISCATOR. The trout is a fish highly valued, both in this and foreign nations. He may be justly said, as the old poet said of wine and we English say of venison, to be a generous fish; a fish that is so like the buck that he also has his seasons, for it is observed that he comes in and goes out of season with the stag and buck. Gesner says his name is of a German offspring, and says he is a fish that feeds clean and purely, in the swiftest streams and on the hardest gravel, and that he may justly contend with all fresh water fish, as the mullet may with all sea fish, for precedency and daintiness of taste; and that being in right season, the most dainty palates have allowed precedency to him.

And before I go farther in my discourse, let me tell you that you are to observe that as there be some barren does that are good in summer so there be some barren trouts that are good in winter; but there are not many that are so, for usually they be in their perfection in the month of May and decline with the buck. Now you are to take notice that in several countries, as in Germany and in other parts, compared to ours, fish do differ much in their bigness and shape and other ways; and so do trouts. It is well known that in the Lake Leman, the Lake of Geneva, there are trouts taken of three cubits long, as is affirmed by Gesner, a writer of good credit, and Mercator says the trouts that are taken in the Lake of Geneva are a great part of the merchandise of that famous city. And you are further to know that there be certain waters that breed trouts remarkable both for their number and smallness. I know a little brook in Kent that breeds them to a number incredible, and you may take them twenty or forty in an hour, but none greater than about the size of a gudgeon. There are also in divers rivers, especially that relate to or be near to the sea, as Winchester or the Thames about Windsor, a little trout called a samlet or skegger trout, in both which places I have caught twenty or forty at a standing, that will bite as fast and as freely as minnows; these be by some taken to be young salmons, but in those waters they never grow to be bigger than a herring.

There is also in Kent near to Canterbury a trout called there a Fordidge trout, a trout that bears the name of the town where it is usually caught, that is accounted the rarest of fish, many of them near the bigness of a salmon, but known by their different color, and in their best season cut very white; and none of these have been known to be caught with an angle, unless it were one that was caught by Sir George Hastings, an excellent angler, and now with God; and he hath told me, he thought that trout bit not for hunger but wantonness; and it is the rather to be believed, because both he then and many others before him have been curious to search into their bellies, what the food was by which they lived; and have found out nothing by which they might satisfy their curiosity.

Concerning which you are to take notice that it is reported by good authors that grasshoppers and some fish have no mouths, but are nourished and take breath by the porousness of their gills, man knows not how; and this may be believed, if we consider that when the raven hath hatched her eggs, she takes no further care, but leaves her young ones to the care of the God of nature, who is said, in the Psalms, "to feed the young ravens that call upon him." And they be kept alive and fed by a dew, or worms that breed in their nests, or some other ways that we mortals know not. And this may be believed of the Fordidge trout which, as it is said of the stork that he knows his season, so he knows his times, I think almost his day, of coming into that river out of the sea, where he lives and, it is like, feeds nine months of the year, and about three in the River of Fordidge. And you are to note that the townsmen are very punctual in observing the very time of beginning to fish for them; and boast much that their river affords a trout that exceeds all others. And just so doth Sussex boast of several fish, as namely a Shelsey cockle, a Chichester lobster, an Arundel mullet, and an Amerly trout.

And now for some confirmation of the Fordidge trout, you are to know that this trout is thought to eat nothing in the fresh water; and it may be the better believed because it is well known that swallows, which are not seen to fly in England for six months in the year but about Michaelmas leave us for a hotter climate, yet some of them that have been left behind their fellows have been found many thousands at a time in hollow trees, where they have been observed to live and sleep out the whole winter without meat; and so Albertus observes that there is one kind of frog that hath her mouth naturally shut up about the end of August and that she lives so all the winter; and though it be strange to some, yet it is known to too many among us to be doubted.

And so much for these Fordidge trouts, which never afford an angler sport, but either live their time of being in the fresh water by their meat formerly gotten in the sea, not unlike the swallow or frog, or by the virtue of the fresh water only; or as the birds of paradise and the chameleon are said to live, by the sun and the air.

There is also in Northumberland a trout called a bull-trout, of a much greater length and bigness than any in these southern parts; and there is in many rivers that relate to the sea salmon-trouts, as much different from others both in shape and in their spots, as we see sheep differ one from another in their shape and bigness, and in the fineness of the wool; and certainly, as some pastures breed larger sheep, so do some rivers by reason of the ground over which they run breed larger trouts.

Now the next thing that I will commend to your consideration is that the trout is of a more sudden growth than other fish. Concerning which you are also to take notice that he lives not so long as the perch and divers other fishes do, as Sir Francis Bacon hath observed in his History of Life and Death.

And next you are to take notice that he is not like the crocodile, which if he lives never so long, yet always thrives till his death; but 'tis not so with the trout, for after he is come to his full growth, he declines in his body, but keeps his bigness or thrives only in his head till his death. And you are to know that he will about (especially before) the time of his spawning get almost miraculously through weirs and flood-gates against the stream, even through such high and swift places as is almost incredible. Next, that the trout usually spawns about October or November, but in some rivers a little sooner or later. Which is the more observable because most other fish spawn in the spring or summer when the sun hath warmed both the earth and water and made it fit for generation. And you are to note that he continues many months out of season; for it may be observed of the trout that he is like the buck or the ox that will not be fat in many months, though he go in the very same pastures that horses do which will be fat in one month; and so you may observe that most other fishes recover strength and grow sooner fat and in season than the trout doth.

And next you are to note that till the sun gets to such a height as to warm the earth and the water the trout is sick and lean and lousy and unwholesome; for you shall in winter find him to have a big head and then to be lank and thin and lean; at which time many of them have sticking on them sugs, or trout-lice, which is a kind of a worm in shape like a clove or pin with a big head, and sticks close to him and sucks his moisture; those, I think, the trout breeds himself, and never thrives till he free himself from them, which is till warm weather comes; and then, as he grows stronger, he gets from the dead, still water into the sharp streams and the gravel and there rubs off these worms or lice, and then as he grows stronger, so he gets him into swifter and swifter streams, and there lies at the watch for any fly or minnow that comes near to him; and he especially loves the May-fly, which is bred of the cod-worm or caddis; and these make the trout bold and lusty, and he is usually fatter and better meat at the end of that month than at any time of the year.

Now you are to know that it is observed that usually the best trouts are either red or yellow, though some, as the Fordidge trout, be white and yet good; but that is not usual. And it is a note observable that the female trout hath usually a less head and a deeper body than the male trout, and is usually the better meat. And note that a hog-back and a little head to any fish, either trout, salmon, or other fish, is a sign that that fish is in season.

But yet you are to note that as you see some willows or palm-trees bud and blossom sooner than others do, so some trouts be in some rivers sooner in season; and as some hollies or oaks are longer before they cast their leaves, so are some trouts in some rivers longer before they go out of season.

And you are to note that there are several kinds of trouts. But these several kinds are not considered but by very few men; for they go under the general name of trouts; just as pigeons do in most places, though it is certain there are tame and wild pigeons; and of the tame there be helmits and runts and carriers and cropers, and indeed too many to name. Nay, the Royal Society have found and published lately that there be thirty and three kinds of spiders; and yet all, for aught I know, go under that one general name of spider. And it is so with many kinds of fish, and of trouts especially, which differ in their bigness and shape and spots and color. The great Kentish hens may be an instance, compared to other hens; and doubtless there is a kind of small trout which will never thrive to be big that breeds very many more than others do that be of a larger size. Which you may rather believe, if you consider that the little wren and titmouse will have twenty young ones at a time, when usually the noble hawk or the musical throstle or blackbird exceed not four or five.

And now you shall see me try my skill to catch a trout; and at my next walking, either this evening or tomorrow morning, I will give you direction how you yourself shall fish for him.

VENATOR. Trust me, master, I see now it is a harder matter to catch a trout than a chub; for I have put on patience and followed you these two hours and not seen a fish stir, neither at your minnow nor your worm.

PISCATOR. Well, scholar, you must endure worse luck sometime, or you will never make a good angler. But what say you now? There is a trout now, and a good one too, if I can but hold him; and two or three turns more will tire him. Now you see he lies still, and the sleight is to land him. Reach me that landing-net. So, Sir, now he is mine own. What say you now? is not this worth all my labor and your patience?

VENATOR. On my word, master, this is a gallant trout; what shall we do with him?

PISCATOR. Marry, e'en eat him to supper. We'll go to my hostess from whence we came; she told me, as I was going out of door, that my brother Peter, a good angler and a cheerful companion, had sent word he would lodge there tonight and bring a friend with him. My hostess has two beds, and I know you and I may have the best. We'll rejoice with my brother Peter and his friend, tell tales, or sing ballads, or make a catch, or find some harmless sport to content us, and pass away a little time without offence to God or man.

VENATOR. A match, good master, let's go to that house, for the linen looks white and smells of lavender, and I long to lie in a pair of sheets that smell so. Let's be going, good master, for I am hungry again with fishing.

PISCATOR. Nay, stay a little, good scholar. I caught my last trout with a worm, now I will put on a minnow and try a quarter of an hour about yonder tree for another, and so walk towards our lodging. Look you, scholar, thereabout we shall have a bite presently, or not at all. Have with you, Sir! On my word, I have hold of him. Oh, it is a great logger-headed chub! Come, hang him upon that willow twig, and let's be going.

*

VENATOR. Well now, good master, as we walk towards the river, give me direction, according to your promise, how I shall fish for a trout.

PISCATOR. My honest scholar, I will take this very convenient opportunity to do it.

The trout is usually caught with a worm or a minnow, which some call a penk, or with a fly, *viz.* either a natural or an artificial fly. Concerning which three I will give you some observations and directions.

And, first, for worms. Of these there be very many sorts, some bred only in the earth, as the earth-worm, others of or amongst plants, as the dug-worm, and others bred either out of excrements or in the bodies of living creatures, as in the horns of sheep or deer, or some of dead flesh, as the maggot or gentle, and others.

Now these be most of them particularly good for particular fishes. But for the trout the dew-worm, which some also call the lob-worm, and the brandling are the chief; and especially the first for a great trout, and the latter for a less. There be also of lob-worms some called squirrel-tails, a worm that has a red head, a streak down the back, and a broad tail, which are noted to be the best because they are the toughest and most lively and live longest in the water; for you are to know that a dead worm is but a dead bait and like to catch nothing, compared to a lively, quick, stirring worm. And for a brandling he is usually found in an old dunghill or some very rotten place near to it, but most usually in cow-dung or hog's-dung, rather than horse-dung, which is somewhat too hot and dry for that worm. But the best of them are to be found in the bark of the tanners which they cast up in heaps after they have used it about their leather.

There are also divers other kinds of worms which for color and shape alter even as the ground out of which they are got; as the marsh-worm, the tag-tail, the flag-worm, the dock-worm, the oak-worm, the gilt-tail, the twachel or lob-worm, which of all others is the most excellent bait for a salmon, and too many to name, even as many sorts as some think there be of several herbs or shrubs or of several kinds of birds in the air. Of which I shall say no more but tell you that what worms soever you fish with are the better for being long kept before they be used. And in case you have not been so provident, then the way to cleanse and scour them quickly is to put them all night in water, if they be lob-worms, and then put them into your bag with fennel. But you must not put your brandlings above an hour in water and then put them into fennel, for sudden use; but if you have time and purpose to keep them long. then they be best preserved in an earthen pot, with good store of moss, which is to be fresh every three or four days in summer and every week or eight days in winter; or at least the moss taken from them and clean washed and wrung betwixt your hands till it be dry, and then put it to them again. And when your worms, especially the brandling, begins to be sick and lose of his bigness, then you may recover him by putting a little milk or cream, about a spoonful in a day, into them by drops on the moss; and if there be added to the cream an egg beaten and boiled in it, then it will both fatten and preserve them long. And note that when the knot which is near to the middle of the brandling begins to swell, then he is sick; and if he be not well looked to, is near dying. And for moss you are to note that there be divers kinds of it which I could name to you, but I will only tell you that which is likest; a buck's-horn is the best, except it be soft white moss which grows on some heaths and is hard to be found. And note that in a very dry time when you are put to an extremity for worms walnut-tree leaves squeezed into water, or salt in water to make it bitter or salt, and then that water poured on the ground where you shall see worms are used to rise in the night will make them to appear above ground presently.

And now, I shall show you how to bait your hook with a worm so as shall prevent you from much trouble and the loss of many a hook too, when you fish for a trout with a running line, that is to say, when you fish for him by hand at the ground. I will direct you in this as plainly as I can, that you may not mistake.

Suppose it be a big lob-worm. Put your hook into him somewhat above the middle and out again a little below the middle. Having so done, draw your worm above the arming of your hook; but note that at the entering of your hook it must not be at the head-end of the worm but at the tail-end of him, that the point of your hook may come out toward the head-end. And having drawn him above the arming of your hook, then put the point of your hook again into the very head of the worm till it come near to the place where the point of the hook first came out. And then draw back that part of the worm that was above the shank or arming of your hook, and so fish with it. And if you mean to fish with two worms, then put the second on before you turn back the hook's-head of the first worm. You cannot lose above two or three worms before you attain to what I direct you; and having attained it, you will find it very useful, and thank me for it. For you will run on the ground without tangling.

Now for the minnow, or penk, he is not easily found and caught till March, or in April, for then he appears first in the river, nature having taught him to shelter and hide himself in the winter in ditches that be near to the river, and there both to hide and keep himself warm in the mud or in the weeds, which rot not so soon as in a running river, in which place if he were in winter, the distempered floods that are usually in that season would suffer him to take no rest, but carry him headlong to mills and weirs to his confusion. And of these minnows, first, you are to know that the biggest size is not the best; and next, that the middle size and the whitest are the best; and then you are to know that your minnow must be so put on your hook that it must turn round when 'tis drawn against the stream, and, that it may turn nimbly, you must put it on a big-sized hook as I shall now direct you, which is thus: put your hook in at his mouth and out at his gill; then, having drawn your hook two or three inches beyond or through his gill, put it again into his mouth and the point and beard out at his tail; and then tie the hook and his tail about very neatly with a white thread, which will make it the apter to turn quick in the water; that done, pull back that part of your line which was slack when you did put your hook into the minnow the second time; I say, pull that part of it back so that it shall fasten the head so that the body of the minnow shall be almost straight on your hook; this done, try how it will turn by drawing it across the water or against a stream; and if it do not turn nimbly, then turn the tail a little to the right or left hand, and try again till it turn quick; for if not, you are in danger to catch nothing; for know, that it is impossible that it should turn too quick. And you are yet to know that in case you want a minnow, then a small loach, or a stickleback, or any other small fish will serve as well. And you are yet to know that you may salt them and by that means keep them fit for use three or four days or longer; and that of salt, bay-salt is the best.

And here let me tell you, what many old anglers know right well, that at some times and in some waters a minnow is not to be got; and therefore let me tell you I have (which I will show to you) an artificial minnow that will catch a trout as well as an artificial fly. And it was made by a handsome woman that had a fine hand, and a live minnow lying by her: the mould or body of the minnow was cloth and wrought upon or over it thus with a needle; the back of it with very sad French green silk, and paler green silk towards the belly, shadowed as perfectly as you can imagine, just as you see a minnow; the belly was wrought also with a needle, and it was, a part of it, white silk; and another part of it with silver thread; the tail and fins were of a quill which was shaven thin; the eyes were of two little black beads; and the head was so shadowed and all of it so curiously wrought and so exactly dissembled that it would beguile any sharp-sighted trout in a swift stream. And this minnow I will now show you, and if you like it, lend it you to have two or three made by it; for they be easily carried about an angler, and be of excellent use; for note that a large trout will come as fiercely at a minnow as the highest-mettled hawk doth seize on a partridge, or a greyhound on a hare. I have been told that one hundred sixty minnows have been found in a trout's belly. Either the trout had devoured so many, or the miller that gave it a friend of mine had forced them down his throat after he had taken him.

Now for flies, which is the third bait wherewith trouts are usually taken. You are to know that there are as many sorts of flies as there be of fruits. I will name you but some of them: as the dun-fly, the stone-fly, the red-fly, the moor-fly, the tawny-fly, the shell-fly, the cloudy or blackish-fly, the flag-fly, the vine-fly; there be of flies, caterpillars and canker-flies and bear-flies; and indeed too many either for me to name or for you to remember. And their breeding is so various and wonderful that I might easily amaze myself and tire you in a relation of them.

And yet I will exercise your promised patience by saying a little of the caterpillar, or the palmer-fly or worm, that by them you may guess what a work it were in a discourse but to run over those very many flies, worms, and little living creatures with which the sun and summer adorn and beautify the river-banks and meadows, both for the recreation and contemplation of us anglers, and which, I think, myself enjoy more than any other man that is not of my profession.

Pliny holds an opinion that many have their birth or being from a dew that in the spring falls upon the leaves of trees, and that some kinds of them are from a dew left upon herbs or flowers; and others from a dew left upon coleworts or cabbages. All which kinds of dews, being thickened and condensed, are by the sun's generative heat most of them hatched and in three days made living creatures; and these of several shapes and colors; some being hard and tough, some smooth and soft; some are horned in their head, some in their tail, some have none; some have hair, some none; some have sixteen feet, some less, and some have none, but (as our Topsel hath with great diligence observed) those which have none move upon the earth or upon broad leaves, their motion being not unlike to the waves of the sea. Some of them he also observes to be bred of the eggs of other caterpillars and that those in their time turn to be butterflies; and again that their eggs turn the following year to be caterpillars. And some affirm that every plant has its particular fly or caterpillar which it breeds and feeds. I have seen, and may therefore affirm it, a green caterpillar, or worm, as big as a small peascod, which had fourteen legs, eight on the belly, four under the neck, and two near the tail. It was found on a hedge of privet, and was taken thence and put into a large box and a little branch or two of privet put to it, on which I saw it feed as sharply as a dog gnaws a bone. It lived thus five or six days and thrived and changed the color two or three times, but by some neglect in the keeper of it, it then died and did not turn to a fly. But if it had lived, it had doubtless turned to one of those flies that some call flies of prey, which those that walk by the rivers may in summer see fasten on smaller flies and I think make them their food. And 'tis observable that as there be these flies of prey which be very large, so there be others, very little, created I think only to feed them, and bred out of I know not what; whose life, they say, nature intended not to exceed an hour, and yet that life is thus made shorter by other flies, or accident.

'Tis endless to tell you what the curious searchers into nature's productions have observed of these worms and flies. But yet I shall tell you what Aldrovandus, our Topsel, and others say of the palmer-worm or caterpillar: that whereas others content themselves to feed on particular herbs or leaves (for most think those very leaves that gave them life and shape give them a particular feeding and nourishment and that upon them they usually abide), yet he observes that this is called a pilgrim or palmer-worm for his very wandering life and various food; not contenting himself, as others do, with any one certain place for his abode nor any certain kind of herb or flower for his feeding, but will boldly and disorderly wander up and down and not endure to be kept to a diet or fixed to a particular place.

Nay, the very colors of caterpillars are, as one has observed, very elegant and beautiful. I shall, for a taste of the rest, describe one of them which I will some time the next month show you feeding on a willow-tree, and you shall find him punctually to answer this very description: his lips and mouth somewhat yellow, his eyes black as jet, his forehead purple, his feet and hinder parts green, his tail two-forked and black, the whole body stained with a kind of red spots which run along the neck and shoulder-blade, not unlike the form of St. Andrew's cross or the letter X made thus crosswise, and a white line drawn down his back to his tail; all which add much beauty to his whole body. And it is to me observable that at a fixed age this caterpillar gives over to eat, and towards winter comes to be covered over with a strange shell or crust called an aurelia, and so lives a kind of dead life without eating all the winter. And as others of several kinds turn to be several kinds of flies and vermin the spring following, so this caterpillar then turns to be a painted butterfly.

*

VENATOR. Master, I can neither catch with the first nor second angle. I have no fortune.

PISCATOR. Look you, scholar, I have yet another. And now, having caught three brace of trouts, I will tell you a short tale as we walk towards our breakfast: a scholar—a preacher I should say—that was to preach to procure the approbation of a parish that he might be their lecturer had got from his fellow-pupil the copy of a sermon that was first preached with great commendation by him that composed and preached it; and though the borrower of it preached it word for word as it was at first, yet it was utterly disliked as it was preached by the second. Which the sermon-borrower complained of to the lender of it; and was thus answered: "I lent you, indeed, my fiddle, but not my fiddle-stick; for you are to know that everyone cannot make music with my words, which are fitted for my own mouth." And so, my scholar, you are to know that as the ill pronunciation or ill accenting of words in a sermon spoils it, so the ill carriage of your line or not fishing even to a foot in a right place makes you lose your labor. And you are to know that though you have my fiddle, that is, my very rod and tacklings with which you see I catch fish, yet you have not my fiddle-stick, that is, you yet have not skill to know how to carry your hand and line nor how to guide it to a right place. And this must be taught you—for you are to remember I told you angling is an art—either by practice or a long observation or both. But take this for a rule: when you fish for a trout with a worm, let your line have so much and not more lead than will fit the stream in which you fish; that is to say, more in a great troublesome stream than in a smaller that is quieter; as near as may be, so much as will sink the bait to the bottom and keep it still in motion, and not more.

But now, let's say grace, and fall to breakfast. What say you, scholar, to the providence of an old angler? Does not this meat taste well? and was not this place well chosen to eat it? for this sycamore-tree will shade us from the sun's heat.

VENATOR. All excellent good, and my stomach excellent good too. And now I remember and find that true which devout Lessius says, "That poor men and those that fast often have much more pleasure in eating than rich men and gluttons, that always feed before their stomachs are empty of their last meat and so rob themselves of that pleasure that hunger brings to poor men." And I do seriously approve of that saying of yours, "That you had rather be a civil, well-grounded, temperate, poor angler than a drunken lord." But I hope there is none such. However, I am certain of this, that I have been at many very costly dinners that have not afforded me half the content that this has done, for which I thank God and you.

And now, good master, proceed to your promised direction for making and ordering my artificial fly.

PISCATOR. My honest scholar, I will do it, for it is a debt due unto you by my promise. And because you shall not think yourself more engaged to me than indeed you really are, I will freely give you such directions as were lately given to me by an ingenious brother of the angle, an honest angle, an honest man, and a most excellent fly-fisher.

You are to note that there are twelve kinds of artificial-made flies to angle with upon the top of the water. Note, by the way, that the fittest season of using these is in a blustering windy day, when the waters are so troubled that the natural fly cannot be seen, or rest upon them. The first is the dun-fly in March; the body is made of dun wool, the wings, of the partridge's feathers. The second is another dun-fly; the body of black wool, and the wings made of the black drake's feathers and of the feathers under his tail. The third is the stone-fly in April; the body is made of black wool made yellow under the wings and under the tail and so made with wings of the drake. The fourth is the ruddy-fly in the beginning of May; the body made of red wool, wrapt about with black silk, and the feathers are the wings of the drake, with the feathers of a red capon also, which hang dangling on his sides next to the tail. The fifth is the yellow or greenish fly, in May likewise; the body made of yellow wool, and the wings made of the red cock's hackle or tail. The sixth is the black-fly, in May also; the body made of black wool, and lapt about with the herle of a peacock's tail, the wings are made of the wings of a brown capon, with his blue feathers in his head. The seventh is the sad yellow-fly in June; the body is made of black wool, with a yellow list on either side, and the wings taken off the wings of a buzzard, bound with black braked hemp. The eighth is the moorish-fly; made with the body of duskish wool, and the wings made of the blackish mail of the drake. The ninth is the tawny-fly, good until the middle of June; the body made of tawny wool, the wings made contrary one against the other, made of the whitish mail of the wild drake. The tenth is the wasp-fly in July; the body made of black wool, lapt about with yellow silk, the wings made of the feathers of the drake or of the buzzard. The eleventh is the shell-fly, good in mid-July; the body made of greenish wool, lapt about with the herle of a peacock's tail, and the wings made of the wings of the buzzard. The twelfth is the dark drake-fly, good in August; the body made with black wool, lapt about with black silk, his wings are made with the mail of the black drake, with a black head. Thus have you a jury of flies likely to betray and condemn all the trouts in the river.

I shall next give you some other directions for fly-fishing such as are given by Mr. Thomas Barker, a gentleman that hath spent much time in fishing; but I shall do it with a little variation.

First, let your rod be light and very gentle. I take the best to be of two pieces.

And let not your line exceed, especially for three or four links next to the hook, I say, not exceed three or four hairs at the most, though you may fish a little stronger above in the upper part of your line. But if you can attain to angle with one hair, you shall have more rises, and catch more fish. Now you must be sure not to cumber yourself with too long a line, as most do. And before you begin to angle, cast to have the wind on your back, and the sun, if it shines, to be before you, and to fish down the stream; and carry the point or top of your rod downward, by which means the shadow of yourself and rod too will be the least offensive to the fish; for the sight of any shade amazes the fish and spoils your sport, of which you must take great care.

In the middle of March—till which time a man should not in honesty catch a trout—or in April, if the weather be dark or a little windy or cloudy, the best fishing is with the palmer-worm, of which I last spoke to you; but of these there be divers kinds, or at least of divers colors. These and the May-fly are the ground of all fly-angling. Which are to be thus made:

First, you must arm your hook with the line in the inside of it; then take your scissors and cut so much of a brown mallard's feather as in your own reason will make the wings of it, you having withal regard to the bigness or littleness of your hook; then lay the outmost part of your feather next to your hook; then the point of your feather next the shank of your hook; and having so done, whip it three or four times about the hook with the same silk with which your hook was armed; and having made the silk fast, take the hackle of a cock or capon's neck or a plover's top, which is usually better; take off the one side of the feather, and then take the hackle, silk, or crewel, gold or silver thread; make these fast at the bent of the hook, that is to say, below your arming; then you must take the hackle, the silver or gold thread, and work it up to the wings, shifting or still removing your finger as you turn the silk about the hook and still looking at every stop or turn that your gold or what materials soever you make your fly of do lie right and neatly; and if you find they do so, then when you have made the head, make all fast; and then work your hackle up to the head and make that fast; and then with a needle or pin divide the wing into two; and then with the arming silk whip it about cross-ways betwixt the wings; and then with your thumb you must turn the point of the feather towards the bent of the hook; and then work three or four times about the shank of the hook; and then view the proportion; and if all be neat and to your liking, fasten.

I confess no direction can be given to make a man of a dull capacity able to make a fly well. And yet I know this, with a little practice, will help an ingenious angler in a good degree. But to see a fly made by an artist in that kind is the best teaching to make it. And then an ingenious angler may walk by the river and mark what flies fall on the water that day, and catch one of them, if he sees the trouts leap at a fly of that kind; and then having always hooks ready-hung with him and having a bag always with him with bear's hair or the hair of a brown or sad-colored heifer, hackles of a cock or capon, several colored silk and crewel to make the body of the fly, the feathers of a drake's head, black or brown sheep's wool, or hog's wool, or hair, thread of gold and of silver, silk of several colors, especially sad-colored, to make the fly's head; and there be also other colored feathers, both of little birds and of speckled fowl—I say, having those with him in a bag and trying to make a fly, though he miss at first, yet shall he at last hit it better even to such a perfection as none can well teach him. And if he hit to make his fly right and have the luck to hit also where there is store of trouts, a dark day, and a right wind, he will catch such store of them as will encourage him to grow more and more in love with the art of fly-making.

VENATOR. But, my loving master, if any wind will not serve, then I wish I were in Lapland, to buy a good wind of one of the honest witches that sell so many winds there and so cheap.

PISCATOR. Marry, scholar, but I would not be there, nor indeed from under this tree. For look how it begins to rain, and by the clouds, if I mistake not, we shall presently have a smoking shower, and therefore sit close. This sycamore-tree will shelter us. And I will tell you, as they shall come into my mind, more observations of fly-fishing for a trout.

But first for the wind, you are to take notice that of the winds the south wind is said to be best. One observes that

> when the wind is south,
> It blows your bait into a fish's mouth.

Next to that the west wind is believed to be the best. And having told you that the east wind is the worst, I need not tell you which wind is the best in the third degree. And yet, as Solomon observes, that "He that considers the wind shall never sow"; so he that busies his head too much about them, if the weather be not made extreme cold by an east wind, shall be a little superstitious. For as it is observed by some that "There is no good horse of a bad color"; so I have observed that if it be a cloudy day and not extreme cold, let the wind sit in what corner it will and do its worst. And yet take this for a rule, that I would willingly fish standing on the lee-shore. And you are to take notice that the fish lies or swims nearer the bottom and in deeper water in winter than in summer; and also nearer the bottom in any cold day, and then gets nearest the low side of the water.

But I promised to tell you more of the fly-fishing for a trout; which I may have time enough to do, for you see it rains May butter. First for a May-fly, you may make his body with greenish-colored crewel or willowish color, darkening it in most places with waxed silk, or ribbed with black hair, or some of them ribbed with silver thread, and such wings for the color as you see the fly to have at that season, nay, at that very day on the water. Or you may make the oak-fly, with an orange-tawny and black ground, and the brown of a mallard's feather for the wings. And you are to know that these two are most excellent flies, that is, the May-fly and the oak-fly. And let me again tell you that you keep as far from the water as you can possibly, whether you fish with a fly or worm, and fish down the stream. And when you fish with a fly, if it be possible, let no part of your line touch the water but your fly only; and be still moving your fly upon the water, or casting it into the water, you yourself being also always moving down the stream. Mr. Barker commends several sorts of the palmer-flies, not only those ribbed with silver and gold, but others that have their bodies all made of black, or some with red, and a red hackle. You may also make the hawthorn-fly, which is all black, and not big, but very small, the smaller the better. Or the oak-fly, the body of which is orange color and black crewel, with a brown wing. Or a fly made with a peacock's feather is excellent in a bright day. You must be sure you want not in your magazine-bag the peacock's feather and grounds of such wool and crewel as will make the grasshopper. And note that usually the smallest flies are the best; and note also that the light fly does usually make most sport in a dark day, and the darkest and least fly in a bright or clear day; and lastly note that you are to repair upon any occasion to your magazine-bag, and upon any occasion vary and make them lighter or sadder according to your fancy or the day.

And now I shall tell you that the fishing with a natural fly is excellent, and affords much pleasure. They may be found thus: the May-fly usually in and about that month near to the river-side, especially against rain; the oak-fly on the butt or body of an oak or ash from the beginning of May to the end of August; it is a brownish fly and easy to be so found, and stands usually with his head downward, that is to say, towards the root of the tree; the small black-fly, or hawthorn-fly, is to be had on any hawthorn bush after the leaves be come forth. With these and a short line, as I showed to angle for a chub, you may dape or dop, and also with a grasshopper, behind a tree or in any deep hole; still making it to move on the top of the water as if it were alive and still keeping yourself out of sight, you shall certainly have sport if there be trouts; yea, in a hot day, but especially in the evening of a hot day.

And now, scholar, my direction for fly-fishing is ended with this shower, for it has done raining. And now look about you, and see how pleasantly that meadow looks; nay, and the earth smells so sweetly too. Come let me tell you what holy Mr. Herbert says of such days and flowers as these, and then we will thank God that we enjoy them, and walk to the river and sit down quietly, and try to catch the other brace of trouts.

> Sweet day, so cool, so calm, so bright,
> The bridal of the earth and sky,
> Sweet dews shall weep thy fall tonight,
>   For thou must die.

> Sweet rose whose hue, angry and brave,
> Bids the rash gazer wipe his eye,
> Thy root is ever in its grave,
>   And thus must die.

Sweet spring, full of sweet days and roses,
A box where sweet compacted lie,
My music shows you have your closes,
                And all must die.

Only a sweet and virtuous soul
Like seasoned timber never gives,
But when the whole world turns to coal,
                Then chiefly lives.

VENATOR. I thank you, good master, for your good direction for fly-fishing and for the sweet enjoyment of the pleasant day, which is so far spent without offence to God or man; and I thank you for the sweet close of your discourse with Mr. Herbert's verses, which, I have heard, loved angling; and I do the rather believe it, because he had a spirit suitable to anglers and to those primitive Christians that you love and have so much commended.

*

No life, my honest scholar, no life so happy and so pleasant as the life of a well-governed angler; for when the lawyer is swallowed up with business and the statesman is preventing or contriving plots, then we sit on cowslip-banks, hear the birds sing, and possess ourselves in as much quietness as these silent silver streams which we now see glide so quietly by us. Indeed, my good scholar, we may say of angling as Dr. Boteler said of strawberries, "Doubtless God could have made a better berry, but doubtless God never did"; and so if I might be judge, God never did make a more calm, quiet, innocent recreation than angling.

BARKER'S DELIGHT
or
THE ART OF ANGLING (1657)

Thomas Barker

NOBLE LORD,

Under favour I will complement and put a case to your Honour. I met with a man, and upon our discourse he fell out with me, having a good weapon, but neither stomach nor skil; I say this man may come home by Weeping cross, I will cause the Clerk to toll his knell. It is the very like case to the gentleman Angler that goeth to the River for his pleasure: this Angler hath neither judgment nor experience, he may come home light laden at his leisure.

A man that goeth to the River for his pleasure, must understand when he cometh there to set forth his tackle: The first thing he must do, is to observe the Sun and the Wind for day, the Moon, the Stars, and the wanes of the Aire for night, to set forth his tackles for day or night, and accordingly to go for his pleasure and some profit.

For example. The Sun proves cloudy, then must you set forth either your ground-bait tackles, or of the brightest of your flyes. If the Sun prove bright and clear, then must you put on the darkest of your flyes; thus must you to work with your flies, light for darkness, and dark for lightness, with the wind in the South, which blowes the fly in the Trouts mouth. Though I set down the wind in the South, I am indifferent where the wind standeth, either with ground-bait or menow, so that I can cast my bait into the River. The very same observation is for night as for day for, if the Moon prove clear, or the Stars glitter in the sky, it is as ill angling that night as if it were at high noon in the midst of the summer, when the Sun shineth at the brightest, wherein there is no hopes of pleasure.

I will begin to angle for the Trout, and discourse his qualitie.

The first thing you must gain must be a neat taper rod light before, with a tender hasel top which is very gentle, with a single hair of five lengths long, one tyed to another, for the bottom of my line, and a line of three haired links for the uppermost part, and so you may kill the greatest Trout that swims, with sea room.

Now I say he that angles with a line made of three haired links for the bottom, and more at the top, may kill fish, but he that angles with a line made of one haired link, shall kill five to the others one; for, the Trout is very quick-sighted, therefore the best way either for night or day is to keep out of sight.

You must angle alwayes with the point of the rod down the stream, for trouts have not quickness of sight so perfect up the stream as they have opposite against them.

But observe the seasonable times. For example, we begin to angle in March: if it prove cloudy, you may angle with the ground baits all day long: but if it prove bright and clear, you must take evening and morning, or else you are not like to do good: so times must be observed and truly understood; for when an angler cometh to the River for his pleasure, and doth not understand to set forth his tackles fit for the time, it is as good keep them in the bag as to set them forth.

Now I am determined to angle with the ground baits, and set my tackles to my rod, and go to my pleasure. I begin at the uppermost part of the stream, carrying my line with an upright hand, feeling my plummet running truly on the ground some ten inches from the hook, plumming my line according to the swiftness of the stream I angle in, for one plummet will not serve for all streams; for the true angling is that the plummet run truly on the ground.

For the bait, the red knotted worm is very good, where Brandlins are not to be had; but Brandlins are better.

Now I will shew you how to make these Brandlins fit to angle with, and to make them lusty and fat, that they may live long on the hook, which causeth the best sport; for that is a chief point, and causeth the best sport.

You must take the yolk of an egg, and some eight or ten spoonfulls of the top of new milk, beaten well together in a porringer, warm it a little untill you see it curdle, then take it off the fire and set it to cool; when it is cold, take a spoon-full and drop it on the moss in an earthen pot, every drop about the bigness of a green pease, shifting your moss twice in the summer, and once a week in the winter. Thus doing, you shall feed your worms and make them fat and lusty, that they will live long and be lusty and lively on your hook. And thus you may keep them all the year long. This is my true experiment for the ground baits, with the running line for the trout.

My Lord, I will now shew the angling with a Menow (called in some places Pincks) for the Trout, which is a pleasant sport, and killeth the greatest fish: The Trout cometh boldly at the bait, as if it were a Mastiffe dog at a Beare; you may angle with greater Tackles and stronger, and be no prejudice in your Angling. A line made of three silks and three hairs twisted for the uppermost part of your line, and a line made of two silks and two hairs twisted for the bottome next your hook, with a swivel nigh the middle of your line, and an indifferent long hook. But if you can attain to angle with a line of foure haired links for the uppermost part, and a line of three haired links for the bottom, for the finer you angle with, it is the better.

Now I must shew you how to bait the menow on your hook: You must put your hook through the lowermost part of the menow's mouth, so draw your hook through; then put the hook in at the mouth again, let the point of the hook come out at the hindmost fin; then draw your line and the menow's mouth will close, that no water get into its belly; you must be alwayes angling with the point of your rod down the stream, drawing your menow up the side of the stream by little & little, nigh the top of the water; the trout seeing the bait cometh at it most fiercely; give a little time before you strike. This is the true way without lead, for many times I have had them come at the lead and forsake the menow. He that trieth shall prove it in time.

My Lord, I will shew you the way to angle with a flye, which is a delightfull sport.

The rod must be light and tender, if you can fit your self with a hasel of one piece, or of two pieces set together in the most convenient manner, light and gentle. Set your line to your rod, for the uppermost part you may use your own discretion, for the lowermost part next your flye it must be of three or four haired links. If you can attain to angle with a line made of one hair, two or three links one tyed to another next your hook, you shall have more rises and kill more fish. Be sure you do not overload your self with lengths of your line. Before you begin to angle make a triall, having the wind on your back, to see at what length you can cast your flye, that the flye light first into the water, and no longer, for if any of the line fall into the water before the flye, it is better uncast than thrown. Be sure you be casting alwayes down the stream with the wind behind you, and the Sun before you. It is a speciall point to have the Sun and Moon before you, for the very motion of the rod drives all the pleasure from you, either by day or by night in all your anglings, both with worms and flyes, there must be a great care of that.

Let us begin to angle in March with the flye. If the weather prove windy or cloudy, there are severall kinds of Palmers that are good for that time.

First, a black Palmer, ribbed with silver. Secondly, a black Palmer ribbed with an orenge-tawny body. Thirdly, a black Palmer made all of black. Fourthly, a red Palmer ribbed with gold. Fifthly, a red Palmer mixed with an orenge-tawny body of cruell. All these flyes must be made with hackles, and they will serve all the year long morning and evening, windy or cloudy. Without these flyes you cannot make a dayes angling good. I have heard say that there is for every moneth in the year a flye for that moneth; but that is but talk, for there is but one monethly flye in the yeare, that is the May-flye. Then if the aire prove clear you must imitate the Hawthorn flye, which is all black and very small, the smaller the better. In May take the May flye, imitate that. Some make it with a shammy body, and ribbed with a black hair. Another way it is made with sandy hogs hair ribbed with black silk, and winged with Mallards feathers, according to the fancy of the angler, if he hath judgement. For first, when it comes out of the shell, the flye is somewhat whiter, then afterwards it grows browner, so there is judgement in that. There is another fly called the Oak-flye that is a very good flye, which is made of orenge colour cruell and black, with a brown wing, imitate that. There is another flye made with the strain of a Peacocks feather, imitating the Flesh-flye, which is very good in a bright day. The Grasse-hopper which is green, imitate that. The smaller these flyes be made, and of indifferent small hooks, they are the better. These sorts which I have set down will serve all the year long, observing the times and seasons, if the angler have any judgement. Note the lightest of your flies for cloudy and dark, and the darkest of your flyes for the brightest dayes, and the rest for indifferent times; a mans own judgement with some experience must guide him. If he mean to kill fish he must alter his flyes according to these directions. Now of late I have found that hogs wooll of several colour makes good bodies, & the wooll of a red heifer makes a good body and beares wooll makes a good body: there are many good furres that make good bodies: and now I work much of hogs wooll, for I finde it floateth best and procureth the best sport.

The naturall flye is sure angling, and will kill great store of trouts with much pleasure. As for the May-flie you shall have him playing alwayes at the rivers side, especially against rain: the Oak-flie is to be had on the but of an oak or an ash, from the beginning of May to the end of August; it is a brownish flie, and standeth alwaies with his head towards the root of the tree, very easie to be found: the small black fly is to be had on every hathorn tree after the buds be come forth: your grasse-hopper which is green is to be had in any medow of grass in June or July. With these flies you must angle with such a rod as you angle with the ground bait: the line must not be so long as the rod drawing your flye as you finde convenient in your angling: When you come to the deep waters that stand somewhat still, make your line two yards long or thereabouts, and dop or drop your flye behind a bush, which angling I have had good sport at; we call it *dopping*.

My Lord sent to me at Sun going down to provide him a good dish of Trouts against the next morning by sixe of the clock, I went to the door to see how the wanes of the aire were like to prove. I returned answer, that I doubted not, God willing, but to be provided at his time appointed. I went presently to the river, and it proved very dark, I drew out a line of three silks and three hairs twisted for the uppermost part, and a line of two hairs and two silks twisted for the lower part, with a good large hook: I baited my hook with two lob-worms, the four ends hanging as meet as I could guess them in the dark, I fell to angle. It proved very dark, so that I had good sport angling with the lob-worms as I do with the flye on the top of the water; you shall hear the fish rise at the top of the water, then you must loose a slack line down to the bottom as nigh as you can guess, then hold your line strait, feeling the fish bite, give time, there is no doubt of losing the fish, for there is not one among twenty but doth gorge the bait; the least stroke you can strike fastens the hook and makes the fish sure; letting the fish take a turn or two you may take the fish up with your hands. The night began to alter and grow somewhat lighter, I took off the lob-worms and set to my rod a white Palmer-flye, made of a large hook; I had sport for the time untill it grew lighter; so I took off the white Palmer and set to a red Palmer made of a large hook; I had good sport until it grew very light: then I took off the red Palmer and set to a black Palmer; I had good sport, made up the dish of fish. So I put up my tackles and was with my Lord at his time appointed for the service.

These three flyes with the help of the lob-worms serve to angle all the year for the night, observing the times as I have shewed you in this night-work, the white flye for darknesse, the red flye in medio, and the black flye for lightnesse. This is the true experience for angling in the night, which is the surest angling of all, and killeth the greatest Trouts. Your lines may be strong, but must not be longer then your rod.

> The rod light and taper, thy tackle fine,
>   Thy lead ten inches upon the line;
> Bigger or lesse, according to the stream,
>   Angle in the dark, when others dream:
> Or in a cloudy day with a lively worm,
>   The Brandlin is best; but give him a turn
> Before thou do land a large wel grown Trout.
>   And if with a flye thou wilt have a bout,
> Overload not with links, that the flye may fall
>   First on the stream, for that's all in all.
> The line shorter than the rod, with a naturall flye:
>   But the chief point of all is the cookery.

Now having taken a good dish of Trouts I presented them to my Lord. He having provided good company, commanded me to turn Cook and dress them for dinner. Whereupon I gave my Lord this bill of fare, which did furnish his table as it was furnished with flesh.

Trouts in broth, which is restorative, which must be boyled in milk, putting to it some large mace, letting it boyle up. Before you put the trouts into the Kettle, the trouts must be drawn and clean washed before you put them in. So keep them with high boyling, untill you think them boyled sufficient. Then you must take a slice or two of good sweet butter and put into your dish, so pour on the broth, having provided the yolks of half a dozen eggs, being very well beaten in a dish or porringer, pour it into your broth, so stir it well; I make no doubt but it will be good broth.

The broth eaten, provide for the sauce some butter, the inner part of a lemmon, the yolk of an egge well beaten together, so pour it into the dish, I make no doubt but it will be well liked of. If they doe not like of this broth, when you boyle other trouts for the service, let the trouts be boyled sufficiently in such liquor as I will shew you now following. You may take the quantity of a quart of the top of the liquor with half a pint of Sack, boyle it together, then provide the yolks of half a dozen eggs well beaten together; beat all this together with a slice or two of good sweet butter; no doubt but this will be very good.

Now we must have two dishes of calvored Trouts hot. For the first course the sauce shall be butter and vinegar, 2 or 3 Anchoves, the bones taken out, beaten together with the yolk of one egge for one of the dishes, with a lemmon squeezed on them. For the other dish the sauce and purtenances shall be a quart of Oysters stewed in half a pint of Whitewine, so put on the fish, then butter and vinegar being well beaten, with the yolk of an egge poured on that, squeezing a lemmon on the fish, there is no question but they will be eaten with delight.

Out of this Kettle we must have two dishes to eat cold for the later course.

THE ANGLER

Washington Irving

IT IS SAID that many an unlucky urchin is induced to run away from his family, and betake himself to a seafaring life, from reading the history of Robinson Crusoe; and I suspect that, in like manner, many of those worthy gentlemen who are given to haunt the sides of pastoral streams with angle rods in hand, may trace the origin of their passion to the seductive pages of honest Izaak Walton. I recollect studying his *Compleat Angler* several years since, in company with a knot of friends in America, and moreover that we were all completely bitten with the angling mania. It was early in the year; but as soon as the weather was auspicious, and that the spring began to melt into the verge of summer, we took rod in hand and sallied into the country, as stark mad as was ever Don Quixote from reading books of chivalry.

One of our party had equalled the Don in the fullness of his equipments; being attired *cap-à-pie* for the enterprise. He wore a broad-skirted fustian coat, perplexed with half a hundred pockets; a pair of stout shoes and leathern gaiters; a basket slung on one side for fish; a patent rod, a landing-net, and a score of other inconveniences, only to be found in the true angler's armoury. Thus harnessed for the field, he was as great a matter of stare and wonderment among the country folk, who had never seen a regular angler, as was the steel-clad hero of La Mancha among the goatherds of the Sierra Morena.

Our first essay was along a mountain brook, among the highlands of the Hudson; a most unfortunate place for the execution of those piscatory tactics which had been invented along the velvet margins of quiet English rivulets. It was one of those wild streams that lavish, among our romantic solitudes, unheeded beauties, enough to fill the sketch book of a hunter of the picturesque. Sometimes it would leap down rocky shelves, making small cascades, over which the trees threw their broad balancing sprays, and long nameless weeds hung in fringes from the impending banks, dripping with diamond drops. Sometimes it would brawl and fret along a ravine in the matted shade of a forest, filling it with murmurs; and, after this termagant career, would steal forth into open day with the most placid demure face imaginable; as I have seen some pestilent shrew of a housewife, after filling her home with uproar and ill-humour, come dimpling out of doors, swimming and courtseying, and smiling upon all the world.

How smoothly would this vagrant brook glide, at such times, through some bosom of green meadow-land among the mountains; where the quiet was only interrupted by the occasional tinkling of a bell from the lazy cattle among the clover, or the sound of a woodcutter's axe from the neighbouring forest.

For my part, I was always a bungler at all kinds of sport that required either patience or adroitness, and had not angled above half an hour before I had completely "satisfied the sentiment," and convinced myself of the truth of Izaak Walton's opinion, that angling is something like poetry—a man must be born to it. I hooked myself instead of the fish; tangled my line in every tree; lost my bait; broke my rod; until I gave up the attempt in despair, and passed the day under the trees, reading old Izaak; satisfied that it was his fascinating vein of honest simplicity and rural feeling that had bewitched me, and not the passion for angling. My companions, however, were more persevering in their delusion. I have them at this moment before my eyes, stealing along the border of the brook, where it lay open to the day, or was merely fringed by shrubs and bushes. I see the bittern rising with hollow scream as they break in upon his rarely invaded haunt; the kingfisher watching them suspiciously from his dry tree that overhangs the deep black millpond, in the gorge of the hills; the tortoise letting himself slip sideways from off the stone or log on which he is sunning himself; and the panic-struck frog plumping in headlong as they approach, and spreading an alarm throughout the watery world around.

I recollect also, that, after toiling and watching and creeping about for the greater part of a day, with scarcely any success, in spite of all our admirable apparatus, a lubberly country urchin came down from the hills with a rod made from a branch of a tree, a few yards of twine, and, as Heaven shall help me! I believe a crooked pin for a hook, baited with a vile earthworm—and in half an hour caught more fish than we had nibbles throughout the day!

But, above all, I recollect the "good, honest, wholesome, hungry" repast, which we made under a beech-tree, just by a spring of pure sweet water that stole out of the side of a hill; and how, when it was over, one of the party read old Izaak Walton's scene with the milkmaid, while I lay on the grass and built castles in a bright pile of clouds, until I fell asleep. All this may appear like mere egotism; yet I cannot refrain from uttering these recollections, which are passing like a strain of music over my mind, and have been called up by an agreeable scene which I witnessed not long since.

In a morning stroll along the banks of Alun, a beautiful little stream which flows down from the Welsh hills, and throws itself into the Dee, my attention was attracted to a group seated on the margin. On approaching, I found it to consist of a veteran angler and two rustic disciples. The former was an old fellow with a wooden leg, with clothes very much but very carefully patched, betokening poverty, honestly come by, and decently maintained. His face bore the marks of former storms, but present fair weather; its furrows had been worn into an habitual smile; his iron-gray locks hung about his ears, and he had altogether the good-humoured air of a constitutional philosopher who was disposed to take the world as it went. One of his companions was a ragged wight, with the skulking look of an arrant poacher, and I'll warrant could find his way to any gentleman's fish-pond in the neighbourhood in the darkest night. The other was a tall, awkward, country lad, with a lounging gait, and apparently somewhat of a rustic beau. The old man was busy in examining the maw of a trout which he had just killed, to discover by its contents what insects were seasonable for bait; and was lecturing on the subject to his companions, who appeared to listen with infinite deference. I have a kind feeling towards all "brothers of the angle," ever since I read Izaak Walton. They are men, he affirms, of a "mild, sweet, and peaceable spirit"; and my esteem for them has been increased since I met with an old *Tretyse of fishing with the Angle,* in which are set forth many of the maxims of their inoffensive fraternity. "Take good hede," sayeth this honest little tretyse, "that in going about your disportes ye open no man's gates, but that ye shet them again. Also ye shall not use this forsayd crafti disport for no covetousness to the encreasing and sparing of your money only, but principally for your solace, and to cause the helth of your body and specyally of your soule."

I thought that I could perceive in the veteran angler before me an exemplification of what I had read; and there was a cheerful contentedness in his looks that quite drew me towards him. I could not but remark the gallant manner in which he stumped from one part of the brook to another; waving his rod in the air, to keep the line from dragging on the ground, or catching among the bushes; and the adroitness with which he would throw his fly to any particular place; sometimes skimming it lightly along a little rapid; sometimes casting it into one of those dark holes made by a twisted root or overhanging bank, in which the large trout are apt to lurk. In the meanwhile he was giving instructions to his two disciples; showing them the manner in which they should handle their rods, fix their flies, and play them along the surface of the stream. The scene brought to my mind the instructions of the sage Piscator to his scholar. The country around was of that pastoral kind which Walton is fond of describing. It was a part of the great plain of Cheshire, close by the beautiful vale of Gessford, and just where the inferior Welsh hills begin to swell up from among fresh-smelling meadows. The day, too, like that recorded in his work, was mild and sunshiny, with now and then a soft-dropping shower, that sowed the whole earth with diamonds.

I soon fell into conversation with the old angler, and was so much entertained, that, under pretext of receiving instructions in his art, I kept company with him almost the whole day; wandering along the banks of the stream, and listening to his talk. He was very communicative, having all the easy garrulity of cheerful old age; and I fancy was a little flattered by having an opportunity of displaying his piscatory lore; for who does not like now and then to play the sage?

He had been much of a rambler in his day, and had passed some years of his youth in America, particularly in Savannah, where he had entered into trade and had been ruined by the indiscretion of a partner. He had afterwards experienced many ups and downs in life, until he got into the navy, where his leg was carried away by a cannon-ball, at the battle of Camperdown. This was the only stroke of real good fortune he had ever experienced, for it got him a pension, which, together with some small paternal property brought him in a revenue of nearly forty pounds. On this he retired to his native village where he lived quietly and independently; and devoted the remainder of his life to the "noble art of angling."

I found that he had read Izaak Walton attentively, and he seemed to have imbibed all his simple frankness and prevalent good humour. Though he had been sorely buffeted about the world, he was satisfied that the world, in itself, was good and beautiful. Though he had been as roughly used in different countries as a poor sheep that is fleeced by every hedge and thicket, yet he spoke of every nation with candour and kindness, appearing to look only on the good side of things; and, above all, he was almost the only man I had ever met with who had been an unfortunate adventurer in America and had honesty and magnanimity enough to take the fault to his own door, and not to curse the country. The lad that was receiving his instructions, I learnt, was the son and heir apparent of a fat old widow who kept the village inn, and of course a youth of some expectation, and much courted by the idle gentleman-like personages of the place. In taking him under his care, therefore, the old man had probably an eye to a privileged corner in the taproom, and an occasional cup of cheerful ale free of expense.

There is certainly something in angling, if we could forget, which anglers are apt to do, the cruelties and tortures inflicted on worms and insects, that tends to produce a gentleness of spirit, and a pure serenity of mind. As the English are methodical, even in their recreations, and are the most scientific of sportsmen, it has been reduced among them to perfect rule and system. Indeed, it is an amusement peculiarly adapted to the mild and highly cultivated scenery of England, where every roughness has been softened away from the landscape. It is delightful to saunter along those limpid streams which wander, like veins of silver, through the bosom of this beautiful country; leading one through a diversity of small home scenery; sometimes winding through ornamented grounds; sometimes brimming along through rich pasturage, where the fresh green is mingled with sweet-smelling flowers; sometimes venturing in sight of villages and hamlets, and then running capriciously away into shady retirements. The sweetness and serenity of nature, and the quiet watchfulness of the sport, gradually bring on pleasant fits

of musing, which are now and then agreeably interrupted by the song of a bird, the distant whistle of the peasant, or perhaps the vagary of some fish, leaping out of the still water, and skimming transiently about its glassy surface. "When I would beget content," says Izaak Walton, "and increase confidence in the power and wisdom and providence of Almighty God, I will walk the meadows by some gliding stream, and there contemplate the lilies that take no care, and those very many other little living creatures that are not only created, but feed (man knows not how) by the goodness of the God of nature, and therefore trust in him."

I cannot forbear to give another quotation from one of those ancient champions of angling, which breathes the same innocent and happy spirit:

> Let me live harmlessly, and near the brink
> Of Trent or Avon have a dwelling-place,
> Where I may see my quill, or cork, down sink,
> With eager bite of pike, or bleak, or dace;
> And on the world and my Creator think:
> Whilst some men strive ill-gotten goods t' embrace;
> And others spend their time in base excess
> Of wine, or worse, in war, or wantonness.
> Let them that will, these pastimes still pursue,
> And on such pleasing fancies feed their fill;
> So I the fields and meadows green may view,
> And daily by fresh rivers walk at will,
> Among the daisies and the violets blue,
> Red hyacinth and yellow daffodil.

On parting with the old angler, I inquired after his place of abode, and happening to be in the neighbourhood of the village a few evenings afterwards, I had the curiosity to seek him out. I found him living in a small cottage, containing only one room, but a perfect curiosity in its method and arrangement. It was on the skirts of the village, on a green bank, a little back from the road, with a small garden in front, stocked with kitchen herbs, and adorned with a few flowers. The whole front of the cottage was overrun with a honeysuckle. On the top was a ship for a weathercock. The interior was fitted up in a truly nautical style, his ideas of comfort and convenience having been acquired on the berth-deck of a man-of-war. A hammock was slung from the ceiling, which, in the daytime, was lashed up so as to take but little room. From the centre of the chamber hung a model of a ship, of his own workmanship. Two or three chairs, a table, and a large sea-chest, formed the principal moveables. About the wall were stuck up naval ballads, such as "Admiral Hosier's Ghost," "All in the Downs," and "Tom Bowling," intermingled with pictures of sea-fights, among which the battle of Camperdown held a distinguished place. The mantlepiece was decorated with sea-shells, over which hung a quadrant, flanked by two wood-cuts of most bitter-looking naval commanders. His implements for angling were carefully disposed on nails and hooks about the room. On a shelf was arranged his library, containing a work on angling, much worn, a Bible covered with canvas, an odd volume or two of voyages, a nautical almanack, and a book of songs.

His family consisted of a large black cat with one eye, and a parrot which he had caught and tamed, and educated himself, in the course of one of his voyages; and which uttered a variety of sea phrases with the hoarse brattling tone of a veteran boatswain. The establishment reminded me of that of the renowned Robinson Crusoe; it was kept in neat order, everything being "stowed away" with the regularity of a ship of war; and he informed me that he "scoured the deck every morning, and swept it between meals."

I found him seated on a bench before the door, smoking his pipe in the soft evening sunshine. His cat was purring soberly on the threshold, and his parrot describing some strange evolutions in an iron ring that swung in the centre of his cage. He had been angling all day, and gave me a history of his sport with as much minuteness as a general would talk over a campaign; being particularly animated in relating the manner in which he had taken a large trout, which had completely tasked all his skill and wariness, and which he had sent as a trophy to mine hostess of the inn.

How comforting it is to see a cheerful and contented old age; and to behold a poor fellow, like this, after being tempest-tost through life, safely moored in a snug and quiet harbour in the evening of his days! His happiness, however, sprung from within himself, and was independent of external circumstances; for he had that inexhaustible good nature, which is the most precious gift of Heaven; spreading itself like oil over the troubled sea of thought, and keeping the mind smooth and equable in the roughest weather.

On inquiring further about him, I learnt that he was a universal favourite in the village, and the oracle of the tap-room; where he delighted the rustics with his songs, and, like Sinbad, astonished them with his stories of strange lands, and shipwrecks, and sea-fights. He was much noticed, too, by gentlemen sportsmen of the neighborhood; had taught several of them the art of angling; and was a privileged visitor to their kitchens. The whole tenor of his life was quiet and inoffensive, being principally passed about the neighbouring streams, when the weather and season were favourable; and at other times he employed himself at home, preparing his fishing tackle for the next campaign, or manufacturing rods, nets, and flies, for his patrons and pupils among the gentry.

He was a regular attendant at church on Sundays, though he generally fell asleep during the sermon. He had made it his particular request that when he died he should be buried in a green spot, which he could see from his seat in church, and which he had marked out ever since he was a boy, and had thought of when far from home on the raging sea, in danger of being food for the fishes—it was the spot where his father and mother had been buried.

I have done, for I fear that my reader is growing weary; but I could not refrain from drawing the picture of this worthy "brother of the angle"; who has made me more than ever in love with the theory, though I fear I shall never be adroit in the practice, of his art; and I will conclude this rambling sketch in the words of honest Izaak Walton, by craving the blessing of St. Peter's master upon my reader, "and upon all that are true lovers of virtue; and dare trust in his providence: and be quiet; and go a angling."

DAME JULIANA BERNERS
and
THEODORE GORDON

John McDonald

DAME JULIANA BERNERS

was an English hunting writer and compiler of the fifteenth century, by legend a nun and noblewoman, to whom the first known essay on sport fishing, *The Treatise of Fishing with an Angle,* has long been attributed.

That Dame Juliana was a real person there is no doubt; her name is attached to the didactic poem on hunting in the *Book of St. Albans* (1486), the first and most famous sporting book printed in English. But the legend that she was of noble rank and Lady Prioress of Sopwell, a nunnery near St. Albans in the Abbey of that name, is without any direct evidence; it has been furiously disputed among antiquarians for centuries. Her connection with fishing is even more nebulous; but *The Treatise of Fishing with an Angle* has wanted an author, and as her name has been the only convenient one, it was adopted for the treatise by fishing writers and librarians, and has outlasted the protest of historians. Her legend is intriguing and in part will perhaps remain forever a mystery.

The thread of connection between Dame Juliana and the *Treatise of Fishing* is the fact that the fishing treatise was first printed in the second *Book of St. Albans* in 1496. The first *Book of St. Albans*—its title conferred, by tradition, from the town where the book was printed—contains treatises on hunting, hawking, and heraldry. When Wynken de Worde reprinted the book ten years later in London, he added the fishing treatise, anonymously, to the collection. The only author's name that appears in either edition is Dame Juliana's, at the end of the book of hunting (the first edition calls her "Dam Julyans Barnes"; the second, "dame Julyans Bernes). Nothing in the styles of the hunting and fishing treatises suggests that they came from the same author; but the whole *Book of St. Albans* in time was attributed to the "author" of the hunting treatise. Her unquestioned authorship of the hunting treatise needs this qualification, that the work, like many in the Middle Ages, was compiled and versified in large part out of earlier hunting treatises.

No earlier evidence of Dame Juliana's existence is known. During the several centuries after her name appeared in print, her legend was created by a number of noted English antiquaries. A gap was made in the records of English history in the first half of the sixteenth century when Henry VIII abolished the monasteries without making provision to save their libraries. Antiquaries attempted to close the gap and restore old glories with a combination of research and imagination. One of these, John Bale, in 1559 described Dame Juliana, without evidence, as an illustrious female who regarded the sports of the field as a source of virtue, honor, and nobility. He stated that she flourished in 1460, and "is said to have edited a small work on Fishing." Raphael Holinshed in his *Chronicles* (1577) said she was "a gentlewoman endowed with excellent gifts both of body and mind." John Pits (1611) described her as a manlike woman of noble rank, "a Minerva in her studies and a Diana in hunting." But the most important statement in the history of the legend was made by William Burton (1575–1645), antiquary and brother of Robert Burton. In his copy of the *Book of St. Albans*, he wrote in longhand that the book was made by Lady Julian Berners of a noted Berners family, giving some details, and said that she was Lady Prioress of Sopwell and that the book was printed in the Abbey of St. Albans. Similar observations were made by a county historian, Sir Henry Chauncy, in his book on Hertfordshire in 1700. All subsequent writing on Dame Juliana derived from these sources.

Controversy raged among antiquaries during the eighteenth and nineteenth centuries as to whether it was possible to conceive of a woman who was both nun and sportswoman. In his great facsimile edition of the second *Book of St. Albans,* in 1810, Joseph Haslewood undertook to resolve the difficulty by supposing that she might have been first one and then the other; at court in her youth engaging in field sports and keeping a commonplace book; afterward retired to a convent, perhaps "from disappointment," there passing the time versifying the rules of sport. Trying thus only to reconcile reasonably the roles of nun and sportswoman, Haslewood put the seal on the legend.

Along with other antiquaries of the eighteenth and nineteenth centuries, Haslewood explicitly denied the possibility that Dame Juliana could have written the *Treatise of Fishing,* but their view could not prevail. The legend of the noble nun, which they and not fishermen had created, was brought into the fishing world for the first time in 1760 by John Hawkins in his introduction to the eighth edition of *The Compleat Angler.* Hawkins appears to have relied on Bale and Pits for his belief in her association with the fishing treatise, and, for the rest, he picked up the assertions of Burton as they had been restated by later antiquaries. Despite the strong efforts of the antiquaries to scotch the attribution Dame Juliana Berners, nun and noblewoman, was established as the first fishing writer and so became famous for the wrong reasons. Her hunting treatise is seldom read and had no great influence on hunting; it was in fact a treatise on the language of hunting rather than on the sport itself. The fame of *Treatise of Fishing* shone on her name.

The appearance of the *Treatise of Fishing* is a remarkable event in the history of fishing. It was written in the early fifteenth century and appears to be original. Before the treatise there is little sign of fishing as a sport. Its codification of the sport dominated the angling world for two centuries, the fifteenth and sixteenth; it was a major influence on Walton and other early fishing writers. As the sole progenitor of the literature of the sport, it thereafter formed the main line of angling tradition. It remains one of the best essays ever written on the sport. The only surviving manuscript version, copied by a scribe around 1450, is in the Yale library, thanks to the late American angling collector, David Wagstaff.

*

THEODORE GORDON (1854–1915)

was a fishing writer, professional fly-tier, "father" of the American dry fly, and creator of the Quill Gordon and other well-known artificial trout flies.

Theodore Gordon, earliest modern American fishing writer and fly-tier, is a pivotal figure in American angling. He introduced the dry fly in the United States in the 1890's, not long after it was developed in England, and although he made this connection with English tradition, he is distinguished also for breaking the nineteenth century American reliance on English fly patterns. Before Gordon, original American flies were usually fancy. Imitation flies were usually copies of English flies. Gordon developed artificial flies imitative of American water insects and gave them an impressionistic style. "I want to see the fly *on the water*," he wrote, "as well as to have specimens." Gordon was conscious of the historic job to be done in his time but was not doctrinal. The theme of his work is in his statement, "The great charm of fly-fishing is that we are always learning."

That part of Gordon's life which is known to us was a fly-fishing idyll. A consuming passion for the sport and poor health sent him to the life of a near-recluse on the Neversink River in the Catskill Mountains of New York not long after the turn of the century. His keen mind and sure fingers—he tied flies by hand—became wholly absorbed and specialized in fly-fishing. "Anglers should keep a diary," he said, and fortunately he left a record in his "Jottings" and "Little Talks" in *Forest and Stream* (predecessor of *Field & Stream*), beginning in 1903, and in the English journal, *Fishing Gazette,* where his earliest note, in 1891, presents succinctly the state of American fishing and its reliance on the English. He also wrote many letters, especially in his later retirement days. Most of them appear to have been lost, but a cache of them was kept by the incomparable

English angling writer, G. E. M. Skues, and smaller bundles by his protégé, Roy Steenrod of Liberty, New York, and Guy Jenkins of New York City. But for these writings and his fly patterns we should know little about Gordon and his work, for almost all else comes from fading memories and legend.

The first substantial record of Gordon curiously marks a turning point in the history of American fly-fishing. It is a letter to him from Frederic M. Halford, the writer in whom the dry-fly revolution centered in England, dated February 22, 1890, just four years after Halford published his *The Theory and Practice of Dry-Fly Fishing*. Halford clipped into a letter a set of his dry flies (preserved by Steenrod and now at the Anglers' Club of New York) and closed with the request, "kindly let me know the result of your experiments." The result was a new era in American fly-fishing.

Gordon makes it evident in this writing that he had read with intense preoccupation most of the American fishing writers of the nineteenth century, as well as the English, and was able to take so much book learning without harm. From books he tells us he learned to tie flies and to fish upstream. But from the stream itself came his decisive learning. He was one of the most brilliant observers of stream life in recorded fishing history, and in his writing he was a teacher who was master of the fishing anecdote. A photograph shows him small, slender, and elegant, fishing beside the girl of whom he wrote: "The best chum I ever had in fishing was a girl, and she tramped just as hard and fished quite as patiently as any man I ever knew." She is another mystery in his life, for he died a bachelor, on May 1, 1915, within the sound of his favorite stream. His monument is the Quill Gordon fly.

THE SELECTIVITY OF TROUT

Art Flick

IN MOST CASES when fish are feeding on a certain species of May fly, or during the period of what we call a "hatch," they are more selective than at other times.

It is then that it will be to the fly fisherman's advantage to know what fly is on the water, as well as its proper representation. With no more study than it takes to learn to differentiate between the various artificials that most fishermen recognize, the important species of May flies can be identified.

Obviously, when you see fish rising to a certain fly, and know exactly what it is, as well as the correct imitation, you will take more and larger trout.

Some writers maintain that fish are less selective when there is a hatch of flies on the water, and that often in such cases they will take almost any fly of a size that corresponds to the natural.

This may be true on certain streams where the fly life is somewhat scarce and the hatches small. Because of this comparative scarcity, the fish will gather in as much food as possible, knowing that there will not be a great deal of it. But in streams where there is an abundance of insect life and the hatches are large, it is a different story. The trout are much more selective and look their food over pretty carefully before taking it.

Most fishermen do not know which of these two conditions they are going to run into, and in fishing it is wise to be prepared for any eventuality.

The fact that you happen to be on a stream where trout are not selective is certainly not a good argument against knowing the natural flies, as well as their imitations. If a trout happens to be rising to anything that looks like food, it will certainly take a good imitation of the natural fly just as quickly as any other fly.

It should be remembered that the way small trout rise to artificials is no criterion, and dry flies should not be judged by their ability to catch the little fellows that do not know what it is all about.

A fly may take seven- to nine-inch trout, but be well-nigh worthless as far as fooling those that are over a foot in length. I believe it is safe to say that from the standpoint of fun and satisfaction, trout from twelve inches up are the size that most of us want to catch.

Fishing pressure on most streams today is so great that a trout must have learned a great deal if it is to grow to fourteen inches. If he is dumb he does not grow to any size, and therefore larger trout are much more selective.

Smaller trout have not reached this degree of selectivity, especially in the streams where legal-sized fish are stocked. Most fish caught today are from seven to ten inches long and have not been away from the hatchery long enough to know what is going on. They will generally rise to anything that comes over them if it looks like food, and I have yet to find a real trout fisherman who got any satisfaction from catching them.

Please do not get the idea that by learning the May flies it will be possible to cope with every condition you will meet in fishing, or that you will be able to catch large trout every time you are on a stream when fish are feeding on duns that are emerging. If you do, you will be disappointed.

Even after a knowledge of May flies is attained, things will often work out other than expected.

I vividly recall an experience I had some years ago on one of my favorite pools. Above the pool is a nice riffle that is just right for *Ephemerella subvaria* (Henrickson or Red Quill). It was just a bit early in the afternoon for these flies to emerge, so my companion and I started fishing with an imitation of the Hendrickson nymph.

We fished them for about a half hour before any naturals started coming, and when the hatch really got under way, trout were taking the duns regularly at the head of the pool.

We changed from nymph to Hendrickson dry flies, and for about an hour we had some excellent fishing. We did not keep track of the number we had caught, and we released all but five, but I should guess that between us we had caught between thirty-five and forty legal fish.

Each of us had hooked and lost a large trout, the size that does not always feed on the surface, but inasmuch as the Hendrickson hatch had just started, we knew that we could depend on them to come regularly for a few days. Of course, we planned to try for the two big fish again on the following day.

We were in the pool at about the same time the next day, but did no fishing, as we were interested in two specific fish and did not want to disturb the pool. There was a slight drizzle, and we felt that this was a good break for us because conditions would be even better than the previous day. Because the flies' wings would take longer to dry, we expected them to remain on the water longer, a condition that always produces better fly fishing.

When the hatch came the stream was covered with flies and fish were feeding all over the pool. It seemed that there were even more fish feeding than on the day before. It was not long before two that we assumed to be those we had hooked on the previous day started to work. They were in the same position and fed like large fish, so we felt quite confident that they were our friends.

After checking a couple of naturals we found that they were the females that were hatching, and put on Hendricksons. Because the natural was identical with those that we had found the day before, there was little doubt in our minds about raising the two large fish. There were so many flies on the stream that it was impossible to distinctly see fish take them, but from the way they were feeding, we were certain they were.

We both cast over our fish, and although they kept right on working, we could not raise either of them. I was sure that the identification had been correct, but try as we might, there was no luck. Because we had not put either of them down, we felt sure that it was a case of faulty presentation, and our two friends kept working at regular intervals.

After about five minutes I decided that something was definitely wrong, and I moved farther up in the pool, where there were numerous smaller fish working. I cast over four different fish but had no better success, and was starting to think that I had made some mistake in technique, but could not dope out what it was.

In the meantime, my companion, as puzzled as I, had changed over to a Red Quill, the artificial of the male Hendrickson; but he still could not raise his fish.

Finally in desperation I took off the dry fly and put on a Hendrickson nymph —why, I do not know. I cast across the stream and let the nymph float down naturally. Just as it made the swing and started to come to the surface, a fish hit it as though his life depended on catching it. The manner of taking was identical to the way a fish rises for a dry fly, as there was a distinct "break," but not made by the trout's tail.

I called to my companion and told him what had happened, and continued to work downstream in the direction of my big fish. In five casts I caught three more fish, and was perfectly satisfied that we had found the answer. While I was releasing the last fish I heard a shout from farther down the pool and saw my partner having the time of his life with a heavy fish. Naturally, I went down to watch the fun, and after quite a few minutes he put his net under his beauty. It was a nineteen-inch brown that had apparently been living off the "fat of the land."

The commotion put my fish down, but we were both satisfied, and tomorrow would be another day.

Why all the fish in that pool were passing up the duns they had taken so readily the previous day and were feeding instead on nymphs is a mystery to me. I had never seen this happen before, nor have I since, with this particular species of May fly. It is one of those mysteries of trout fishing, and I doubt that anyone can furnish a logical reason for it.

Incidentally, when the big fish was dressed we found that although his stomach was actually crammed with food, he had only three winged flies in it, the rest being nymphs of the Hendrickson fly. The flies that he had picked up were probably some that had drowned, and were floating just under the surface of the stream.

Another of the things that I am unable to find the answer to is the way trout sometimes act with *Iron fraudator* (Quill Gordon). It is the first important May fly to appear on almost all streams, and coming as it does early in the season, it has special appeal to the dry-fly fisherman. At this time of the year fish are starting to look for great quantities of food, and with higher water temperatures their appetites are large.

The normal emergence time of this fly is about one-thirty P.M., Eastern Standard Time, the hatch usually starting at about that time. Occasionally there will be a small hatch in the morning, between ten and eleven, depending on how cold the water is, but seldom have I seen fish feed on them.

Very often I have been on a pool in the morning when there was a fair-sized hatch, and yet there was not a fish feeding as nearly as I could determine. Still, in the very same pool in the afternoon the trout would take every fly that came over them, and they were identical with the flies that had been on the water in the morning. Strangely enough, they will not take a wet-fly imitation in the morning either, so that is not the answer.

All of us have sat in on discussions and friendly arguments pertaining to the way fish, trout in particular, look at things. When this answer is found, we will probably know why they are so selective on certain occasions and comparatively careless on others. This subject is probably one of the most controversial in trout fishing.

So far, I have not seen sufficient proof to satisfy me that anyone has even come close to the solution. There are many theories on the subject, but that is all they are, and I have yet to see one that could not be blown full of holes.

For example, many of us have placed flies in a small aquarium and looked up at them through the glass and water, in varying degrees of light, checking angles and so forth.

What does this amount to, after all? The way a fly floating thus appears to the human eye is one thing, but how can it be said positively that such is the way the same object will appear to a trout?

A large group of fishermen contend that trout cannot differentiate between one color and another. Because I cannot definitely prove they are wrong, I will not argue with them about it. However, if such is the case, I find it hard to explain why a trout will take one fly after having refused another that was dressed in exactly the same manner, with the exception of the body. For example, the size of the Hendrickson and Red Quill are the same, as are the hackles and wings. Why will fish refuse one and take the other? I do not know, do you? I doubt that there is a fisherman in the country who has not at some time or other had the same experience in selectivity.

Because I am on some trout stream nearly every day of the open season, I have a lot more time to experiment than do most people. I fool away so much time in this manner that I am only half as good a fisherman as I should be, for the amount of time I am at it. Nevertheless, I do not consider time spent in this way as wasted. We all fish because we get enjoyment out of it, and I get as much fun out of trying to solve some hitherto unexplained problem as I do in catching fish.

Although I have been studying it for quite a few years, I actually know nothing more about how a trout's vision compares to ours than I did when I started.

There is not a standard pattern of dry fly that I have not tried to improve upon, trying slightly different dressings. Except for minor changes, I have not been very successful. For example, in the tying of the Quill Gordon, I have found the fly more effective when tied with the quill from the eye of a peacock feather than when made with any other material. This in spite of the fact that the other dressing of the fly was exactly the same.

Whether or not this difference in effectiveness was due to the darker stripe in the peacock quill, giving the body of the fly the light and dark stripe, I do not profess to know. However, I am perfectly satisfied that the fly with this body, over a period of time, will produce larger and better fish.

If a trout's vision is even slightly comparable to ours, why is it that this same fly, the Quill Gordon, does not closely resemble to us the natural that it imitates? Fish will take it consistently when the natural is on the water, but I doubt if any person who did not know anything about the subject would ever think one a copy of the other, seeing them together.

This is true of most dry flies and nymphs, and to us they do not look anything like the naturals they represent, but they are apparently so suggestive to the fish that they are effective.

Having nothing definite to go by on this subject of vision and selectivity, I will continue to flounder along according to the experiences of others, and my own, until such time as a talking trout will be discovered that can give me the right dope. Possibly someday a mere mortal may discover the answer, but I hope that day never comes. Think of all the swell arguments we would miss!

Another matter that comes under this same heading is the proper color of leaders, from the standpoint of their visibility to trout.

One fisherman will swear that the most effective color is mist, and the next will argue that dark brown is the only shade to use. The result is that leaders are stained and dyed every color of the rainbow.

The fisherman who likes the darker shades says, "Look at that leader on the water, you cannot see it." Very true, we cannot, but we see it against the dark stream bottom. A fish, on the other hand, will see it from the opposite angle, looking up at it, with the sky as a background. According to that, it should be more readily seen by a trout than would one of mist color, or even natural gut.

As far as I am concerned, the color of a leader means very little. None of us, in fishing for a rising trout, would deliberately put the leader over the fish, knowing that it would become frightened. If, on the other hand, we are trying to "pound up" fish, we are putting our fly in the spots where we expect to find a trout.

It has been my experience that the only really important thing about leaders is to remove the glare, and if gut is treated to remove this objectionable feature, color is of no consequence to me. Now that nylon has replaced gut, I find that Tintex dye does a nice job on the new material. I like green, but this is a matter of personal preference. The main thing is, it seems to cut down on glare. If you make your own tippets, they can be made more limp by boiling them during the dyeing process for exactly *one minute,* no longer. This will remove the wiriness from your 3X, 4X, and 5X tippets. But care must be used not to overboil them. One minute will not harm platyl in the least.

When you are next complaining about the selectivity of trout, bear this thought in mind: Were it not for this fortunate trait, how long would our stream fishing last? It would not be many years before our waters would be completely fished out, and I doubt that any of you would welcome that condition. In most cases, fish are scarce enough now in streams open to public fishing.

THE HIDDEN HATCH

Vincent C. Marinaro

"THE SMALLEST OF THE MAYFLIES" is the way the genus Caenis is often described. "The white curse" is another name often applied to it by British flyfishermen—and with good reason.

Caenis is the most exasperating as well as the most fascinating of all the insects that trout eat and flyfishermen try to imitate. It is unique, not only in its tiny size but also in several aspects of its life cycle—aspects that are important to fishermen.

Of all the mayflies, Caenis alone completes the metamorphosis from dun to spinner while it is in the air, and often just a few minutes after hatching from the nymph stage. If you are keen-eyed and observant you can sometimes see great numbers of spinners still dragging the nymphal shuck as they fly to and fro.

Caenis' entire life and purpose as a winged insect is completed in a single forenoon: it hatches from the nymphal stage, changes from dun to spinner, mates, lays its eggs, and then falls to the water and dies, thus becoming a special attraction to the eager trout.

In both the length of its hatching season and the regularity of its emergence, Caenis is the most dependable of the mayflies. From the middle of July until well into October the tiny insects hatch every morning without fail. On any stream where Caenis is well established, the number of hatching insects is enormous.

Caenis is not easy to see, either in the air or on the water. But if your angle of view is just right on any bright morning during Caenis season, you'll see what appears to be a solid wall of glinting, shining, sun-struck wings extending for twenty feet above the river. The wall will shift and undulate and weave with the vagaries of the air currents.

In the early part of the Caenis season the hatch and the resultant rise of trout are of rather short duration, not more than two to three hours. As the season advances, the daily hatch of duns and fall of spinners becomes more and more

118

extensive until it reaches well into noontime, providing some five to six hours of steady fishing.

At the peak of the season the morning cycle of hatching nymphs, molting duns, and falling spinners becomes so heavy that by around noon the great mass of spinners becomes compressed near the surface of the water and the insects begin to fall in great numbers. The surface literally becomes carpeted from bank to bank with the dead and dying spinners. If a good stock of trout is in the river, the rise to these dying spinners is really something to see.

Before this last stage, the rise is rather orderly, but on the final massive fall of spinners the trout become frenzied in their eagerness to get as many Caenis as possible. They hang close to the surface, shifting back and forth and side to side as rapidly as they can, mouths wide open and slobbering as they gulp gobs of the dying spinners. The habits of Caenis and the reaction they cause in trout seem to be the same the world over.

I never see this astonishing performance without thinking of Frank Sawyer, the famous British riverkeeper who made a special study of Caenis on the river Avon and described his trout as just staying on the surface gobbling like a duck. I cannot think of a better expression.

How many Caenis do you think one trout can get in half a day's feeding? Frank Honish, who for years has studied the Caenis fishing on his beloved Little Lehigh River at Allentown, Pennsylvania, assures me that a steadily feeding trout can get 2,000 to 3,000 insects in a single morning.

Autopsies on trout gorged with Caenis reveal bulging stomachs and masses of insects lining throat, mouth, and gills. Similar observations are recorded by the British fishing writers, who have contended with "the white curse" for many generations. In America there has been no widespread interest in Caenis until recent years.

It is really an obscure insect, one of the kind that Charlie Fox, writer and conservationist of Carlisle, Pennsylvania, likes to call a "hidden hatch." Caenis is likely to be ignored, especially where hatches of bigger, showier mayflies are prevalent. The larger hatches are easier to imitate and to fish.

Justin and Fannie Leonard included Caenis as one of the important food items for trout in their fine book, *May-flies of Michigan Trout Streams,* published in 1962. It is certainly an important insect on many of our Pennsylvania streams. John Alevras of Bloomfield, New Jersey, tells me that it is also abundant on New York trout streams.

As you've probably guessed by now, fishing a Caenis hatch presents some very unusual problems. The tiny size of the insect is one of them. Tying these minute imitations in sizes 22, 24, and 28 is likely to be a source of despair to many amateur tyers. To me it is old hat because of my long familiarity with the tiny terrestrials. You'll surmount this problem if you feel as I do that there is no finer fishing in the world than dry-fly fishing with tiny artificials and fine gut.

The next serious problem arises from the sheer abundance of insects on the water. Your artificial is competing with so many of the naturals that getting the attention of the trout seems hopeless. You have only to observe how numerous are the naturals that get by him while he is taking just one to realize how serious this problem is.

I have a few rules that I observe religiously to beat these odds, and I offer them with the hope that they will help you too.

First, be on time for the beginning of the morning rise. On the waters that I fish the rise starts between 7 and 8 A.M., daylight saving time. The comparatively sparse display of insects gives you a chance to get a trout's attention. Do not waste your time on small trout. Pick out a good one, and start working on him immediately.

Second, remain until the very end of the hatch, when all the spinners have been washed away. Often you will find a good trout that is still looking for "just one more."

Third, check minor lines of drift where insects are comparatively sparse. Good trout often occupy side channels and pockets that offer good cover, even though these spots have fewer insects.

Fourth, watch your trout's feeding rhythm. Each trout has a definite feeding pace marked by regular intervals between rises. If you make your pitch out of step with his desire to rise he will not take your fly. Remember that a trout has little energy reserve compared with warm-blooded animals. Rhythmical feeding is the only way he can profitably use his energy; taking such small insects in any other way would be a metabolic disaster to him.

The only time a trout can break this rhythm profitably is at the end of the spinner fall, when he can down a mouthful of insects at a gulp. Think of it: a trout must move his entire body every time he eats something little bigger than a pinhead, a process that often goes on for many hours. If humans had to eat that way, eating would be dreadfully exhausting.

How big a trout can you hope to take on these tiny flies? To me a twelve- to fourteen-inch trout in good condition taken on Caenis and a 7X tippet is a fine achievement. I have taken trout up to eighteen inches long on this tackle. I got three eighteen-inchers in one week during the 1967 season, and two more in 1968. They were all wild, burly, limestone trout.

I have heard of bigger trout being taken on Caenis but have never seen them. When I hear such stories I always feel a little ashamed and resolve to do better the next time. My trouble is that someone is always around when I get a good fish, and he always insists on measuring it down to the last fraction. Once in a while I am allowed a quarter-inch leeway just to round out the figures. But seriously, any time I get an eighteen-inch, heavy-bodied wild trout on 7X leader and a No. 22 or 24 hook, I am a proud fisherman, especially if I catch it in weed-choked, logjammed waters like the Letort, which flows near my home in Mechanicsburg, Pennsylvania.

Technically, one of the eighteen-inchers that I got in 1968 wasn't caught on Caenis. Dennis Nawrocki and George Green of Carlisle were fishing with me that morning on the Letort. We caught a few nice trout, and when the hatch and fall of spinners was over we started back toward our cars. On the way back I broke off my No. 24 Caenis and put it in my flybox. When I turned for a last look at the water I caught the wink of a rise near a pile of debris. I reached into the flybox and picked out the first thing at hand—a tiny floating ant—and tied it to my 7X leader point.

A long downstream float was needed to get the fly over the fish. Two throws went badly. The third was just right, with enough slack in the leader to drift the fly over the trout. As the ant reached the edge of the jam, a long brown shape rose slowly from the cover and sipped the ant in very delicately.

For the next half-hour the trout explored every weed bed in that stretch of water, and I had many apprehensive moments trying to keep my leader free of weed balls and trying to keep the trout from smashing the leader with his tail. Finally, George netted him for me. Though the trout wasn't caught on a complete Caenis ring, he *was* caught on 7X leader with a tiny hook during the Caenis hatch.

This story has an interesting sequel that points up the great strength of a well-conditioned limestone trout. I have said that trout do not have a great reserve of energy. Even so, for a short while they can exert tremendous power.

After we landed the trout I decided that I wanted to photograph him while he was still alive. First, however, I would have to go home and get my camera. So I put the fish in a cotton-mesh live-bag and put the bag in the water under a bed of watercress. George Green offered to stay and keep an eye on the fish.

While I was gone, George's wife joined him. I returned a short time later, and they met me with somber faces and a tale of woe. While they'd been sitting there they had heard a terrific commotion in the water. They had hurried over to see what it was and had seen my big trout out of the bag and making his way to freedom. I examined the bag and found a big hole in the bottom. Yet, before putting the fish inside I had examined the bag very carefully, even putting my forearm inside and hitting the mesh with my fist. The trout had literally lashed the netting to shreds with his powerful tail.

Now you may ask, why use 7X leader? Why not 6X, which has an enormous margin of strength over 7X? The more experience I have with trout, the more I am convinced that they are not leader-shy—disturbed by the leader's thickness. What disturbs them is a leader that snakes or streaks across the currents. And 7X drags as much as 4X.

I decided long ago that the size of the tippet should be determined by the size of the fly. To behave properly on the surface, size 24 dry flies need 7X tippets. On the other hand, you simply cannot manage the big grasshopper and cricket imitations on such fine leader. You need 3X, 4X, or 5X tippets for such imitations, and plenty of shy trout are caught on those sizes on the Letort and similar waters.

The tiny Caenis dun rides the water so lightly that it doesn't even dent the surface film. I can never hope to achieve that kind of performance with the imitation, but I try to get as close to it as possible. A 7X tippet presses the tiny imitation into the surface film less than does a 6X; a 6X presses less than a 5X; and so on.

What about using larger imitations—showing the trout something bigger and different to divert his attention from those ridiculous specks? I have no quarrel with fishermen who believe in this theory, but it has never worked for me. I find that trout are very narrow-minded feeders when a specific hatch is involved.

How do you handle a three-pound trout on such delicate rigging? Can it be done consistently? Certainly, except for those situations where leader of any size is of no avail. There is nothing you can do about a big determined trout that dives into a log jam, wraps the leader around an obstruction, and breaks off without further ceremony. Such incidents have happened to me many times; I hope that they will happen again!

Many years ago when I was working out the now familiar terrestrial patterns (Jassids, Ants, etc.) in small sizes (see "Jassids—New Approach to Fly Fishing," *Outdoor Life*, March, 1958), I was forced to use very fine natural silkworm gut to make these flies behave properly. In those days fine gut was diamond-drawn to as fine as 8X. Under the N.A.A.C.C. table of standards, this 8X material was rated at a breaking strength of four ounces. Imagine the problem of trying to handle a good-size fish on that kind of material. Today, nylon leader of the same diameter is rated at 7X and is four times as strong, far more uniform, and limp enough to allow a fly to float more freely and without drag.

Ordinary methods of handling fish did not work with fine silkworm gut. I was smashed time after time until I discovered what I was doing wrong. The trouble lay in the fact that an upright rod creates a lot of friction on a free-running line, and this friction uses up too much of the margin of safety of fine gut.

Strangely, only a few anglers in the history of flyfishing seem to have discovered this fact and used it to advantage. One of the most famous of these—and perhaps the most successful salmon fishermen of all time—was A. H. E. Wood of Scotland, inventor of greased-line and low-water fishing for salmon. Wood invariably put his rop tip about one foot above the surface of the water and kept it there during a fight with a salmon. He caught thousands of salmon, many on 1X silkworm gut (N.A.A.C.C. test: 1½ pounds), using the low rod and no more pressure than that of the currents and the reel check. When queried about his low-rod technique Wood said: "After all, there is little sense in continually pulling upwards as though you were trying to lift the fish out of the river; and it only makes him more determined to get his head down and fight hard."

I feel the same way. I like to keep a big fish as calm and quiet as possible and lick him by nagging him to death a little at a time. On a low rod and loose line he becomes confused, and you can gently tow him out of danger by tugging lightly on the line with your thumb and forefinger.

Stiffness or softness of a rod has little bearing on the matter of fighting a trout on a delicate leader. If anything, the soft rod creates more friction and drag on the line than a stiff one does, because under full bend the soft rod assumes a more nearly complete circle, with the line bearing hard on every guide. The stiff rod bends only a little, usually near the top, creating severe line friction on only one or two guides.

Lowering the rod when you are using an ultrafine tippet gives you a chance to adjust the drag with mathematical precision because you are playing your fish directly from the reel, which usually has tension adjustments. On the reel itself you need no more than one ounce of drag to prevent the line from overrunning. And remember that this drag may build up to two and a half or three ounces as the line runs out and comes closer to the core of the reel. Always adjust your reel with a full drum, not an empty one.

Another real danger to your fine tippet occurs when a strong fish makes a long run downriver and then suddenly turns and heads back up. This maneuver throws a wide loop in the line against which the current pushes with tremendous force. The lowered rod reduces this hazard a great deal, since the line will peel more freely from the reel.

One of the worst dangers is the jumping fish. Any hooked gamefish soon discovers what is bothering him, and he'll often make a jump and try to fall on the leader or smash it with his tail. Here, again, the lowered rod allows the line to yield directly from the reel.

It is virtually impossible for a fish to throw a hook on a slack line. Hooks sometimes get a light hold on a mere thread of tissue and then tear out when the fisherman doesn't yield with the rod. I have landed many good fish that were barely hooked.

The most spectacular performance I ever saw involving a trout hooked on Caenis tackle happened in July 1968. Dennis Nawrocki, George Green, John Faller, and I had gone to a small limestone stream near Carlisle, Pennsylvania, for a morning of Caenis fishing. We began fishing near the upstream end of a very long meadow. Dennis was fishing a short distance below me, and suddenly I heard him give a whoop. I turned and was astonished to see a powerful trout plowing a furrow downstream and Dennis with rod pointing downstream running madly over the rough terrain after the fish. Then both of them disappeared around a bend in the stream.

I took out after them as fast as my rickety joints would allow, all the while shouting a warning to Dennis about the dangers below the bend. Dennis was not familiar with this water. Below that bend was a sunken footbridge that caught and held debris that was washed downstream. If the trout got to the footbridge, all would be lost.

The trout stopped a few yards short of the bridge, and John Faller and I got out on it and flogged the water with our nets, trying to keep the fish upstream. The flogging succeeded for a while, but then the fish turned and blasted his way through the debris under our feet. I turned and was relieved to see Dennis's white line deep in the water and running downstream.

We pondered the situation for a few moments. Then, when the fish had stopped, I suggested to Dennis that he separate his line from the reel while I fished the line out of the water below the bridge with a long pole.

It worked. Dennis came below the bridge and refastened his line to the reel. Shortly thereafter we were able to net the fish many yards below the bridge.

Thus ended the prettiest race I ever saw between man and trout. Dennis and that trout—a deep-girthed small-headed beautifully colored brown—must have run a quarter of a mile downstream.

So much for handling fish on Caenis tackle. Now let's look at the flies themselves.

The smallest practical imitation that I have used successfully is a No. 24. I've tried 28's, but I had such poor results in hooking and holding fish that I no longer use them.

I also had very poor results with the 24's until I began doctoring the hooks a little. The only 24's that I've been able to get have turned-down eyes, which close the bite of the hooks considerably. With a tiny jeweler's pliers I take hold of the neck of the hook just behind the eye and bend the eye upward a trifle, thus opening the bite. Next, with the hook in the vise, I push the shank laterally to either side to get the point out of alignment with the shank, thus opening the bite some more. I break a few hooks this way, but the results are really worthwhile. Finally, I sharpen the hook point by honing it gently with a hard Arkansas engraver's pencil.

Now we are ready to construct our imitation. The Leonards have reported six species of Caenis. The British claim four, but for 100 years they have treated all four species as one. For practical purposes we can do the same.

The Caenis mayfly exists in four variations: male and female dun, and male and female spinner. By far the most important imitation is that of the female spinner, which falls to the water in vast numbers. The male spinner usually falls on land and is comparatively unimportant.

The female spinner has clear glassy wings; rear segments of the body are a translucent grayish white; the thorax is black and humped. The freshly emerged duns riding the currents are well taken by the trout, but here we can treat both sexes as one since they are so similar in appearance, their outstanding feature being the smoky-blue wings. My favorite pattern for the dun is a simple and ancient fly, the Blue Upright:

Hook: No. 22 or 24.
Tails: three very short blue-dun fibers, slanting downward to raise the hook as much as possible.
Body: stripped bicolor peacock quill.
Hackle: one or two tiny blue-dun hackles no more than ⅛ inch long in the fiber to make a total hackle spread of ¼ inch. Three or four turns are sufficient.

Natural blue-dun hackle is preferable, of course. I am still eking out a few flies from an ancient blue-dun neck. How I wish I had another one that was just like it.

As an alternate pattern, if you have only large blue-dun hackles, you can bunch some fibers together and make blue wings in the same way that lemon wood-duck fibers are used. One or two turns of a tiny badger or cream hackle can be added to float the fly.

The following is one of Frederic Halford's fine patterns. It imitates very well the white curse, which is really the female spinner of the species:

Hook: No. 22 or 24.
Hackle: a tiny badger hackle, over three turns of black ostrich herl worked at the shoulder.
Body: black tying silk with flat silver tag.

No tails are mentioned by Halford, but I would add three short blue-dun fibers, as for the previous pattern.

The following pattern is a great favorite with many local fishermen, primarily to imitate the female spinner:

Hook: No. 22 or 24.
Tails: three fibers of palest blue dun.
Body: grayish white fur, sparsely applied.
Thorax: a few turns of bronze peacock herl.
Hackle: badger or palest cream or blue dun.

Here is one of G. E. M. Skues's favorite patterns:

Hook: No. 22 or 24.
Wings: palest starling.
Body: white silk.
Hackle: a tiny white cock's hackle.

My favorite pattern for the female spinner is as follows:

Hook: No. 24.
Tails: three fibers of palest blue dun or palest cream hackle.
Body: two layers of clear white horsehair; start at the center of the shank, wind to the bend, then back to center again.
Thorax: black fur or black Angus wool (wonderful stuff that I collected from a barbed-wire fence).
Hackle: two or three turns of a tiny blue dun or palest cream hackle.

On all spinner patterns, keep the hackle thin. If the hackle turns out so thick that it obscures the body, cut away some fibers at top and bottom.

No matter what pattern you use, do not lose confidence in it if it is not immediately taken. Caenis fishing requires a lot of precision casting, and even then your fly is just one item among the many naturals that will be floating by the trout. So don't give up. The important thing is to get the trout to see your fly.

Finally, a few words about the strike—a fearful word in the language of the flyfisherman if he knows all that it implies. A. H. E. Wood used a very unusual and successful method of setting the hook. He put the rod low and to the side of the fish and let the current pull the hook into the corner of the trout's mouth—and he took a lot of time to do it. The corner hold is the best of all, but we do not have enough current in our meadow streams to use the Wood method.

The best method I know of is to move the rod low and to the rear of the trout until the line is taut. That's all. The little hook will be drawn back to the corner of the fish's mouth, where it will imbed itself firmly in the tough tissue in that area. The important point is to be deliberate. Your trout won't really come into contact with that little hook until he drops back and squeezes the water out of his mouth through his gills.

Caenis fishing is not a story of behemoth trout and two-handed adventure. It is an extremely sophisticated sport involving delicate tackle and the precise handling thereof. It can be very frustrating, but to me it will be forever the most fascinating kind of fishing.

THE CARP

Leslie P. Thompson

MY INTRODUCTION TO CARP FISHING happened as follows: One afternoon in early May some thirty-odd years ago while driving through the country not far from my home I came upon a small pond by the roadside. Stepping from the car I surveyed the surrounding landscape. On my left a hundred yards away ran the Charles River; close to the road on my right was a pretty little pond scarcely an acre in extent; a pleasant prospect and for the moment peaceful and quiet.

Suddenly my attention was directed to the far shore of the pond, where from nowhere appeared the figure of a boy stripping off his clothes in feverish haste. In he went and shot through the water hand over hand. This was no silly practice of gymnastics learned in a swimming-tank; each stroke showed the grim force of necessity, for before him, with the speed of an eight-oar racing shell, moved a long bamboo pole. The mysterious creature pulling on the line was somewhat handicapped in planning an escape, for the outlet to the river under the road was well screened and the neat little artificial lake offered not sanctuary of weed or rush along its shores, and the long pole with an occasional bob and dip, sped hither and thither thus giving the young swimmer a distinct advantage in the chase. Biding his time and seizing a favorable opportunity, the boy grasped the bamboo butt and with pole over shoulder waded ashore and, floundering on the grass, was a six-pound carp!

I'll confess to a rather rapid readjustment of aesthetic values before I began to appreciate the beauty of the fish which lay at my feet. The New Englander finds the height of piscine beauty in the salmon and the trout. Here was something quite different—something outlandishly picturesque in character, and immediately there came to mind handsome paintings and exquisite carvings by Chinese masters; then came a vision of a procession winding through an ancient city street in far Cathay, and above a multi-colored throng, glorious paper monsters waved in the breeze. A new world of vast horizons opened before me, and on the way home I dreamed of great golden fish bending the bamboo, and I thought—who knows!—perhaps some day one of these exotic beauties may find its way into my landing net.

That evening from a shelf in my study I selected the few books in which carp and carp fishing were mentioned. My findings were meagre enough, but I studied that little with great interest. Early American writers had little to say on the subject, and that was easily understood, for the species in question—the common European carp (*Cyprinus carpio*) was not brought to this country until a few years before the middle of the nineteenth century.* In the *American Angler's Guide*—published in 1845—John J. Brown wrote about the carp as follows: "This beautiful fish is not a native of our country; but as they have been imported from England by a number of persons in many parts of the United States, for the purpose of stocking their ponds, and protection having been given them by the laws of the State of New York, they will undoubtedly become an object of the Angler's pleasure." . . . Prophetic Mr. Brown! In 1860 Frank Forester saw no such bright prospect, and had little to say in praise of the "scaley foreigner," which escaping from private fish ponds had found its way into the Hudson River. Thaddeus Norris in 1865 described various members of the carp family found in the United States but made no mention of fishing for European carp in this country. In 1875 Genio Scott referred to the carp in a most interesting description of pisciculture among the Chinese, and European monks of the Middle Ages, and pictured a European carp in a plate showing fish of the family *Cyprinidae,* but no mention was made of the introduction of *Cyprinus carpio* in this country.

In America it is only quite recently that the carp has been thought worthy of

* Very likely soon after 1830, from time to time, there were small importations of the common European carp, most of the shipments coming from Germany. In the 1870s this fish was planted in fairly large numbers in the city parks of Washington, D.C., and Baltimore, Maryland. Through the years they have spread from the Atlantic to the Pacific and are now found in nearly every state in the Union.

capture by rod and line, but in the old country, for over four hundred years, angling for carp has been considered a fine art. Izaak Walton wrote with great enthusiasm about the "Queen of Rivers," how to lure this "very subtle fish" with various baits, and "how to make this Carp, that is so curious to be caught, so curious a dish of meat, as shall make him worth all your labor and patience." As I continued to take books from the shelf and read of carp fishing in recent years, I was held spellbound by the account given of the landing of a carp—the climax of Hugh Sheringham's masterpiece, *At Dawn of Day*. Irresistibly swept on by the combined influence of Walton and Sheringham, I became within the minute a "carp addict" *—a lost soul! That night, the last book to engage my attention was *Coarse Fish Angling* which I found to be a goldmine of information, for the Trent Otter (J. W. Martin) gave explicit directions concerning baits and tackle. Before proceeding with his instructions, the author remarks, "Carp fishing and carp catching are two distinct things and must not be confounded. Big ones are wide awake to the angler's proceedings, and after we have exhausted our resources and got to the end of our patience, that big carp is still snug on the bottom of the lake." (I'm inclined to believe the *river* carp is equally if not more difficult of capture.)

On the shore of the little pond near the Charles, on the evening following my midnight reading orgy, I joined a group of fishermen—workers in the silk-mill above the falls. I studied their methods and listened to wondrous tales of mighty battles and broken tackle. Now and again great fish would swirl on the water's smooth surface, and once a giant went high in the air, falling with a resounding splash that rocked the placid pool from end to end.

No fish were taken that evening, nor the next, nor the next, but within the week, on paste made of dough and honey, I brought to a net a small three-pounder.

In the years following this event, I visited the pool from time to time, but my float remained motionless, and no fishermen were seen on the shore. The waters of the pond overflowed through a culvert under the road, then opened into a little brook that ran to the river. I was told of an exceptionally heavy flood which, breaking the barrier, had allowed the escape of every fish in the pond.

Without doubt, above and below on the Charles River, similar escapes have occurred, especially during a period soon after the Civil War when French-roofed houses, iron stags, summer houses, fountains and ornamental fish ponds were the fashion. Only the other day, while seated by the side of an ancient angler, I was told of a private fish pond of considerable size in Medfield which contained a

---

* "Carp addict" appears in *Confessions of a Carp Fisher*, a most interesting and charming little volume published by Eyre & Spottiswoode, London, 1950. Both the text by "BB" and the illustrations by Denys Watkins-Pitchford fit the subject to perfection and do it full justice.

No enthusiastic carp fisher should fail to read Arthur Ransom's account of an adventure on a little duck-pond in England, p. 159, *Rod and Line*, published in 1929 by Jonathan Cape, London. *Rod and Line* by Arthur Ransom is always within easy reach on my book-shelf, and how many happy hours it has given me!

large number of carp, but for one reason or another, several years ago the fish were liberated and allowed to drop down a brook and into the river.

Thus, I believe, the Charles was stocked with carp, and to-day they are found in many places all the way from a few miles from the source to the big dam at the lower end of the Cambridge Basin in the City of Boston. Muddy River flowing through the Fenway holds many a fine fish. Possibly our fish commissioners at one time planted carp in the river along with trout and Mississippi cat-fish, but of that I have no record.

After learning that fish had escaped from my little pond by the roadside, for *fifteen* years I searched the waters of the river looking for signs of carp, and I fished for them in several places where on the shore I found evidence of the carp-fisher's activities—trampled banks, forked sticks and potato peelings. Once at dawn, above the pumping station at Dedham, I was joined by a native of Poland—a fine intelligent fisherman with every detail of his gear in perfect order. His tackle was identical with mine; he had learned the art from his grandfather in the old country, my little knowledge had been gained from books. We took no fish that morning, but my friend told of good catches in recent years and whispered in my ear deep secrets of the craft including the use of various baits, among them the priceless whole kernels of stewed corn found in cans, which bait thenceforth became my favorite. Once in late May, at the same swim, I had two good runs but failed to set the hook, and finally after many unsuccessful expeditions my efforts were rewarded.

This from my diary—7th September 1935. The Charles River at Dedham, Mass.—*Weather,* fair, warm, calm, light S.W. wind—*Water,* fairly low and a bit clouded with algae. *Fish,* One Carp—length twenty-seven and a half inches, weight eleven and a half pounds. *Bait,* corn "Niblets." *Tackle,* ten and a half foot two-handed fly-rod. *Reel,* quadruple multiplyer holding a hundred yards of fifteen pound test undressed silk line. *Hook,* No. 5 Sproat.

Record of the day—On the river at 9 a.m. where, at the old stand above the bridge at the pumping station, I fish for carp for two hours . . . not a touch. Down to the Dedham Boat House where I hire a boat and cast for black bass until noon . . . no luck. I am told by the boat-house keeper that the Poles from Norwood occasionally catch a carp from the meadow just below the bridge nearby.

A hearty snack of mixed grill and beer at Dedham village, and at 1.30 p.m. I am settled comfortably on a camp stool on the river bank in the meadow. After throwing a handful of corn into the swim, I enjoy ten minutes of perfect peace. Then . . . the float trembles, it stops, it trembles again; five minutes, and on retrieving the line, I find no corn on the hook. The re-baited hook is cast to the same spot fifty feet from the shore. Half a minute and again the float trembles, a moment and the line slides away ten feet—twelve feet—fifteen feet; I tighten and the hook sets into something that appears to be uncommonly solid; then away goes the fish at lightning speed down and across the river using up most of the hundred yards of line. He pauses under a canoe occupied by two members of the Audubon Society innocently peering through binoculars at a downy woodpecker; the bird watchers are quite unaware of a monster held in leash a few inches directly beneath them. Pressure on the line moves the fish, and up and down the river he goes, never stopping, never weakening, he's strong as a young bull, and I move up and down the bank following his flight. Rushes and pickerel-weed line the shore, but not too far away is a little opening of gravelly beach; there I must coax him. The bow of the bass net looks small, but the net is deep and into it he is gently guided from my stand knee-deep in the river.

The mixed grill and beer is a cannon-ball on my stomach, and floundering ashore, I'm obliged to retreat and lie down in the shade of a pine tree. In the playing and landing of a fish, never have I become so excited; salmon and trout have been played and netted, and I have remained cool and calm; why should this "scaley foreigner" throw me into a fever!

8th September—Late afternoon. Around the kitchen table the family gathers, and following my enthusiastic lead, admire the swelling flanks covered by big shining scales, the symmetrical lines of a body of no mean bulk, and the rather fetching little Mongolian mustaches depending from the sides of a rounded mouth that appears to be on the point of whistling a merry tune. With *The Compleat Angler* before me, the fish is dressed according to Izaak Walton's directions which I am determined faithfully to follow even to the recipe for cooking the "Queen of Rivers." So off we go to the village, and from grocery and provision store clean the shelves of every known condiment and spice—sweet marjoram, thyme and parsley, rosemary and savory, whole onions. The grocer fails at our demand for twelve pickled oysters, but three anchovies are proudly produced. Mr. Volpe at the wine shop supplies flasks of Chianti, their fat bellies dressed in straw trimmed with gay colors. Then comes a gallon of California claret in which, along with a hundred savory ingredients, the carp is to be boiled *whole* in a great iron pot; and we must not forget salt, cloves, mace and the rinds of oranges and lemons.

The invited guests are greeted by a delicate foreign fragrance which steals into every room in the house, and cheered and refreshed by drinks served in the gunroom, at seven o'clock the company is seated round the board. In comes a silver platter supporting an arrangement of form and color which well deserves being immortalized on canvas by the brush of the greatest of old Dutch masters. And flanking the platter on the right is a dish of boiled new potatoes, on the left, a bowl of garden lettuce and fresh tomatoes. On a side table, as well as a Camembert cheese and a big crusty loaf of Italian bread, is every ingredient which a good French dressing requires.

We fall to, and taste "this curious dish of meat," and having tasted, we all agree it has well repaid our trouble and charges, our labor and our patience. Every plate of the entire company is replenished as the rich red Tuscan wine goes round.

> Guid wife gae fetch ma fishin gear,
> And flask o' barley bree. . . .*

* These lines are taken from *Songs of the Edinburgh Angling Club.*

Here it may not be out of place to describe in detail the fishing gear and baits which I use when fishing for carp in the Charles.

Taken to the river on all occasions is a twelve-ounce rod nine feet nine inches long patterned after the salmon spinning rods used in the old country, and if a fish of uncommon size had been spotted, the ten-foot fourteen-ounce J. J. Hardy spinning rod is placed in the car. Again, if basking carp have been discovered in a certain still pool, then a stout ten-foot fly-rod, complete with single action reel, fly-line and backing, becomes a useful addition. When in use the spinning rod has seated, five inches from the extreme butt, an American, quadruple, multiplying reel holding a hundred yards of undressed braided silk or nylon line of fifteen pound test; the last fifty yards are well greased, for a floating line, while it lasts, is a great comfort. Threaded on the line is a sliding float of cork— "blimp"-like in form—three and a quarter inches long and one and a half inches in diameter. Thrust through its centre longitudinally is a hollow reed extending five-eighths of an inch beyond each end.* When the lead is resting on the bottom, no "stopper" on the line is required, for the sliding float finds the proper depth automatically. Directly below the float, the line is passed through a drilled bullet weighing three-quarters of an ounce. Next comes a glass bead to act as a buffer against the knot forming the upper end of a loop at the end of the line. Looped through this is a nine-inch snell of gut or nylon on which is neatly bent a No. 4 or 5 Sproat of well-tempered stout wire.

* The stem of an old-fashioned corn-cob pipe serves the purpose admirably. Straps of thin sheet brass may be bent and bound over the openings at each end to save the reed from splitting. Through the metal a hole is drilled just large enough to allow free passage of the line. With these additions, the float rides to better advantage.

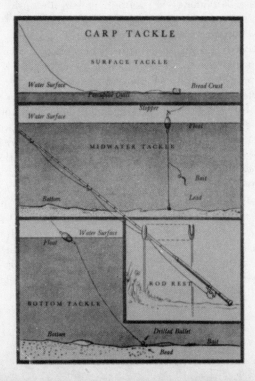

THE HATCH-THOMPSON CORN CARRIER OR GROUND BAITER

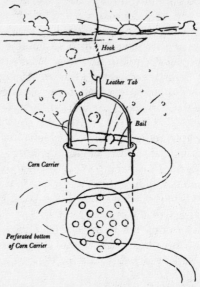

Anglers fishing for carp in clear still waters and light-tackle enthusiasts may find the gear described above unwarrantably stout and heavy. But when fishing a big float in a running river, a reasonable amount of lead is necessary to guard against tripping the bait along the bottom, and a stout rod mounting a reel without a sliding drag is often needed in keeping a heavy fish from snags, weeds, rushes and heavily bushed banks.

And now—the baits. Heading the list are the whole kernels of stewed corn; they are easily procured, and threaded on the hook, hold well and are not *too* attractive to hornpout, sunfish, dace, pickerel, bass, and trout, although on rare occasions I have taken samples of each species on this bait. Once I was not a little surprised at bringing ashore a fresh-water clam, both corn and hook had disappeared between tightly closed shells. When fishing with corn, small turtles are sometimes a nuisance, and a hooked snapping-turtle of great size is a major calamity. As a rule the carp is a vegetarian, and when in the mood, may be tempted by potatoes, corn, peas, and beans as well as dough, breadcrusts, plum cake, and bits of fruit and berries. On certain occasions he becomes carnivorous and shows an appetite for grubs and worms. The taste of an insect may not be entirely unknown to him; at any rate, counterfeit insects under certain unusual conditions have been accepted as food. Clippings in my scrapbook tell of carp taken on artificial flies both wet and dry; nevertheless, I believe that fly-fishing for carp in most waters would be disappointing if not entirely unsuccessful. Occasionally carp have been reported taken on slow-moving streamers, spoons and underwater plugs, which suggests a limited fish diet. Finally, this curious fish may be justly rated omnivorous, otherwise he would balk entirely at the strange pastes mixed according to ancient recipes which contain ingredients of a most revolting nature. He may not be a dainty fish, but you'll find him, like J. Bagstock, "de-vilish sly"!

To return to the gear. While fishing for carp, only in moments of activity is the rod held in the hand, and a rod rest built to the following specifications saves searching the country round for forked sticks. The Rod Rest—A smooth round stick of maple two feel long is shod with the empty cartridge of an army rifle—the pointed hard-jacketed bullet remaining intact. The stick is tapered to five-sixteenths of an inch at the other end, on which is slipped, into a hole bored for the purpose, a rounded block of wood one inch in diameter and four inches long in which is cut a V-shaped notch capable of holding in a firm position, at an angle of 45°, the rod, its butt resting on the ground. In transport the shaft is slipped into a compartment of the rod-case; the top—easily detached—is dropped into the tackle-bag.

Tied together in a snug bundle are the rods, the net, and the gaff. The Net—From a pear-shaped hickory bow sixteen inches across hangs a deep net capable of holding comfortably fish from two to ten pounds in weight, the stout ash handle is three feet ten and a half inches long shod with a crutch-rubber. The Gaff—A similar shaft mounts a generous gaff, for who knows when a record carp may take the bait!

The carp fisher under stress may think and act quickly and to good purpose, but the battle over, he likes to take his ease, hence a comfortable camp-stool becomes a necessity.

Every item of the equipment being carefully checked, we are ready to start for the river. Bait, rods, rod-rest, net and gaff; camp-stool and tackle bag containing everything that makes for comfort and perhaps success in fishing.

Through the seasons after taking the eleven and a half pounder at Dedham, the whole length of the Charles was explored and several swims were discovered which produced some fine fish. But after taking these fish, the news went abroad, and subsequent visits to famous spots found the banks trampled and lined with forked sticks. Thereafter these places produced, as a rule, small fish only—the big ones having moved to quieter waters. On many expeditions I was joined by old friends, and new friendships were formed at the riverside. One day an English mechanic—a champion carp fisher—told of record catches. His best fish, taken at Medfield on a night-crawler, weighed thirty-nine and a half pounds! Another day a Russian was discovered standing on the river bank, still as a fishing heron; a seasoned fisherman who knew his trade, for he had brought ashore several carp of over twenty pounds. Views on tackle and technique were exchanged as well as recipes for cooking. His "Fried Carp Meat Balls—Russe" did not find great favor at my table. Again I spent a delightful afternoon with Adam Kasanovitch—a master in the art of preparing potatoes for bait. Adam knew my old friend Joe Adamowski, and his admiration for his fellow countryman Ignace Paderewski knew no bounds. "Ah!" he exclaimed, "he's One Big Shot."

Other fishermen of lesser accomplishments were encountered from time to time; their gear usually consisted of a hand line—the hook baited with potato or dough, and always accompanying this simple tackle was a rod and float, the hook baited with worm, on which were taken sun-fish, perch, horn-pout, eels and suckers, each and all being dumped into a big boiling pot which never left the fire in the homes of these thrifty fishermen. Scenting "scaley fish," a Jewish Rabbi might pull up at a popular swim and jump from a truck laden with live barnyard fowls in coops. Beside a hand-line, *two* rods plainly hinted at an inclination toward a wholesale business.

TO MY COMPANIONS ON THE CHARLES

How sweet the meadows, what perfect peace
Steals o'er the angler as he throws his baits
To lure the wise, the ever cunning Carp,
And on his pleasure silently awaits.

But see the float! it has for hours
Been idly swimming on reflected skies
Begin to tremble as in fright
And grim events it seems to advertise.

In dim cool depths, a giant sheathed in bronze
Moves to his doom, by sordid greed beset,
A fine skilled hand, and tackle nicely balanced,
Soon have him flound'ring in the waiting net.

And once more peace, that perfect peace returns
To meadows green the little battle o'er,
A mother duck, her brood in close formation,
Swims through the reeds along the distant shore.

One would scarcely think that the practice of a quiet sport like carp fishing would ever lead to high adventure and night alarms. But listen! Here are a few selections from my diary.

CARPE DIEM *

Of all the fish that swim the watery mead,
Not one in cunning can the Carp exceed.

* Published in the *Atlantic Monthly* for May, 1943.

Date: 20th June 1939.

Place: Medfield Meadows, Charles River. Water low and reasonably clear.

Weather: Cloudy, Warm, Clearing after rain in the morning and the sun showing.

Fish: One Carp. Weight 18 lb. 1 oz.

Bait: Corn niblets on Number 5 hook.

Rod: 10½ ft. Spinning rod.

Reel: American multiplyer holding 100 yds. 15-pound test silk line.

Record of the Day: My favorite carp-swim, near the railroad bridge at Dover, has been discovered and now looks like a buffalo wallow: many forked sticks line the bank. I must find a *quiet* place.

The map leads me to a broken-down bridge on a narrow country road several miles up-river. Arriving at Medfield Meadows at 4:00 P.M. and standing on the bridge I study the water; below is a fair current and a number of dace are dimpling the surface—I cannot see far up-river because of a sharp bend and a screen of trees and bushes.

As I am standing there looking and studying, I hear quiet voices beyond the trees—an old and husky voice and a young one. Then a tremendous splash. The husky voice remarks, "That must be one of the big carp I've been telling you about."

I assemble my gear carefully; camp-stool, green-topped rod rest, long-shafted gaff, stewed corn—all complete. Crossing the broken bridge and going beyond the trees, I discover two honest anglers fishing for horn-pout. The older man, in white overalls, is not only an honest angler but an honest painter—house, not portrait. "Yes, that must have been a big carp that splashed—all of fifteen pounds."

Seated on the camp-stool (I've given up the old striped one and changed to one with a brown seat and green woodwork which harmonizes rather better with the hickory-shafted, green-topped rod rest and the bethabara-butted and split-bamboo-tipped rod), I fill the long-handled spoon with juicy corn from the special corn-jar, and with a flip and carry-through stroke shower niblets on the surface of the water. They sink to the bottom. Five or six minutes, and the baited hook, the drilled bullet, and the sliding float follow.

The hours roll by, punctuated from time to time by a pout taken by the pair eighty yards upstream. At 7.30 p.m. the float trembles, a run, and the hook is in a six-inch "shiner." I admire his brassy sides and red fins and return him to the river.

At 8.00 p.m. the float trembles again, stops, trembles once more, than moves away six feet, ten feet, fifteen feet, and the hook is in something solid which fortunately does *not* bolt downstream as is the custom of *Cyprinus carpio.* Possibly the round pool in which the very slow current circles about in an eddy four feet below me accounts for this obliging behavior of the big fish. Both bethabara and bambo are getting good exercise, but finally the fish sails slowly near the surface, under the bank, and the point of the gaff is under her, just behind the gills. The afternoon has been hot, and I have removed my short rubber carp-boots; my stockinged feet give me a good toe-hold.

She is on the grass, and my friends up-river move down to have a look. During the play they have remained perfectly stationary—never a shout, never a word of direction; in short, they are fishermen.

Old and husky voice says, "Something should be done about this." I agree but remind him that my car is quite a distance down the road and across the bridge. He walks to his basket, and after a few words of apology concerning glasses, we do something about it. It is getting dark, but before we leave, my host, glancing at the gaff, says, "You expected to get one," and I say, "Yes, I did."

It is pretty late when I get home. Margaret is asleep, but Jack is in the bathtub, and his right arm looks strong. On the bathroom scales The Carp goes exactly eighteen pounds one ounce. A hen fish in fine condition—not a scale missing—heavy with roe.

ST. BOTOLPH CLUB, 22ND JUNE 1939

The flesh is firm and sweet—not a trace of "pondy" flavor. The temperamental chef in the kitchen insists on serving it with his own sauce. Well, there are two schools of thought: he likes his, I like mine. Mine is D. T.'s receipt in *The Compleat Angler*, John Major's Edition, 1824. The enormous roe, like a sheet of golden corn bread, is delicious, however, either as an *hors d'oeuvre* or with the fish, and Monsieur C., fellow member of the Hook and Slice Club, mighty driver of golf balls and wine expert, produces the proper Bordeaux wine.

Hearty congratulations of the small fishing fraternity, and the usual hostile and antagonistic attitude of the dull common herd. Yes, they have seen them at Fontainebleau, and they have warts on their noses (I mean the carp). A friend in New York only the other day sent them a forty-pound salmon from the Cascapedia. Nevertheless, each one gobbles three helpings of Carp au Walton, while they are talking about themselves, Czechoslovakia, and Franklin Roosevelt.

ICE CHEST AT MIDNIGHT

Date: 28th June 1940.

Place: Medfield Meadows, Charles River, Swim of the Broken Bridge. Water fairly high but clear.

Weather: 4 p.m. Cool, threatening rain. Evening, heavy showers.

Fish: One Carp. Weight 10 lb. Bait, corn.

Record of the Day: Fishing from four in the afternoon to seven in the evening, an occasional carp is taken—small ones of three-quarters of a pound. Then comes the rain; I put on a rubber shirt and am about to pack up the gear when a good fish jumps in the cove up-river—a gun-shot away. Making my way to a new stand opposite the fish, I cast out and wait, the rain comes down in torrents and a retreat is indicated. I start to pull in, and feeling a slight resistance, I strike, and then the fun begins. He's putting up a stronger fight than my record eighteen-pounder, and that is hard to understand for the new J. J. Hardy spinning rod is a powerful weapon. At last he is under control, when to my dismay I discover I've left the gaff at the old stand. A finger is slipped under the gill-cover; how this is managed I do not know, for the steep bank is slippery as grease. It's accomplished, however, and I'm off to fried clams and a bottle of Feigensphan P.O.N. at The Colonial on the road to Dedham. Examination after landing reveals the No. 5 Sproat stuck on the *outside* of the fish's mouth, which accounts for the long and strong struggle.

On the way home I stop at an old friend's house in Dedham. Young Lovering and his wife are at the theatre but a sleepy and rather frightened housemaid opens the ice-chest door and in slides the big Carp. . . . A roguish little eye, peeping from a bottom shelf, nearly causes a fainting spell when Elizabeth seeks the refreshment of a midnight glass of milk. This reported to me, hysterically, over the telephone next morning.

MAGIC

This adventure happened when a limited supply of gasoline was allowed for pleasure vehicles.

Date: 25th July 1943.

Place: Newton Upper Falls, Charles River, Puddingstone Run.

Weather: 9 A.M. Clearing after gentle showers.

Fish: One Carp. Weight 7 lb. Bait, corn.

Record of the day: At nine o'clock the sun shines and the water is pretty as Puddingstone Run. A number of carp are about, but all are in a finicky mood, and it is not until just before noon that a seven-pounder is brought to net. Dispatched with the priest, he is slipped into a paper shopping-bag, which I am soon to discover is not the best thing in the world for transporting freshly caught fish. All goes well on the half-mile march to the bus stop until halfway up the last steep hill where I stop to rest in the shade of a tree. Through a gate at the roadside comes a pretty little girl with golden hair. "What's 'at?" says she, pointing to the bag. The hot noon-day sun has had its effect, and I reply, " 'at's a big fissy, wanna see?" The wretched carrier is lifted, and out through the water-soaked paper pops the carp. A frightened glance down the pike shows the approaching bus. One corner of a bandanna is knotted through the gills of the fish, the opposite corner, after several turns of the big handkerchief around a finger, is made fast to the bag handles. There hangs my prize in a bottomless bag, safe from prying eyes.

A breathless run to the top of the hill, and stepping aboard the Greyhound, I find myself in the midst of a jolly crowd of soldiers and sailors with their sweethearts. Immediately I become conscious of smiling glances filled with undisguised curiosity, for, without doubt, this strange passenger, burdened with half a ton of impedimenta in great variety is a novel spectacle. Then. . . . Presto! Shades of Merlin and Malagigi, was there *ever* such magic! From the finger of a hand raised high, to retain a balance in the swaying bus, the bandanna slips its coils and when it tightens at full length, there exposed to view is the lower section and tail of a four-foot monster.

OTTERS

The otter is seldom seen at close range in our part of the country.

Date: 26th July 1947.

Place: Dover, Mass. The Old Swim on the Charles.

Record of the Day: Up with the sun—a perfect summer morning. On the river at seven o'clock and for two hours the float is motionless, never a leaping carp shows up the long reach, never a dimple on the still surface. Mysterious!

Suddenly the quiet of the morning air is shattered by the sound of a terrific disturbance in the water below the bridge. I am about to investigate the cause, when up through the far arch appear three terrifying creatures, sleek heads and shining eyes, first above the surface, then below, and going at the rate of an express train. Visions of a wrecked circus van, from which sea-lions have escaped, flash through the mind—but no! Those fierce glances are not those of a playful sea-lion. *Otters!* By all that's holy! But what huge animals! Up the shore, then across and up the river and out of sight.

Packing up the gear, I drive three miles up-stream and settle in the shade of the big elm on the Norwood Road, for without doubt, every fish in the Old Swim is dying of fright. Will these savage monsters put an end to the fishing in the quiet meadows for the rest of the season?

A GREAT INVENTION—BAITING THE SWIM FOR CARP *

Date: September 1944.

Place: Newton Upper Falls, Charles River, Dora's Swim.

> You see the ways the fisherman doth take
> To catch the fish: what engines doth he make!
> —JOHN BUNYAN

A big one is rolling at a distance of forty yards under the far bank. His appetite must be whetted with a spoonful of corn, he must peck at a kernel or two as an *hors d'oeuvre* before attacking the banquet—five kernels in a row on a No. 5 Sproat.

* Published in the *Fishing Gazette*, 30th March, 1946, 171 High Street, Beckenham, Kent, England.

Flicking corn with a wooden spoon, be its handle ever so long and springy, and the carry-through stroke ever so perfect, fails to throw the furthermost grain over forty feet; the pattern is ragged and covers too great an area.

One evening as we are sitting by the river, I tell my companion of the difficulties connected with baiting a swim at long range. Many a bright idea has flitted through my mind, many a method has been tried and found wanting; I have even flirted with the idea of encasing the grains of corn in a ball of sand and clay the exact size and weight of a regulation baseball—by hook or crook becoming acquainted with Ted Williams, luring him to the stream-side—all will be merry.

My friend at my side then makes a valuable suggestion. "Why not," says he, "in some way attach a spoonful of corn to the hook and cast it across the river?" The possibilities of a bundle made of niblets, wrapped in tissue paper, similar to the little Fourth of July torpedoes, are discussed, and the next evening exhaustive experiments are made along these lines, but no great success attends the performance, for, sometimes there are bombs bursting in air when *one* layer of paper is used; *two* layers, and the corn is held too long before the wet paper disintegrates sufficiently to release the contents. Besides, attaching the "torpedo" to the hook with a piece of precious casting line is a tedious and messy operation.

And then—the great inspiration! Rushing home, the vacuum top of a Chili sauce bottle is discovered in the pantry. Down the sink-drain goes the sauce, in the ash-can goes the bottle. A piece of stout spring-brass wire is cunningly fitted as a bail for the little bucket and holes are drilled in the bottom; a slotted leather tab to hold the hook is fixed to the bail.

The next evening by the riverside, a shaking hand fills the container—a heaping load. A rhythmic swing backward—then forward, and out shoots the line, sliding float, drilled bullet and hook with the precious cargo trailing. A splash in the exact spot near yonder bank, and the perilous journey is made without mishap—no casualties of kernels in transit, for the corn, having learned a valuable lesson from close association with the intelligent angler, has achieved that blessed state—inertia, which combats successfully the propelling force of the steely wrist and the resilient bamboo. And now the little bucket—itself fallen into pleasant immobility, which finally comes, willy-nilly, to all things great and small—pierces the surface of another element. The bucket's specific gravity is great, it sinks rapidly and parts company with the semi-buoyant corn which is hustled out of its cozy nest by jets of water which spurt through holes in the bottom. And the pattern on the river floor? Perfect!—not too large, not too small—and of even distribution.

Now retrieve the empty carrier and unhook it. Light a pipe, tell a story, sing a song and catch a carp; and should he weigh twenty pounds, knock him on the head and give a dinner party, or—if you do not feel like giving a dinner party—let him go!

The outside of the carrier is enameled a billiard-cloth green—the inside is white. Were I an Indian Prince, I would have one fashioned of pure gold; beneath the lip and encircling the vessel would be carved a frieze of leaping carp. A ruby or an emerald or two encrusted would do no harm, and with a treble hook trailing, a bass or pickerel might be picked up on the way in.

BREAD CRUST AND THE FLY ROD

Date: 25th May 1945.
Place: Newton Upper Falls on the Charles, Still Pool.
Weather: Cool. Wind W. Sunshine and showers.
Fish: One carp of 5 lb. Full of well-formed roe.
Record of the Day: I decide to fish Still Pool as the water is too high to try the running stream. From time to time a carp rolls, near the left, right, the far bank, and again in the middle. From 2 to 4.30 p.m. I fish in a conventional manner—bait on the bottom—not a touch; fish are showing all about me—most exasperating; one fellow is particularly annoying, for he swirls at five-minute intervals not more than twenty feet away and close to the bank on which I am sitting. Thinking that, perhaps with the season well advanced, the ooze and vegetation on the bottom has become thick enough to cover the bait, and as there is no current and little wind, I put a stopper on the float a foot above the baited hook and swing it gently over this destroyer of equanimity. He takes it without hesitation, and I bring a five-pounder ashore.

The wind is freshening and moves the float at too great a pace, so I resort to another rig. The sinker at the end of the line, that it may rest on the bottom, the hook a foot or two above that and a stationary float fixed at a proper depth. Not successful, for every time a cast is made, a smart little turtle, who has been keenly observing operations, swims rapidly up to the red-topped float (I didn't know they could make such speed), noses it, then up-ends, follows the line to the hook and steals the bait. "Oh, very well," say I, so I throw out in the centre of the pool fifty feet away, and I'm blessed if that intelligent creature doesn't streak it to the float, give it a bunt, up-end and down the line to enjoy another feast. A very interesting game, but it doesn't feed a starving family on a meatless Sunday.

While nibbling a pilot-biscuit, I shy a few rather large crumbs into the water nearby, and am entertained by watching a clumsy old snapping-turtle sucking them in from the surface. I throw another piece farther down, near the bank, and a four-pound carp takes it with a swirl. I must remember this—carp are *not always* bottom feeders. An idea! When I go to the Still Pool again, I'll encase a No. 5 Sproat in a floating crust of bread. A fly-rod and a greased line—why not! I've caught big chub on the Connecticut by using these tactics.

Date: 26th May 1945.
Place: Still Pool on the Charles.
Weather: Fair and warm, light S.W. breeze from 12 m. to 2.30 p.m. when the wind shifts to the *East* and stays there for the rest of the afternoon.

Fish: Three Carp. One of 4½ lb., two of 4 lb. each.
Record of the Day:

> The pleasantest angling is to see the fish
> Cut with her golden oars the silver stream
> And greedily devour the treacherous bait.
> —WILLIAM SHAKESPEARE

The floating bread-crust works! "Minor Tactics" have come to Carp Fishing. I arrive at Still Pool at noon. Warm, sunny and calm. The carp are swirling and, from the high bank, I can see several cruising near the surface directly in front of me, not more than a dozen feet from the shore. With a stout greenheart fly-rod carrying a well-greased fly line and a porcupine quill fitted close above a snelled hook on which is impaled a good tough crust of Italian bread, I creep up behind a bush and cast out. The dry bread-crust floats well, and there it remains unmolested for several minutes. Presently a carp approaches and inspects it; the water is still, the light is right, I can see the smallest detail, even the expression of his crafty eyes. No, he's not frightened* at this something that has fallen so lightly on the water. Crafty and cunning he may be, but at the same time, like some of his brothers with arms and legs instead of fins and tails, he is *greedy*. Still cautious, however, he will not hurriedly bolt the tasty morsel baked by that great artist Mazola; he is suspicious, he will wait and watch. And he has not long to wait, for from behind the bush comes a second crust—a harmless, hookless crust—which is first nosed, then swallowed by another carp close by. This is too much for my greedy playfellow who unhesitatingly sucks in crust number one, and after a most satisfactory play—he's not towing an ounce of lead and a float the size of a lemon—he is gently led into the net and brought ashore, his scales of pale gold gleaming in the sunshine.† Four and one-half pounds, not a big fish but he has given pretty sport.

After a leisurely lunch in the shade of a tree two other fair carp are taken in this fascinating manner; and then every fish in the pool goes off the feed, it's now half past two, and the east wind blows cool on my back. Then follows three hours of fishing with floating crust and corn on the bottom without a nibble from a real fish, but I'm obliged to leave a hook in the mouth of a whacking old snapping-turtle, for these noisome reptiles have taken the stage. Did that shift of wind put the fish down? I'm inclined to think so, but I do not know.

---

* Carp lying close to the surface are easily disturbed, but when lying near the bottom, several feet under water—especially in a running river—the "plop" of an ounce of lead does not appear to frighten them. I've often wondered at this behaviour in such a shy fish, but it must be remembered that these fish are accustomed to tremendous commotions when their mates are in a leaping mood. I have observed, however, that the constant hammering of a swim is likely to clear it of big fish.

† The scales on the flanks of small carp from the Charles—fish up to five and six pounds—are usually of pale gold. Larger fish, as a rule, are darker, showing scales of rich bronze.

P.S. Every time I lead a fish to the shore, it is closely followed in its every move by another fish—not two or three, *one*. His or her mate?

> And a salty tear from a rheumy eye
> Ran down the crimson cheek.

CARP IN THE KITCHEN

In the breast of every fisherman lurks the heart of a savage, when with great satisfaction he catches and kills his fish. It is only when he enters the kitchen, with its long shelf of cook books, that he becomes a civilized being.

RECIPE FOR COOKING A FIVE-POUND CARP

A delicious dish requiring comparatively little labor and patience in its preparation. The Roe Sauce is a perfect complement to the meat, accentuating, as it does to a marked degree, the delicate flavor.

Clean and skin like a perch or black-bass, cutting out the fins, and chopping off the head and tail. If a roe fish, remove roe carefully preserving the incasing membrane.

Put fish in a thick iron or aluminum covered pot and almost cover with water. Add heaping teaspoonful of "All Spice," a few bay leaves, teaspoonful of salt, a little black pepper, a few cloves, a sliced onion, rinds of half an orange and half a lemon.

Boil hard for fifteen minutes, and then add two wine glasses of sherry and simmer for another fifteen minutes.

The Sauce—To be cooked and stirred constantly over a reasonably hot fire. One cup of heavy cream, butter the size of an egg, two egg yolks; add one or two spoonfuls of broth from the carp-kettle, season with salt—not too much, not too little—teaspoon of English mustard, dash of paprika. Thicken with roe of the fish (remove membrane, leaving the roe free, and stir well into the sauce). Add glass of sherry. Lacking roe, a slight thickening of flour may be used. Pour over fish on platter, surround by lettuce leaves and garnish with sliced lemons—and "much good do you." Note: For a twenty-pounder multiply ingredients by four.

The Roe Sauce alone, served on toast, makes a fine dish.

The milt of a male carp, broiled like a sweetbread and served on toast, is a dish beyond compare!

Thanks to the charming lady who made this discovery in a French cook book.

The French are a thrifty race. The following is gathered from an old French cook book.

A carp taken from running water is preferred. However, if you receive a *gift* of one, which is still alive, coming from stagnant water, "cause it to swallow two spoonfuls of strong vinegar . . . rum or cognac may be substituted for the vinegar. It is possible that the carp will not particularly fancy the aromatic spirits, but they give an excellent flavor to the fish." And so on, not leaving out the smallest detail that may lead to the success of this wholesome bit of cookery. We are warned against "a greenish stone-like unit" found near the head of the fish. Remove it! For it gives a sour taste to the flesh.

Then follows a recipe for Carpe au Bleu, a masterpiece of the chef's art. Served *hot* to-day, *cold* with mayonnaise tomorrow. Note: I am indebted to Frederick A. Celler for translating and contributing this interesting information.

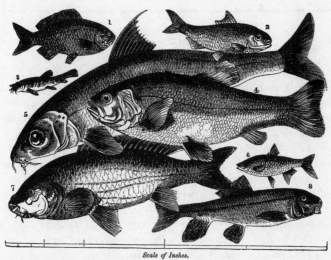

Scale of Inches.

THE CARP FAMILY.—1. Golden Carp, or Goldfish, *Cyprinus auratus*. 2. The Roach, *Leuciscus rutilus*. 3. The Loach, or Beardie, *Cobitis barbatula*. 4. The Tench, *Tinca vulgaris*. 5. The Barbel, *Barbus vulgaris*. 6. New York Shiner, *Cyprinus crysoleucas*. 7. Common Carp, *Cyprinus carpis*. 8. Common New York Sucker, *Catostomus communis*.

GOURMET SALMON, TROUT, AND BASS

Colonel Henry A. Siegel

SALMON

BOTH FOR SPORT AND EATING, the salmon is the king of freshwater fish. The difference between fresh and frozen salmon is as pronounced as that between a fine beer and the "near beer" of Prohibition that elicited the famous Will Rogers comment: "Whoever named it was a poor judge of distance." If at all possible, bring your salmon back home on ice and "in the round"—that is, uncleaned with the gills left in (as opposed to other fish; since there is no pepsin, there is no decay problem, and any cutting increases the action of bacteria). They may safely be kept on ice at least two weeks, and I have kept some as long as three when ice was added daily. If you must freeze salmon, freeze them individually in containers of water; the next best method is true flash freezing.

Salmon smoked on the Miramichi by Claire and Archie Jardine are every bit as good as the Scottish import—which sells for between nine and twelve dollars a pound here. Such smoking requires a twenty-four-hour brine and forty-eight-hour smoke; under normal conditions it will keep only three or so weeks in the refrigerator before the formation of mold. If the mold is not too extensive, it may safely be wiped off with a cloth saturated with vinegar.

I was lamenting this fact to Ernie Schwiebert several years ago, while we were checking the quality of the potables at the Antrim Lodge Bar in Roscoe. He put me on to the greatest discovery since that of cracked ice—an easy and sure-fire method of keeping smoked salmon for at least one year. Take several widemouthed jars with screw caps, and, after rinsing them out thoroughly, place slices (in the case of grilse, bits and pieces) of the salmon in the jars. Pack well. Now add enough olive oil to cover completely, and be sure that no air remains. Replace the caps and put the jars on the bottom shelf of your refrigerator until needed. If you don't like the flavor of olive oil, the salmon may be drained on paper towels, and you will discover that the fish has not absorbed any of the oil. (*Saumon fumé* at any of the great restaurants in Europe or America is served with a cruet of olive oil, capers, and a pepper grinder.) The olive oil may be filtered and reused without any deleterious effects.

Poached Salmon

This is a method of cooking, not catching, fish. If you are a devout salmon fisherman, or expect to become one, buy a fish poacher (what the French call a *poissonnière*), an oblong utensil with a removable grid so that the whole fish may be removed without being broken from the kettle and drained; the poacher also has a lid. If you are only going to cook salmon every year or so, wrap the fish in cheesecloth and curve him so that he'll fit around the inside of the largest pot in your kitchen—perhaps the one you use for cooking spaghetti. Large poachers are expensive, and they also take a large amount of court-bouillon; but they will serve for several grilse. A very large salmon may be cut in two, and when the platter is decorated as the striking centerpiece for a large party, the cut is easily masked with strips of pimento or mayonnaise forced through one of the various nozzles of a pastry bag.

The basic recipe for court-bouillon is: 1 bottle dry white wine, 1 quart water, 1 tablespoon salt, 2 carrots and 2 onions sliced thin, a few cracked peppercorns, 2 or 3 cloves, 2 bay leaves, 4 celery tops, and 1 teaspoon thyme. I like to add a fish head and any fish bones or tails. One-half cup vinegar may be used instead of the wine. Bring to a boil and let simmer for 30 minutes. Double or triple this recipe if needed; the liquid should just cover the fish.

Your fish should have been cleaned and rinsed by now (don't scale salmon but remove the skin after the fish is cooked), and is ready to go into the poacher. Lift out the rack, put the fish on it, and lower it into the liquid. Bring back to simmering (185° to 195° F), and with the lid on, cook for 12 to 15 minutes for a grilse, 15 to 20 minutes for a salmon.

If the fish is served hot, use Hollandaise sauce. Served cold (my favorite), let the sauce be homemade mayonnaise. A chilled bottle of white Rhône or Rhine or Moselle wine goes well with both, and both can be accompanied with a dish of cucumber salad.

My recipe for mayonnaise: Rinse a mixing bowl with very hot water and then dry. Beat 2 egg yolks—with a silver or stainless fork. Add ½ teaspoon salt, a pinch of pepper, ½ teaspoon Colman's mustard, and 2 teaspoons lemon juice or vinegar. Beat well. Put ½ cup olive oil and ½ cup bland vegetable oil in a measuring cup, and add the mixed oils drop by drop at first, beating constantly. You may later add the oil more rapidly, but always keep the mixture fairly thick. When all the oil has been poured, add 1 or 2 teaspoons more lemon juice or vinegar. Still more may be added if your taste calls for such. For green mayonnaise, add finely chopped herbs as follows: 1 tablespoon chives, 2 tablespoons parsley, 1 tablespoon tarragon (if dried, 1 teaspoon), and 1 teaspoon dill to the finished sauce. Add a few drops of green cake coloring for deeper green.

Grilled Salmon

To cook a salmon in this fashion, the fish should be split from the *top* and cleaned. Do not remove the backbone. Rub both sides with butter or oil and salt and pepper, and put the fish on a well-greased hinged broiler—the same kind you use for steaks. Place over a charcoal fire that has reached the gray stage, flesh down, for a few minutes; then turn the broiler over, add a mixture of butter, juice of a lemon, and a small handful of minced parsley. The fish should cook slowly, and will take about half an hour. When the backbone shows signs of lifting easily when you take a fork to it, the fish is done. Do not overcook—it will dry out.

Salmon Florentine

In a saucepan melt ½ stick butter, add ¼ cup flour, and stir until blended and smooth. Scald 1½ cups milk and add to the roux, stirring again until smooth. Season with a pinch of salt, ½ teaspoon Coleman's mustard and several good dashes of tabasco and Angostura bitters. Mix in a cup of grated cheese (I like Romano and Parmesan half and half). Put 2 cups cooked, drained, and chopped spinach in a buttered casserole, add the sauce and 2 cups flaked cooked salmon. Sprinkle with another ½ cup grated cheese and bake uncovered in a moderate oven for 15 minutes.

Salmon Chowder

After letting the cook at Boyd's Fishing Lodge on the Miramichi beat me at a few games of cribbage, I wheedled this fine recipe out of him.

Boil a cleaned grilse in lightly salted water for 10 minutes, using 4 cups of water. Remove the fish and set aside. Strain the broth, add 4 cups each of finely diced potatoes and onions; if you have some celery, add 3 stalks, also diced. Simmer until the potatoes feel done when tested with a knife (about 10 minutes). While the potatoes simmer, bone and skin your fish, keeping it in man-sized pieces. Add 1 stick of butter, 4 cups of evaporated milk, and the chunks of salmon; then salt and pepper to taste. Reheat to a simmer. Do not let boil! Serve with pilot crackers and cold ale or beer—and be prepared for demands for seconds.

TROUT

Nothing in the edible world loses flavor more rapidly than trout. Until you have tasted wild trout cooked just out of the stream, you have simply never tasted trout. Trout, if they are left whole and wrapped in an absorbent paper such as newspaper or paper toweling, will keep in a creel as well as any method I know of—especially if your creel allows for good passage of air. If you can get the fish into an ice chest (but not in direct contact with the ice), so much the better. All fish keep better when coated with a mixture of oil and soy sauce before being placed into the refrigerator; this produces no "fishy" odor, and the soy sauce doesn't add any flavor.

Fried Trout

Richard Salmon in his fine book *Fly Fishing for Trout* devotes two pages to the proper method of cooking bacon. I'll be brief: Fry bacon slowly over a moderate fire. There is no better fat for frying trout (or any other fish) than properly rendered bacon fat.

After the fish have been cleaned and dried, dip them in milk, then roll them in seasoned cornmeal or cracker crumbs. Use a large cast-iron skillet and have about ⅛ of an inch of bacon fat sizzling hot when you drop in the fish. Shake the pan several times to be sure that the fish are not sticking. As soon as they begin to curl, turn them; keep turning until the fish will lie flat. Smaller trout should be fried quickly; that way they will be golden brown on the outside and still moist on the inside. Larger trout should be fried slower, so that they will cook through.

For sauce: Pour out the bacon fat and wipe the pan with paper towels. Put in 1 or 2 tablespoons butter for each fish, and about twice that amount of lemon juice; add freshly ground black pepper and heat until the butter is a medium brown. If there is any watercress, add that as a garnish.

Blue Trout

Trout for this the most famous of trout recipes *must* be freshly killed. Many of the French restaurants that specialize in this simple but delectable dish are situated directly beside a trout stream—or have a tank in which the trout are kept alive. When boiled in a vinegar solution, such fresh trout will turn a beautiful shade of blue.

To serve 6, take 6 freshly killed and cleaned trout (8 to 10 inches is the best size) and wipe them with wine vinegar. Prepare a court-bouillon as in the salmon section, but use 3 quarts water and 1½ cups wine vinegar; triple all the other ingredients. After simmering for the period recommended, return to a boil. Plunge the trout into the liquid, then return to simmer. Cook until the fish feel soft when tried with a fork; this can vary from 4 to 10 minutes. Remove the fish from the liquid, using great care that they remain whole; then drain. Serve with Hollandaise or melted butter and the best white wine you can afford.

Bean-Hole Trout

This is a good method of cooking your camp breakfast while you fix dinner. Before you make the campfire, dig a pit to accommodate the trout for your morning meal. After it has been cleaned, each trout should have some butter and lemon juice placed inside, and both sides salted and peppered. Wrap each fish in foil, using enough so that the package will be completely sealed. When placed in the pit, the fish should be about three inches apart, and if there is more than one layer, the layers should have about that same amount of earth between them. Don't try more than two layers: the heat won't penetrate. Place the same amount of dirt on top, and then build your fire on top of the now-covered pit.

In the morning, your trout should be properly cooked. If they aren't to your taste, curse me; and then make the adjustments necessary for your next try. If they are too well done, add more dirt on top; if they aren't done enough, use less dirt. Since I don't know how late you sleep or how big you make your fires, I can't be more exact: but bean-hole trout for breakfast can be well worth your efforts.

BLACK BASS (large- and small-mouth)

The flavor of bass usually depends on the water the fish are taken from, but by filleting them after you have removed the skin, you can reduce such differences to a minimum.

Fillet of Bass Meunière

Roll 10 seasoned fillets in flour or fine cornmeal. Sauté in 3 or 4 tablespoons hot butter until the fillets are golden brown on both sides. Remove and keep as warm as possible. Heat another 3 tablespoons butter until dark brown, add juice of medium-sized lemon and 2 tablespoons finely chopped parsley, and pour over the fish.

Fillet of Bass au Gratin

Use 3 pounds fillets for this dish. Roll each fillet in seasoned flour. Line a well-buttered casserole with a tablespoon each of chopped parsley and chopped onion mixed. Place the fillets on this, add ½ cup dry vermouth, and dot with butter. Cover with bread crumbs to which has been added grated sharp cheese and some melted butter. Cover and bake in a hot oven 20 minutes. Uncover and cook another 5 minutes or until the top is nicely browned. Save dishes by serving your fillet of bass au gratin right from the casserole.

EXCALIBUR: THE STEELHEAD*

Paul O'Neil

THE REST OF THE WORLD'S TROUT may be taken in summer, to the sound of birds and the pleasant hum of insects, but the steelhead—the big, sea-going rainbow of the Northwest coasts—is winter's child. To know him you must gird as for war and wade the rivers when they are bitter cold—in sleet-filled gloom, or in freezing blue weather when the leafless alders gleam in pale sunlight along the streams, and ice forms in the guides of your rod. To know the steelhead, you should hurt with cold and nurse a little fear of the numbing current which pushes against your waders; it can pull you down and make you gasp and drown you, as steelhead streams methodically drown a few of your fellow fishermen with every passing year.

The steelhead may be pursued in fairer weather, and in easier ways. He runs as far south as the Sacramento River in California. Some of his number run in the early spring, and, in such rivers as the Snake and Oregon's famed Rogue, he runs in the summer, too. But he is a northern fish; when he leaves the sea to spawn, he comes mostly to the rivers of Oregon, Washington, British Columbia, and Alaska, and he migrates chiefly during December, January, and February. The fisherman who has not met him when it is cold has not been properly introduced. Winter sets the stage for him and makes him unique.

* Reprinted by permission of *Sports Illustrated* from the March 11, 1957, issue. © 1957 by Time Inc.

There is ominous drama in the very look of a chill, green river on a dark and stormy afternoon, and a man fighting cold and snow to wade it is being properly conditioned for his moment of revelation. For the steelhead is a fish which makes an impact upon the adrenalin-producing glands rather than the intellect. He is always big (six to thirty pounds), and he burns with savage energy from the limitless feed of the ocean he has left behind. He can hurtle into the air a split second after he is hooked, and flash hugely out in the murk, like the sword Excalibur thrust up from the depths—at once a gleaming prize and a symbol of battle. At that sight, and at the first astounding wrench of the rod, the fisherman is rewarded for his hardihood: he is suddenly warm and reckless, and simultaneously possessed of mindless desperation and rocketing hope.

Men in the grip of this atavistic elation sometimes find themselves doing extraordinary things. A steelhead out in moving water at the end of a six-pound test leader and a nine-pound monofilament line transmits a horrifying sense of power to the rod. Many an otherwise conservative fellow has found himself heedlessly following his fish downstream—laboring wildly along a gravel bar while up to the waist in icy water, body half buoyant, weightless feet feeling desperately for bottom, bucking rod held high and numbed hands working the reel with reverence to get back precious line.

Men have tripped, gone down with a splash, and come up with hardly a change of expression to carry on the struggle; they have run along river banks, hurdling rocks and thrashing out into the water around log jams, in their effort to turn, control, and finally dominate their trout. A lot of them have lost. A few have literally hurled their rods into the stream at the awful second when the line went irrevocably slack. But of course a lot of men—and women, too—have won battles with a big fish in bad water, have guessed when it was time to say, "Now it's you or me," have increased the pressure, controlled the startling submarine disturbance at the end of the line, have endured the trout's last jump and its surface splashing, and have finally reached it—silver, iridescent, and enormous—on shelving gravel or frozen sand and have reached for its gills like a prospector bending at last over the mother lode. And afterwards have relaxed, before an evening fire, in a glow of weariness and euphoria.

Not every struggle with a steelhead is so difficult, for the fish is a creature of moods, and water and weather vary. But the measure of the big trout is his impact upon man, individually and en masse. It is dramatic in the extreme. During the last ten years steelhead fishing has become a near mania in the Northwest. One man in ten in western Washington braves the wintry cold to fish the steelhead streams, and a quarter of a million do so along the West Coast as a whole.

Hundreds of night-shift workers at the Boeing Airplane Company's plants in Seattle and Renton keep rods in their cars and fish on their way home in the morning. Doctors, lawyers, bankers, and engineers fish for steelhead, talk about steelhead and dream about steelhead from November to March. Many a visitor from afar has caught the virus, and many a Northwesterner, trapped in the cities of the East and South, goes on mooning about winter fishing year after year. A lot of people who never fish—but like to eat—applaud the steelhead too. Baked or broiled, he is a delight to the palate; juicy, succulent, similar to salmon in color, taste and texture but with a delicate hint of rainbow trout flavor which is difficult to describe but wonderful to experience.

Like many another public figure, the steelhead elicits fervent testimonials. Ex-President Herbert Hoover has been a steelheader for decades (his favorite streams: the Klamath and the Rogue), and Jim Phelan nurses memories of fishing the Skagit during his gaudy years as football coach at the University of Washington. Clark Gable is still recovering emotionally from his first steelhead, a bright fish which he took on a dry fly and which jumped eleven times before he finally landed it. Supreme Court Justice William O. Douglas (who has a weather-beaten fishing shack in Washington's Quillayute River wilderness) considers the big trout the "champion of champions" and talks raptly of his "first great jump, and the maddening race downstream in fast water."

Although he is a game fish, the steelhead also has a marked influence upon business. Sporting goods stores not only sell tons of fishing gear calculated to make certain his demise, but also retail pamphlets with maps of streams, detailed descriptions of holes and drifts, and even intelligence on the attitudes of farmers whose fields abut the stream. Newspapers run almost daily pronunciamentos on fishing conditions. Motels near distant rivers do a brisk business. Department stores cater to the steelheader's need for voluminous costuming—the rites of preparing for the wintry stream have become almost as formalized as those of the ancient knight preparing for the lists.

In his efforts to armor himself against the cold, many a fisherman has turned to long underwear of quilted Dacron, or of materials which incorporate thousands of insulating air cells, and to heavy woolen "feel gloves"—so called because both thumbs and forefingers have panels of thin nylon which permit the angler to remain sensitive to the reel. He must have waders or hip boots, a slicker, thick woolen socks, fishing vest, a sou'wester, wool shirt and heavy sweaters as well, and, once laboriously girded for the fray, he often stuffs two or three hand warmers (which burn lighter fluid) into his pockets to create islands of heat around his muffled torso. "They are," says Dr. Fred Cleveland of Seattle's Mason Clinic, "the greatest comfort to man since the invention of woman."

This furor seems only logical, for the steelhead (*Salmo irideus gairdneri*) which was almost ignored during the Northwest's early decades, is one of the world's toughest and most brilliant game fish and a prince of the beautiful salmonoid family. Pound for pound, he is lustier and more enduring than any of the six strains of Pacific salmon. Unlike them, he does not face inevitable death after spawning—if he can maintain more than sixty per cent of his body weight in migration up a stream, he will get back to the sea, rebuild his strength, grow bigger and return to spawn again.

Exhaustion tests have shown that he can swim for minutes in water fast enough to wash the big king salmon downstream. He is bold: at sea, even as a small fish, he does not school up like Pacific salmon but swims alone. In streams, he is a heavy-water fish, and moves by preference in deep, fast-moving currents. He is hardy: steelhead have come into coastal streams with their body cavities ripped open by sharks and have still hit a lure and have fought gallantly. He is an amazing jumper. Pacific salmon have never surmounted Shipherd's Falls, a roaring, sixty-foot cataract in Washington's Wind River (although they now negotiate it by fish ladder), but the steelhead is able to pick his way up by leaping from one small pocket of water, four, five, or six feet to the next, often jumping at odd angles to hit the targets he must sense but cannot possibly see as he launches himself.

The steelhead and his blood brother, the rainbow trout, seem quite obviously to be the same fish. When they are small they are absolutely indistinguishable. Though the steelhead turns a bright silver in the sea, he gradually darkens again when he returns to his river, and the bold, red rainbow stripe reappears down his sides. Why, fishermen have asked for decades, do some rainbows go to sea and some stay content to live out their lives in fresh water?

For the answer it is necessary to go back millions of years to the ice age—to a time before the existence of the fresh-water streams up which the steelhead and other anadromous fishes now make their adventurous voyages into the coastal valleys. A prehistoric sea trout spawned in brackish waters at the feet of glaciers, and from him both strains of fish have descended. As the glaciers receded, and rivers formed, these prehistoric trout went farther and farther inland to spawn. During the immense period of time this process involved, some of them—the rainbows—became physically accustomed to fresh water, perhaps after being landlocked by slides or disturbance of terrain, and doubtless then only after finding water containing enough minerals and feed to allow the strongest to survive. The steelhead, however, went on returning to the ocean.

Over the centuries—despite their identical appearance—the two strains of trout have developed differences in organic function. The body fluids of both must still contain 75/100ths of one per cent salt if they are to live—the same percentage which existed in the brackish waters from which their common ancestor stemmed. To maintain this balance, the fresh-water rainbow has developed gills and kidneys capable of conserving salt and throwing off water. But the ocean is two per cent saline, and the organs of the sea-going steelhead perform a reverse function—they throw off salt and conserve water. A rainbow will die after a half hour in the ocean. But a little steelhead, who looks exactly like him, develops a salt deficiency when he is seven and one-half to eight inches long (and probably other needs, as well, since his streams are low in cobalt, iodine, and calcium). He grows restless, he loses appetite, his scales become deciduous, and he heads downstream for the sea, where he grows prodigiously.

In some respects, he is probably closer to the famed Atlantic salmon—which, despite its name, is a trout, too—than to his own blood brothers, the rainbow. Anglers who have caught both tend to speak of them only in contrast, but fisheries experts, confronted by a Pacific steelhead and an Atlantic salmon, both fresh from the ocean (and thus a common silver color) have been unable to decide which was which; they are, in essence, the same fish. For all his similarity to the Atlantic salmon, however, the steelhead has adapted himself to his own environment in distinctive ways during his eon of adventuring from the Pacific into the western valleys of the North American continent.

All steelhead spawn in the early spring, but they swim up rivers of varying length to do so. Since some, as a consequence, must start their journeys earlier than others, they have divided themselves into three separate races: the great race of winter-run fish, which enter streams in the cold months; the summer-run fish, which come into rivers in July and August; and a group which runs into the Columbia River in April and May.

All of these fish are virtually indistinguishable to the eye (although body shapes and coloring may vary subtly from one watershed to the next), and all carry amazing supplies of fuel as they start upstream. For sheer performance, however, the spring- and summer-run fish are seldom matched in nature; they come from the ocean prepared to stay in fresh water from eight to eleven months, and some of them to swim all the way into the wilds of Idaho or eastern British Columbia, there to perform the reproductive function—and they are prepared to manage all these labors without any feeding worthy of the name.

Men have caught scores of steelhead, and have inevitably found their stomachs empty; thus it is popularly supposed in many quarters that they do not feed at all in rivers. Actually they do, and at times on very odd fodder—mice and birds' feathers, for instance—and it is this instinct which makes them attack bait and lures which Pacific salmon will refuse in streams. But the flesh and internal cavities of steelhead are so packed with vital oils, fats, salts, and minerals when they leave the sea that their stomachs are squeezed almost to the point of uselessness by the riches in their bodies. There is logic in this: the rivers contain little feed during the cold months, and even in the summertime the coastal streams of the Northwest lack the heavy insect life and big fly hatches of more easterly waters.

During all his time in the river, the steelhead is marvelously governed—both as a game fish and as a creature intent on reproducing his own kind—by water temperatures. A steelhead is only infinitesimally warmer than the water in which he swims. He will die after a while in water colder than 36° because his metabolism slows to a point at which it cannot compete with the natural forces of breakdown in his body. At 39° he is logy and unresponsive; at 40°, if hooked, he will often be disappointingly easy to land, but at 42° or 43° he will go berserk at the first feel of the snubbing rod.

He comes into rivers and does most of his upstream traveling in them when they are high, protectively discolored and generally unfishable; not because he cannot swim in shallows but because streams almost invariably grow cold when they are low and clear in the winter. The sea stays at 45°, and he tends to linger off rivermouths, like a man hesitating to step into a cold bath, until they warm and flood with rain. Once in fresh water he will pause in holes and runs when freezes set in; thus the angler, who needs clear water, is eternally forced out in horrible weather, both when streams are dropping or when they first begin to warm (a word used only relatively) and rise.

Each occasional increase in stream temperatures, too, brings the female fish closer to ripeness. Steelhead have a passion for survival; the parent fish spawn in the main channels of streams under moving and aerated water where there is little chance that drought can expose the nest or redd. Female steelhead construct these incubators by lying on their sides over gravel bottom and undulating rhythmically—thus creating a hydraulic force which dredges a depression in the stream bed for them. The nests are four or five feet long and eighteen inches deep; when the eggs are ejected and fertilized, the current washes the disturbed gravel back into the depression and covers them.

Once they are buried, the eggs will hatch in fifty days at an average water temperature of 50°—but will take five days longer for each degree of cold below this level. As a result, the tiny, newly hatched fish are seldom thrown into the world until spring has really begun. Even so, they lead a rugged life. They must fight their way up through a foot and a half of sand and gravel after emerging from the egg, and, once free in the water, they become the pawns of fatalistic instinct. Though only three-fourths of an inch long, they start confidently downstream to seek a place of their own along the banks and shallows; those which cannot find unoccupied growing space swim serenely on into salt water and perish, sacrifices to the need for an uncrowded river and the demands of their luckier brothers and sisters.

Of all the anadromous fishes of the Pacific, the steelhead serves the severest apprenticeship for the sea; western salmon leave the stream by the time they are a year old, some of them after only ninety days. But the steelhead stays two years, and only the fittest of his number survive. He goes seaward, moreover, only in March, April or May. If he develops the physiological need for salt water later in the year he will stubbornly resist it until the next spring and will die rather than violate his timetable. He is born with an instinct for hiding himself—no matter how restless he is, he will not start for the ocean except in the dark of the moon, or on cloudy nights or when the water is murky from rains.

In the ocean the steelhead feeds greedily on shrimp and herring, avoids—if he can—marauding sharks and seals, and grows tremendously. In twenty or twenty-one months he weighs from six to eleven pounds and heads back toward land, guided to his own stream (there are 142 steelhead rivers in Washington alone) by that mysterious homing instinct common to all salmonoid fishes. An appointed few of his number, linger for yet another year in the ocean. These reluctant fish are nature's insurance against some home-stream disaster which might wipe out the run, and they follow the next winter, bearing seed which would re-establish their strain. They—and those steelhead which are able to spawn more than once—are the angler's prizes; they weigh twenty, twenty-five, even thirty pounds and are awesome creatures to cross.

The pursuit of steelhead has gone on in the Northwest for over half a century but for most of that time only the hardiest and most dedicated of fishermen braved the cold along the wintry streams. The only lure used was a walnut-size cluster of salmon eggs—a commodity which imparts a gloriously fishy stench to the person. Some fishermen "plunked" them—that is, sank a baited hook and a chunk of lead in a deep hole and simply waited for a fish to hook himself. Most anglers "drifted"—that is, they cast a lightly weighted bait across a stream and allowed it to bump along the bottom in a long arc. Plunking was slow. Drifting demanded long practice, sometimes years of it, for a steelhead does not strike salmon eggs, but only mouths them delicately, and proper use of a level-wind reel is not learned in a day.

In the years after World War II, however, two handy and efficient devices suddenly set off today's stampede to the steelhead streams. The spinning reel made every dub an expert caster, and a Seattle barber named Willis B. Korff invented a curious new lure, the Cherry Bobber, which permitted a tyro to hook a steelhead. The original bobber was simply a round piece of wood, the size and color of a cherry, which sported a rotating brass spinner, and a naked treble hook. For reasons best known to himself, the steelhead snatched at this gadget with alacrity when it was drifted near him on the bottom, and usually did so with a jerk which instantly informed the angler that he was jugular-to-jugular with the foe.

The steelhead boom has been growing ever since; when compared to the tradition-governed and selective convocations of the Atlantic salmon fisherman, it is an anarchistic phenomenon, full of the fever and opportunism of an early western land rush. The private water and club rules of Scottish and Canadian salmon streams do not exist in the Northwest—every man, woman, and child has access to streams and the right to take steelhead—and there are no revered and ancient methods.

The Cherry Bobber has been followed by the "clown bobber," a smaller wooden bead painted yellow with red spots, the Hoh Bug, a lure carved from cottonwood roots, and the "spinning bobber," which is equipped with vanes, somewhat like a Devon. It has been discovered that the steelhead will hit small spoons—that he will, in fact, hit a bare hook which has been festooned with a few threads of fluorescent red or lime-green wool yarn.

All these lures are drifted on the bottom, like the salmon eggs which the skilled and recalcitrant oldtimers still use. But in this evolution of technique drift fishing grows increasingly sportier—more and more fishermen are adopting a five-and-one-half- or six-ounce glass rod which is stiff in the butt and sensitive in the tip, light monofilament lines (since they are easier to cast), even lighter leaders (to prevent breaking the line itself when the hook snags) and as little weight as possible in the interests of a free and natural drift.

Almost every innovation, in fact, seems to lead drift fishing closer to sporting ideals; a yarn-covered hook, after all, is a sort of wet fly even though it is cast differently and weighted with a bit of lead. And a stubborn and long-suffering minority of purists has meanwhile been borrowing from the drifters to prove that steelhead, which have long been taken on flies in the warm, summer-run streams, can also be taken with them in the winter when they stay deep in the chill current and when insect life is nonexistent. The trick: "shooting" light monofilament behind quick-sinking fly lines (some of them made of glass) to get distance and depth, and "dredging the bottom" with wet flies in such local patterns as Brad's Brat and Stillaguamish Belle.

The unique and heartening aspect of the steelhead stampede, however, is concerned with the life and times of the steelhead himself. The big trout, who might very well have been on his way to extinction under the present remorseless attack, is actually increasing mightily. Thanks to a burly near-genius named Clarence Pautzke, there are more fish in many streams in 1957 than there were before steelhead fishing began. Pautzke—a former University of Washington football player who is now the Washington State Game Department's chief fisheries biologist—has shrewdly capitalized on two aspects of the steelhead's life (that he will automatically go to sea when he reaches a certain size and that as a mature fish he needs little or no feed in streams) to prove that unlimited runs of big, fighting fish can be installed in any steelhead river.

The reasoning which led him to his triumph—unprecedented in three thousand years of fish culture—seems simple enough in retrospect. In stocking any stream, man is limited by the amount of feed available; put two thousand fish in water capable of supporting only one thousand, and half will die or will be stunted. This is as true of young steelhead during their formative times in streams as any other trout. But, Pautzke thought, why not raise the fish in ponds until they actually felt the urge to go to salt water, use the streams merely as chutes to send them out to the ocean's rich feeding grounds, wait two years, and—presto—get back hundreds, thousands, even millions of big, healthy trout?

It has worked. Guided, in part, by some earlier work by Dr. Lauren R. Donaldson, of the University of Washington School of Fisheries, and Thor Gudjonsson (a former graduate student, now Director of Fisheries Research for Iceland), Pautzke force-feeds his small fish and brings them to the sea-going stage in one year instead of two.

To protect them when they go downstream, he has banned spring fishing for fresh-water trout on scores of streams. This was a necessity, since a little sea-bound steelhead is virtually indistinguishable from a legal-size, eight-inch rainbow, but it was not accomplished without setting off a fearful roar of protest from thwarted opening-day anglers. Pautzke cunningly stilled the clamor by putting rainbows in Washington's numerous lowland lakes (where they grew bigger than they ever had in the streams) and by using them to divert and satisfy the rush of spring trout fishermen. The tons of eight-inch steelhead which are sloshed into Washington's streams from a huge tank truck each spring no longer need run a gantlet of fly rods. By planting one million fish a year, Pautzke has added 100,000 gleaming steelhead (which some fishermen call Pautzke's Pets) to the normal run. With more money and more equipment he expects to produce a million lusty big fish; Oregon and British Columbia are, meanwhile, instituting downstream stocking programs, too.

This philosophy of producing rather than conserving fish is at the heart of the whole exciting steelhead boom, and its greatest departure from the attitudes and methods of Eastern and European salmon culture. Pautzke, a man who looks, and often talks like a Cowlitz Valley logger, would doubtless shake the very soul of a conservation-minded Scottish laird. He haunts the streams, often with rod in hand, and exults at the sight of steelhead on the bank. "Look at those beautiful bastards," he sometimes shouts. "Catch them all. There's more where they came from!"

The steelhead, himself, puts it differently. "Catch me," he says with his first leap, "if you can."

SALMON IN CONNEMARA AND IN DEVON

Arnold Gingrich

Fishing, if 1 a fisher may protest,
Of pleasures is the sweetest, of sports the best,
Of exercises the most excellent,
Of recreations the most innocent,
But now the sport is marred, and wott ye why?
Fishes decrease, and fishers multiply.

—THOMAS BASTARD, in
Chrestoleros, 1598

MOST TROUT FISHERMEN I KNOW, in these latter days of greatly heightened fishing pressure on streams, where the anglers appear to outnumber the fish, approach their sport with the attitude of the gambler who, on being told that the roulette wheel was crooked, said: "I know, but what can I do? It's the only wheel in town."

The alternative, to the monotony and frustration of seasonal servitude spent whipping the riffs and eddies of overfished or fished-out streams, is to take off for as long as you can get away, for one of the places where the fishing is, well, never guaranteed—as we all learn sometime, and some sooner than others—but so carefully tended and preserved and reserved that, by contrast at least, it's likely to seem so wonderful that you remain in a state of euphoria verging on beatitude for a year after you get back, and figure you're still way ahead on points even if you go fishless for the rest of the season.

Ireland is one recommendation. A great advantage it has is that your wife will probably like it, and if the only way you can get in any far-away fishing is by combining it with a vacation trip, then Ireland is a good bet. So many people just assume that fishing takes you to such interesting places, but in general the places with the most interesting fishing are the least likely to be interesting for any other reason. Ireland is a blessed exception.

Now that the jets overfly it, Shannon Airport is more of a treat than it was when all the flights by the northern route had to stop there. And it still is, as it was then, the world's greatest bargain basement, and particularly succulent to the tastes and wants of women shoppers. The restaurant there, too, is one of the best anywhere, and if you were to come away from the bargain counters of the duty-free shopping center for no longer than it takes to sample their bread and their tea, you still might go away saying it was one of the taste sensations of your life. Irish bread and Irish butter are both so superb that, whenever you get back to them, you wonder how in the meantime you could have made do with less. Their tea, too, is highly habit-forming, made, as our ghillie Laurence O'Malley said, "strong enough to trot a horse upon." And as for Irish coffee—not that you have to go to Shannon Airport any more to get it—it will still remind you of Shannon wherever you get it afterward, if you first sampled it there. With its witty recipe and its inimitable flavor, it's as close to nectar as the gods will ever let us get:

> Cream rich as a brogue,
> Coffee strong as a friendly hand,
> Sugar sweet as the tongue of a rogue,
> Whisky smooth as the wit of the land.

Before you ever get to where you're going to fish, you're very likely to be so well disposed, and so is your wife, that the fishing may seem better than it is. For one thing, since salmon fishing has been so long known as the sport of kings, you'll feel that in one respect at least you're living up to its name, if you do it from a hotel that is a castle, like Ballynahinch, at Ballinafad, County Galway, or Ashford Castle, at Cong, County Mayo. Paradoxically, the best fishing at Ashford Castle is, or at least was, away over in the very shadow of Ballynahinch in Connemara, some thirty miles west of Cong, where Noel Huggard, the proprietor of Ashford Castle, has, or at any rate had, a magnificent beat, or stand, at the "butt" of Lough Derryclare, at the point where it forms a bubble in the flow of the

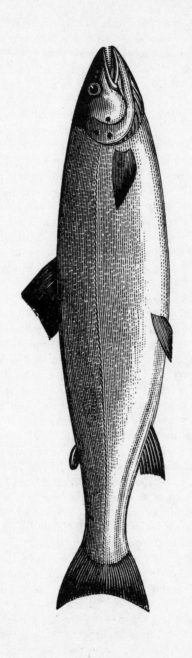

Ballynahinch River to the sea. This, and the other beats on the Ballynahinch River that belong to Ballynahinch Castle, are superb spots for the postgraduate trout fisherman who wants to take salmon on his trout tackle. The fish are unlikely to run much over ten pounds, but will give you a very lively show on any rod under five ounces, and a real picnic on rods under three.

Ashford Castle itself is on Lough Corrib, at Cong, which is in County Mayo, just over the line to the east of Connemara, and most of its guests fish from boats, on the lake. So before you go there, unless you're ready to settle for boat fishing, you'd better check to see whether Noel Huggard still has any river beats for salmon, such as he had in the past, or can arrange some for you. If he can, then Ashford Castle is the place to stay. You come to the castle through the twisting streets of Cong, the picturesque little village where the movie *The Quiet Man* was made. As you go past the pub of the film, which turns out to be a general store in actuality, you see the spot in the river where the film showed the priest engaged in a Homeric battle with a salmon. We both suspected that salmon of being no fish when we saw the film, and sure enough we met him personally when we got to Ashford Castle; a six-footer named Laurence O'Malley, one of Ashford's ghillies. He it was who was tugging like a Trojan, out of sight of the camera, at the other end of the priest's line, in a scene that was funny but wouldn't have fooled one fisherman in ten thousand. You turn in to the gatehouse at the entrance to the grounds of Ashford Castle, passing the majestic ruins of the Royal Abbey of Cong, which dates from the twelfth century, when it was erected on the site of a twice-burned monastery founded in A.D. 623. The oldest part of the castle dates back to the year 1228, and this and successive additions to it had fallen into ruin by 1852, the year of the great famine, when Guinness, the famous brewer of Guinness Stout, bought it from the Ashford Estate and set about restoring it. His son, Lord Ardilaun, spent well over a million prewar pounds on the castle alone, before his death in 1915, to say nothing of what he spent on the grounds, which by his time had grown to 35,000 acres.

As a hotel, Ashford Castle dates back only to the early summer of 1939, when it was acquired, with three hundred acres of the surrounding grounds, from the trust representing the Guinness interests, by Noel Huggard, whose family owns other distinctive hotels in Waterville and Killarney. He and his wife Angela are the perfect prototypes of a county hunting couple, and staying as a hotel guest in their company gives you the illusion of living in a sporting and holiday residence of more than baronial affluence. For this "small hotel" is small only in the sense that the space set aside for the accommodation of the paying guests is proportionate, in relation to the sprawling splendor of the whole, to the exposed portion of an iceberg. For Ashford Castle has its own farm, dairy, slaughterhouse, and butchery, as well as a fishery and salmon smoking plant. Its grounds include a maze, a beach, a cinema, a tackle shop, flower gardens, and vegetable gardens, as well as an ornamental Japanese garden, a deer park, an eel weir, tennis courts and garages, and a slipway for seaplanes. Edward VII spent a month there, as a Guinness guest. Today's guest is likely to feel that the treatment now can hardly be less royal than it was then. Paul Gallico, for instance, went there once for a week and stayed three months.

Noel Huggard has fished for salmon all his life, and if he sizes you up as a truly addicted angler, which he can do after one swift glance at your fly boxes, he will send you to his choicest beat, the stand at the Derryclare Butts. If he sizes you up as a Sunday fisherman, he'll stick you in a boat and figure you'll be happier there, and of course quite possibly you will, because it's no trick at all to pull in hefty brown trout, mighty salmon, or fearsome pike, trolling in Lough Corrib, practically within the shadow of his castle walls. But once you've left the lush greenery of County Mayo and begin the climb into the highlands of Connemara, where there's almost always a rainbow somewhere over the winding roads, over the heather and the gorse, and once you've crossed the bog from the high road down to the butt of Derryclare, you'll have the time of your fishing life—that is, you will if you go any time from mid-April to the end of May, when the salmon are almost sure to be in.

If your tackle is as light as it should be for maximum enjoyment—a bamboo trout rod with a tippet of no more than 2X—you'll lose a lot of salmon, because you can't follow them off the jetties where you hook them, but you'll be storing up memories, in the process, that will last you for decades. And losing them in decent proportion to the number you land is the only way to be sporting about this fishing, because the fish belong to the hotel, and the ghillie works for the hotel all the time and for you only while you're there. The ghillie gaffs the fish, and a fish gaffed is a fish done for. Jane had an eleven-pounder, which took her twenty-three minutes to play, on her two-piece 8-foot 4¼-ounce Orvis, with a 16-foot leader tapered to 2X, hooked on a size 4 Mar Lodge. The fish had given her a great show, running out the backing beyond the first hundred yards. The backing was black for the first hundred yards; beneath it I had wound another hundred yards of white backing around the core of her Landex reel, and she and Laurence O'Malley both shouted across the jetty, to where I was fishing from the other side, that the fish was running all the backing out. I shouted back that it couldn't, but they insisted that it was, as they saw what they thought was the bare reel spool appearing beneath the last black strands of the first hundred yards. Within seconds the argument was settled, as the fish tore on out, and the white backing unreeled to follow him. That will give you an idea of the head of steam that a spring-run Irish salmon, fresh in and with the sea lice still on him, can build up when you're playing him on tackle light enough that you don't dare do anything but let him run.

When the fish was reeled in to where the leader was starting to come through the guides, Jane said: "Laurence, that's a noble fish—I want to release him."

Laurence, poised with the gaff, gave her such a black Irish look as to make it questionable whether he intended to use the gaff on the fish or on her, and muttering something about the one way to put an end to any such talk as that, strode in over his boot tops to gaff the fish with merciless finality.

Our salmon at Derryclare ran ten, eleven, and fourteen pounds, and that's about the range you can expect most of them to be, although they have been taken there as small as six and as large as twenty. One wonderful afternoon in mid-June of 1936, three rods took ten salmon there, from six and a half to twenty, and in 1921 one rod killed thirty-six salmon there between mid-April and the end of May. The record of the Ballynahinch Castle fishing is even more impressive, one rod having taken fourteen salmon there in a day. Their stretch consists of the Ballynahinch River, below Derryclare, flowing for about three miles from Lake Ballynahinch into Cashel Bay; the beats consist of a series of pools and flats, practically every yard of which is fishable except in spate, down to the Tombeeola Bridge.

Between Ashford Castle and Ballynahinch Castle you pass through the Joyces' country, which at first hearing you of course associate with *Ulysses,* until you find out that it is so named because it is full of Joyces, not one of whom ever heard of James. North of Ashford Castle, and a bit east, is Lough Carra, between Ballinrobe and Castlebar, all full of associations if you're old enough to be a George Moore fan; but he wasn't a fisherman, and there's no special attraction there for the angler. Lough Carra does have some very big brown trout, averaging twice the size of those of Conn and Corrib, but as far as I'm concerned all three are just so much more boat fishing. But where you go in Ireland depends largely on when you can get away, and for how long. If you have a month, you can get around to several districts.

The big fish are in the Blackwater, of course, and especially in the famous beat at Careysville, owned by the Lismore Estates Company, Lismore, County Waterford. Four salmon of over 50 pounds were taken in the Blackwater between 1903 and 1930. There were even more of that size, six to be exact, taken in that same period from the Shannon, but the hydroelectric scheme ruined the fishing there for a matter of decades after that, and the Shannon has only recently shown signs of coming back. So if it's size that matters to you most, then your first choice practically has to be the Blackwater, between Fermoy and Lismore. Your next choice would probably, on this basis, be the Suir from Carrick to Clonmel, where the largest Irish salmon ever caught on rod and reel, a fifty-seven-pounder, was taken back in 1874.

But while there's a status-factor, in that there's a certain amount of dining-out to be done on the mere fact that you've fished the Blackwater, I'd opt for Connemara if I had time for only one district. Connemara is Iceland, but with trees, for the wild and rugged aspect of its lanscape, and for the quick comings and goings of its showers and its sunshines. There's something awesomely Wagnerian about the lowering clouds that wreath the hills among which you wind and turn, in Connemara as in Iceland. And there's the same effect on the fish, it seems: I often noticed, in both places, how the emergence of the sun for a brief bright interval between the overcast and the showers would seem to wake them up like an alarm clock, and as the sun broke through you'd tend to grip your rod a little tighter, bracing for the sudden savage pull that so often came at just that moment. The two places are alike, too, in the infrequency with which you encounter raffic other than horse-drawn, as you motor to and from your fishing spots. In Ireland, however, the carts turn out to be pulled, more often than not, by donkeys. But when it comes to the frequency with which you pass pubs, then all resemblance ceases. In Ireland the pubs are delightful, and seemingly omnipresent, and on the days when you've taken salmon, you are a clod if you don't stop in at some of them, to buy your ghillie a Guinness. In Iceland, on the other hand, since there are no pubs to be passed, you have your own Black Death right on the stream, in any Icelander's haversack, so there's no occasion for this ritual that adds such a warm touch to the Irish fishing.

Much depends on time and money, but if neither is too limited, an ideal month in Ireland, from mid-April to mid-May, could be divided, more or less equally according to how the luck sped you on or held you back, among these four spots, any of which can be reached within three hours' driving time from Shannon. First, a week fishing out of either Ashford Castle or Ballynahinch Castle—and I say first because there's always the chance that things might be popping enough at either that you'd say the hell with the rest of the schedule and just stay on. Second, a week on the Blackwater, anywhere you can get on it, from Mallow to Lismore. Third, a week at the Butler Arms, Waterville, County Kerry, fishing the Currane. It would be good to have this particular week abut the week at Ashford Castle, since the same family owns both places and if you wanted to arrive early or late at either, depending on the way your luck was going, you could let them straighten out your schedule between them. Fourth, a week on the Ilen, at Skibbereen, if only for the piquancy it would lend your future small talk, to be able to refer to "one time at Skibbereen." If any of the last three didn't work out, when it came time to nail down definite dates and reservations, you could always take a week on the Maigue, fishing out of the hotel at Adare, County Limerick. It's a lovely little village and the hotel is quaint. It's very close to Shannon, and you could make it either your first week after arrival, while the dates for some of the other places might be firming up, or your last before leaving.

Whatever you do, and before you do anything, get a copy of *The Angler's Guide to Ireland,* published by the Bord Failte Eirann (the Irish Tourist Board), which is frequently revised, comprehensive and knowledgeable, utterly without puffery, and tells you all you need to know, in angling terms, about all the places you might want to fish. As anglers' reading it is delightful: it tells all about the right flies and the right sizes for the different times and places, and is as witty as it is wise.

As refreshing as Connemara, in its remoteness, its utter "awayness" from any angling scenes or surroundings you're likely to have known at home, is Devon, to which I was sent by a book about fishing, so if you should ever happen to go there after, if not directly because of, reading this, then it would be a double dose of poetic justice. In Devon you feel that you're five hundred miles and five hundred years away from everything you've ever seen or known. Every inn seems to date from 1450, and every church seems to date from 1140. You drive on the left because it's in England, but the distinction is academic, since there's really neither right nor left to roads that have only a middle. You poke about the lovely Devon countryside, going to and from your fishing, in narrow country lanes that seem like so many green tunnels, with their borders of hedges that are anywhere from shoulder to head high. You meet other cars, of course, but when you do you'll get out and he'll get out, and you have a nice friendly and ever so sporting discussion concerning the relative distances which one of you will have to drive backwards to get to the nearest of those occasional spots wide enough to permit you to pass each other in your opposed directions. These chance encounters turn out to be a large part of the fun, and in between times you're enjoying the narrow winding roads in a way that you'd long since forgotten roads could be enjoyed. You find yourself trying to remember whether it was Chesterton or Belloc who memorialized "the rolling English drunkard who laid out the rolling English roads."

Getting there was half the fun, just as the Cunard people say about crossing the Atlantic, though in my case it turned out to apply to crossing England, by a slow train out of Waterloo Station. I had read about Hatherleigh, in Devon, in Bernard Venables's then newest book, *The Angler's Companion,* published in London in 1958 by George Allen & Unwin, Ltd., and distributed in this country by Macmillan. The British Railways people in New York seemed to know no more about Hatherleigh than I did; in fact, much less, since I had just been reading Venables, and apparently they hadn't, so they said the best they could do would be to sell me a ticket to Torrington, thirteen miles away, and I would have to shift for myself from there, by cart or by cab or however. Bless them forever for their ignorance, because the slow train to Devonshire wound up toward the Bristol Channel and back down again, making a sort of shepherd's crook beyond Exeter, until it came back down again to Torrington. That part of the ride must have consumed more than an hour of the five hours and some minutes that the train took, in all, to come from London.

It was the best part of the trip. Up to Exeter the stops had been for towns, whereas beyond, the train seemed to be stopping for every cow-crossing. Literally, those last fifteen or twenty stops seemed almost all to have to do with picking up milk pails. But the train ride was, in and of itself, so wonderful—with the hominess of its old-fashioned plush-lined compartment, the unhurried pleasure of frequent ambles back and forth to the restaurant car, which seemed to be run, like a Central European café, on the principle that you were welcome at all hours, however little or much you cared to eat or drink on any one visit to it— so that, between the two places, we were both sorry when the journey ended, like coming to the last page of a book you have loved.

It was only after we'd been in Hatherleigh a while, and were thinking about the arrangements for our return trip to London, that we discovered that Exeter, which we had passed through before undertaking that last shepherd's-crook ride up along the Bristol Channel for the lovely last hour of the trip, is only nine miles from Hatherleigh. Since the hour we would have saved, if we had got off originally at Exeter, would have lost us a dozen memorable sights, and would itself have no doubt been forgotten within a day, we both felt grateful for the ignorance of the British Railways clerk in New York who had booked us to Torrington—"as near as you can get" to Hatherleigh from London. Since the only possible point of traveling for pleasure is the way it papers the walls of memory, that slow train to Devonshire had given us the extra dividend of an hour's added pleasure.

That was 1959, and the trains may no longer be so bucolic. I remember, a year or so ago, being told that the only good train left in this country is *The Lark*, from Los Angeles to San Francisco, and that in this day of being uncomfortably buffeted about, faster than you care to go, from pure jet to turboprop and back again, it would be worth taking, just as a pleasure trip. *The Lark* didn't leave until nine at night, but it would be wonderful, I was told, to get on it any time after six o'clock in the evening, dine leisurely and well, enjoy the sights of the beautiful coast from the big dining-car windows, and then get off in the morning in San Francisco. Since I had successive dates in the two cities, I decided to try it. It wasn't easy. I had to book my ticket from Los Angeles to San Francisco and pay for it in advance from New York, and then go pick it up at the station in Los Angeles. This had to be done before a given hour or the reservation might lapse, despite the fact that the ticket had been paid for. When I got to the station to pick up the ticket, I asked the man at the ticket window about dining on *The Lark* "any time after six o'clock."

"Well, hell, the train don't go till nine," he answered.

"I know," I said, "but I was told that one of the big attractions is the nice dinner you serve from six o'clock on."

"They *is* a snack car," he admitted, "where they might could give you a san'wich 'n' a coke 'er somethin' by say maybe quarter *of* nine."

So much for the wonderful tips you get from your friends about travel. The next time I saw my friend who had touted me onto *The Lark*, I asked him if he had been larking me, or had it been that long since he had taken *The Lark* himself.

"Oh well," he confessed upon reflection, "it must be five or six years since I've taken it, come to think of it."

So, come to think of it, in this epoch of change that wonderful slow train to Devonshire, out of Waterloo Station, perhaps should not be urged upon you too insistently as being the better half of the fun of getting to Hatherleigh. Maybe, although at the time nothing could have seemed less likely, even Hatherleigh itself has changed. And we all know—don't we?—how fishing can change, not only from season to season but even from one day to the next.

Our Christmas card lists reveal the fact that, even in the course of these relatively few years of its long history, the George Hotel at Hatherleigh (established 1450) has changed, at least to the extent that its very gentle proprietor, Mr. Herbert Simmons, is no longer there. So, before you go to Hatherleigh, you'd better check the guide called *Fishing in Britain and Northern Ireland,* put out by the British Travel Association, to see whether the George Hotel is still listed. If it isn't, or if they can't or won't have you, or if the place has been torn down, you're still all right. Try the Half Moon Inn, the hotel in Sheepwash—I swear I'm not making this up—which is as close to this particular spot on the Torridge as the George Hotel in Hatherleigh is. The Half Moon, Sheepwash, Devon.

But before I assume that you're going, just listen to what got me to go there, and see if you can resist it any more than I could. Hear now Bernard Venables, in *The Angler's Companion,* a book you ought to read anyway, if you ever go to England:

> Close to Devon's north coast on the Cornish border the River Torridge starts. At its mouth it empties into Bideford Bay, sharing an estuary with the Taw. Between it runs a circuitous course, making a great horseshoe into the warm and rolling Devon hinterland. It is not a great river as Wye and Tay are great; there is no sense of majesty, wild or stately, which is often the association of salmon fishing. It is a small river by such standards; it runs intimately with its landscape rather than with splendour. Its prospects usually are short ones, steep and enclosed.

> But it has a beauty, of its special Devon kind, to enchant and still a troubled mind. In its deep valley, under the tree hung crests, there is a seclusion as gently rurally perfect as is to be found in England. The river runs quietly, except in spates, swirling a little, in places breaking over the stones, but only seldom being riotous, making a lulling dappling sound. The sheep in the fields that hang on the falling faces of the hills bleat gruffly, pigeons coo; the lark rises in a placid ecstasy. The buzzard flies in leisurely sweeps, quartering the valley and calling continuously in its mournful mewing voice. At Hatherleigh, in April, where the river is on the bend of its horseshoe shape, the feeling of the valley's removal from the harsher farther world saps all sense of urgency.

> There, there is a beat that the author knows. The road runs to it from Hatherleigh, running narrowly and inconsequentially, into the valleys and over the hills, up into the looming sight of Dartmoor, down into the high-hedged hollows, past a village, past a pretty pub. Then falling twisting under a shade of trees and past stone cottages to a bridge where the water starts, an ancient narrow massive bridge, patched with golden lichen on the stone, grown with ferns, little and leathery, in the crevices.

> The beat runs upstream from there, with the bank on the narrow flatness of the close-turfed meadow under the forest of the sudden hillside. The road is little frequented; off the road and up the bank, even that small traffic is forgotten, and there will be no more intrusion than, once in a while, the bailiff treading his mildly admonitory rounds, insuring that the fisherman does not lawlessly fish without a license.

> The river's run of spring fish is at its best in April, and that is as happy a circumstance as there could be. Under the edge of the hand of the hill, against the hedges, down to the water, there are the primroses; the milkmaids

grow with them, and out across the meadow. There are the early purple orchids, and on the warmer days there are the first bees humming and the brimstone butterfly on the wing. Then, to confirm the rising glow of hope, a salmon jumps in the pool above the bridge.

Where the fishing usually starts, in the pool by the hut, by a bend in the river, the water has so promising a look on a fine April day, and when the level is right, that it can hardly be envisaged that a salmon will not be caught—and indeed, on that pool, one often is caught. It is so encouraging a pool to fish, unlike the vast expanses on some greater rivers; its nature can be encompassed by the studying eye. Where the fish are known to lie, the reason for their lying is plainly to be seen—so often not the case in salmon fishing. Each cast is made in warm expectancy. The fly is coaxed and worked along the submerged sheltering shelf of rock, with expectation tingling in the senses from moment to moment. But, when the joyful emergency does come, the rod does throb and bend, and then presently the fish—always so unimaginably big—does show, there is always the same amazed delight that so big and far-travelled a fish could come out of this small river. But indeed, this sense of scarcely believable revelation is an inseparable part of all salmon fishing so far as the author is concerned. Every salmon caught is as hard to believe as the first one was.

There is, broadly, and for no reason that has so far emerged precisely, a connection between the size of a river and the size of its salmon. The Torridge is not a big fish river. In the spring some will weigh no more than eight pounds; most will be about ten or twelve pounds. One of fifteen pounds is a big fish.

Oh 'tis true, 'tis true. Oh excellent author, oh venerable and venerated Venables, every blessed least word turned out to be true, down to the last one, for no fish exceeded fourteen pounds. And the beat described was instantly recognizable, from "the looming sight of Dartmoor" on, around the bends and past the hedges, and the pretty village and the pub, until the ancient narrow lichened stone bridge hove into view. Going over the hills from Hatherleigh, we soon learned enough Devonian weather lore to know that if you can see Dartmoor plain, then tomorrow there'll be rain. Dartmoor, where there's a big prison, is probably a grim sight close up, but it's beautiful from far off, though its beauty may be lost on you if you have something on for the morrow that can be spoiled by rain. In the blessed Devon sunshine, when we ran the little Wolseley up to the crest of that one hill, we always hoped to see it wreathed in mist. In Devon, though, much as I hate to indulge in the pathetic fallacy, even the rain somehow seems friendlier than it ever felt anywhere else. For one thing, after you've been there for more than a day or so, you find yourself dressing for it, and for another, as in the classic case of hitting yourself on the head with a hammer, it's so wonderful when it stops.

It was on that beat, in lambent sunshine between the flowering trees, that Jane cast not wisely but so well, across the river and into the *crise* of a tennis elbow, and it was on that beat, so well portrayed in words by Venables, that the last word of his prophecy was fulfilled, for the bailiff, the man from the river board, duly found us there on his "mildly admonitory round," and though he was polite and friendly, almost genial, in exchanging gossip about what fish had been taken when in the previous few days, he still didn't fail to bring the conversation at last around to the point where, after a deprecatory little cough, he said: "Of course you both have your licenses." And upon being assured that we did, he still wondered if we "didn't mind" showing them to him. So every word that Bernard Venables wrote about Hatherleigh and the Torridge was true. How many angling books, do you suppose, would pass such a test?

But there were other beats in the vicinity, no less wonderful, that he had not mentioned, and one of them was at another bend in the river, at Iddesleigh, bordering the plowed fields of Mr. James Banbury, a gentleman farmer with racing cars in one of his barns. Mr. Jim, wearing riding breeches and a venerable tweed jacket, and using a small tractor as his cockhorse, would come riding over his hills to point out the best lies on his water, and there the stream was even smaller, making the fish seem even more "unimaginably big." The one trouble with Mr. Jim's water, almost every time we fished it, was that it was full of jumping salmon, but jumping in that high pole-vaulter's leap that always means they are jumping for joy, or to get rid of sea lice, or for no good reason at all, except that the one thing they won't do then is take a fly. When they leap in the low arc of a man diving off a bank, instead of a high board, then they mean business and you'll take them, but you won't as long as they're jumping.

At one of the favorite salmon lies on his water, which Mr. Jim was kind enough to point out to me, I saw a salmon that looked "unimaginably big," as advertised by Bernard Venables, meaning that it probably ran about fourteen pounds, and this one, for once, was holding still and not jumping out of the stream like the popping kernels in a pan of popcorn, as so many of the others had been. I cast to him, very carefully, using Mr. Jim's favorite fly, a number 5 low-water Black Doctor. The fly lit well above him, and I was grateful to see that it was swinging on a straight line, with no slack, just below the surface, where in a few seconds it would pass right over his head—upon which a fourteen-inch brown trout swirled up from nowhere and made off with it.

Oh irony—back home on the Beaverkill or the Esopus, I'd have wanted to give that fourteen-inch brownie at least a fourteen-gun salute, but here on the Torridge, where he came between me and a fish that might well have gone as many pounds as he represented in inches, I cursed him roundly, and couldn't wait to get him in and brush him off the hook. I tossed him back so cavalierly, giving him the bum's rush without a thought as to how and where he landed in the water, in contrast to the loving stroking I would normally give such a fish when heading him gently back upstream to give him the benefit of the revivifying effect of the current, that after a few minutes I began cursing myself. That was only after the salmon, utterly unperturbed, had twice snooted the same fly when it swung over his nose on subsequent casts that achieved his lie without in any way being impeded or intercepted. I cursed myself for having given in, if only in a momentary fit of temper, to the salmon fisher's snobbish attitude toward trout.

This is a one-way snobbism, for though I've often heard salmon fishermen speak contemptuously of trout, and had in this instance just done so myself, though fortunately in nobody's hearing—unless you want to count the trout himself—still I have never heard a trout angler speak of salmon in any tone other than one of worshipful awe. Maybe I might have, if I had been privileged to spend a lot of time hanging around the Houghton Club quarters at Stockbridge on the Test, but at least I never heard an American trouter low-rate the salmon. Perhaps this is because trout never seem as easy to catch as when they're encountered in a salmon river, and most trout fishermen only rarely get a chance to go after salmon. Nobody has ever bragged about catching a sucker since the time of Texas Guinan, nor has anybody, I imagine, ever had one mounted. But there are times and places—and this day on Mr. Jim's water on the Torridge was one—where trout are to salmon as suckers are to trout. It's just that there are no times and places where anything else in the same water makes a sucker out of a salmon. There are those, and Lord Grey of Fallodon was one of them, who contend that a sea trout is pound for pound an even better adversary than a salmon. But the comparison is never made in any invidious way, and it's always carefully stated to the effect that they love not salmon the less, but only sea trout more.

The same snob value that accrues to salmon, in waters that they share with trout, also accrues to trout, and I've always thought most unfairly, in waters that they share with grayling. Mention a grayling to an American trout fisherman and his eyes will light up. But on the classic English chalk streams, like the Test and the Itchen, they'll look at you askance if you're so naïve and provincial as to get enthusiastic about a grayling. Yet there's hardly a sight to be seen anywhere more beautiful than, say in Austria, a grayling between you and the sun, shaking a shower of diamonds from that lavender dorsal fin. But a grayling admittedl· is a relative cinch to tempt into striking, compared to the almost legendary difficulty of fooling a chalk-stream trout.

I had long since learned, in Iceland, that in ratio of performance to size—the index of performance, as they say in automobile racing—there's nothing finer with fins than a sea trout. But if one comes between you and a bigger sea-run member of the same *salmo* family, then you're ready to cuss him out for a cussed nuisance. Twice this happened in Connemara, when a perky "white trout" of about fourteen inches—could it have been the same one?—came between me and a salmon that appeared to be about to take my fly. It may have been the same sea trout, though it was a salmon in a different lie, and interested, both times, in a different fly, a Black Dose once and a Thunder & Lightning the other time. God, was I mad! Long afterward, though, when you're away from fish and fishing entirely, and find yourself looking back in your mind's eye at different waters you've fished, you may recall him or them, as I do now those two or that same "white trout," with a pleasant fondness verging on downright affection. At the moment of fishing, however, all that seems to count is the scarcity value of the particular fish you're after. Though if we still had salmon by the thousands coming up and down our Eastern coastal rivers as far south as Delaware, as they once did, instead of being coaxed back by the dozen into a few Maine rivers, as they have been in recent years, we wouldn't stand in such awe of them. But today, as Al McClane says, you practically feel as if you ought to tip your hat at the sight of them.

And as for grayling, it is only since Alaska's statehood that we can now say again that we have them in more than one state. At the turn of the century we had them in Michigan, where there's a town named after them, where my father as a young man fished for them. It was along about that time that Michigan gave quantities of grayling for stocking purposes to Montana, where they were threatened with extinction. Then, not too many years back, after grayling had long been extinct in Michigan, Montana tried to reciprocate. But it was too late. The lumber barons had in the interim done too much dirty work. The Montana grayling wouldn't "take" again, in those same Michigan waters that their forebears had come from in the first place. So now, if you want to fish for grayling, you must go either out to Montana or up to Alaska. Actually, if you live in the East, it's almost simpler, in this phase of the jet age, to go after them in England, or even in Bavaria or Austria.

The English, in an extension of that same sporting snobbery already noted, persist in classing the lordly grayling as a "coarse fish," which, to any American who has ever so much as seen a grayling, seems to be the ultimate in insults. On the other hand, Englishmen will happily fish for, and in some instances even blithely eat, certain species, such as chub, dace, roach, and rudd, that we would consider not only "coarse," but positively vulgar. The grayling is neither. I caught, and immediately afterward cooked, a beautiful big fat one once on the Itchen just above Winchester, and it was heaven out of water.

There are no grayling on the Torridge, but it is a great sea trout river, though very few had been seen in April when we were there. Mr. Jim was all for having us back in June, for the run of the "peal," as they are called in Devon. In Ireland, when you say "peal" you mean grilse, which they refer to as "salmon peal," whereas they call the peal of the Devonshire man by their own Irish term, white trout. To add to the confusion, just a few miles away from North Devon, in Wales, they call the sea trout "sewin." And, of course, wherever you see "salmon trout" on the menu, you know it means sea trout, even if you don't know that they are also known by such varying regional or developmental names as herling, whitling, sprat, scad, mort, pug, herring-sprod, and finnock. It's a progressive puzzlement.

The invaluable Bernard Venables, whom I shall forever include in my prayers for having led me to the Torridge, says in *The Angler's Companion*—and what a companion it became—that the Torridge is a good sea trout river:

From time to time a peal will be taken in April, invariably a big one; but the real run starts in June, and then the fish swarm up the river if there is water for them. Thereafter they will continue to come until the end of the season. Many fishermen, once the sea-trout run has started, will bother no more about the salmon. The sea-trout, taken by fly on the shallows after dark, offer such wonderful sport. They may be taken at other times and by other means, spinning; but it is by fly fishing that the cream of the sport is had.

The Torridge can be so beautiful in April, it's hard to imagine what it would be by June. If Byron could have known this lovely river, where the salmon are to be taken from between banks so benignly close together, in surroundings of such pastoral beauty, it is hard to believe that he could ever have called angling "the cursedest, coldest and the stupidest of sports."

THE KING OF THE MACKEREL

Charles Holder

TUNA ANGLING is purely a modern sport which I suggested ten or twelve years ago at the island of Santa Catalina, California, and, like many manly sports, it flashed into popularity and almost world-wide fame. The tuna is the horse-mackerel, the giant of the mackerel tribe, the doughty head of the family *Scombridae;* an ocean wanderer, a pelagic swash-buckler of the sea; now feeding upon bluefish, menhaden, or herring in the Atlantic, gorging itself with the great flying-fish or squid in the Pacific; everywhere a terror to the smaller denizens of the deep. For centuries it has been caught in great nets in the Mediterranean Sea, on whose shores it is considered a dainty; and from the mouth of the St. Lawrence to Cape Cod it is more or less common in summer and occasionally harpooned, its crescent-shaped tail being seen on many a longshore fish-house from Cape Breton to Swampscott, a talisman of good luck.

As to the time for tuna fishing, there is a difference of opinion. Some anglers are on the ground at daylight; others follow the schools at all times. I have had better luck, that is, more strikes, early in the morning on a rising tide, but the tuna is fickle game. At times it bites vigorously, then will cease without rhyme or reason, during which exasperating period schools of hundreds may be passed and crossed, the fish absolutely ignoring the various devices of the angler. The fishing-ground may be said to be from the point of Avalon Bay to Long Point, a distance of four miles, and from fifty feet to a mile offshore. The tuna is a strategist, and this shoreline, with its numerous open bays, the mouths of canyons, constitutes a series of traps, into which they can charge the flying-fishes; and when they are feeding, they can be caught on the edge of the kelp within twenty feet of the shore. The tuna does not travel in a single large school. That they arrive in a body is doubtless true, but when once on the ground they divide into small squadrons of from fifty to two hundred and are apparently preparing to spawn, playing on the surface, and on calm days, which are the rule in spring, they can be seen for a long distance, the spike dorsal out of the water, followed by the upper lobe of the sharp crescent tail. They are so tame that a boat can approach within fifteen or twenty feet of them before they sink, and it is an easy matter to follow and circle the school.

In fishing we are on the beach at daylight. To the east great bands of vermilion are piercing the sky, and the entire heavens are blazing with a rosy light, the advance guard of the sun that presently comes up over the Sierras on the mainland like a ball of fire. The boatman, who is just in with fresh flying-fishes, reports tunas all along shore, and a few moments later we are shoving off, seated in the stern of a wide-beamed yawl. She is rigged with a two-horse-power engine, but the boatman rows out into the bay, stopping to fasten on the leaders as we over-reel. This accomplished, he rows on while we unreel the entire line to soak it—an essential, as a dry line will burn off under the rush of a fish when the leather brake is applied. We are not out of the bay when a flying-fish is seen coming directly toward us, then another, and still another.

"Look out, sir!" cries the boatman.

Look out, indeed. Two fliers pass over the boat, my companion and I dodging them, catching one, and then, not ten feet from us, a torpedo seems to explode, and the still water flies into the air a mass of gleaming foam. Quickly another rod is taken, the living flier hooked on and cast. We are surely caught unprepared, yet zeee-ee-zee! a swirl of waters, a wail from the steel throat of the big reel, and the game is away. Gone? yes, gone, and if it must be acknowledged, two tuna men, who imagined they were cool under any circumstances, but have been robbed of bait and one hundred feet of line, and all in a moment, now sit dumfounded, then laugh at this phase of fisherman's luck. Manifestly the tunas could not wait for any lengthy preparation; they came in to meet us; we have met the enemy and we are theirs. The moral is, not to start from the beach until everything is in readiness and to be prepared for a strike the moment the bait is over, and all the time. A school of half a dozen tunas has entered the bay charging the flying-fishes, and is off up the coast, where we follow. Once around the point the tuna ground stretches away from point to point, four miles or more, of as beautiful water as the eye ever rested upon, with high rocky cliffs and blue-tinted mountains to the left, and everywhere as smooth as glass. Tunas are in a short time sighted, some leaping into the air, and as we move down the coast a heavy sea appears to be breaking on the Long Point rocks. But it is merely tunas feeding, each tuna as it rushes creating a whitecap; as hundreds are seen, the sight is a marvelous simulation of a storm on a sea of glass.

A flying-fish now comes soring over the ocean a foot above it, and we know that just below is an eagle-eyed nemesis ready to pounce upon it like a tiger. We know that the tuna and its mate are swimming at an angle, canted, or, as the boatman says, with a "list," that its big, black, hypnotic eye may follow each move of the flier. The latter has soared nearly two hundred yards and begins to flag; its tail drops lower and lower, then touches the water to beat it furiously, at which there comes a rush of waters as the tuna attempts to seize its game. But the flying-fish in these few seconds of impact has stored a fresh supply of force, or inertia, and now soars away in a slightly different direction, a foot above the surface, the tuna still beneath it, uncertain whether to leap or to wait until the weary victim shall drop into its maw. It is here that we are treated to the lofty leaps of the tuna. If the latter is swimming deep in the chase, it occasionally dashes upward after the soaring fish, often missing it and rising ten or more feet into the air—a magnificent spectacle. Attaining its limit it turns gracefully and drops headlong into the sea. I have seen such a fish strike the flying-fish and send it whirling upward like a pinwheel. Again, the tuna will seize its prey in mid-air, as will a man-of-war bird.

While we have been digressing on came the flying-fish, crossing our bait by a lucky chance, or by the strategy of the boatman. We could almost feel the premonitory crash; every nerve was tingling with expectation; then twenty feet from the bait there was a rush, the tunas had sighted them, and for several feet they raced along, for there were two (generally the case), hurling the water, arrows aimed at the baits. They had been deflected from the flier, and while the water swirled astern, the cry of two reels rose on the morning air. Vainly the leather thumb-brakes were pushed upon the line; the latter slipped beneath it in feet and yards, then one reel became silent, the slack line telling the story of a flaw, or possibly too much thumb-power, or a rusty leader. Despite every effort the tuna tore the line from the reel, the boatman backing with all his strength, endeavoring to force sternway on the boat before the line was fully exhausted. Five hundred feet had slipped away and the boat was sliding through the water at a rapid rate when suddenly the line slackened, the game was gone. No, the line was doubling in, and springing to my feet I witnessed a splendid movement of the gamy fish, one which I have never seen repeated. The tuna had turned and was literally charging the boat, *el toro* of the sea, coming on like a gleam of light, its sharp dorsal cutting the water. I reeled with all my speed, knowing that if I was caught on the turn with an unknown amount of slack line, the end might come; but fifty feet had not been gained before the tuna was within fifteen feet of the boat, then seeing me it turned and was away like an arrow from a bow. The big reel groaned as the crash came, but the brake was thrown off and my thumb played upon the leather pad with rare good luck, with just sufficient force to prevent overrunning. I gained enough line during this spectacular performance to stop the fish at three hundred feet, and held it by the thread of line while it towed the boat out to sea. A mile it took us, now plunging into the deep heart of the channel, to rise again with throbs which came on the tense line like heart-beats and found an echoing response. I gained ten feet to lose five, then would lose twenty to recover all, and more by vigorous "pumping," as the fish sulked and labored at the bottom of the sea. Suddenly I felt the line humming, vibrating like the cord of some musical instrument as the great fish rose, and as it reached the surface with a mighty swerve that gave the boatman active work to keep us astern to the game, it turned and again charged me. I rose, reeling rapidly as I watched the splendid trick; for trick it was, an attempt to take me unawares, running in on the line to break it if possible in the outrush. Again the fish turned hard by the boat and dashed away, this time inshore, towing us a mile or more, and within fifty feet of the rocks and their beard of kelp, where I succeeded in turning it, and now gained so rapidly that I had the fish within a short distance of the boat. The boatman was fingering his gaff, when, with a magnificent rush, the tuna tore from the reel three hundred feet of line, undoing the strenuous labor of nearly two hours. The fish appeared to be seized with a frenzy. It rushed around the boat at long range, plunged deep into the blue water as though searching the bottom for some obstacle upon which to rub the line, then rising with a strange bounding motion which was imparted to the rod, again charged the boat.

For three hours I fought this superb fish, during which it towed the boat from near Evalon to Long Point, then several miles in and out, repeatedly charging, never giving signs of weakening, always bearing away with its full force. At the end of three hours I again brought the fish to within fifty feet of the boat, when it again broke away and towed us four miles south, occasionally stopping to rush in, and once carried us out into rough water, towing the boat stern first against the heavy seaway so rapidly that I expected to see her fill; but by sheer good luck I turned the fish, and at the end of four hours brought it to gaff. Slowly it circled the boat and for the first time we saw that the fish was what we had suspected, of unusual size. As it slowly swam along, its big back of a deep blue, its white belly occasionally gleaming as it turned, its finarettes flashing gold, it presented a magnificent spectacle, a compensation for the hardest struggle I had ever made. Nearer it came, then it was turned at the quarter, boatman's gaff slid beneath, and the big hook struck home. It was a clever gaff, but with a tremendous surge the tuna sounded, shivering the handle in the gaffer's hands, and was away taking the wreck with it. Fortunately I stopped the rush, and a few moments later again had the tuna alongside. This time a new gaff held it, the gamy creature, never conquered, never discouraged, lashing the water, hurling it over us, a last defiance. A nervous gaffer would have lost the fish at this stage, but the boatman held fast, and stepping on the gunwale pressed it down to the waters' edge and cleverly slid the quivering, struggling tuna into the boat, where it pounded the planking with such vigorous blows that the small craft trembled from stem to stern. As its fine proportions were revealed, I realized that we had landed the largest tuna ever taken with a rod. Its actual weight was about one hundred and eighty-seven pounds; its scale-record weight on shore after bleeding was one hundred and eighty-three pounds; its length was six feet four inches. This catch suggested the Tuna Club, and for two years this fish was the record catch of this organization. I have taken a number of tunas since, and have seen a large number caught, but have never known a fish that so thoroughly exemplified the word "game"; and in justice to this splendid fish, which is now in the possession of a Chicago angler, I must confess that a few moments more would have placed me *hors de combat*.

Among the exciting personal experiences incident to this sport which I recall was being capsized by a tuna nearly a mile offshore. I was trying the experiment of tuna fishing with a light jointed rod, seven and two-thirds feet long, weighing about fifteen ounces, which I used for yellowtail. I hooked my fish, and after a beautiful surface play of forty minutes brought it to gaff. Jim Gardner, the boatman, gaffed it cleverly and landed it, when the fish made a convulsive leap and fell upon the gunwale, capsizing the boat, which sank beneath us, rising bow up, covering the water with gaffs, oars, and other wreckage of the angler's art. My companion, Mr. Townsend of Philadelphia, could not swim, and was otherwise embarrassed by a heavy overcoat; and as the boat rolled over and evidently would not hold three, Gardner and I started to swim to the launch, which had been lying off, some distance away, and which was now coming up, while Mr. Townsend rested upon the bottom of the boat, assuring us that he was all right. As I neared the launch I heard the boatman's wife, who was aboard, scream that her husband was drowning, and turning, saw that Gardner had disappeared. Visions of certain big hammerhead sharks flashed through my mind; but as I stopped, endeavoring to look down into the blue depths, up he came, and I discovered that he still held my tuna by the gaff; in fact, he had never relinquished his grasp upon the handle, and was towing the fish, the latter, as it occasionally plunged downward, taking the plucky gaffer out of sight—a performance extraordinary in its nature, which was repeated three times. Each time Gardner, who was a professional swimmer previous to his boating career, dragged the tuna to the surface, and after an exciting and exhausting swim we were picked up, the launch and fisherman from shore reaching us about the same moment, Gardner securing a rope which his wife tossed him. I was burdened with a heavy corduroy hunting-suit and leggings, and found that I could not lift myself aboard, nor could the two men haul me in, so I was lashed to the rail, Gardner throwing his legs about the propeller. In this position we rested a moment, then by a supreme effort I was hauled in, and while the crew held me by the legs, I leaned over; and as Gardner lifted up the still struggling fish, I thrust my arm into its mouth and grasped it firmly by the gills; Gardner took a half hitch about its tail with a rope, and the men hauled upon my legs, and with a resounding cheer we dropped the leaping tuna into the cockpit—a laughable climax to a seemingly irrational and impossible fish story.

MARLIN OFF THE MORRO:
A CUBAN LETTER

Ernest Hemingway

THE ROOMS on the northeast corner of the Ambos Mundos Hotel in Havana look out, to the north, over the old cathedral, the entrance to the harbor, and the sea, and to the east to Casablanca peninsula, the roofs of all houses in between and the width of the harbor. If you sleep with your feet toward the east, this may be against the tenets of certain religions, the sun, coming up over the Casablanca side and into your open window, will shine on your face and wake you no matter where you were the night before. If you do not choose to get up you can turn around the other way in the bed or roll over. That will not help for long because the sun will be getting stronger and the only thing to do is close the shutter.

Getting up to close the shutter you look across the harbor to the flag on the fortress and see it is straightened out toward you. You look out the north window past the Morro and see that the smooth morning sheen is rippling over and you know the trade wind is coming up early. You take a shower, pull on an old pair of khaki pants and a shirt, take the pair of moccasins that are dry, put the other pair in the window so they will be dry next night, walk to the elevator, ride down, get a paper at the desk, walk across the corner to the cafe and have breakfast.

There are two opposing schools about breakfast. If you knew you were not going to be into fish for two or three hours, a good big breakfast would be the thing. Maybe it is a good thing anyway but I do not want to trust it, so drink a glass of vichy, a glass of cold milk and eat a piece of Cuban bread, read the papers and walk down to the boat. I have hooked them on a full stomach in that sun and I do not want to hook any more of them that way.

We have an ice-box that runs across the stern of the boat with bait iced down on one side and beer and fruit iced on the other. The best bait for big marlin is fresh cero mackerel or kingfish of a pound to three pounds weight. The best beer is Hatuey, the best fruits, in season, are Filipino mangoes, iced pineapple, and alligator pears. Ordinarily we eat the alligator pears for lunch with a sandwich, fixing them with pepper and salt and a freshly squeezed lime. When we run into the beach to anchor, swim and cook a hot lunch on days when fish are not running you can make a French dressing for the pears, adding a little mustard. You can get enough fine, big avocados to feed five people for fifteen cents.

The boat is the Anita, thirty-four feet long, very able in a sea, with plenty of speed for these fish, owned and skippered by Capt. Joe Russell of Key West who brought the first load of liquor that ever came into that place from Cuba and who knows more about swordfish than most Keywesters do about grunts. The other man on board is the best marlin and swordfisherman around Cuba, Carlos Gutierrez, of Zapata, thirty-one, Havana, fifty-four years old, who goes Captain on a fishing smack in the winter and fishes marlin commercially in the summer. I met him six years ago in Dry Tortugas and first heard about the big marlin that run off Cuba from him. He can, literally, gaff a dolphin through the head back-handed and he has studied the habits of the marlin since he first went fishing for them as a boy of twelve with his father.

As the boat leaves the San Francisco wharf, tarpon are rolling in the slip. Going out of the harbor you see more of them rolling near the live fish cars that are buoyed alongside the line of anchored fishing smacks. Off the Morro in the entrance to the harbor there is a good coral bottom with about twenty fathoms of water and you pass many small boats bottom fishing for mutton fish and red snappers and jigging for mackerel and occasional kingfish. Outside the breeze freshens and as far as you can see the small boats of the marlin fishermen are scattered. They are fishing with four to six heavy handlines in from forty to seventy fathoms drifting for the fish that are travelling deep. We troll for the ones that are on the surface feeding, or travelling, or cruising fifteen or twenty fathoms down. They see the two big teasers or the baits and come up with a smash, usually going head and shoulders out of water on the strike.

Marlin travel from east to west against the current of the Gulf Stream. No one has ever seen them working in the other direction, although the current of the Gulf Stream is not so stable; sometimes, just before the new moon, being quite slack and at others running strongly to the westward. But the prevailing wind is the northeast trade and when this blows the marlin come to the top and cruise with the wind, the scythe tail, a light, steely lavender, cutting the swells as it projects and goes under; the big fish, yellow looking in the water, swimming two or three feet under the surface, the huge pectoral fins tucked close to the flanks, the dorsal fin down, the fish looking a round, fast-moving log in the water except for the erect curve of that slicing tail.

The heavier the current runs to the eastward the more marlin there are; travelling along the edge of the dark, swirling current from a quarter of a mile to four miles off shore; all going in the same direction like cars along a highway. We have been fighting a fish, on days when they were running well, and seen six others pass close to the boat during a space of half an hour.

As an indication of how plentiful they are, the official report from the Havana markets from the middle of March to the 18th of July this year showed eleven thousand small marlin and one hundred and fifty large marlin were brought into the market by the commercial fishermen of Santa Cruz del Norte, Jaruco, Guanabo, Cojimar, Havana, Chorrera, Marianao, Jaimanitas, Baracoa Banes, Mariel, and Cabañas. Marlin are caught at Matanzas and Cardenas to the east and at Bahai Honda to the west of the towns mentioned but those fish are not shipped to Havana. The big fish had only been running two weeks when this report was compiled.

Fishing with rod and reel from the middle of April through the 18th of July of this season we caught fifty-two marlin and two sailfish. The largest black marlin was 468 pounds, and 12 feet 8 inches long. The largest striped marlin was 343 pounds and 10 feet 5 inches. The biggest white marlin weighed 87 pounds and was 7 feet 8 inches in length.

The white marlin run first in April and May, then come the immature striped marlin with brilliant stripes which fade after the fish dies. These are most plentiful in May and run into June. Then come the black and striped marlin together. The biggest run of striped marlin is in July and as they get scarce the very big black marlin come through until into September and later. Just before the striped marlin are due to run the smaller marlin drop off altogether and it seems, except for an occasional school of small tuna and bonito, as though the Gulf Stream were empty. There are so many color variations, some of them caused by feed, others by age, others by the depth of water, in these marlin that anyone seeking notoriety for himself by naming new species could have a field day along the north Cuba coast. For me they are all color and sexual variations of the same fish. This is too complicated a theory to go into a letter.

The marlin hit a trolled bait in four different ways. First, with hunger, again with anger, then simply playfully, last with indifference. Anyone can hook a hungry fish who gives him enough line, doesn't backlash and sets the hook hard enough. What happens then is something else. The main thing is to loosen your drag quickly enough when he starts to jump and make his run, and get the boat after him as he heads out to sea. The hungry marlin smashes at the bait with bill, shoulders, top fin and tail out. If he gets one bait he will turn and charge the other. If you pull the bait out of his mouth he will come for it again as long as there is any bait on the hook.

The angry fish puzzled us for a long time. He would come from below and hit the bait with a smash like a bomb exploding in the water. But as you slacked line to him he has dropped it. Screw down on the drag and race the bait in and he would slam it again without taking it. There is no way to hook a fish acting that way except to strike hard as he smashes. Put the drag on, speed up the boat and sock him as he crashes it. He slams the bait to kill it as long as it seems to be alive.

The playful marlin, probably one who has fed well, will come behind a bait with his fin high, shove his bill clear out of water and take the bait lightly between his bill and pointed lower jaw. When you turn it loose to him he drops it. I am speaking of absolutely fresh bait caught that same day; if the bait were stale you might expect them all to refuse it once they had tasted it. This sort of fish can often be made to hit by speeding the boat up and skipping the bait over the top of the water with the rod. If he does take it, do not give him too much line before you hit him.

The indifferent fish will follow the bait for as many as three or four miles. Looking the baits over, sheering away, coming back to swim deep down below them and follow, indifferent to the bait, yet curious. If such a fish swims with his pectoral fins tucked close to his sides he will not bite. He is cruising and you are on his course. That is all. The minute a marlin sees the bait, if he is going to strike, he raises his dorsal fin and spreads those wide, bright blue pectorals so that he looks like some great, under-sea bird in the water as he follows.

The black marlin is a stupid fish. He is immensely powerful, can jump wonderfully and will break your back sounding but he has not the stamina of the striped marlin, nor his intelligence. I believe they are mostly old, female fish, past their prime and that it is age that gives them that black color. When they are younger they are much bluer and the meat, too, is whiter. If you fight them fast, never letting up, never resting, you can kill them quicker than you could ever kill a striped marlin of the same size. Their great strength makes them very dangerous for the first forty minutes. I mean dangerous to the tackle; no fish is dangerous to a man in a launch. But if you can take what they have to give during that time and keep working on them they will tire much quicker than any striped marlin. The 468 pounder was hooked in the roof of the mouth, was in no way tangled in the leader, jumped eight times completely clear, towed the boat stern first when held tight, sounded four times, but was brought to gaff at the top of the water, fin and tail out, in sixty-five minutes. But if I had not lost a much larger striped marlin the day before after two hours and twenty minutes, and fought a black one the day before for forty-five I would not have been in shape to work him so hard.

Fishing in a five-mile-an-hour current, where a hooked fish will always swim against the current, where the water is from four hundred to seven hundred fathoms deep, there is much to learn about tactics in fighting big fish. But one myth that can be dissipated is the old one that the water pressure at one thousand feet will kill the fish. A marlin dies at the bottom only if he has been hooked in the belly. These fish are used to going to the bottom. They often feed there. They are not built like bottom fish which live always at the same depth but are built to be able to go up and down in any depth. I have had a marlin sound four hundred yards straight down, all the rod under water over the side, bent double with that weight going down, down, down, watching the line go, putting on all pressure possible on the reel to check him, him going down and down until you are sure every inch of line will go. Suddenly he stops sounding and you straighten up, get onto your feet, get the butt in the socket and work him up slowly, finally you have the double line on the reel and think he is coming to gaff and then the line begins to rip out as he hooks up and heads off to sea just under the surface to come out in ten long, clean jumps. This after an hour and a half of fight. Then to sound again. They are a fish all right. The 343 pounder jumped 44 times.

You can fish for them in Cuba from April all through the summer. Big ones will be accidental until the middle of June and we only saw four broadbill all season. But in July and August it is even money any day you go out that you will hook into a fish from three hundred pounds up. Up means a very long way up. The biggest marlin ever brought into the market by the commercial fishermen weighed eleven hundred and seventy-five pounds with head cut off, gutted, tail cut off and flanks cut away; eleven hundred and seventy-five pounds when on the slab, nothing but the saleable meat ready to be cut into steaks. All right. You tell me. What did he weigh in the water and what did he look like when he jumped?

3

A FIERCE AND GENTLE PASSION

". . . you will search far to find a fisherman to admit that a taste for fishing, like a taste for liquor, must be governed lest it come to possess its possessor."

—SPARSE GREY HACKLE

MR. THEODORE CASTWELL

G. E. M. Skues

MR. THEODORE CASTWELL, having devoted a long, strenuous and not unenjoyable life to hunting to their doom innumerable salmon, trout, and grayling in many quarters of the globe, and having gained much credit among his fellows for his many ingenious improvements in rods, flies, and tackle employed for that end, in the fullness of time died and was taken to his own place.

St. Peter looked up from a draft balance sheet at the entry of the attendant angel.

"A gentleman giving the name of Castwell. Says he is a fisherman, your Holiness, and has 'Fly-Fishers' Club, London' on his card."

"Hm-hm," says St. Peter. "Fetch me the ledger with his account."

St. Peter perused it.

"Hm-hm," said St. Peter. "Show him in."

Mr. Castwell entered cheerfully and offered a cordial right hand to St. Peter.

"As a brother of the angle—" he began.

"Hm-hm," said St. Peter. "I have been looking at your account from below."

"I am sure I shall not appeal to you in vain for special consideration in connection with the quarters to be assigned to me here."

"Hm-hm," said St. Peter.

"Well, I've seen worse accounts," said St. Peter. "What sort of quarters would you like?"

"Do you think you could manage something in the way of a country cottage of the Test Valley type, with modern conveniences and, say, three quarters of a mile of one of those pleasant chalk streams, clear as crystal, which proceed from out the throne, attached?"

"Why, yes," said St. Peter. "I think we can manage that for you. Then what about your gear? You must have left your fly rods and tackle down below. I see you prefer a light split cane of nine foot or so, with appropriate fittings. I will indent upon the Works Department for what you require, including a supply of flies. I think you will approve of our dresser's productions. Then you will want a keeper to attend you."

"Thanks awfully, your Holiness," said Mr. Castwell. "That will be first-rate. To tell you the truth, from the Revelations I read, I was inclined to fear that I might be just a teeny-weeny bit bored in heaven."

"In h-hm-hm," said St. Peter, checking himself.

It was not long before Mr. Castwell found himself alongside an enchantingly beautiful clear chalk stream, some fifteen yards wide, swarming with fine trout feeding greedily: and presently the attendant angel assigned to him had handed him the daintiest, most exquisite, light split-cane rod conceivable—perfectly balanced with the reel and line—with a beautifully damped tapered cast of incredible fineness and strength, and a box of flies of such marvelous tying as to be almost mistakable for the natural insects they were to simulate.

Mr. Castwell scooped up a natural fly from the water, matched it perfectly from the fly box, and knelt down to cast to a riser putting up just under a tussock ten yards or so above him. The fly lit like gossamer, six inches above the last ring; and next moment the rod was making the curve of beauty. Presently, after an exciting battle, the keeper netted out a beauty of about two and a half pounds.

"Heavens," cried Mr. Castwell. "This is something like."

"I am sure his Holiness will be pleased to hear it," said the keeper.

Mr. Castwell prepared to move upstream to the next riser when he noticed that another trout had taken up the position of that which he had just landed, and was rising. "Just look at that," he said, dropping instantaneously to his knee and drawing off some line. A moment later an accurate fly fell just above the neb of the fish, and instantly Mr. Castwell engaged in battle with another lusty fish. All went well, and presently the landing net received its two and a half pounds.

"A very pretty brace," said Mr. Castwell, preparing to move on to the next string of busy nebs which he had observed putting up around the bend. As he approached the tussock, however, he became aware that the place from which he had just extracted so satisfactory a brace was already occupied by another busy feeder.

"Well, I'm damned," said Mr. Castwell. "Do you see that?"

"Yes, sir," said the keeper.

The chance of extracting three successive trout from the same spot was too attractive to be forgone, and once more Mr. Castwell knelt down and delivered a perfect cast to the spot. Instantly it was accepted and battle was joined. All held, and presently a third gleaming trout joined his brethren in the creel.

Mr. Castwell turned joyfully to approach the next riser round the bend. Judge, however, his surprise to find that once more the pit beneath the tussock was occupied by a rising trout, apparently of much the same size as the others.

"Heavens," exclaimed Mr. Castwell. "Was there ever anything like it?"

"No, sir," said the keeper.

"Look here," said he to the keeper, "I think I really must give this chap a miss and pass on to the next."

"Sorry, it can't be done, sir. His Holiness would not like it."

"Well, if that's really so," said Mr. Castwell, and knelt rather reluctantly to his task.

Several hours later he was still casting to the same tussock.

"How long is this confounded rise going to last?" inquired Mr. Castwell. "I suppose it will stop soon."

"No, sir," said the keeper.

"What, isn't there a slack hour in the afternoon?"

"No afternoon, sir."

"What? Then what about the evening rise?"

"No evening rise, sir," said the keeper.

"Well, I shall knock off now. I must have had about thirty brace from that corner."

"Beg pardon, sir, but his Holiness would not like that."

"What?" said Mr. Castwell. "Mayn't I even stop at night?"

"No night here, sir," said the keeper.

"Then do you mean that I have got to go on catching these damned two-and-a-half pounders at this corner forever and ever?"

The keeper nodded.

"Hell!" said Mr. Castwell.

"Yes," said his keeper.

THE CULPRIT

Anton Chekhov

A PUNY LITTLE PEASANT, exceedingly skinny, wearing patched trousers and a shirt made of ticking, stands before the investigating magistrate. His hairy, pock-marked face, and his eyes, scarcely visible under thick, overhanging brows, have an expression of grim sullenness. The mop of tangled hair that has not known the touch of a comb for a long time gives him a spiderish air that makes him look even grimmer. He is barefoot.

"Denis Grigoryev!" the magistrate begins. "Step nearer and answer my questions. On the morning of the seventh of this present month of July, the railway watchman, Ivan Semyonovich Akinfov, making his rounds, found you, near the hundred-and-forty-first milepost, unscrewing the nut of one of the bolts by which the rails are fastened to the sleepers. Here is the nut! . . . With the said nut he detained you. Is this true?"

"Wot?"

"Did all this happen as stated by Akinfov?"

"It did, sure."

"Very well; now, for what purpose were you unscrewing the nut?"

"Wot?"

"Stop saying 'wot' and answer the question: for what purpose were you unscrewing the nut?"

"If I didn't need it, I wouldn't've unscrewed it," croaks Denis, with a sidelong glance at the ceiling.

"What did you want that nut for?"

"The nut? We make sinkers of these nuts."

"Who are 'we'?"

"We, folks. . . . The Klimovo peasants, that is."

"Listen, brother; don't play the fool with me, but talk sense. There's no use lying to me about sinkers."

"I never lied in my life, and here I'm lying . . ." mutters Denis, blinking. "But can you do without a sinker, Your Honor? If you put live bait or worms on a hook, would it go to the bottom without a sinker? . . . So I'm lying," sneers Denis. "What the devil is the good of live bait if it floats on the surface? The perch and the pike and the eel-pout will bite only if your line touches bottom, and if your bait floats on the surface, it's only a bullhead will take it, and that only sometimes, and there ain't no bullhead in our river . . . That fish likes plenty of room."

"What are you telling me about bullhead for?"

"Wot? Why, you asked me yourself! Up our way the gentry catch fish that way, too. Even a little kid wouldn't try to catch fish without a sinker. Of course, somebody with no sense might go fishing without a sinker. No rules for fools."

"So you say you unscrewed this nut to make a sinker of it?"

"What else for? Not to play knucklebones with!"

"But you might have taken a bit of lead or a bullet for a sinker . . . a nail . . ."

"You don't pick up lead on the road, you have to pay for it, and a nail's no good. You can't find nothing better than a nut . . . It's heavy, and it's got a hole."

"He keeps playing the fool! As though he'd been born yesterday or dropped out of the sky! Don't you understand, you blockhead, what this unscrewing leads to? If the watchman hadn't been on the lookout, the train might have been derailed, people would have been killed—*you* would have killed people."

"God forbid, Your Honor! Kill people? Are we unbaptized, or criminals? Glory be to God, sir, we've lived our lives without dreaming of such a thing, much less killing anybody . . . Save us, Queen of Heaven, have mercy on us! What are you saying, sir?"

"And how do you suppose train wrecks happen? Unscrew two or three nuts, and you have a wreck!"

Denis sneers and screws up his eyes at the magistrate incredulously.

"Well! How many years have all of us here in the village been unscrewing nuts, and the Lord's protected us; and here you talk about wrecks, killing people. If I'd carried off a rail or put a log in the way, then maybe the train might've gone off the track, but . . . ppfff! a nut!"

"But try to get it into your head that the nut holds the rail fast to the sleepers!"

"We understand that . . . We don't unscrew all of 'em . . . We leave some . . . We don't do things without using our heads . . . We understand."

Denis yawns and makes the sign of the cross over his mouth.

"Last year a train was derailed here," says the magistrate. "Now it's plain why!"

"Beg pardon?"

"I say that it's plain why the train was derailed last year . . . Now I understand!"

"That's what you're educated for, our protectors, to understand. The Lord knew to whom to give understanding . . . Here you've figured out how and what, but the watchman, a peasant like us, with no brains at all, he gets you by the collar and pulls you in. You should figure it out first and then pull people in. But it's known, a peasant has the brains of a peasant. . . . Write down, too, Your Honor, that he hit me twice on the jaw, and on the chest, too."

"When your house was searched they found another nut. . . . At what spot did you unscrew that, and when?"

"You mean the nut under the little red chest?"

"I don't know where you kept it, but it was found. When did you unscrew it?"

"I didn't unscrew it; Ignashka, one-eyed Semyon's son, he gave it to me. I mean the one that was under the chest, but the one that was in the sledge in the yard, that one Mitrofan and I unscrewed together."

"Which Mitrofan?"

"Mitrofan Petrov . . . Didn't you hear of him? He makes nets and sells them to the gentry. He needs a lot of those nuts. Reckon a matter of ten for every net."

"Listen. According to Article 1081 of the Penal Code, deliberate damage to a railroad, calculated to jeopardize the trains, provided the perpetrator of the damage knew that it might cause an accident—you understand? Knew! And you couldn't help knowing what this unscrewing might lead to—is punishable by hard labor."

"Of course, you know best . . . We're ignorant folk . . . What do we understand?"

"You understand all about it! You are lying, faking!"

"Why should I lie? Ask in the village if you don't believe me. Only bleak is
caught without a sinker. And a gudgeon's no kind of fish, but even gudgeon
won't bite without a sinker."

"Tell me about bullhead, now," says the magistrate with a smile.

"There ain't no bullhead in our parts. . . . If we cast our lines without a sinker,
with a butterfly for bait, we can maybe catch a chub that way, but even that not
often."

"Now, be quiet."

There is silence. Denis shifts from one foot to the other, stares at the table
covered with green cloth, and blinks violently as though he were looking not at
cloth but at the sun. The magistrate writes rapidly.

"Can I go?" asks Denis, after a silence.

"No. I must put you in custody and send you to prison."

Denis stops blinking and, raising his thick eyebrows, looks inquiringly at the
official.

"What do you mean, prison? Your Honor! I haven't the time; I must go to the
fair; I must get three rubles from Yegor for lard!"

"Be quiet; don't disturb me."

"Prison . . . If I'd done something, I'd go; but to go just for nothing! What
for? I didn't steal anything, so far as I know, I wasn't fighting . . . If there's any
question about the arrears, Your Honor, don't believe the elder . . . Ask the permanent member of the Board . . . the elder, he's no Christian."

"Be quiet."

"I'm quiet as it is," mutters Denis; "as for the elder, he's lied about the assess-
ment, I'll take my oath on it . . . We're three brothers: Kuzma Grigoryev, then
Yegor Grigoryev, and me, Denis Grigoryev."

"You're disturbing me . . . Hey, Semyon," cries the magistrate, "take him out."

"We're three brothers," mutters Denis, as two husky soldiers seize him and lead
him out of the chamber. "A brother don't have to answer for a brother. Kuzma
don't pay, so you, Denis, have to answer for it . . . Judges! Our late master the
general is dead—the Kingdom of Heaven be his!—or he'd have shown you judges
what's what . . . You must have the know-now when you judge, not do it any
which way . . . All right, flog a man, but justly, when it's coming to him."

MURDER

Sparse Grey Hackle

"IF FISHING INTERFERES with your business, give up your business," any angler will tell you, citing instances of men who have lost health and even life through failure to take a little recreation, and reminding you that "the trout do not rise in Greenwood Cemetery," so you had better do your fishing while you are still able. But you will search far to find a fisherman to admit that a taste for fishing, like a taste for liquor, must be governed lest it come to possess its possessor; that an excess of fishing can cause as many tragedies of lost purpose, earning power and position as an excess of liquor. This is the story of a man who finally decided between his business and his fishing, and of how his decision was brought about by the murder of a trout.

Fishing was not a pastime with my friend John but an obsession—a common condition, for typically your successful fisherman is not really enjoying a recreation, but rather taking refuge from the realities of life in an absorbing fantasy in which he grimly if subconsciously re-enacts in miniature the unceasing struggle of primitive man for existence. Indeed, it is that which makes him successful, for it gives him that last measure of fierce concentration, that final moment of unyielding patience which in angling so often make the difference between fish and no fish.

John was that kind of fisherman, more so than any other I ever knew. Waking or sleeping, his mind ran constantly on the trout and its taking, and back in 1932 I often wondered whether he could keep on indefinitely doing business with the surface of his mind and fishing with the rest of his mental processes—wondered, and feared that he could not. So when he called me one spring day and said, "I'm tired of sitting here and watching a corporation die; let's go fishing," I know that he was not discouraged with his business so much as he was impatient with its restraint. But I went with him, for maybe I'm a bit obsessed myself.

That day together on the river was like a thousand other pages from the book of any angler's memories. There was the clasp and pull of cold, hurrying water on our legs, the hours of rhythmic casting, and the steady somnambulistic shuffling which characterizes steelworkers aloft and fly fishermen in fast water. Occasionally our heads were bent together over a fly box; at intervals our pipes wreathed smoke, and from time to time a brief remark broke the silence. We were fishing "pool and pool" together, each as he finished walking around the other to a new spot above him.

Late afternoon found me in the second pool below the dam, throwing a long line up the still water. There was a fish rising to some insect so small that I could not detect it, so I was using a tiny gray fly on a long leader with a 5x point. John came by and went up to the dam pool and I lost interest in my refractory fish and walked up to watch, for there was always a chance of a good fish there. I stopped at a safe distance and sat down on a rock with my leader trailing to keep it wet, while John systematically covered the tail of the pool until he was satisfied that there were no fish there to dart ahead and give the alarm, and then stepped into it.

As he did so his body became tense, his posture that of a man who stalks his enemy. With aching slowness and infinite craft he began to inch up the pool and as he went his knees bent more and more until he was crouching. Finally, with his rod low to the water and one hand supporting himself on the bottom of the stream, he crept to a casting position and knelt in mid-current with water lapping under his elbows, his left sleeve dripping unheeded as he allowed the current to straighten his line behind him. I saw that he was using the same leader as mine but with a large No. 12 fly.

"John, using 5x?" I breathed. Without turning his head he nodded almost imperceptibly.

"Better break off and reknot," I counseled softly, but he ignored the suggestion. I spoke from experience. Drawn 5x gut is almost as fine as a human hair, and we both knew that it chafes easily where it is tied to a fly as heavy as No. 12, so that it is necessary to make the fastening in a different spot at frequent intervals in order to avoid breaking it.

I kept silence and watched John. With his rod almost parallel to the water he picked up his fly from behind him with a light twitch and then false-cast to dry it. He was a good caster; it neither touched the surface nor rose far above it as he whipped it back and forth.

Now he began lengthening his line until finally, at the end of each forward cast, his fly hovered for an instant above a miniature eddy between the main current and a hand's breadth of still water which clung to the bank. And then I noticed what he had seen when he entered the pool—the sudden slight dimple denoting the feeding of a big fish on the surface.

The line came back with a subtle change from the wide-sweeping false casts, straightened with decision and swept forward in a tight roll. It straightened again and then checked suddenly. The fly swept round as a little elbow formed in the leader, and settled on the rim of the eddy with a loop of slack upstream of it. It started to circle, then disappeared in a sudden dimple and I could hear a faint sucking sound.

It seemed as if John would never strike although his pause must have been but momentary. Then his long line tightened—he had out fifty feet—as he drew it back with his left hand and gently raised the rod tip with his right. There was slight pause and then the line began to run out slowly.

Rigid as a statue, with the water piling a little wave against the brown waders at his waist, he continued to kneel there while the yellow line slid almost unchecked through his left hand. His lips moved.

"A big one," he murmured. "The leader will never hold him if he gets started. I should have changed it."

The tip of the upright rod remained slightly bent as the fish moved into the circling currents created by the spillway at the right side of the dam. John took line gently and the rod maintained its bend. Now the fish was under the spillway and must have dived down with the descending stream, for I saw a couple of feet of line slide suddenly through John's hand. The circling water got its impetus here and this was naturally the fastest part of the eddy.

The fish came rapidly toward us, riding with the quickened water, and John retrieved line. Would the fish follow the current around again, or would it leave it and run down past us? The resilient rod tip straightened as the pressure was eased. The big trout passed along the downstream edge of the eddy and swung over the bank to follow it round again, repeated its performance at the spillway, and again refused to leave the eddy. It was troubled and perplexed by the strange hampering of its progress but it was not alarmed, for it was not aware of our presence or even of the fact that it was hooked, and the restraint on it had not been enough to arouse its full resistance.

Every experienced angler will understand that last statement. The pull of a game fish, up to the full limit of its strength, seems to be in proportion to the resistance which it encounters. As I watched the leader slowly cutting the water, I recalled that often I had hooked a trout and immediately given slack, whereupon invariably it had moved quietly and aimlessly about, soon coming to rest as if it had no realization that it was hooked.

I realized now that John intended to get the "fight" out of his fish at a rate slow enough not to endanger his leader. His task was to keep from arousing the fish to a resistance greater than the presumably weakened 5x gut would withstand. It seemed as if it were hopeless, for the big trout continued to circle the eddy, swimming deep and strongly against the rod's light tension, which relaxed only when the fish passed the gateway of the stream below. Around and around it went, and then at last it left the eddy. Yet it did not dart into the outflowing current but headed into deep water close to the far bank. I held my breath, for over there was a tangle of roots, and I could imagine what a labyrinth they must make under the surface. Ah, it was moving toward the roots! Now what would John do—hold the fish hard and break off; check it and arouse its fury; or perhaps splash a stone in front of it to turn it back?

He did none of these but instead slackened off until his line sagged in a catenary curve. The fish kept on, and I could see the leader draw on the surface as it swam into the mass of roots. Now John dropped his rod flat to the water and delicately drew on the line until the tip barely flexed, moving it almost imperceptibly several times to feel whether his leader had fouled on a root. Then he lapsed into immobility.

I glanced at my wrist watch, slowly bent my head until I could light my cold pipe without raising my hand, and then relaxed on my rock. The smoke drifted lazily upstream, the separate puffs merging into a thin haze which dissipated itself imperceptibly. A bird moved on the bank. But the only really living thing was the stream, which rippled a bit as it divided around John's body and continually moved a loop of his yellow line in the disturbed current below him.

When the trout finally swam quietly back out of the roots, my watch showed that it had been there almost an hour and a quarter. John slackened the line and released a breath which he seemed to have been holding all that while, and the fish re-entered the eddy to resume its interminable circling. The sun, which had been in my face, dropped behind a tree, and I noted how the shadows had lengthened. Then the big fish showed itself for the first time, its huge dorsal fin appearing as it rose toward the surface and the lobe of its great tail as it turned down again; it seemed to be two feet long.

Again its tail swirled under the surface, puddling the water as it swam slowly and deliberately, and then I thought that we would lose the fish, for as it came around to the downstream side of the eddy it wallowed an instant and then headed toward us. Instantly John relaxed the rod until the line hung limp and from the side of his mouth he hissed, "Steady!"

Down the stream, passing John so closely that he could have hit it with his tip, drifted a long dark bulk, oaring along deliberately with its powerful tail in the smooth current. I could see the gray fly in the corner of its mouth and the leader hanging in a curve under its belly, then the yellow line floating behind. In a moment he felt of the fish again, determined that it was no longer moving, and resumed his light pressure, causing it to swim around aimlessly in the still water below us. The sun was half below the horizon now and the shadows slanting down over the river covered us. In the cool, diffused light the lines on John's face from nostril to mouth were deeply cut and the crafty folds at the outer corners of his lids hooded his eyes. His rod hand shook with a fine tremor.

The fish broke, wallowing, but John instantly dropped his rod flat to the water and slipped a little line. The fish wallowed again, then swam more slowly in a large circle. It was moving just under the surface now, its mouth open and its back breaking water every few feet, and it seemed to be half turned on its side. Still John did not move except for the small gestures of taking or giving line, raising or lowering his tip.

It was in the ruddy afterglow that the fish finally came to the top, beating its tail in a subdued rhythm. Bent double, I crept ashore and then ran through the brush to the edge of the still water downstream of the fish, which now was broad on its side. Stretching myself prone on the bank, I extended my net at arm's length and held it flat on the bottom in a foot of water.

John began to slip out line slowly, the now beaten trout moving feebly as the slow current carried it down. Now it was opposite me and I nodded a signal to John. He moved his tip toward my bank and cautiously checked the line. The current swung the trout toward me and it passed over my net.

I raised the rim quietly and slowly, and the next instant the trout was doubled up in my deep-bellied net and I was holding the top shut with both hands while the fish, galvanized into a furious flurry, splashed water in my face as I strove to get my feet under me.

John picked his way slowly down the still-water, reeling up as he came, stumbling and slipping on the stones like an utterly weary man. I killed the trout with my pliers and laid it on the grass as he came up beside me and stood watching it with bent head and sagging shoulders for a long while.

"To die like that!" he said as if thinking aloud. "Murdered—nagged to death; he never knew he was fighting for his life until he was in the net. He had strength and courage enough to beat the pair of us but we robbed him a little at a time until we got him where we wanted him. And then knocked him on the head. I wish you had let him go."

The twilight fishing, our favorite time, was upon us but he started for the car and I did not demur. We began to take off our wet shoes and waders.

"That's just what this depression is doing to me!" John burst out suddenly as he struggled with a shoelace. "Niggling me to death! And I'm up here fishing, taking two days off in the middle of the week, instead of doing something about it. Come on; hurry up. I'm going to catch the midnight to Pittsburgh; I know where I can get a contract."

And sure enough he did.

A WEDDING GIFT

John Taintor Foote

GEORGE BALDWIN POTTER is a purist. That is to say, he either takes trout on a dry fly or he does not take them at all. He belongs to a number of fishing clubs, any member of which might acquire his neighbor's wife, beat his children, or poison a dog and still cast a fly, in all serenity, upon club waters; but should he impale on a hook a lowly though succulent worm and immerse the creature in those same waters it would be better that he send in his resignation at once, sooner than face the shaken committee that would presently wait upon him.

George had become fixed in my mind as a bachelor. This, of course, was a mistake. I am continually forgetting that purists rush into marriage when approaching or having just passed the age of forty. The psychology of this is clear.

For twenty years, let us say, a purist's life is completely filled by his efforts to convert all reasonable men to his own particular method of taking trout. He thinks, for example, that a man should not concern himself with more than a dozen types of standard flies. The manner of presenting them is the main consideration. Take any one of these flies, then, and place it, by means of an eight-foot rod, a light, tapered line, and a mist-colored leader of reasonable length, on fast water—if you want trout. Of course, if you want to listen to the birds and look at the scenery, fish the pools with a long line and an eight-foot leader. Why, it stands to reason that____

The years go by as he explains these vital facts patiently, again and again, to Smith and Brown and Jones. One wet, cold spring, after fighting a muddy stream all day, he reexplains for the better part of an evening and takes himself, somewhat wearily upstairs. The damp and chill of the room at whatever club he may be fishing is positively tomblike. He can hear the rain drumming on the roof and swishing against the windows. The water will be higher than ever tomorrow, he reflects, as he puts out the lights and slides between the icy sheets. Steeped to the soul in cheerless dark, he recalls numbly that when he first met Smith and Brown and Jones they were fishing the pools with a long line. That

195

was, let's see—fifteen—eighteen—twenty years ago. Then he must be forty. It isn't possible! Yes, it is a fact that Smith and Brown and Jones are still fishing the pools with a long line.

In the first faint light of dawn he falls into an uneasy, muttering slumber. The dark hours between have been devoted to intense thought and a variety of wiggles which have not succeeded in keeping the bedclothes against his shoulder blades.

Some time within the next six months you will remember that you have forgotten to send him a wedding present.

George, therefore, having arrived at his fortieth birthday, announced his engagement shortly thereafter. Quite by chance I ran across his bride-to-be and himself a few days before the ceremony, and joined them at lunch. She was a blonde in the early twenties, with wide blue eyes and a typical rose-and-white complexion. A rushing, almost breathless account of herself, which she began the moment we were seated, was curious, I thought. It was as though she feared an interruption at any moment. I learned that she was an only child, born and reared in Greater New York; that her family had recently moved to New Rochelle; that she had been shopping madly for the past two weeks; that she was nearly dead, but that she had some adorable things.

At this point George informed me that they would spend their honeymoon at a certain fishing club in Maine. He then proceeded to describe the streams and lakes in that section at some length—during the rest of the luncheon, as a matter of fact. His fiancée, who had fallen into a wordless abstraction, only broke her silence with a vague murmur as we parted.

Owing to this meeting I did not forget to send a wedding present. I determined that my choice should please both George and his wife through the happy years to come.

If I had had George only to consider, I could have settled the business in two minutes at a sporting-goods store. Barred from these for obvious reasons, I spent a long day in a thoroughly exhausting search. Late in the afternoon I decided to abandon my hopeless task. I had made a tremendous effort and failed. I would simply buy a silver doodad and let it go at that.

As I staggered into a store with the above purpose in view, I passed a show case devoted to fine china, and halted as my eyes fell on a row of fish plates backed by artfully rumpled blue velvet. The plates proved to be hand painted. On each plate was one of the different varieties of trout, curving up through green depths to an artificial fly just dropping on the surface of the water.

In an automatic fashion I indicated the plates to a clerk, paid for them, gave him my card and the address, and fled from the store. Some time during the next twenty-four hours it came to me that George Potter was not among my nearest and dearest. Yet the unbelievable sum I had left with that clerk in exchange for those fish plates could be justified in no other way.

I thought this fact accounted for the sort of frenzy with which George flung himself upon me when next we met, some two months later. I had been week-ending in the country and encountered him in the Grand Central Station as I emerged from the lower level. For a long moment he wrung my hand in silence, gazing almost feverishly into my face. At last he spoke:

"Have you got an hour to spare?"

It occurred to me that it would take George an hour at least to describe his amazed delight at the splendor of my gift. The clock above Information showed that it was 12:45. I therefore suggested that we lunch together.

He, too, glanced at the clock, verified its correctness by his watch, and seized me by the arm.

"All right," he agreed, and was urging me toward the well-filled and somewhat noisy station café before I grasped his intention and tried to suggest that we go elsewhere. His hand only tightened on my arm.

"It's all right," he said; "good food, quick service—you'll like it."

He all but dragged me into the café and steered me to a table in the corner. I lifted my voice above an earnest clatter of gastronomical utensils and made a last effort.

"The Biltmore's just across the street."

George pressed me into my chair, shoved a menu card at me and addressed the waiter.

"Take his order." Here he jerked out his watch and consulted it again. "We have forty-eight minutes. Service for one. I shan't eat anything; or, no—bring me some coffee—large cup—black."

Having ordered mechanically, I frankly stared at George. He was dressed, I now observed, with unusual care. He wore a rather dashing gray suit. His tie, which was an exquisite shade of gray-blue, was embellished by a handsome pearl. The handkerchief, appearing above his breast pocket, was of the same delicate gray-blue shade as the tie. His face had been recently and closely shaven, also powdered; but above that smooth whiteness of jowl was a pair of curiously glittering eyes and a damp, a beaded brow. This he now mopped with his napkin.

"Good God," said I, "what it is, George?"

His reply was to extract a letter from his inside coat pocket and pass it across the table, his haunted eyes on mine. I took in its few lines at a glance:

> Father has persuaded me to listen to what you call your explanation. I arrive Grand Central 2:45, daylight saving, Monday.
>
> ISABELLE.

Poor old George, I thought; some bachelor indiscretion; and now, with his honeymoon scarcely over, blackmail, a lawsuit, heaven only knew what.

"Who," I asked, returning the letter, "is Isabelle?"

To my distress, George again resorted to his napkin. Then, "My wife," he said.

"Your wife!"

George nodded.

"Been living with her people for the last month. Wish he'd bring that coffee. You don't happen to have a flask with you?"

"Yes, I have a flask." George brightened. "But it's empty. Do you want to tell me about your trouble? Is that why you brought me here?"

"Well, yes," George admitted. "But the point is—will you stand by me? That's the main thing. She gets in"—here he consulted his watch—"in forty-five minutes, if the train's on time." A sudden panic seemed to seize him. His hand shot across the table and grasped my wrist. "You've got to stand by me, old man— until the ice is broken. That's all I ask. Just stick until the train gets in. Then act as if you knew nothing. Say you ran into me here and stayed to meet her. I'll tell you what—say I didn't seem to want you to stay. Kid me about wanting her all to myself, or something like that. Get the point? It'll give me a chance to sort of—well, you understand."

"I see what you mean, of course," I admitted. "Here's your coffee. Suppose you have some and then tell me what this is all about—if you care to, that is."

"No sugar, no cream," said George to the waiter; "just pour it. Don't stand there waving it about—pour it, pour it!" He attempted to swallow a mouthful of steaming coffee, gurgled frightfully and grabbed his water glass. "Great jumping Jehoshaphat!" he gasped, when he could speak, and glared at the waiter, who promptly moved out into the sea of diners and disappeared among a dozen of his kind.

"Steady, George," I advised as I transferred a small lump of ice from my glass to his coffee cup.

George watched the ice dissolve, murmured "Idiot" several times, and presently swallowed the contents of the cup in two gulps.

"I had told her," he said suddenly, "exactly where we were going. She mentioned Narragansett several times—I'll admit that. Imagine—Narragansett! Of course I bought her fishing things myself. I didn't buy knickers or woolens or flannel shirts—naturally. You don't go around buying a girl breeches and underwear before you're married. It wouldn't be—well, it isn't done, that's all. I got her the sweetest three-ounce rod you ever held in your hand. I'll bet I could put out sixty feet of line with it against the wind. I got her a pair of English waders that didn't weigh a pound. They cost me forty-five dollars. The rest of the outfit was just as good. Why, her fly box was a Truxton. I could have bought an American imitation for eight dollars. I know a lot of men who'll buy leaders for themselves at two dollars apiece and let their wives fish with any kind of tackle. I'll give you my word I'd have used anything I got for her myself. I sent it all out to be packed with her things. I wanted her to feel that it was her own —not mine. I know a lot of men who give their wives a high-class rod or an imported reel and then fish with it themselves. What time is it?"

"Clock right up there," I said. But George consulted his watch and used his napkin distressingly again.

"Where was I?"

"You were telling me why you sent her fishing things out to her."

"Oh, yes! That's all of that. I simply wanted to show you that from the first I did all any man could do. Ever been in the Cuddiwink district?"

I said that I had not.

"You go in from Buck's Landing. A lumber tug takes you up to the head of Lake Owonga. Club guides meet you there and put you through in one day—twenty miles by canoe and portage up the west branch of the Penobscot; then nine miles by trail to Lost Pond. The club's on Lost Pond. Separate cabins, with a main dining and loafing camp, and the best squaretail fishing on earth —both lake and stream. Of course, I don't fish the lakes. A dry fly belongs on a stream and nowhere else. Let me make it perfectly clear."

George's manner suddenly changed. He hunched himself closer to the table, dropped an elbow upon it and lifted an expository finger.

"The dry fly," he stated, with a new almost combative ring in his voice, "is designed primarily to simulate not only the appearance of the natural insect but its action as well. This action is arrived at through the flow of the current. The moment you move a fly by means of a leader you destroy the_____

I saw that an interruption was imperative.

"Yes, of course," I said; but your wife will be here in_____"

It was pitiful to observe George. His new-found assurance did not flee—flee suggests a withdrawal, however swift—it was immediately and totally annihilated. He attempted to pour himself some coffee, take out his watch, look at the clock, and mop his brow with his napkin at one and the same instant.

"You were telling me how to get to Lost Pond," I suggested.

"Yes, to be sure," said George. "Naturally you go in light. The things you absolutely have to have—rods, tackle, waders, wading shoes, and so forth, are about all a guide can manage at the portages in addition to the canoe. You pack in extras yourself—change of underclothes, a couple of pairs of socks, and a few toilet articles. You leave a bag or trunk at Buck's Landing. I explained this to her. I explained it carefully. I told her either a week-end bag or one small trunk. Herb Trescott was my best man. I left everything to him. He saw us on the train and handed me tickets and reservations just before we pulled out. I didn't notice in the excitement of getting away that he'd given me three trunk checks all stamped 'Excess.' I didn't notice it till the conductor showed up, as a matter of fact. Then I said, 'Darling, what in heaven's name have you brought three trunks for?' She said—I can remember her exact words—'Then you're not going to Narragansett?'

"I simply looked at her. I was too dumfounded to speak. At last I pulled myself together and told her in three days we'd be whipping the best squaretail water in the world. I took her hand, I remember, and said, 'You and I together, sweetheart,' or something like that."

George sighed and lapsed into a silence which remained unbroken until his eye happened to encounter the face of the clock. He started and went on:

"We got to Buck's Landing, by way of Bangor, at six in the evening of the following day. Buck's Landing is a railroad station with grass growing between the ties, a general store and hotel combined, and a lumber wharf. The store keeps canned peas, pink-and-white-candy, and felt boots. The hotel part is—well, it doesn't matter except that I don't think I ever saw so many deer heads; a few stuffed trout, but mostly deer heads. After supper the proprietor and I got the three trunks up to the largest room: We just got them in and that was all. The tug left for the head of the lake at seven next morning. I explained this to Isabelle. I said we'd leave the trunks there until we came out, and offered to help her unpack the one her fishing things were in. She said, 'Please go away!' So I went. I got out a rod and went down to the wharf. No trout there, I knew; but I thought I'd limber up my wrist. I put on a Cahill Number Fourteen—or was it Sixteen____"

George knitted his brows and stared intently but unseeingly at me for some little time.

"Call it a Sixteen," I suggested.

George shook his head impatiently and remained concentrated in thought.

"I'm inclined to think it was a Fourteen," he said at last. "But let it go; it'll come to me later. At any rate, the place was alive with big chub—a foot long, some of 'em. I'll bet I took fifty—threw 'em back, of course. They kept on rising after it got dark. I'd tell myself I'd go after one more cast. Each time I'd hook a big chub, and—well, you know how the time slips away.

"When I got back to the hotel all the lights were out. I lit matches until I got upstairs and found the door to the room. I'll never forget what I saw when I opened that door—never! Do you happen to know how many of the kind of things they wear a woman can get into one trunk? Well, she had three and she'd unpacked them all. She had used the bed for the gowns alone. It was piled with them—literally piled; but that wasn't a starter. Everywhere you looked was a stack of things with ribbons in 'em. There were enough shoes and stockings for a girls' school; silk stockings, mind you, and high-heeled shoes and slippers." Here George consulted clock and watch. "I wonder if that train's on time," he wanted to know.

"You have thirty-five minutes, even if it is," I told him; "go right ahead."

"Well, I could see something was wrong from her face. I didn't know what, but I started right in to cheer her up. I told her all about the chub fishing I'd been having. At last she burst into tears. I won't go into the scene that followed. I'd ask her what was the matter and she'd say, 'Nothing,' and cry frightfully. I know a lot of men who would have lost their tempers under the circumstances, but I didn't; I give you my word. I simply said, 'There, there,' until she quieted down. And that isn't all. After a while she began to show me her gowns. Imagine —at eleven o'clock at night, at Buck's Landing! She'd hold up a dress and look over the top of it at me and ask me how I liked it, and I'd say it was all right. I know a lot of men who wouldn't have sat there two minutes.

"At last I said, 'They're all all right, darling,' and yawned. She was holding up a pink dress covered with shiny dingle-dangles, and she threw the dress on the bed and all but had hysterics. It was terrible. In trying to think of some way to quiet her it occurred to me that I'd put her rod together and let her feel the balance of it with the reel I'd bought her—a genuine Fleetwood, mind you—attached. I looked around for her fishing things and couldn't find them. I'll tell you why I couldn't find them." George paused for an impressive instant to give his next words the full significance due them. "They weren't there!"

"No?" I murmured weakly.

"No," said George. "And what do you suppose she said when I questioned her? I can give you her exact words—I'll never forget them. She said, 'There wasn't any room for them.'" Again George paused. "I ask you," he inquired at last, "I ask you as man to man; what do you think of that?"

I found no adequate reply to this question and George, now thoroughly warmed up, rushed on.

"You'd swear I lost my temper then, wouldn't you? Well, I didn't. I did say something to her later, but I'll let you be the judge when we come to that. I'll ask you to consider the circumstances. I'll ask you to get Old Faithful in your mind's eye."

"Old Faithful?" I repeated. "Then you went to the Yellowstone later?"

"Yellowstone! Of course not! Haven't I told you we were already at the best trout water in America? Old Faithful was a squaretail. He'd been in the pool below Horseshoe Falls for twenty years, as a matter of record. We'll come to that presently. How are we off for time?"

"Thirty-one minutes," I told him. "I'm watching the clock—go ahead."

"Well, there she was, on a fishing trip with nothing to fish with. There was only one answer to that—she couldn't fish. But I went over everything she'd brought in three trunks and I'll give you my word she didn't have a garment of any sort you couldn't see through.

"Something had to be done and done quick, that was sure. I fitted her out from my own things with a sweater, a flannel shirt, and a pair of knicker-bockers. Then I got the proprietor up and explained the situation. He got me some heavy underwear and two pairs of woolen stockings that belonged to his wife. When it came to shoes it looked hopeless, but the proprietor's wife, who had got up, too, by this time, thought of a pair of boy's moccasin's that were in the store and they turned out to be about the right size. I made arrangements to rent the room we had until we came out again to keep her stuff in, and took another room for the night—what was left of it after she'd repacked what could stay in the trunks and arranged what couldn't so it wouldn't be wrinkled.

"I got up early, dressed, and took my duffle down to the landing. I wakened her when I left the room. When breakfast was ready I went to see why she hadn't come down. She was all dressed, sitting on the edge of the bed. I said, 'Breakfast is ready, darling,' but I saw by her face that something was wrong again. It turned out to be my knickers. They fitted her perfectly—a little tight in spots—except in the waist. They would simply have fallen off if she hadn't held them up.

"Well, I was going in so light that I only had one belt. The proprietor didn't have any—he used suspenders. Neither did his wife—she used—well, whatever they use. He got me a piece of clothesline and I knotted it at each end and ran it through the what-you-may-call-'ems of the knickers and tied it in front. The knickers sort of puckered all the way round, but they couldn't come down —that was the main thing. I said, 'There you are, darling.' She walked over and tilted the mirror of the bureau so that she could see herself from head to foot. She said, 'Who are going to be at this place where we are going?' I said, 'Some of the very best dry-fly men in the country.' She said, 'I don't mean them; I mean the women. Will there be any women there?''

"I told her, certainly there would be women. I asked her if she thought I would take her into a camp with nothing but men. I named some of the women: Mrs. Fred Beal and Mrs. Brooks Carter and Talcott Ranning's sister and several more.

"She turned around slowly in front of the mirror, staring into it for a minute. Then she said, 'Please go out and close the door.' I said, 'All right, darling; but come right down. The tug will be here in fifteen minutes.'

"I went downstairs and waited ten minutes, then I heard the tug whistle for the landing and ran upstairs again. I knocked at the door. When she didn't answer I went in. Where do you suppose she was?"

I gave it up.

"In bed!" said George in an awe-struck voice. "In bed with her face turned to the wall; and listen, I didn't lose my temper as God is my judge. I rushed down to the wharf and told the tug captain I'd give him twenty-five dollars extra if he'd hold the boat till we came. He said all right and I went back to the room.

"The breeches had done it. She simply wouldn't wear them. I told her that at a fishing camp in Maine clothes were never thought of. I said, 'No one thinks of anything but trout, darling.' She said, 'I wouldn't let a fish see me looking like that.'" George's brow beaded suddenly. His hands dived searchingly into various pockets. "Got a cigarette? I left my case in my other suit."

He took a cigarette from me, lighted it with shaking fingers and inhaled deeply.

"It went on like that for thirty minutes. She was crying all the time, of course. I had started down to tell the tug captain it was all off, and I saw a woman's raincoat hanging in the hall. It belonged to some one up in one of the camps, the proprietor told me. I gave him seventy-five dollars to give to whoever owned it when he came out, and took it upstairs. In about ten minutes I persuaded her to wear it over the rest of her outfit until we got to camp. I told her one of the women would be able to fix her up all right when we got there. I didn't believe it, of course. The women at camp were all old-timers; they'd gone in as light as the men; but I had to say something.

"We had quite a trip going in. The guides were at the head of the lake all right—Indian Joe and a new man I'd never seen, called Charlie. I told Joe to take Isabelle—he's one of the best canoemen I ever saw. I was going to paddle bow for my man, but I'd have bet a cooky Indian Joe could stay with us on any kind of water. We had to beat it right through to make camp by night. It's a good stiff trip, but it can be done. I looked back at the other canoe now and then until we struck about a mile of white water that took all I had. When we were through the other canoe wasn't in sight. The river made a bend there, and I thought it was just behind and would show up any minute.

"Well, it didn't show up and I began to wonder. We hit our first portage about ten o'clock and landed. I watched downstream for twenty minutes, expecting to sight the other canoe every instant. Then Charlie, who hadn't opened his head, said, 'Better go back,' and put the canoe in again. We paddled downstream for all that was in it. I was stiff with fright. We saw 'em coming about three miles lower down and back-paddled till they came up. Isabelle was more cheerful-looking than she'd been since we left New York, but Joe had that stony face an Indian gets when he's sore.

"I said, 'Anything wrong?' Joe just grunted and drove the canoe past us. Then I saw it was filled with wild flowers. Isabelle said she'd been picking them right off the banks all the way long. She said she'd only had to get out of the boat once, for the blue ones. Now, you can't beat that—not in a thousand years. I leave it to you if you can. Twenty miles of stiff current, with five portages ahead of us and a nine-mile hike at the end of that. I gave that Indian the devil for letting her do such a thing, and tipped the flowers into the Penobscot when we unloaded for the first portage. She didn't speak to me on the portage, and she got into her canoe without a word.

"Nothing more happened going in, except this flower business had lost us two hours, and it was so dark when we struck the swamp at Loon Lake that we couldn't follow the trail well and kept stumbling over down timber and stepping into bog holes. She was about fagged out by then, and the mosquitoes were pretty thick through there. Without any warning she sat down in the trail. She did it so suddenly I nearly fell over her. I asked her what was the matter and she said, 'This is the end'—just like that—'this is the end!' I said, 'The end of what, darling?' She said, 'Of everything!' I told her if she sat there all wet and muddy she'd catch her death. She said she hoped so. I said, 'It's only two miles more, darling. Just think, to-morrow we'll be on the best trout water in the world!' With that she said, 'I want my mother, my darling mother,' and bowed her head in her hands. Think it over, please; and remember, I didn't lose my temper. You're sure there's nothing left in your flask?"

"Not a drop, George," I assured him. "Go ahead; we've only twenty-five minutes."

George looked wildly at the clock, then at his watch.

"A man never has it when he wants it most. Have you noticed that? Where was I?"

"You were in the swamp."

"Oh, yes! Well, she didn't speak after that, and nothing I could say would budge her. The mosquitoes had got wind of us when we stopped and were coming in swarms. We'd be eaten alive in another ten minutes. So I told Joe to give his pack to Charlie and help me pick her up and carry her. Joe said, 'No, by damn!' and folded his arms. When an Indian gets sore he stays sore, and when he's sore he's stubborn. The mosquitoes were working on him good and plenty, though, and at last he said, 'Me carry packs. Charlie help carry—that.' He flipped his hand over in the direction of Isabelle and took the pack from Charlie.

"It was black as your hat by now, and the trail through there was only about a foot wide with swamp on each side. It was going to be some job getting her out of there. I thought Charlie and I would make a chair of our arms and stumble along with her some way; but when I started to lift her up she said, 'Don't touch me!' and got up and went on. A blessing if there ever was one. We got to camp at ten that night.

"She was stiff and sore next morning—you expect it after a trip like that—besides, she'd caught a little cold. I asked her how she felt, and she said she was going to die and asked me to send for a doctor and her mother. The nearest doctor was at Bangor and her mother was in New Rochelle. I carried her breakfast over from the dining camp to our cabin. She said she couldn't eat any breakfast, but she did drink a cup of coffee, telling me between sips how awful it was to die alone in a place like that.

"After she'd had the coffee she seemed to feel better. I went to the camp library and got *The Dry Fly on American Waters*, by Charles Darty. I consider him the soundest man in the country. He's better than Pell or Fawcett. My chief criticism of him is that in his chapter on Streams East of the Alleghenies—east of the Alleghenies, mind you—he recommends the Royal Coachman. I consider the Lead-Wing Coachman a serviceable fly on clear, hard-fished water; but the Royal—never! I wouldn't give it a shade over the Professor or the Montreal. Just consider the body alone of the Royal Coachman—never mind the wings and hackle—the body of the Royal is____"

"Yes, I know, George," I said; "but____"

I glanced significantly at the clock. George started, sighed, and resumed his narrative.

"I went back to the cabin and said, 'Darling, here is one of the most intensely interesting books ever written. I'm going to read it aloud to you. I think I can finish it to-day. Would you like to sit up in bed while I read?' She said she hadn't strength enough to sit up in bed, so I sat down beside her and started reading. I had read about an hour, I suppose, when she did sit up in bed quite suddenly. I saw she was staring at me in a queer, wild way that was really startling. I said, 'What is it, darling?' She said, 'I'm going to get up. I'm going to get up this instant.'

"Well, I was delighted, naturally. I thought the book would get her by the time I'd read it through. But there she was, as keen as mustard before I'd got well into it. I'll tell you what I made up my mind to do, right there. I made up my mind to let her use my rod that day. Yes, sir—my three-ounce Spinoza, and what's more, I did it."

George looked at me triumphantly, then lapsed into reflection for a moment. "If ever a man did everything possible to—well, let it go. The main thing is, I have nothing to reproach myself with—nothing. Except—but we'll come to that presently. Of course, she wasn't ready for dry flies yet. I borrowed some wet flies from the club steward, got some cushions for the canoe and put my rod together. She had no waders, so a stream was out of the question. The lake was better, anyway, that first day; she'd have all the room she wanted for her back cast.

"I stood on the landing with her before we got into the canoe and showed her just how to put out a fly and recover it. Then she tried it." A sort of horror came into George's face. "You wouldn't believe any one could handle a rod like that," he said huskily. "You couldn't believe it unless you'd seen it. Gimme a cigarette.

"I worked with her a half hour or so and saw no improvement—none whatever. At last she said, 'The string is too long. I can't do anything with such a long string on the pole.' I told her gently—gently, mind you—that the string was an eighteen-dollar double-tapered Hurdman line, attached to a Gebhardt reel on a three-ounce Spinoza rod. I said, 'We'll go out on the lake now. If you can manage to get a rise, perhaps it will come to you instinctively.'

"I paddled her out on the lake and she went at it. She'd spat the flies down and yank them up and spat them down again. She hooked me several times with her back cast and got tangled up in the line herself again and again. All this time I was speaking quietly to her, telling her what to do. I give you my word I never raised my voice—not once—and I thought she'd break the tip every moment.

"Finally she said her arm was tired and lowered the rod. She'd got everything messed up with her last cast and the flies were trailing just over the side of the canoe. I said, 'Recover your cast and reel in, darling.' Instead of using her rod, she took hold of the leader close to the flies and started to pull them into the canoe. At that instant a little trout—couldn't have been over six inches— took the tail fly. I don't know exactly what happened, it was all over so quickly. I think she just screamed and let go of everything. At any rate, I saw my Spinoza bounce off the gunwale of the canoe and disappear. There was fifty feet of water just there. And now listen carefully: not one word did I utter—not one. I simply turned the canoe and paddled to the landing in absolute silence. No reproaches of any sort. Think that over!"

I did. My thoughts left me speechless. George proceeded:

"I took out a guide and tried dragging for the rod with a gang hook and heavy sinker all the rest of the day. But the gangs would only foul on the bottom. I gave up at dusk and paddled in. I said to the guide—it was Charlie—I said, 'Well, it's all over, Charlie.' Charlie said, 'I brought Mr. Carter in and he had an extra rod. Maybe you could borrow it. It's a four-ounce Meecham.' I smiled. I actually smiled. I turned and looked at the lake. 'Charlie,' I said, 'somewhere out there in that dark water, where the eye of man will never behold it again, is a three-ounce Spinoza—and you speak of a Meecham.' Charlie said, 'Well, I

just thought I'd tell you.' I said, 'That's all right, Charlie. That's all right.' I
went to the main camp, saw Jean, the head guide and made arrangements to
leave the next day. Then I went to our cabin and sat down before the fire. I
heard Isabelle say something about being sorry. I said, 'I'd rather not talk about
it, darling. If you don't mind, we'll never mention it again.' We sat there in
silence, then, until dinner.

"As we got up from dinner, Nate Griswold and his wife asked us to play
bridge with them that evening. I'd told no one what had happened, and Nate
didn't know, of course. I simply thanked him and said we were tired, and we
went back to our cabin. I sat down before the fire again. Isabelle seemed restless.
At last she said, 'George.' I said, 'What is it, darling?' She said, 'Would you like
to read to me from that book?' I said, 'I'm sorry, darling; if you don't mind
I'll just sit here quietly by the fire.'

"Somebody knocked at the door after a while. I said, 'Come in.' It was
Charlie. I said, 'What is it, Charlie?' Then he told me that Bob Frazer had been
called back to New York and was going out next morning. I said, 'Well, what
of it?' Charlie said, 'I just thought you could maybe borrow his rod.' I said, 'I
thought you understood about that, Charlie.' Charlie said, 'Well, that's it. Mr.
Frazer's rod is a three-ounce Spinoza.'

"I got up and shook hands with Charlie and gave him five dollars. But when
he'd gone I began to realize what was before me. I'd brought in a pint flask of
prewar Scotch. Prewar—get that! I put this in my pocket and went over to
Bob's cabin. Just as I was going to knock I lost my nerve. I sneaked away from
the door and went down to the lake and sat on the steps of the canoe landing.
I sat there for quite a while and took several nips. At last I thought I'd just go
and tell Bob of my loss and see what he said. I went back to his cabin and
this time I knocked. Bob was putting a few odds and ends in a shoulder pack.
His rod was in its case, standing against the wall.

"I said, 'I hear you're going out in the morning." He said, 'Yes, curse it, my
wife's mother has to have some sort of a damned operation or other.' I said,
'How would a little drink strike you, Bob?' He said, 'Strike me! Wait a minute!
What kind of a drink?' I took out the flask and handed it to him. He unscrewed
the cap and held the flask to his nose. He said, 'Great heavens above, it smells
like____' I said, 'It is.' He said, 'It can't be!' I said, 'Yes, it is.' He said, 'There's
a trick in it somewhere.' I said, 'No, there isn't—I give you my word.' He tasted
what was in the flask carefully. Then he said, 'I call this white of you, George,'
and took a good stiff snort. When he was handing back the flask he said, 'I'll
do as much for you some day, if I ever get the chance.' I took a snifter myself.

"Then I said, 'Bob, something awful has happened to me. I came here to
tell you about it.' He said, 'Is that so? Sit down.' I sat down and told him. He
said, 'What kind of a rod was it?' I said, 'A three-ounce Spinoza.' He came over
and gripped my hand without a word. I said, 'Of course, I can't use anything
else.' He nodded, and I saw his eyes flicker toward the corner of the room
where his own rod was standing. I said, 'Have another drink, Bob.' But he

just sat down and stared at me. I took a good stiff drink myself. Then I said, 'Under ordinary circumstances, nothing on earth could hire me to ask a man to____' I stopped right there.

'Bob got up suddenly and began to walk up and down the room. I said, 'Bob, I'm not considering myself—not for a minute. If it was last season, I'd simply have gone back to-morrow without a word. But I'm not alone any more. I've got the little girl to consider. She's never seen a trout taken in her life— think of it, Bob! And here she is, on her honeymoon, at the best water I know of. On her honeymoon, Bob!' I waited for him to say something, but he went to the window and stared out, with his back to me. I got up and said good-night and started for the door. Just as I reached it he turned from the window and rushed over and picked up his rod. He said, 'Here, take it,' and put the rod case in my hands. I started to try to thank him, but he said, 'Just go ahead with it,' and pushed me out the door."

The waiter was suddenly hovering above us with his eyes on the dishes.

"Now what do you want?" said George.

"Never mind clearing here," I said. "Just bring me the check. Go ahead, George."

"Well, of course, I can't any more than skim what happened finally, but you'll understand. It turned out that Ernie Payton's wife had an extra pair of knickers and she loaned them to Isabelle. I was waiting outside the cabin while she dressed next morning, and she called out to me, 'Oh, George, they fit!' Then I heard her begin to sing. She was a different girl when she came out to go to breakfast. She was almost smiling. She'd done nothing but slink about the day before. Isn't it extraordinary what will seem important to a woman? Gimme a cigarette."

"Fifteen minutes, George," I said as I supplied him.

"Yes, yes, I know. I fished the Cuddiwink that day. Grand stream, grand. I used a Pink Lady—first day on a stream with Isabelle—little touch of sentiment —and it's a darn good fly. I fished it steadily all day. Or did I try a Seth Green about noon? It seems to me I did, now that I recall it. It seems to me that where the Katahdin brook comes in I____"

"It doesn't really matter, does it, George?" I ventured.

"Of course, it matters!" said George decisively. "A man wants to be exact about such things. The precise details of what happens in a day's work on a stream are of real value to yourself and others. Except in the case of a record fish, it isn't important that you took a trout; it's exactly how you took him that's important."

"But the time, George," I protested.

He glanced at the clock, swore softly, mopped his brow—this time with the blue-gray handkerchief—and proceeded.

"Isabelle couldn't get into the stream without waders, so I told her to work along the bank a little behind me. It was pretty thick along there, second growth and vines mostly; but I was putting that Pink Lady on every foot of good water and she kept up with me easily enough. She didn't see me take many trout, though. I'd look for her, after landing one, to see what she thought of the way I'd handled the fish, and almost invariably she was picking ferns or blueberries, or getting herself untangled from something. Curious things, women. Like children, when you stop to think of it."

George stared at me unseeingly for a moment.

"And you never heard of Old Faithful?" he asked suddenly. "Evidently not, from what you said a while ago. Well, a lot of people have, believe me. Men have gone to the Cuddiwink district just to see him. As I've already told you, he lay beside a ledge in the pool below Horseshoe Falls. Almost nothing else in the pool. He kept it cleaned out. Worst sort of cannibal, of course—all big trout are. That was the trouble—he wanted something that would stick to his ribs. No flies for him. Did his feeding at night.

"You could see him dimly if you crawled out on a rock that jutted above the pool and looked over. He lay in about ten feet of water, right by his ledge. If he saw you he'd back under the ledge, slowly, like a submarine going into dock. Think of the biggest thing you've ever seen, and that's the way Old Faithful looked, just lying there as still as the ledge. He never seemed to move anything, not even his gills. When he backed in out of sight he seemed to be drawn under the ledge by some invisible force.

"Ridgway—R. Campbell Ridgway—you may have read his stuff, Brethren of the Wild, that sort of thing—claimed to have seen him move. He told me about it one night. He said he was lying with just his eyes over the edge of the rock, watching the trout. Said he'd been there an hour, when down over the falls came a young red squirrel. It had fallen in above and been carried over. The squirrel was half drowned, but struck out feebly for shore. Well, so Ridgway said—Old Faithful came up and took Mister Squirrel into camp. No hurry; just came drifting up, sort of inhaled the squirrel and sank down to the ledge again. Never made a ripple, Ridgway said; just business.

"I'm telling you all this because it's necessary that you get an idea of that trout in your mind. You'll see why in a minute. No one ever had hold of him. But it was customary, if you fished the Cuddiwink, to make a few casts over him before you left the stream. Not that you ever expected him to rise. It was just a sort of gesture. Everybody did it.

"Knowing that Isabelle had never seen trout taken before, I made a day of it —naturally. The trail to camp leaves the stream just at the falls. It was pretty late when we got to it. Isabelle had her arms full of—heaven knows what— flowers and grass and ferns and fir branches and colored leaves. She'd lugged the stuff for hours. I remember once that day I was fighting a fourteen-inch fish in swift water and she came to the bank and wanted me to look at a ripe blackberry—I think it was—she'd found. How does that strike you? And listen! I said, 'It's a beauty, darling.' That's what I said—or something like that. . . . Here, don't you pay that check! Bring it here, waiter!"

"Go on, George!" I said. "We haven't time to argue about the check. You'd come to the trail for camp at the falls."

"I told Isabelle to wait at the trail for a few minutes, while I went below the falls and did the customary thing for the edification of Old Faithful. I only intended to make three or four casts with the Number Twelve Fly and the hair-fine leader I had on, but in getting down to the pool I hooked the fly in a bush. In trying to loosen it I stumbled over something and fell. I snapped the leader like a thread, and since I had to put on another, I tied on a fairly heavy one as a matter of form.

"I had reached for my box for a regulation fly of some sort when I remembered a fool thing that Billy Roach had given me up on the Beaverkill the season before. It was fully two inches long; I forget what he called it. He said you fished it dry for bass or large trout. He said you worked the tip of your rod and made it wiggle like a dying minnow. I didn't want the contraption, but he'd borrowed some fly oil from me and insisted on my taking it. I'd stuck it in the breast pocket of my fishing jacket and forgotten it until then.

"Well, I felt in the pocket and there it was. I tied it on and went down to the pool. Now let me show you the exact situation." George seized a fork. "This is the pool." The fork traced an oblong figure on the tablecloth. "Here is Old Faithful's ledge." The fork deeply marked this impressive spot. "Here are the falls, with white water running to here. You can only wade to this point here, and then you have an abrupt six-foot depth. 'But you can put a fly from here to here with a long line,' you say. No, you can't. You've forgotten to allow for your back cast. Notice this bend here? That tells the story. You're not more than twenty feet from a lot of birch and whatnot, when you can no longer wade. 'Well then, it's impossible to put a decent fly on the water above the sunken ledge,' you say. It looks like it, but this is how it's done: right here is a narrow point running to here, where it dwindles off to a single flat rock. If you work out on the point you can jump across to this rock—situated right here— and there you are, with about a thirty-foot cast to the sunken ledge. Deep water all around you, of course, and the rock is slippery; but—there you are. Now notice this small cove, right here. The water from the falls rushes past it in a froth, but in the cove it forms a deep eddy, with the current moving round and round, like this." George made a slow circular motion with the fork. "You know what I mean?"

I nodded.

"I got out on the point and jumped to the rock; got myself balanced, worked out the right amount of line and cast the dingaree Bill had forced on me, just above the sunken ledge. I didn't take the water lightly and I cast again, but I couldn't put it down decently. It would just flop in—too much weight and too many feathers. I suppose I cast it a dozen times, trying to make it settle like a fly. I wasn't thinking of trout—there would be nothing in there except Old Faithful—I was just monkeying with this doodle-bug thing, now that I had it on.

"I gave up at last and let it lie out where I had cast it. I was standing there looking at the falls roaring down, when I remembered Isabelle, waiting up on the trail. I raised my rod preparatory to reeling in and the what-you-may-call-'em

made a kind of a dive and wiggle out there on the surface. I reached for my reel handle. Then I realized that the thingamajig wasn't on the water. I didn't see it disappear, exactly; I was just looking at it, and then it wasn't there. 'That's funny,' I thought, and struck instinctively. Well, I was fast—so it seemed—and no snags in there. I gave it the butt three or four times, but the rod only bowed and nothing budged. I tried to figure it out. I thought perhaps a water-logged timber had come diving over the falls and upended right there. Then I noticed the rod take more of a bend and the line began to move through the water. It moved out slowly, very slowly, into the middle of the pool. It was exactly as though I was hooked on to a freight train just getting under way.

"I knew what I had hold of then, and yet I didn't believe it. I couldn't believe it. I kept thinking it was a dream, I remember. Of course, he could have gone away with everything I had any minute if he'd wanted to, but he didn't. He just kept moving slowly, round and round the pool. I gave him what pressure the tackle would stand, but he never noticed a little thing like that; just kept moving around the pool for hours, it seemed to me. I'd forgotten Isabelle; I admit that. I'd forgotten everything on earth. There didn't seem to be anything else on earth, as a matter of fact, except the falls and the pool and Old Faithful and me. At last Isabelle showed up on the bank above me, still lugging her ferns and whatnot. She called down to me above the noise of the falls. She asked me how long I expected her to wait alone in the woods, with night coming on.

"I hadn't had the faintest idea how I was going to try to land the fish until then. The water was boiling past the rock I was standing on, and I couldn't jump back to the point without giving him slack and perhaps falling in. I began to look around and figure. Isabelle, said, 'What on earth are you doing?' I took off my landing net and tossed it to the bank. I yelled, 'Drop that junk quick and pick up that net!' She said, 'What for, George?' I said, 'Do as I tell you and don't ask questions!' She laid down what she had and picked up the net and I told her to go to the cove and stand ready.

"She said, 'Ready for what?' I said, 'You'll see what presently. Just stand there.' I'll admit I wasn't talking quietly. There was the noise of the falls to begin with, and—well, naturally I wasn't.

"I went to work on the fish again. I began to educate him to lead. I thought if I could lead him into the cove he would swing right past Isabelle and she could net him. It was slow work—a three-ounce rod—imagine! Isabelle called, 'Do you know what time it is?' I told her to keep still and stand where she was. She didn't say anything more after that.

"At last the fish began to come. He wasn't tired—he'd never done any fighting, as a matter of fact—but he'd take a suggestion as to where to go from the rod. I kept swinging him nearer and nearer the cove each time he came around. When I saw he was about ready to come I yelled to Isabelle. I said, 'I'm going to bring him right past you, close to the top. All you have to do is to net him.'

"When the fish came round again I steered him into the cove. Just as he was swinging past Isabelle the stuff she'd been lugging began to roll down the bank. She dropped the landing net on top of the fish and made a dive for those leaves and grasses and things. Fortunately the net handle lodged against the bank, and after she'd put her stuff in a nice safe place she came back and picked up the net again. I never uttered a syllable. I deserve no credit for that. The trout had made a surge and shot out into the pool and I was too busy just then to give her any idea of what I thought.

"I had a harder job getting him to swing in again. He was a little leery of the cove, but at last he came. I steered him toward Isabelle and lifted him all I dared. He came up nicely, clear to the top. I yelled, 'Here he comes! For God's sake, don't miss him!' I put everything on the tackle it would stand and managed to check the fish for an instant right in front of Isabelle.

"And this is what she did: it doesn't seem credible—it doesn't seem humanly possible; but it's a fact that you'll have to take my word for. She lifted the landing net above her head with both hands and brought it down on top of the fish with all her might!"

George ceased speaking. Despite its coating of talcum powder, I was able to detect an additional pallor in his countenance.

"Will I ever forget it as long as I live?" he inquired at last.

"No, George," I said, "but we've just exactly eleven minutes left."

George made a noticeable effort and went on:

"By some miracle the fish stayed on the hook; but I got a faint idea of what would have happened if he'd taken a real notion to fight. He went around the pool so fast it must have made him dizzy. I heard Isabelle say, 'I didn't miss him, George'; and then—well, I didn't lose my temper; you wouldn't call it that exactly. I hardly knew what I said. I'll admit I shouldn't have said it. But I did say it; no doubt of that; no doubt of that whatever."

"What was it you said?" I asked.

George looked at me uneasily.

"Oh, the sort of thing a man would say impulsively—under the circumstances."

"Was it something disparaging about her?" I inquired.

"Oh, no," said George, "nothing about her. I simply intimated—in a somewhat brutal way, I suppose—that she'd better get away from the pool—er—not bother me any more is what I meant to imply."

For the first time since George had chosen me for a confidant I felt a lack of frankness on his part.

"Just what did you say, George?" I insisted.

"Well, it wasn't altogether my words," he evaded. "It was the tone I used, as much as anything. Of course, the circumstances would excuse—Still, I regret it. I admit that. I've told you so plainly."

There was no time in which to press him further.

"Well, what happened then?" I asked.

"Isabelle just disappeared. She went up the bank, of course, but I didn't see her go. Old Faithful was still nervous and I had to keep my eye on the line. He quieted down in a little while and continued to promenade slowly around the pool. I suppose this kept up for half an hour more. Then I made up my mind that something had to be done. I turned very carefully on the rock, lowered the tip until it was on a line with the fish, turned the rod under my arm until it was pointing behind me and jumped.

"Of course, I had to give him slack; but I kept my balance on the point by the skin of my teeth, and when I raised the rod he was still on. I worked to the bank, giving out line, and crawled under some bushes and things and got around to the cove at last. Then I started to work again to swing him into the cove, but absolutely nothing doing. I could lead him anywhere except into the cove. He'd had enough of that; I didn't blame him, either.

"To make a long story short, I stayed with him for two hours. For a while it was pretty dark; but there was a good-sized moon that night, and when it rose it shone right down on the pool through a gap in the trees fortunately. My wrist was gone completely, but I managed to keep some pressure on him all the time, and at last he forgot about what had happened to him in the cove. I swung him in and the current brought him past me. He was on his side by now. I don't think he was tired even then—just discouraged. I let him drift over the net, heaved him out on the bank and sank down beside him, absolutely all in. I couldn't have got to my feet on a bet. I just sat there in a sort of daze and looked at Old Faithful, gleaming in the moonlight.

"After a half-hour's rest I was able to get up and go to camp. I planned what I was going to do on the way. There was always a crowd in the main camp living room after dinner. I simply walked into the living room without a word and laid Old Faithful on the center table.

"Well, you can imagine faintly what happened. I never got any dinner—couldn't have eaten any, as a matter of fact. I didn't even get a chance to take off my waders. By the time I'd told just how I'd done it to one crowd, more would come in and look at Old Faithful; and then stand and look at me for a while; and then make me tell it all over again. At last everybody began to dig up anything they had with a kick in it. Almost every one had a bottle he'd been hoarding. There was Scotch and gin and brandy and rye and a lot of experimental stuff. Art Bascom got a tin dish pan from the kitchen and put it on the table beside Old Faithful. He said, 'Pour your contributions right in here, men.' So each man dumped whatever he had into the dish pan and everybody helped himself.

"It was great, of course. The biggest night of my life, but I hope I'll never be so dog-tired again. I felt as though I'd taken a beating. After they'd weighed Old Faithful—nine pounds five and a half ounces; and he'd been out of water two hours—I said I had to go to bed, and went.

"Isabelle wasn't in the cabin. I thought, in a hazy way, that she was with some of the women, somewhere. Don't get the idea I was stewed. But I hadn't had anything to eat, and the mixture in that dish pan was plain TNT.

"I fell asleep as soon as I hit the bed; slept like a log till daylight. Then I half woke up, feeling that something terrific had happened. For a minute I didn't know what; then I remembered what it was. I had landed Old Faithful on a three-ounce rod!

"I lay there and went over the whole thing from the beginning, until I came to Isabelle with the landing net. That made me look at where her head should have been on the pillow. It wasn't there. She wasn't in the cabin. I thought perhaps she'd got up early and gone out to look at the lake or the sunrise or something. But I got up in a hurry and dressed.

"Well, I could see no signs of Isabelle about camp. I ran into Jean just coming from the head guide's cabin and he said, 'Too bad about your wife's mother.' I said, 'What's that?' He repeated what he'd said, and added, 'She must be an awful sick woman.' Well, I got out of him finally that Isabelle had come straight up from the stream the evening before, taken two guides and started for Buck's Landing. Jean had urged her to wait until morning, naturally; but she'd told him she must get to her mother at once, and took on so, as Jean put it, that he had to let her go.

"I said, 'Let me have Indian Joe, stern, and a good man, bow. Have 'em ready in ten minutes.' I rushed to the kitchen, drank two cups of coffee and started for Buck's Landing. We made the trip down in seven hours, but Isabelle had left with her trunks on the 10:40 train.

"I haven't seen her since. Went to her home once. She wouldn't see me; neither would her mother. Her father advised not forcing things—just waiting. He said he'd do what he could. Well, he's done it—you read the letter. Now you know the whole business. You'll stick, of course, and see me through just the first of it, old man. Of course, you'll do that, won't you? We'd better get down to the train now. Track Nineteen."

George rose from the table. I followed him from the café, across the blue-domed rotunda to a restraining rope stretched before the gloomy entrance to Track Nineteen.

"George," I said, "one thing more: just what did you say to her when she____"

"Oh, I don't know," George began vaguely.

"George," I interrupted, "no more beating about the bush. What did you say?"

I saw his face grow even more haggard, if possible. Then it mottled into a shade resembling the brick on an old colonial mansion.

"I told her____" he began in a low voice.

"Yes?" I encouraged.

"I told her to get the hell out of there."

And now a vision was presented to my mind's eye; a vision of twelve fish plates, each depicting a trout curving up through green waters to an artificial fly. The vision extended on through the years. I saw Mrs. George Baldwin Potter ever gazing upon those rising trout and recalling the name on the card which had accompanied them to her door.

I turned and made rapidly for the main entrance of the Grand Central Station. In doing so I passed the clock above Information and saw that I still had two minutes in which to be conveyed by a taxicab far, far from the entrance to Track Nineteen.

I remember hearing the word "quitter" hurled after me by a hoarse, despairing voice.

THE LADY OR THE SALMON?

Andrew Lang

THE CIRCUMSTANCES which attended and caused the death of the Hon. Houghton Grannom have not long been known to me, and it is only now that, by the decease of his father, Lord Whitchurch, and the extinction of his noble family, I am permitted to divulge the facts. That the true tale of my unhappy friend will touch different chords in different breasts, I am well aware. The sportsman, I think, will hesitate to approve him; the fair, I hope, will absolve. Who are we, to scrutinise human motives, and to award our blame to actions which, perhaps, might have been our own, had opportunity beset and temptation beguiled us? There is a certain point at which the keenest sense of honour, the most chivalrous affection and devotion, cannot bear the strain, but breaks like a salmon line under a masterful stress. That my friend succumbed, I admit; that he was his own judge, the severest, and passed and executed sentence on himself, I have now to show.

I shall never forget the shock with which I read in the *Scotsman,* under "Angling," the following paragraph:

"Tweed—Strange Death of an Angler—An unfortunate event has cast a gloom over fishers in this district. As Mr. K—, the keeper on the B—water, was busy angling yesterday, his attention was caught by some object floating on the stream. He cast his flies over it, and landed a soft felt hat, the ribbon stuck full of salmon-flies. Mr. K— at once hurried upstream, filled with the most lively apprehensions. These were soon justified. In a shallow, below the narrow, deep and dangerous rapids called 'The Trows,' Mr. K— saw a salmon leaping in a very curious manner. On a closer examination, he found that the fish was attached to a line. About seventy yards higher he found, in shallow water, the body of a man, the hand still grasping in death the butt of the rod, to which the salmon was fast, all the line being run out. Mr. K— at once rushed into the stream, and dragged out the body, in which he recognised with horror the Hon. Houghton Grannom, to whom the water was lately let. Life had been for some minutes extinct, and though Mr. K— instantly hurried for Dr. —, that gentleman could only attest the melancholy fact. The wading in 'The Trows' is extremely danger-ous and difficult, and Mr. Grannom, who was fond of fishing without an at-tendant, must have lost his balance, slipped, and been dragged down by the weight of his waders. The recent breaking off of the hon. gentleman's contem-plated marriage on the very wedding-day will be fresh in the memory of our readers."

This was the story which I read in the newspaper during breakfast one morn-ing in November. I was deeply grieved, rather than astonished, for I have often remonstrated with poor Grannom on the recklessness of his wading. It was with some surprise that I received, in the course of the day, a letter from him, in which he spoke only of indifferent matters, of the fishing which he had taken, and so forth. The letter was accompanied, however, by a parcel. Tearing off the outer cover, I found a sealed document addressed to me, with the superscription, "Not to be opened until after my father's decease." This injunction, of course, I have scrupulously obeyed. The death of Lord Whitchurch, the last of the Grannoms, now gives me liberty to publish my friend's *Apologia pro morte et vita sua.*

"Dear Smith" (the document begins), "Before you read this—long before, I hope—I shall have solved the great mystery—if, indeed, we solve it. If the water runs down to-morrow, and there is every prospect that it will do so, I must have the opportunity of making such an end as even malignity cannot suspect of being voluntary. There are plenty of fish in the water; if I hook one in 'The Trows,' I shall let myself go whither the current takes me. Life has for weeks been odious to me; for what is life without honour, without love, and coupled with shame and remorse? Repentance I cannot call the emotion which gnaws me at the heart, for in similar circumstances (unlikely as these are to occur) I feel that I would do the same thing again.

"Are we but automata, worked by springs, moved by the stronger impulse, and unable to choose for ourselves which impulse that shall be? Even now, in decreeing my own destruction, do I exercise free-will, or am I the sport of heredi-tary tendencies, of mistaken views of honour, of a seeming self-sacrifice, which, perhaps, is but selfishness in disguise? I blight my unfortunate father's old age; I destroy the last of an ancient house; but I remove from the path of Olive Dunne the shadow that must rest upon the sunshine of what will eventually, I trust, be a happy life, unvexed by memories of one who loved her passionately. Dear Olive! how pure, how ardent was my devotion to her none knows better than you. But Olive had, I will not say a fault, though I suffer from it, but a quality, or rather two qualities, which have completed my misery. Lightly as she floats on the stream of society, the most casual observer, and even the enamoured be-holder, can see that Olive Dunne has great pride, and no sense of humour. Her dignity is her idol. What makes her, even for a moment, the possible theme of ridicule is in her eyes an unpardonable sin. This sin, I must with penitence confess, I did indeed commit. Another woman might have forgiven me. I know not how that may be; I throw myself on the mercy of the court. But, if another could pity and pardon, to Olive this was impossible. I have never seen her since that fatal moment when, paler than her orange blossoms, she swept through the porch of the church, while I, dishevelled, mud-stained, half-drowned—ah! that memory will torture me if memory at all remains. And yet, fool, maniac, that I was, I could not resist the wild, mad impulse to laugh which shook the rustic spectators, and which in my case was due, I trust, to hysterical but *not* unmanly emotion. If any woman, any bride, could forgive such an apparent but most unintentional insult, Olive Dunne, I knew, was not that woman. My abject letters of explanation, my appeals for mercy, were returned unopened. Her parents pitied me, perhaps had reasons for being on my side, but Olive was of marble. It is not only myself that she cannot pardon, she will never, I know, forgive herself while my existence reminds her of what she had to endure. When she receives the intelligence of my demise, no suspicion will occur to her; she will not say 'He is fitly punished'; but her peace of mind will gradually return.

"It is for this, mainly, that I sacrifice myself, but also because I cannot endure the dishonour of a laggard in love and a recreant bridegroom.

"So much for my motives: now to my tale.

"The day before our wedding-day had been the happiest in my life. Never had I felt so certain of Olive's affections, never so fortunate in my own. We parted in the soft moonlight; she, no doubt, to finish her nuptial preparations; I, to seek my couch in the little rural inn above the roaring waters of the Budon.

> Move eastward, happy earth, and leave
>   Yon orange sunset fading slow;
> From fringes of the faded eve
>   Oh, happy planet, eastward go,

I murmured, though the atmospheric conditions were not really those described by the poet.

> Ah, bear me with thee, smoothly borne,
>   Dip forward under starry light,
> And move me to my marriage morn,
>   And round again to—

" 'River in grand order, sir,' said the voice of Robins, the keeper, who recognised me in the moonlight. 'There's a regular monster in the Ashweil,' he added, naming a favourite cast; 'never saw nor heard of such a fish in the water before.'

" 'Mr. Dick must catch him, Robins,' I answered; 'no fishing for me to-morrow.'

" 'No, sir,' said Robins, affably. 'Wish you joy, sir, and Miss Olive, too. It's a pity, though! Master Dick, he throws a fine fly, but he gets flurried with a big fish, being young. And this one is a topper.'

"With that he gave me good-night, and I went to bed, but not to sleep. I was fevered with happiness; the past and future reeled before my wakeful vision. I heard every clock strike; the sounds of morning were astir, and still I could not sleep. The ceremony, for reasons connected with our long journey to my father's place in Hampshire, was to be early—half-past ten was the hour. I looked at my watch; it was seven of the clock, and then I looked out of the window: it was a fine, soft, grey morning, with a south wind tossing the yellowing boughs. I got up, dressed in a hasty way, and thought I would just take a look at the river. It was, indeed, in glorious order, lapping over the top of the sharp stone which we regarded as a measure of the due size of water.

"The morning was young, sleep was out of the question; I could not settle my mind to read. Why should I not take a farewell cast, alone, of course? I always disliked the attendance of a gillie. I took my salmon rod out of its case, rigged it up, and started for the stream, which flowed within a couple of hundred yards of my quarters. There it raced under the ash tree, a pale delicate brown, perhaps a little thing too coloured. I therefore put on a large Silver Doctor, and began steadily fishing down the ash-tree cast. What if I should wipe Dick's eye, I thought, when, just where the rough and smooth water meet, there boiled up a head and shoulders such as I had never seen on any fish. My heart leaped and stood still, but there came no sensation from the rod, and I finished the cast, my knees actually trembling beneath me. Then I gently lifted the line, and very elaborately tested every link of the powerful casting-line. Then I gave him ten minutes by my watch; next, with unspeakable emotion, I stepped into the stream and repeated the cast. Just at the same spot he came up again; the huge rod bent like a switch, and the salmon rushed straight down the pool, as if he meant to make for the sea. I staggered on to dry land to follow him the easier, and dragged at my watch to time the fish; a quarter to eight. But the slim chain had broken, and the watch, as I hastily thrust it back, missed my pocket and fell into the water. There was no time to stoop for it; the fish started afresh, tore up the pool as fast as he had gone down it, and, rushing behind the torrent, into the eddy at the top, leaped clean out of the water. He was seventy pounds if he was an ounce. Here he slackened a little, dropping back, and I got in some line. Now he sulked so intensely that I thought he had got the line round a rock. It might be broken, might be holding fast to a sunken stone, for aught that I could tell; and the time was passing, I knew not how rapidly. I tried all known methods, tugging at him, tapping the butt, and slakening line on him. At last the top of the rod was slightly agitated, and then, back flew the long line in my face. Gone! I reeled up with a sigh, but the line tightened again. He had made a sudden rush under my bank, but there he lay again like a stone. How long? Ah! I cannot tell how long! I heard the church clock strike, but missed the number of the strokes. Soon he started again downstream into the shallows, leaping at the end of his rush—the monster. Then he came slowly up, and 'jiggered' savagely at the line. It seemed impossible that any tackle could stand these short violent jerks. Soon he showed signs of weakening. Once his huge silver side appeared for a moment near the surface, but he retreated to his old fastness. I was in a tremor of delight and despair. I should have thrown down my rod, and flown on the wings of love to Olive and the altar. But I hoped that there was time still—that it was not so very late! At length he was failing. I heard ten o'clock strike. He came up and lumbered on the surface of the pool. Gradually I drew him, plunging ponderously, to the gravel beach, where I meant to 'tail' him. He yielded to the strain, he was in the shallows, the line was shortened. I stooped to seize him. The frayed and overworn gut broke at a knot, and with a loose roll he dropped back towards the deep. I sprang at him, stumbled, fell on him, struggled with him, but he slipped from my arms. In that moment I knew more than the anguish of Orpheus. Orpheus! Had I, too, lost my Eurydice? I rushed from the stream, up the steep bank, along to my rooms. I passed the church door. Olive, pale as her orange-blossoms, was issuing from the porch. The clock pointed to 10:45. I was ruined, I knew it, and I laughed. I laughed like a lost spirit. She swept past me, and, amidst the amazement of the gentle and simple, I sped wildly away. Ask me no more. The rest is silence."

Thus ends my hapless friend's narrative. I leave it to the judgment of women and of men. Ladies, would you have acted as Olive Dunne acted? Would pride, or pardon, or mirth have ridden sparkling in your eyes? Men, my brethren, would ye have deserted the salmon for the lady, or the lady for the salmon? I know what I would have done had I been fair Olive Dunne. What I would have done had I been Houghton Grannom I may not venture to divulge. For this narrative, then, as for another, "Let every man read it as he will, and every woman as the gods have given her wit."

STUBB KILLS A WHALE

Herman Melville

IF TO STARBUCK the apparition of the Squid was a thing of portents, to Queequeg it was quite a different object.

"When you see him 'quid," said the savage, honing his harpoon in the bow of his hoisted boat, "then you quick see him 'parm whale."

The next day was exceedingly still and sultry, and with nothing special to engage them, the Pequod's crew could hardly resist the spell of sleep induced by such a vacant sea. For this part of the Indian Ocean through which we then were voyaging is not what whalemen call a lively ground; that is, it affords fewer glimpses of porpoises, dolphins, flying-fish, and other vivacious denizens of more stirring waters, than those off the Rio de la Plata, or the in-shore ground off Peru.

It was my turn to stand at the foremast-head; and with my shoulders leaning against the slackened royal shrouds, to and fro I idly swayed in what seemed an enchanted air. No resolution could withstand it; in that dreamy mood losing all consciousness, at last my soul went out of my body; though my body still continued to sway as a pendulum will, long after the power which first moved it is withdrawn.

Ere forgetfulness altogether came over me, I had noticed that the seamen at the main and mizen mast-heads were already drowsy. So that at last all three of us lifelessly swung from the spars, and for every swing that we made there was a nod from below from the slumbering helmsman. The waves, too, nodded their indolent crests; and across the wide trance of the sea, east nodded to west, and the sun over all.

Suddenly bubbles seemed bursting beneath my closed eyes; like vices my hands grasped the shrouds; some invisible, gracious agency preserved me; with a shock I came back to life. And lo! close under our lee, not forty fathoms off, a gigantic Sperm Whale lay rolling in the water like the capsized hull of a frigate, his broad, glossy back, of an Ethiopian hue, glistening in the sun's rays like a mirror. But lazily undulating in the trough of the sea, and ever and anon tranquilly sprouting his vapory jet, the whale looked like a portly burgher smoking his pipe of a warm afternoon. But that pipe, poor whale, was thy last. As if struck by some enchanter's wand, the sleepy ship and every sleeper in it all at once started into wakefulness; and more than a score of voices from all parts of the vessel, simultaneously with the three notes from aloft, shouted forth the accustomed cry, as the great fish slowly and regularly spouted the sparkling brine into the air.

"Clear away the boats! Luff!" cried Ahab. And obeying his own order, he dashed the helm down before the helmsman could handle the spokes.

The sudden exclamations of the crew must have alarmed the whale; and ere the boats were down, majestically turning, he swam away to the leeward, but with such a steady tranquility, and making so few ripples as he swam, that thinking after all he might not as yet be alarmed, Ahab gave orders that not an oar should be used, and no man must speak but in whispers. So seated like Ontario Indians on the gunwales of the boats, we swiftly but silently paddled along; the calm not admitting of the noiseless sails being set. Presently, as we thus glided in chase, the monster perpendicularly flitted his tail forty feet into the air, and then sank out of sight like a tower swallowed up.

"There go flukes!" was the cry, an announcement immediately followed by Stubb's producing his match and igniting his pipe, for now a respite was granted. After the full interval of his sounding had elapsed, the whale rose again, and being now in advance of the smoker's boat, and much nearer to it than to any of the others, Stubb counted upon the honor of the capture. It was obvious, now,

that the whale had at length become aware of his pursuers. All silence of cautiousness was therefore no longer of use. Paddles were dropped, and oars came loudly into play. And still puffing at his pipe, Stubb cheered on his crew to the assault.

Yes, a mighty change had come over the fish. All alive to his jeopardy, he was going "head out"; that part obliquely projecting from the mad yeast which he brewed.

"Start her, start her, my men! Don't hurry yourselves; take plenty of time—but start her; start her like thunder-claps, that's all," cried Stubb, spluttering out the smoke as he spoke. "Start her, now; give 'em the long and strong stroke, Tashtego. Start her, Tash, my boy—start her, all; but keep cool, keep cool—cucumbers is the word—easy, easy—only start her like grim death and grinning devils, and raise the buried dead perpendicular out of their graves, boys—that's all. Start her!"

"Woo-hoo! Wa-hee!" screamed the Gay-Header in reply, raising some old war-whoop to the skies; as every oarsman in the strained boat involuntarily bounced forward with the one tremendous leading stroke which the eager Indian gave.

But his wild screams were answered by others quite as wild. "Kee-hee! Kee-hee!" yelled Daggoo, straining forwards and backwards on his seat, like a pacing tiger in his cage.

"Ka-la! Koo-loo!" howled Queequeg, as if smacking his lips over a mouthful of Grenadier's steak. And thus with oars and yells the keels cut the sea. Meanwhile, Stubb retaining his place in the van, still encouraged his men to the onset, all the while puffing the smoke from his mouth. Like desperadoes they tugged and they strained, till the welcome cry was heard—"Stand up, Tashtego!—give it to him!" The harpoon was hurled. "Stern all!" The oarsmen backed water; the same moment something went hot and hissing along every one of their wrists. It was the magical line. An instant before, Stubb had swiftly caught two additional turns with it round the loggerhead, whence, by reason of its increased rapid circlings, a hempen blue smoke now jetted up and mingled with the steady fumes from his pipe. As the line passed round and round the loggerhead; so also, just before reaching that point, it blisteringly passed through and through both of Stubb's hands, from which the hand-cloths, or squares of quilted canvas sometimes worn at these times, had accidentally dropped. It was like holding an enemy's sharp two-edged sword by the blade, and that enemy all the time striving to wrest it out of your clutch.

"Wet the line! wet the line!" cried Stubb to the tub oarsman (him seated by the tub) who, snatching off his hat, dashed the sea-water into it. More turns were taken, so that the line began holding its place. The boat now flew through the boiling water like a shark all fins. Stubb and Tashtego here changed places—stem for stern—a staggering business truly in that rocking commotion.

From the vibrating line extending the entire length of the upper part of the boat, and from its now being more tight than a harpstring, you would have thought the craft had two keels—one cleaving the water, the other the air—as the boat churned on through both opposing elements at once. A continual cascade

played at the bows; a ceaseless whirling eddy in her wake; and, at the slightest motion from within, even but of a little finger, the vibrating, cracking craft canted over her spasmodic gunwale into the sea. Thus they rushed; each man with might and main clinging to his seat, to prevent being tossed to the foam; and the tall form of Tashtego at the steering oar crouching almost double, in order to bring down his centre of gravity. Whole Atlantics and Pacifics seemed passed as they shot on their way, till at length the whale somewhat slackened his flight.

"Haul in—haul in!" cried Stubb to the bowsman! and, facing round towards the whale, all hands began pulling the boat up to him, while yet the boat was being towed on. Soon ranging up by his flank, Stubb, firmly planting his knee in the clumsy cleat, darted dart after dart into the flying fish; at the word of command, the boat alternately sterning out of the way of the whale's horrible wallow, and then ranging up for another fling.

The red tide now poured from all sides of the monster like brooks down a hill. His tormented body rolled not in brine but in blood, which bubbled and seethed for furlongs behind in their wake. The slanting sun playing upon this crimson pond in the sea, sent back its reflection into every face, so that they all glowed to each other like red men. And all the while, jet after jet of white smoke was agonizingly shot from the spiracle of the whale, and vehement puff after puff from the mouth of the excited headsman; as at every dart, hauling in upon his crooked lance (by the line attached to it), Stubb straightened it again and again, by a few rapid blows against the gunwale, then again and again sent it into the whale.

"Pull up—pull up!" he now cried to the bowsman, as the waning whale relaxed in his wrath. "Pull up!—close to!" and the boat ranged along the fish's flank. When reaching far over the bow, Stubb slowly churned his long sharp lance into the fish, and kept it there, carefully churning and churning, as if cautiously seeking to feel after some gold watch that the whale might have swallowed, and which he was fearful of breaking ere he could hook it out. But that gold watch he sought was the innermost life of the fish. And now it is struck; for, starting from his trance into that unspeakable thing called his "flurry," the monster horribly wallowed in his blood, over-wrapped himself in impenetrable, mad, boiling spray, so that the imperilled craft, instantly dropping astern, had much ado blindly to struggle out from that phrensied twilight into the clear air of the day.

And now abating in his flurry, the whale once more rolled out into view; surging from side to side; spasmodically dilating and contracting his spout-hole, with sharp, cracking, agonizing respirations. At last, gush after gush of clotted red gore, as if it had been the purple lees of red wine, shot into the frighted air; and falling back again, ran dripping down his motionless flanks into the sea. His heart had burst!

"He's dead, Mr. Stubb," said Daggoo.

"Yes; both pipes smoked out!" and withdrawing his own from his mouth, Stubb scattered the dead ashes over the water; and, for a moment, stood thoughtfully eyeing the vast corpse he had made.

A FISHING EXCURSION

Guy de Maupassant

PARIS WAS BLOCKADED, desolate, famished. The sparrows were few, and anything that was to be had was good to eat.

On a bright morning in January, Mr. Morissot, a watchmaker by trade, but idler through circumstances, was walking along the boulevard, sad, hungry, with his hands in the pockets of his uniform trousers, when he came face to face with a brother-in-arms whom he recognized as an old-time friend.

Before the war, Morissot could be seen at daybreak every Sunday, trudging along with a cane in one hand and a tin box on his back. He would take the train to Colombes and walk from there to the Isle of Marante where he would fish until dark.

It was there he had met Mr. Sauvage who kept a little notion store in the Rue Notre Dame de Lorette, a jovial fellow and passionately fond of fishing like himself. A warm friendship had sprung up between these two and they would fish side by side all day, very often without saying a word. Some days, when everything looked fresh and new and the beautiful spring sun gladdened every heart, Mr. Morissot would exclaim "How delightful!" and Mr. Sauvage would answer "There is nothing to equal it."

Then again on a fall evening, when the glorious setting sun, spreading its golden mantle on the already tinted leaves would throw strange shadows around the two friends, Sauvage would say "What a grand picture!"

"It beats the boulevard!" would answer Morissot. But they understood each other quite as well without speaking.

The two friends had greeted each other warmly and had resumed their walk side by side, both thinking deeply of the past and present events. They entered a *café*, and when a glass of absinthe had been placed before each Sauvage sighed.

"What terrible events, my friend!"

"And what weather!" said Morissot sadly; "this is the first nice day we have had this year. Do you remember our fishing excursions?"

"Do I! Alas! when shall we go again!"

After a second absinthe they emerged from the *café,* feeling rather dizzy—that light-headed effect which alcohol has on an empty stomach. The balmy air had made Sauvage exuberant and he exclaimed, "Suppose we go!"

"Where?"

"Fishing."

"Fishing! Where?"

"To our old spot, to Colombes. The French soldiers are stationed near there and I know Colonel Dumoulin will give us a pass."

"It's a go; I am with you."

An hour after, having supplied themselves with their fishing tackle, they arrived at the colonel's villa. He had smiled at their request and had given them a pass in due form.

At about eleven o'clock they reached the advance-guard, and after presenting their pass, walked through Colombes and found themselves very near their destination. Argenteuil, across the way, and the great plains toward Nanterre were all deserted. Solitary the hill of Orgemont and Sannois rose clearly above the plains —a splendid point of observation.

"See," said Sauvage pointing to the hills. "The Prussians are there."

Prussians! They had never seen one, but they knew that they were all around Paris, invisible and powerful; plundering, devastating, and slaughtering. To their superstitious terror they added a deep hatred for this unknown and victorious people.

"What if we should meet some?" said Morissot.

"We would ask them to join us," said Sauvage in true Parisian style.

Still they hesitated to advance. The silence frightened them. Finally Sauvage picked up courage.

"Come, let us go on cautiously."

They proceeded slowly, hiding behind bushes, looking anxiously on every side, listening to every sound. A bare strip of land had to be crossed before reaching the river. They started to run. At last, they reached the bank and sank into the bushes, breathless but relieved.

Morissot thought he heard some one walking. He listened attentively, but no, he heard no sound. They were indeed alone! The little island shielded them from view. The house where the restaurant used to be seemed deserted; feeling reassured, they settled themselves for a good day's sport.

Sauvage caught the first fish, Morissot the second; and every minute they would bring one out which they would place in a net at their feet. It was indeed miraculous! They felt that supreme joy which one feels after having been deprived for months of a pleasant pastime. They had forgotten everything—even the war!

Suddenly, they heard a rumbling sound and the earth shook beneath them. It was the cannon on Mont Valérien. Morissot looked up and saw a trail of smoke, which was instantly followed by another explosion. Then they followed in quick succession.

"They are at it again," said Sauvage shrugging his shoulders. Morissot, wh
was naturally peaceful, felt a sudden, uncontrollable anger.

"Stupid fools! What pleasure can they find in killing each other!"

"They are worse than brutes!"

"It will always be thus as long as we have governments."

"Well, such is life!"

"You mean death!" said Morissot laughing.

They continued to discuss the different political problems, while the canno
on Mont Valérien sent death and desolation among the French.

Suddenly they started. They had heard a step behind them. They turned an
beheld four big men in dark uniforms, with guns pointed right at them. The
fishing-lines dropped out of their hands and floated away with the current.

In a few minutes, the Prussian soldiers had bound them, cast them into a boa
and rowed across the river to the island which our friends had thought deserte
They soon found out their mistake when they reached the house, behind whic
stood a score or more of soldiers. A big burly officer, seated astride a chair, smok
ing an immense pipe, addressed them in excellent French. "Well, gentlemen
have you made a good haul?"

Just then, a soldier deposited at his feet the net full of fish which he had take
care to take along with him. The officer smiled and said: "I see you have don
pretty well; but let us change the subject. You are evidently sent to spy upon m
You pretended to fish so as to put me off the scent, but I am not so simple. I hav
caught you and shall have you shot. I am sorry, but war is war. As you passed th
advance-guard you certainly must have the password; give it to me, and I wi
set you free."

The two friends stood side by side, pale and slightly trembling, but they ar
swered nothing.

"No one will ever know. You will go back home quietly and the secret wi
disappear with you. If you refuse, it is instant death! Choose!"

They remained motionless, silent. The Prussian officer calmly pointed to th
river.

"In five minutes you will be at the bottom of this river! Surely, you have
family, friends waiting for you?"

Still they kept silent. The cannon rumbled incessantly. The officer gave order
in his own tongue, then moved his chair away from the prisoners. A squad o
men advanced within twenty feet of them, ready for command.

"I give you one minute, not a second more!"

Suddenly approaching the two Frenchmen, he took Morissot aside and whis
pered: "Quick—the password. Your friend will not know; he will think I change
my mind." Morissot said nothing.

Then taking Sauvage aside he asked him the same thing, but he also was silent
The officer gave further orders and the men leveled their guns. At that moment
Morissot's eyes rested on the net full of fish lying in the grass a few feet away. Th
sight made him faint and, though he struggled against it, his eyes filled with tears

Then turning to his friend: "Farewell! Mr. Sauvage!"

"Farewell! Mr. Morissot."

They stood for a minute, hand in hand, trembling with emotion which they were unable to control.

"Fire!" commanded the officer.

The squad of men fired as one. Sauvage fell straight on his face. Morissot, who was taller, swayed, pivoted, and fell across his friend's body his face to the sky, while blood flowed freely from the wound in the breast. The officer gave further orders and his men disappeared. They came back presently with ropes and stones, which they tied to the feet of the two friends, and four of them carried them to the edge of the river. Thy swung them and threw them in as far as they could. The bodies weighted by stones sank immediately. A splash, a few ripples, and the water resumed its usual calmness. The only thing to be seen was a little blood floating on the surface. The officer calmly retraced his steps toward the house muttering. "The fish will get even now."

He perceived the net full of fish, picked it up, smiled, and called, "Wilhelm!"

A soldier in a white uniform approached. The officer handed him the fish saying: "Fry these little things while they are still alive; they will make a delicious meal."

And having resumed his position on the chair, he puffed away at his pipe.

A SEPARATE AND VARIED BREED

"At the outset, the fact should be recognized that the community of fishermen constitute a separate class or subrace among the inhabitants of the earth."

—GROVER CLEVELAND

TOMORROW'S THE DAY

Corey Ford

TOMORROW IS THE MOMENT he's been waiting for. Tomorrow the fisherman will emerge from his annual six-months' hibernation, which began with the close of last year's trout season, and head once more for that favorite pool he has brooded about all winter. Tomorrow—nor rain, nor snow, nor sleet—the law comes off.

Is all in readiness for the Jehovian clang of his alarm-clock at 4 A.M.? Has he made good use of the idle winter months? Does he have his tackle in shape, his gear laid out, his reel oiled, his line all greased? By way of answer, let us glance into the home of a typical angler as the great event draws near. . . .

'Tis the night before opening day—let Clement Moore sue me—and all through the house not a creature is stirring except for his spouse, who has gotten up half an hour ahead to start the coffee and make some peanut-butter sandwiches. His waders are hung by the chimney with care, in hopes that the patches he finally got around to gluing on last midnight will be dry by morning. His freshly varnished rod—he's been meaning to get the job done ever since last September—dangles from the chandelier, still too sticky to handle. His leaders are soaking overnight in the bathtub so that they will be thoroughly soft by the time he gets to the stream tomorrow and remembers where he left them. His boots are up in the attic if he could only find them, his one pair of wading socks have holes in both heels, and somebody, I said somebody, has deliberately mislaid his creel. His line is wound in a cat's cradle around the bedposts, his flies lie in a jumbled heap on the bedside stand, and he has collapsed on the pillow to grab a few minutes' shut-eye before his partner arrives.

Out on the lawn there arises a clatter as a jeep halts in front and his partner sounds the horn vigorously, waking everyone else in the neighborhood and eventually the fisherman himself. He springs from his bed, struggling to untangle himself from the trout line in which he has become thoroughly enmeshed. Sleepily he thrusts his right foot into the left leg of his trousers, shoves an arm through the neckband of his shirt, crams everything else in sight into his landing net, and rushes downstairs, shouting to his wife to please kindly try to recall just what in blazes she did with his pipe. After a frantic search the pipe is discovered between his teeth, where he left it last night when he went to sleep, and he hauls on his waders and starts out the front door, returning almost immediately to unhook his suspenders from the newel-post.

The jeep is half-way to Sullivan County before he remembers that he put his trout reel on the hall table so that he would be sure to see it, his fishing jacket is still hanging on the coat rack, and he forgot to bring the peanut-butter sandwiches. "Next year," he says bitterly, because in addition he has just remembered that his license is in the pocket of the fishing jacket, "next year I won't leave everything till the last minute. Next year I'll get ready in time."

For the benefit of the repentant angler, therefore, I have listed a few things he can do to get ready for the coming trout season. If he will follow these hints carefully, and make a point of going upstairs each night as soon as dinner is over and spending the next five or six hours locked up all alone in his den, he will find that his gear is in perfect shape when opening day arrives. He will also find that his wife has left him and gone home to Mother.

Care of Tackle. Every year a number of articles are written on the care and preservation of fishing tackle. The angler should read all these articles carefully, nodding his head from time to time and murmuring sagely: "That's a pretty good idea," or "This fellow sure knows what he's talking about." After reading each article, he should clip it out of *Field & Stream* and file it away in a large folder entitled: "Opening Day—things to do in preparation for." This file will come in handy later to wrap fish in.

One of the most important things to do in preparation for opening day, of course, is to sort over your collection of trout flies and rearrange them so that you can put your hands on any pattern you want without delay. To accomplish this task, turn all your fly boxes upside down and dump the contents in a heap on the tackle-room table. Pour yourself a small spot of Scotch, because this job will probably take quite a while, and paw over the assortment of flies before you. Select a No. 14 fan-wing Cahill, hold it aloft and turn it slowly from side to side, trying to recollect where you worked it last. Let's see, now, wasn't that the fly you used to take that 3-pound squaretail on the Albany, right out from under Dan Holland's nose? Place it back reverently on the pile, pour yourself another jigger of Scotch, and pick up a No. 12 Quill Gordon. This would be the one you borrowed from Mac to hook that 24-inch grayling on Tanalian Creek in Alaska. Return it to the heap on the table, fill the jigger glass again, and pick out a small Black Gnat. Paul Clowes gave you that one, the time you took the 4-pound rainbow on the North Fork of the Snake. This black-and-white fly is the one Sid Hayward tied for you from the hair of your own bird dog. This Blue Dun is the one you used last year with Austin Scott on the Connecticut.

Continue brooding thus over the collection, occasionally refilling your glass as you tell over your favorite patterns one by one, until your wife shouts upstairs that it's three o'clock, for heaven's sakes, and aren't you ever coming to bed? Dump the flies back in the boxes, and plan to sort them out tomorrow night instead. After all, you've got all winter.

Equally important, in getting ready for opening day, is to go through the pockets of your fishing jacket and remove all the superfluous items that have collected in them during the past season. There is nothing more cumbersome than a loaded fishing jacket, its sides bulging so that you can barely move your arms to cast. The best way is to empty all the contents from the pockets, sort them over carefully one by one, and put back only those essential items which you could not possibly do without, such as:

1. A piece of string, about ten inches long. (You never can tell when you'll need a piece of string.)

2. A hunk of copper wire. (You never know when you'll want a hunk of copper wire.)

3. A button. (You'd better keep that, because it probably came off something.)

4. A pack of stale tobacco, half full. (Might come in handy if you ever run out of tobacco.)

5. An empty tin box that you could use sometime to keep spare flies in; a red bandanna handkerchief, smelling slightly of fish, in case you want to wrap something up; a botle of fly dope with some sticky brown stuff in the bottom, in case you need to renew the prescription; a swivel, in case you ever want a swivel; a reel with the handle missing, in case you find the handle again; part of a chocolate bar, which has melted and stuck to the inside of your pocket so that you can't get it out; a broken scales, which could easily be fixed; a key to something, if you could only remember what it fits, and several nice-looking streamer flies with the barbs broken off, because it seems a shame to throw them away.

6. A safety-pin, which you reluctantly decide to get rid of, because after all you've got to get rid of something. (Later on, when your galluses break in the middle of the stream, you will discover that the one thing in the world you need is a safety-pin.)

Repairing Waders. Only one thing is worse than discovering at the last moment that there is a hole in one leg of your waders, and that is discovering there are holes in both legs. Veteran fishermen wince at the very thought of striding across a pool and feeling their waders fill with ice-cold water. In order to avoid this, many fishermen fill their waders with warm water before stepping into the stream.

There are several ways of finding out whether your waders leak. One method is to fill the bathtub with water, put on your waders, and sit down in the tub. This method is not entirely satisfactory, since the immersion of the fisherman results in a corresponding displacement of water that elevates the level in the tub to a point slightly higher than the waist of the waders, causing him to assume a rather silly expression when his wife glances into the bathroom and asks him acidly just what he thinks he's doing, and wouldn't he like her to bring him one of Junior's celluloid ducks?

A better method is to take the waders down into the cellar, pull them inside out, and hang them from a couple of nails in the ceiling. Fill a bucket with water, pour it into the waders, and watch closely to see whether a leak appears. Draw another bucket of water, pour it down inside, and inspect the legs carefully. Continue to fill the waders with water until the nails in the ceiling give way, dropping the waders and flooding the cellar floor to a depth of several inches. Quietly wade back upstairs.

Probably the best method is to wait till you get to the stream. If there's a hole in your waders that lets the water in, cut another hole just below it to let the water out again. You'll end up just as dry as anybody else.

Preparing the Fishing Hat. The most indispensable item in any fisherman's equipment is his hat. This ancient relic, with its battered crown and well-frayed band, preserves not only the memory of every trout he ever caught, but also the smell. In case his wife ever carries out her threat to give it away to the garbage collector, the fisherman may proceed as follows:

After a hasty visit to the lawyer's to institute divorce proceedings against his wife (this step is automatic), he should repair to the nearest hat store and purchase the first headgear he sees. If it does not fit, yank it down over the skull until the stitches give way, so that it feels better. Rip out the silk lining and hand it back to the clerk, roll the rest of the hat into a tight ball, and sit on it all the way home in order to start breaking it in. Later, as time permits, the following additional care is recommended:

1. Impregnate it thoroughly with fish slime, asafetida, old axle grease, diesel oil, citronella and hair tonic.

2. Festoon the band with barbed flies until it resembles a moulting hen.

3. Fill the crown with water and let it stand in the sun a few days until the seams start coming apart.

4. Place it in the driveway, crank up the garden tractor, and drive it back and forth over the hat, shoveling on an occasional forkful from the compost heap. Knead thoroughly.

5. Last but not least, place it on a stump and shoot it with a 10-gauge magnum at approximately fifty feet. If the fisherman uses double oo buck, and his aim is right, the result should be a hat which he needn't be ashamed to wear on any stream.

Here, then, are a few things the prudent angler can do to get himself set for the arrival of opening day. Does he take advantage of the suggestions I have carefully listed above? Does he profit from his past mistakes, and spend his nights over the winter to good purpose? Will he have his tackle all ready in plenty of time next year, instead of leaving everything as usual till the last minute?

For the answer to these fascinating questions, turn back and start over again at the beginning of this article.

FISHING'S JUST LUCK

Elmer Ransom

SAM IS NATURALLY ORNERY AND CONTENTIOUS. Anybody who knows about winter trout will tell you that a sinking plug, most times, has got it all over a floater—that is, over a so-called crippled minnow. But you can't argue with Sam—the perfect fisherman. He harbors some fool notion that if you catch a fish with an under-water lure, you've done something low and indecent; slipping up on the blind side, so to speak. Take brook trout for instance. Sam will loosen his belt in contemplation of the fish you've cooked, thankful that he limited his breakfast to twelve battercakes, three eggs, four slices of bacon, and two cups of coffee—not to mention a goodly bait of that universal southern dish, hominy grits.

Then, while he folds himself around pound after pound of your fish, he'll revile you for using a wet fly. One time, in Canada, he even refused to eat more than four fish because he claimed that I'd used worms. As if worms would hurt the flavor of a fish. Pfff!

He reminds me of a vegetarian who wears a fur coat and leather shoes. Consistency, that's what he lacks—consistency.

He helped me with the canoe, lifting the light end, of course, the bum, and he fussed over the tackle and cushions while I got the motor and the gasoline. He blew on his hands to warm them and muttered something about winter being the time for hunting, and about Framp needing a work-out. Framp is his pointer dog, and he suits Sam to a T. Framp's got ants in his breeches, too, and snoots all winter fishermen.

The Perfect Fisherman appropriated the two cushions and made himself comfortable. We drifted with the tide while I cranked the motor.

"Let's get going," he shouted, after I'd yanked the rope a fourth time. I looked at him bitterly and went back to cranking. The motor *would* cut up with Sam along, and after I'd bragged that it always started on the first turn.

He let me crank for five minutes—deliberately before he said: "And why not turn on the gas? It does use gas, doesn't it?"

I didn't answer him. I acted dignified and turned on the gas, and we roared

up Broad River with the tide behind us and the wind in our faces. Which meant
a rough trip.

Sam fumbled in the bottom of the boat for something and, seeing my chance,
I quartered the canoe into a curling whitecap, and ducked my head. The spray
drummed into my rain shirt. Looking up, I saw Sam wiping behind his ears, and
read his lips.

"Damn it," he was saying. "You did that on purpose." He had no proof. I
pretended not to understand. Wasn't I astern, taking spray all the time, while he
was dry and comfortable forward?

He reached for my parka—my gorgeous red parka, intended, on other occasions, as colorful proof that I was a man and not a moose—and pulled it over his
head, leaving the hood around his shoulders. He knew darned well I wouldn't
wet him if he had that parka on.

We were after winter trout, which are your old friends the sea trout, spotted
squeateague, spotted weakfish, or, if you are a college professor, *Cynoscion nebu-
losus.*

And the guy who named them weakfish had a distorted sense of humor. Like
calling Jack Dempsey a sissy.

The immortal Jordan, who ought to know, says of them: "As a game fish the
squeateague is the greatest of the family. No saltwater fish of our Atlantic coast
affords more sport to the angler than this species."

The winter trout has other points in his favor. No man can forbid your fishing
the waters in which he abounds and no state legislature can require a license for
his taking. Poor man, rich man, beggar man, thief—he's there for all who have
the love of the salt in their bones, and the skill to take him. He may strike
gently or with a reckless, hilarious abandon. Always, he puts up a grand battle.

He moves from place to place so that many fellows of the angle may have their
chance, but he does admit a healthy partiality to more southern waters. Who
wouldn't? Over much of his range he may be taken every month in the year. In
the waters of Georgia and South Carolina the months from October through
January are best.

He hankers after artificial lures. I know because I am a doodle-bug fisherman
when the occasion demands, never knowingly denying a hungry fish the morsel
of his choice. Time and again I've seen experienced plug fishermen, using black-
bass casting tackle, with the right sort of artificial minnow, wallop a bait fisherman operating from the same boat.

Take it or leave it, two of us, using sinking plugs, caught 157 on one tide. Oh,
we didn't keep them all. But there was no ethical reason why we shouldn't had
we been so inclined, for commercial fishermen take thousands of pounds daily in
their nets, offering them in most markets serving the Atlantic seaboard. There
is no possible chance for the rod-and-reel fishermen to deplete the species; the
blue fish and the netters kill more in one day than the rod-and-reel fishermen do
in a season—not to mention the professionals who go "striking" at night with a
brilliant light and a three-pronged gig. So ease your conscience, if you have a

good catch, and take a few to your friends. The situation is different from that prevailing with freshwater fish.

Sure, I love the winter trout. He has put the salt spray in my nostrils when my mind was lower than the belly of a snake and every damn thing gone wrong. He has fought me, fed me, rejuvenated me, brought me back believing there was some sense to this twisted warp called life.

There are, perhaps, a few fish of his size that fight better. Certainly, the striped bass, royalty incarnate, and possibly that grand old aristocrat the channel bass (known as school bass in the smaller weights). But the stripers are most often hard to find, and the channel bass more temperamental.

Locate a shell bank at low tide and fish it as the tide covers it, or stop at almost any bridge or trestle over southern salt water, and at the right season and tide you will be likely to strike winter trout. And always, peel your eye for the terns and gulls. Where they congregate, diving to the surface for small morsels, you'll find that a school is working, and the minnows on which they feed are leaping to escape them. Work your lure slowly through this water, and you may have a strike on every cast until the school moves away or ceases to feed.

Avoid fishing in the full or the new moon. Don't ask me why. Possibly it is because the higher tides permit the fish to gorge themselves in the covered marshes, or maybe it is just as Uncle Jake says: "Dey mouth is sore, suh. Dey yenty gwine strike much."

This day Sam and I were going to fish near the Seaboard trestle on Broad River, a wide estuary of the sea that cuts away from Port Royal Sound, behind Parris Island, in the South Carolina Low Country. We rode a sponson-equipped canoe—a good, safe boat for rough water—powered by a light twin outboard.

We took four casting rods. And why four rods? Because, in fishing the salt, you can never be quite sure what is going to strike. One time I hooked a monster cabio. No, I didn't land him. Another day a small tarpon took my lure in waters where tarpon were almost unknown.

Our reels were regular quadruple multiplying casting reels, carrying a hundred yards of eighteen-pound-test silk line, hard braided. Cuttyhunk lasts longer, and in the six thread is fairly satisfactory, but it is definitely more difficult to cast, most likely to backlash.

Of lures there is no end, from the home-made clothespin plug or the imitation mud minnow, both of which are given their elusive motion by the manipulation of the rod tip, to gaudy creations warranted to outwiggle a strip-tease dancer. It was this matter of lures that was to start our next argument, but then something had to start any argument if Sam were to remain happy. Me? I don't argue unless Sam goads me into it by one of his absurd contentions with which I don't agree.

After fighting the chop for four miles, I cut the motor near the trestle and yelled for Sam to let the anchor go.

It wasn't my fault that he snubbed the rope too close and the anchor dragged in the swift tide, throwing us out of position, but he bellyached no end about pulling it in again. As though handling the anchor in twenty feet of water was any job at all compared to skippering the canoe four miles against a head wind.

Six or eight people were fishing from the trestle. While we maneuvered to position two fish were caught. I shouted "What luck?" The hopeful cry of all fishermen.

"Plenty," exulted a big guy on the trestle.

He took a long swig from a flask (drat him), and then held up a string of fish that would make any man's eyes bug out. I could see that we were late.

Sam snapped his floater close to the trestle, gave it an expert flip. It was just too bad but I had to break the news sometime.

"In this wind," I told him as gently as I could, "they won't be striking on top."

He turned a stony eye my way, and averred that I'd misled him. I merely shrugged my shoulders. What are you ever going to do with a stubborn man?

I dropped my sinking plug close to the trestle, let it ride down, and slowly, almost bumping the bottom, I retrieved with a jerking motion. At the third flip, I had a smashing strike. The fish ran to starboard, and Sam let his line get in the way.

I lost the fish and, naturally, very firmly told Sam what I thought of a guy who was so jealous that he would do a thing of this kind. He paid me no attention, whatever, for the trestle fraternity was doing business right along, and Sam gets excited when fish are being caught. Disregarding my appropriate remarks, he hissed. "If these fish won't hit a surface lure I'm going to drown you." His reputation was at stake.

And would you believe it? Sam threw that floater close to the trestle, and for a second I thought the bridge was falling down. The whole school must have ganged up on that one plug. Sam said, "Ha!" snapped his wrist, and set the hook.

"Don't press him, you dumbbell," I urged. "Your hook will pull out."

He eyed me coldly, out of one corner, and replied: "Are *you* advising *me!*" That's just the way he said it. He didn't ask it either.

The fish swept under the anchor rope, and Sam did a Houdini, passing the rod after the fish while I grabbed his leg to keep him inboard. I didn't mind about Sam, but he had my parka on.

Some guys have all the luck. I'm telling you, Sam did everything wrong. Everything! And still he landed the fish. Then he smoothed his hair, set his hat on straight and told me to take his picture.

Sam's not much to look at in my opinion, but one of these iridescent beauties, spotted and gleaming in the winter sunshine, is a model fit for the camera of a king. With a long, able body, pointed head, fighting mouth, and one or two keen canine teeth in the projecting lower jaw, he has all the swift and savage beauty of the under-water, with its age-long, immutable law that only the fit survive. And keep your hands out of that mouth and away from the sharp gillrakes.

"Well," Sam said, giving me the evil eye, "what is it to be?"

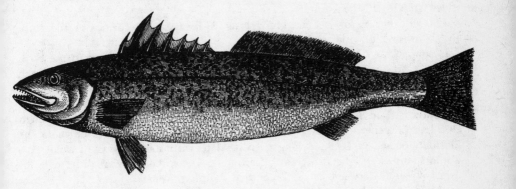

My conscience didn't hurt me at all. Not one bit. He was asking for it. This surface strike was sheer accident, and science was bound to triumph.

"Low man pays for shells, transportation, and grub next Saturday," I suggested.

He wet his lips in greedy contemplation. "And some raw meat for Framp," he added, sticking his neck out.

The tide began to slacken. The fishing is always more furious at the turn, either low or high tide.

I bumped the plug on the bottom, and a fish struck and ran toward the boat. He was a bit smaller than the fish Sam had landed. Then I hooked a fish on each of six successive casts and landed five of them.

Sam's temper was about to get the best of him. But then it was his own fault. It always is. I advised that he change to an under-water plug, being far enough ahead to be generous with advice. Next Saturday we might drive down to the Florida line where I had a long overdue date with some coveys of quail. We would spend the night at a good little hotel I knew about. What did I care for Sam's expense? Between strikes I mouthed the plan over.

"All right," he bellowed, "all right." Sounding like he meant anything but all right. "You hooked me but just wait, I'll get you." Just like Sam, holding a grudge when all he had to do was to listen to what a fisherman told him.

Being mad, he wasn't ready for the next strike. I don't know what he snagged, but it broke his line on the first long rush, and the fish and Sam's floater disappeared toward Port Royal Sound.

He grunted. That fish might mean the pot. Oh yeah! And suppose I'd landed the one he tangled in his line. He had a lot to grouch over, now didn't he? He scrambled around the bottom looking for his box of floaters. He came up, solemn eyed and accusing, asking where I'd put them. Yes, where I'd put them! Ain't that just like Sam? They were on the mantel at the shack.

"You did it on purpose," he complained bitterly. "You knew they'd strike on top."

It was this unwarranted bickering that caused my backlash. I had worked the lure close to the boat when the granddaddy of them all hit my plug. He jerked the reel handle out of my hand, slapped the rod on the side of the boat, smashing the tip, thumbed his fins at me in disgust and swam away.

"Look what you've done," I bellowed. Sam actually grinned. The camera clicked as I worked to untangle the snarl. When I looked up Sam was casting a sinking plug.

I heard him grunt. His rod arched, and there was something lively on the far end of his line. I looked away. I couldn't bear to see it. The man had hooked two fish on a single cast, one on each gang of hooks. No telling what he'd catch if he really put some hooks on a plug.

"Take your time," he called as I fought the backlash. He brought in another fish and added: "Time out for a picture." I looked at him witheringly but he didn't wither.

"Dry fly fisherman," I said with appropriate sarcasm. "Floating plug! I knew you'd crook me if you got a chance."

"Now, now," he answered comfortably. "Just take your time with that snarl while papa brings home the bacon."

He snapped up the rod tip again, and set the hook with a satisfying "Ugh!" and then as the fish began to cut up he added: "I'm thinking of the grub, the meat for Framp, the shells and the gas and oil that you are going to buy next Saturday. Would you like to make a small wager that your potlicker pup finds one covey to Framp's two?"

I told him where he could go.

My rod was rigged when a fish struck Sam close to the boat. Now a winter trout does his fighting mostly under the water, but this one surprised Sam; I'd say the fish even scared him. He yanked that fish hard enough to loosen the tonsils of a tarpon. But do you think the fish got away? He did not. Instead he gave one frenzied leap and flopped in the boat.

"Count 'em, my lad," Sam exulted, "or even weigh 'em if you wish. They have scales." Which was an old and rotten pun. "We are now even and all your shenanigans have gained you nothing. Honesty is the best policy. You ought to try it sometime."

I didn't say what I was thinking. Instead I cast close to the bridge, and very expertly began to retrieve with that sure, slow wiggle of mine which, if I do say it as shouldn't, is known among the winter trout themselves as "the great irresistible."

Of course Sam had no chance. He had never fished the salt before. He fished too fast. He wouldn't let his lure sink far enough. He didn't hoochie-koochie his plug to give it fish appeal. Anybody could tell that. I would have felt sorry for him if he hadn't been so ornery.

Even when he caught the next fish I grinned at him encouragingly. For a novice he hadn't done too bad. I was one down but I even the count in less than five minutes.

Then the fish stopped striking as completely as though someone had rung a dinner bell downriver. The tide was running out swiftly by now. I hung up on an oyster shell and lost my plug. Sam accused me of getting excited. We cast for forty minutes more without a strike. The lucky stiff. The fish *would* move off just in time to save his hide.

The sun dropped low and the biting chill crept into my bones. A *rum chaud* was to be had at the shack, steaming and savory.

"Oh, hum," Sam yawned. "You're a lucky guy."

He pulled on the anchor, blaming me that the water was cold and wet. I put my rod in its rack on the side of the canoe, pushed the motor down, turned on the gas—please note that—primed her. As I was about to twist her tail, Sam made one last, lazy, indifferent cast.

He started the lure in when suddenly his rod tip slapped the water. The reel handle banged against his knuckles. He gasped as the line ran out and out.

"After him, you big stiff," he shouted, "he's taking all my line."

I saw a swirl, the flip of a tail as the fish "nodded," and I groaned.

A channel bass, at the wrong place, on the wrong plug, at the wrong tide and time, but, above all else, by the wrong fisherman.

When the fish was in the boat, six pounds of it, Sam muttered something about next Saturday, pulled up the hood of my parka, curled himself comfortably into a ball under the bow and out of the wind, and went to sleep while I drove the boat home.

Science? Fishing is just luck.

THE FISHERMAN'S SONG

Thomas D'Urfey

Of all the world's enjoyments,
   That ever valued were;
There's none of our employments
   With fishing can compare:
      Some preach, some write,
      Some swear, some fight,
   All, golden lucre courting.
But fishing still bears off the bell,
   For profit or for sporting.
Then who a jolly fisherman, a fisherman will be
      His throat must wet,
      Just like his net,
To keep out cold at sea.

The country squire loves running
   A pack of well-mouthed hounds:
Another fancies gunning
   For wild ducks in his grounds:
      This hunts, that fowls,
      This hawks, Dicks bowls,

No greater pleasure wishing,
But Tom that tells what sport excels,
  Gives all the praise to fishing.
      Then who a jolly fisherman, . . .

A good Westphalia gammon
  Is counted dainty fare;
But what is't to a salmon
  Just taken from the Ware?
      Wheat ears and quails,
      Cocks, snipes, and rails,
    Are prized, while season's lasting,
But all must stoop to crayfish soup,
    Or I've no skill in tasting.
      Then who a jolly fisherman, . . .

Keen hunters always take to
  Their prey with too much pains;
Nay, often break a neck too,
  A penance for no brains:
      They run, they leap,
      Now high, now deep,
    Whilst he, that fishing chooses,
With ease may do't, nay, more to boot,
    May entertain the muses.
      Then who a jolly fisherman, . . .

And though some envious wranglers,
  To jeer us will make bold;
And laugh at patient anglers,
  Who stand so long i' th' cold:
      They wait on Miss,
      We wait on this,
    And think it easy labour;
And if you'd know, fish profits too,
    Consult our Holland neighbour.
Then who a jolly fisherman, a fisherman will be
      His throat must wet,
      Just like his net,
  To keep out cold at sea.

A PICKEREL YARN

Fred Mather

TWO PRITCHARD BROTHERS, Tom and Harry, came from England and started to make and repair fishing tackle in Fulton street, New York, so long ago that the nearest date I can fix for it is the one so dear to our childhood: "Once upon a time." They are not recorded in the Chinese "Book of the Lily," which was written at the beginning of all things, and so must have come to New York after that period; but it was very long ago. The little shop upstairs was kept busy by anglers who knew of their skill, and also by some of the large fishing tackle houses, which found it more convenient than to send small jobs by express to their factories; and so the brothers found plenty of work to their hands while they lived.

The little shop was a place where one might drop in at any time and feel sure of meeting some of the old-time anglers of the city, and the talk would run on the nearby trout streams, rods, ferrules, flies, the prospect of a run of weakfish, the tides, the last big catch of sheepshead at the wreck of the Black Warrior, and such other things as are discussed where anglers most do congregate. There is no such place in New York city now, and never will be until an angler's club is formed. I meet anglers occasionally in the different fishing tackle emporiums, but they are there on business and not for social talk, as was the case at Pritchards'. We needed such a place then and we need a club now.

Of Tom Pritchard I knew little; he was the eldest, wore gray muttonchop whiskers and attended to business; therefore, as Dame Juliana Berners says, "I write the less of him." When I first knew Harry, some thirty years ago, he must have been a boy of about fifty years old, as convivial as opportunity offered and always ready to tell a story, the impediment in his speech increasing as he neared the climax, when his jaws would work but refuse to deliver a sound until he pressed his fists into his hips and yelled the finale, and this added point to all his yarns. As he put it: "I can s-s-s-sing and I can w-w-whistle, but I'm a s-s-sinner if I can t-t-talk." Frank Endicott once made Harry this proposition: "If you can't talk, don't try; you're too old to learn new tricks. When you've got a fishing yard to spin, just sing the introduction and descriptive part, and when you get to the last of it—where we are all willing to strain our credulity to believe you—just 'whistle o'er the lave o' it,' as the Scotch song goes. This will be a great relief to you, and will leave much veracity to your credit with all of us."

Harry was the man who was fishing for black bass on Greenwood Lake when a drunken "guide" tried to bail out the perforated bait car which hung overboard, as has been related, but he had amplified the story with detail and climax until we enjoyed it as something of which we had never heard. But this is a digression.

"N-now Hi'll tell you a t-t-true s-s-story, an' Hi don't c-care hif you b-b-believe hit or not. You halways puts m-me down for l-l-lyin', hanyway, an' Hi d-d-do' know has hits hany use to t-t-tell you hanythink m-m-more, you wouldn't b-b-believe me, hanyway."

"Go on, Harry," said Endicott, "we always believe you when we are sure you are telling a truthful yarn, and we, as brothers of the angle, realize the fact that there is an angler's license as well as a poet's. Please unfold this truthful yarn; it will place a great balance to your credit."

"Harry," said I, "the trouble with you is your excessive modesty. You evidently never expected me to believe that you killed a forty-foot shark on a sixteen-ounce rod while fishing for small fish in the waters of India, but your glowing account of your four hours' fight with the monster after it had dragged you from the boat, and how you reeled in an gave line while treading water, bore the stamp of authenticity. Then, too, your reeling the great fish in and getting on its back, drowning it by pulling off your boots and jamming them into two of the gill openings, suffocating the fish with hands and feet in the other gill slits while you awaited death when the shark sank, is in memory as distinct as when you told it. I do not doubt the slightest detail, and have often rejoiced at your opportune rescue by the native fishermen, and your restoration to your regiment in Her Majesty's service. Please don't think that we entertain doubts of the truthfulness of your stories, even if such doubts sometimes cross your own mind."

"T-t-that's good. You think Hi don't halways b-b-b-believe my hown s-s-stories. P'r'aps Hi don't b-believe 'em hev'ry time; hall Hi ask is for you to b-b-b-believe 'em."

"Let me explain," said I, "the funny man of the press has done much to injure the veracity of the angler. He has gone so far as to brand a palpable lie as a 'fish story,' thereby throwing discredit upon our guild. In his ignorance that a whale is not a fish he, in his skepticism, goes back many centuries, but now, Harry, let me go beyond the latter-day reporter, who has exhausted his wit upon the appetite of the goat, the disturbing influence of the mother-in-law, and the wholly fictitious accounts of the wealth of the plumber and the ice-man, into the question of the truthfulness of the fisherman. Is he less given to exaggeration than his brother who handles the gun? Is he more unworthy of belief than men who engage in other forms of sport or of business? I'll answer my own questions by saying that he is not, and in proof of this will point to the fact that I have even believed some of your stories."

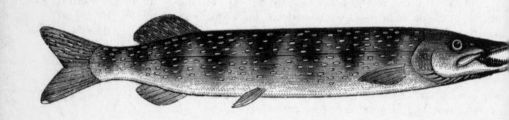

"I move the previous question," said Mr. Endicott, "all this talk that Mather has shot off is irrelevant and not at all to the point. If Harry has a story to tell it should take precedence of all. Go on, Harry, and tell your story. I'll agree to believe a third of it and Mr. Scott and Fred will believe the other two-thirds. In that way the whole story will be believed without injuring our capacity for believing any stories that others present may inflict on us. Let her go!"

"Well, this here ain't much of a s-s-story, an' I don't care w-w-whether you b-b-believe or not, cause, it's as true as I sit 'ere on this stool, an' that's no lie. Y' see Hi was afishin' for p-p-pickerel up hon Greenwood Lake, hall by my lonesome, han I was a ketchin' s-s-small ones right fast han a keepin' c-c-count by sayin' that m-m-makes nine han' this un's t-t-ten, in that kind o' way ha 'avin' fun—."

"Hold on, Harry," said Endicott, "we want more detail. How big were these small pickerel, and what bait were you using?"

"Hi was b-b-baitin' with live minners, or k-k-killies has they calls 'em hin the salt-water. Hi hain't got h-h-hany of 'em left to prove they was my b-b-bait, but Hi'll hask you to t-t-take my word for 'em. The p-p-pickerel was a-r-r-r-runnin' hextra small that d-d-day, han' the first s-s-singular thing that struck me was their r-r-regular size, han' I m-m-measured 'em. Hi'm a s-s-sinner hif they wasn't hall just heleven an' a harf h-h-hinches long to a fraction; and I sez to mys-s-self, sez Hi, this here's hall one s-s-school, hall hout o' one litter, but they're b-b-big henuff to take 'ome,' so Hi fishes on."

"How many did you get on this remarkable day?" asked Mr. Scott.

"Hi'm a c-c-comin' to that hif you'll gi' me a c-c-chance. Y'see, Hi was hout for three days' f-f-fishin', an' Hi wanted to keep my f-f-fish halive till I left for 'ome; so Hi 'ad a fish car halongside, han' the p-p-pickerel were dropped into that as fast as Hi p-p-pulled 'em in. They was a-bitin' f-f-fast, an' about s-s-sundown Hi thought the car must be p-p-putty full, for Hi had counted f-f-forty-three, an' Hi'd quit. One m-m-more took hold, han' has 'e was a-kickin' hon the bottom of the boat Hi takes a look in the c-c-car, han' what do you think Hi s-s-see?"

"Well, Harry," said Endicott, "as I have followed the story, I should say that you must have seen forty-three pickerel in a mass and nothing more, because you have not mentioned taking in snapping turtles and other monsters. What else could you have seen? There's nothing remarkable in your yarn so far, that you should preface it, as you did, with the remark that we might not believe it. As far as I am concerned, I am willing to believe not only the third, to which I agreed, but the whole story as well. What did you see?"

"N-n-n-nothing!"

"But," said Mr. Scott, "you put the fish in the car; where were they?"

"Hin the b-b-boat. There was a slat hoff the b-b-bottom of that c-c-car, han' Hi'd been a-c-c-catchin' the same p-p-pickerel hall day, han' 'e____"

Harry's vocal organs gave out. We gravely shook hands, remarked upon the state of the weather and left him trying to finish the story.

THE ONE-EYED POACHER'S LEGAL SALMON

Edmund Ware Smith

INCREDIBLE THOUGH IT MAY seem to those who know him, the one-eyed poacher once deliberately caught a salmon by legal means. It is even more incredible that Uncle Jeff allows me to set down the disgraceful episode in a more or less loose arrangement of words. However, he seemed to feel that his experience belongs among Coongate legends, and he finally gave in.

"It didn't happen in my own country," he stated nobly, "so it don't really count agin me."

It seems that a number of right-minded salmon fishermen had organized an expedition to the Southwest Miramichi, New Brunswick, and had coaxed Uncle Jeff into going along as friend and philosopher, expenses paid, to round out the staff of excellent native guides.

The party boarded the night train for Fredericton, and Uncle Jeff spent his first and only night aboard a Pullman, tucking his shoes neatly in the little green hammock, and laying his glass eye on the window ledge, where it stared accusingly at him during the long, dark hours.

It must be said, in fairness to the one-eyed poacher, that he was not truly tempted to go salmon fishing with a fly rod, or any other kind of rod. Thus he had foresightedly brought along his telescopic salmon spear, fashioned in Boody Chambers' blacksmith shop in Privilege out of different sizes of iron pipe and the rocker barb of a harpoon which he had stolen from an antique shop in Bangor. The spear rested in the hammock along with his shoes, clanking musically against the window as the night wore away.

But the real, or deeper reason, why Uncle Jeff had consented to go on the trip was that it was during Prohibition times, and he understood that the New Brunswick Liquor Commission possessed an adequate supply of Hernando's Fiery Dagger rum. With Fiery Dagger as a goal, he could tolerate the idiotic equipment which his employers had brought along for salmon fishing. There were rods in long cases—single-handed ones, and the old two-handers; leaders of assorted lengths; and aluminum boxes full of dainty creations called Dusty Millers, Jock Scotts, Thunder and Lightnings, and the like.

Arriving in Fredericton, the party proceeded at once to the Queen Hotel. Uncle Jeff was assigned a room, and he deposited his luggage consisting of the salmon spear and a tattered jacket, and stalked hastily around the corner and down the street to the heavenly Liquor Commission. But, as so often happened, hard luck dogged him from the very start. There was no Hernando's Fiery Dagger.

"Never heard of it," said the clerk politely. "Who makes it?"

"The Universal Solvent & Vitriol Company, of Slant-eye, Minnesota," said Uncle Jeff, mournfully.

The clerk didn't seem to know the concern, and offered Uncle Jeff his choice of Scotches, ryes, and gins which were considered potable by common people. The one-eyed poacher finally selected a bottle and returned to the Queen Hotel, where he drained it dry during the hours of waiting. The label said the stuff was ninety proof—but that, to Hernando's Fiery Dagger, was as water.

However, the salmon fishermen noted that Mr. Coongate began singing in the smoking car on the train going up to Half Moon. At Half Moon the party debarked in the pitch darkness by the bridge, and encamped for the night in a small cabin by the sweet, musically whispering river.

No one slept so peacefully as did the one-eyed poacher. Mosquitoes and midges, propellers whining, dove toward him only to crumple in mid-air and crash when they came within range of his breath. He dreamed his favorite dream of salmon spearing by torchlight. This was followed by a nightmare in which it was revealed to him that there was no alcoholic beverage of any kind in possession of anyone on the trip.

He awoke in pain. He had lost his glass eye. It was morning—and his nightmare proved to be true. Absolutely, horribly, and incontestably true. Perilously, and damnably true—with one, solitary exception, which made it truer still.

The leader of the expedition was a tall, gentle, and stately Professor of English Literature in an Eastern university. His dignity was at times almost equal to Uncle Jeff Coongate's, and this was one of the times. While Uncle Jeff couldn't believe himself suffering from a hangover—only one bottle of that watery stuff— his one eye nevertheless rolled, and his gnarled hands brushed irritably at a file of little men which seemed bent on marching around on the rawhide laces of his boots, or swamp slippers, as he called them.

It was then that Professor Marshall appeared at the canoes drawn up on the river bank, opened a small pack, and removed a bottle, which he held up to be viewed by his friends, including Uncle Jeff.

The beauties of the great river, of the early morning mist, of the firs and hardwoods, were temporarily lost to the one-eyed poacher. Clutching his salmon spear for support, he cleared his throat, and reassembled his tongue.

"Perfesser," he asked majestically, "is that there a quart bottle?"

"It is," said Professor Marshall, beaming.

Uncle Jeff's one eye bleared, watered, and focused once more. It—his eye—was within fourteen inches of the bottle.

"Has it got a green label on it, with orange stripes, and daggers all around the border?"

"It has."

Uncle Jeff gulped and drew the inevitable, heaven-sent conclusion. "Then, it's —by God, sir—it's Hernando's Fiery Dagger rum!"

"It is indeed, Mr. Coongate."

Never had a river looked so beautiful to Thomas Jefferson Coongate. Never had mere breathing been so delectable, nor a sky so miraculously blue and cloud-free.

"Perfesser," said the old-timer, "if I could have jest a tech of Hernando's— here, I'll go fetch a pint dipper for it—my stomach would be better. I et somethin' last night. Turnips, I guess."

"We didn't have turnips, Uncle Jeff. It was carrots."

"Carrots, then," said Mr. Coongate, his hand twitching toward the bottle.

But the one-eyed poacher was doomed to disappointment. Professor Marshall gently, if perhaps over-temperately, explained that the Hernando's Fiery Dagger was in the nature of a prize. It was to be given to the man catching the largest fish.

"Largest today, Perfesser?" inquired Uncle Jeff hopefully.

"Largest for the trip."

"That means we got to wait five days," said the stricken man, wilting in the stern of his canoe.

They lunched at noon not far from McKiel Brook, where a further tragedy was revealed to Uncle Jeff. In one of the several pools along a rapid called Push-and-be-damned, he had spied the dorsal fin of a salmon which, according to his estimate, would go twenty-five pounds. Tactfully suggesting that the fishing was sure to be better a hundred yards beyond his discovery, the one-eyed poacher sided into a grassy landing, slid his spear down the leg of his pants where it nestled like something quite at home, and crept up the river bank through the second growth to a point overlooking his prize salmon. The fish was nervous, as well it might have been. It nosed into the current, and Uncle Jeff caught the silver flash of its immense side.

It was broad daylight—a fact which irked Uncle Jeff and made him feel uncomfortable. Torchlight was his way, but with care he might succeed. He unsheathed his spear and extended it. The salmon seemed uncommonly peaceful. Uncle Jeff moved the spear into position so slowly that even the salmon didn't, apparently, detect danger. The great fish had met its master—or, rather, it hadn't quite met him, for Uncle Jeff felt a prickling sensation in the back of his neck which caused him to suspect he was not alone.

Rolling his head around, he perceived, standing directly behind him, the tall figure of Professor Marshall, two of his companions, and three guides. Although lying flat on his boiler-plate stomach, Uncle Jeff Coongate managed to bow with considerable majesty—a feat which only he could have achieved prone.

"Howdy, boys," said he, grinning amiably. "Any luck?"

The New Brunswick guides, being law-abiding, and treasuring the bounties of their river, glared. Professor Marshall and his companions had difficulty controlling smiles, and eventually quit trying.

"It's with rod and reel, Mr. Coongate," said Professor Marshall. "The contest, I mean."

"Oh—that so?" said Uncle Jeff, rising to his feet and brushing bark, dirt and two beetles from his raiment. "Why didn't you say so, first off?"

"I thought it was understood."

"I understood different," said the one-eyed poacher, aggrievedly concealing his spear. "Besides, I ain't got no rod, nor no reel."

"I know," said Professor Marshall, "so I have brought you one. Here you are."

The one-eyed poacher touched the horrid gear—a sixty-five dollar, double-handed salmon rod, equipped with a fine reel, a nine-foot leader, and a beautifully smooth, double-tapered line. The old poacher waved the rod disgustedly. Something whizzed by his hat, and he grabbed at it, and caught it in his horny palm. It seemed to be attached to the leader, and he inspected it indignantly.

"What in hell's that?" he asked.

"A salmon fly—a Jock Scott."

To Uncle Jeff, this was the crowning insult. He sighed, and wiped his eye with his sleeve, as he mentally compared this dainty bit of fluff and steel with the large and lethal barb of his salmon spear.

He had been very cunningly trapped. It looked as though he would have to go fishing as the law decreed, whether he wanted to or not. Adding another spice to his misery, he ruefully recalled that some extravagant soul—probably Professor Marshall—had even bought him a New Brunswick fishing license.

But he determined to live down these various indignities, and for the next few days, though grim and saturnine, he went fishing with a fly, while downstream floated bits of foliage and larger treetops which he sheared off on his Olympian backcasts.

On the fifth and last day, the party arrived at Burnt Hill Brook, having run Slate Island Rapids in a rising river. The sacred bottle of Hernando's Fiery Dagger was still tragically intact, but a young fellow named Beaver Smith was piling up a terrific lead. The score, by weights, ran as follows, at three in the afternoon of the fifth day, position—mouth of Burnt Hill Brook:

> Professor Marshall, 9 lbs.
> John Emmet, 11 lbs., 2 ozs.
> Beaver Smith, 14¼ lbs.
> Harrison Kane, 8 lbs.
> Thomas Jefferson Coongate, 3 lbs.
> (grilse caught while fly dragged as
> the angler cut some chewing tobacco).

Uncle Jeff sat on the high ledge above the river that fateful afternoon longing for just one hour alone with his salmon spear. During his meditation, a whoop came from below, where Beaver Smith, to clinch matters, was in the process of landing a salmon which was incontestably heavier than his 14¼ pounder—except that someone had lost the scales.

Proudly bearing his great fish, Beaver stalked up to Uncle Jeff and dangled it before him.

"Not bad, hey Uncle Jeff?"

"Huh!"

"Heft him."

"Hell with him."

"Feeling low, old-timer?"

"Somethin' I et."

But it was along about in here somewhere that the invincible scheme-light must have flared like a Very light in the lone, malignant eye of the poacher from Privilege. And while this light was of itself a deadly and capable thing, it was for once assisted by a stroke of luck, or at least a brief chain of circumstances.

There is a pool in the Miramichi a couple of hundred yards or so below the entrance of Burnt Hill Brook. It is named the Cocktail Pool, and for reasons obvious enough, Uncle Jeff drifted disconsolately thence. The name of the pool was about as close as he could get to a drink of anything, but it gave him a slight comfort, as, with his first backcast, he wrenched a large limb from a maple, and on the forward cast shot it across the river, a matter of fifty yards or better.

On his next cast, gravity and the gods assisting, the old poacher's limp and battered Jock Scott actually landed in the water. He eyed the fly gloomily as it sank. It sank above, and about three feet upstream of, a bored salmon. And—oh, hell, you know how it goes. This salmon had been lying there doggo for three days. Then the river began to rise, and the salmon either liked it, or he didn't like it. Anyway, he moved a little out of position, and there was this confounded mess of feathers right above him, and he sneered at it, and as it floated down, he grew annoyed with life, surfaced his nose, sucked, pressed his lips together, and suddenly felt his neck practically leave its socket, and his vertebrae come apart, one by one. In short, this particular salmon was taking the original Nantucket Sleigh Ride, by courtesy of Thomas Jefferson Coongate. Uncle Jeff has remarked elsewhere that, if you handle a fly rod right, it's practically as effective as spearing.

Weight for weight, probably no salmon was ever beached quicker. Beached is hardly the word. *This* salmon was treed! It fell through the foliage, slithering from limb to limb, into Uncle Jeff's lap. He clutched it in both arms, but he needn't have. The fish was dead before it ever left the water. Why the gear held together is either a major mystery, or a major compliment to the manufacturers of American fishing tackle, *en masse*.

Well, the story ought to end here. But it refuses, on behalf of Uncle Jeff. His salmon ought, definitely and positively, to outweigh Beaver Smith's largest. But it was clearly not as large as Beaver's; at least not quite. Anybody could see it with the naked eye—but Uncle Jeff's wasn't naked. It wore a veil of a baleful blue color, and its owner might have been holding four aces, a pair of treys, or a sawed-off shotgun.

The excited group around him didn't faze him. He remained calm, superior, superb.

"It's a marvelous fish, Uncle Jeff!" cried Beaver himself.

"It's bright," remarked Professor Marshall, "but at the same time, it seems a little thin."

"I stretched him a mite, when I treed him," remarked the one-eyed poacher modestly. "But he was chunky, oncet."

"Beaver's is heavier," said the professor, hefting both specimens, and looking academic.

"Sure it is. You can tell," said John Emmet, himself testing the weights.

Harrison Kane, Beaver, the guides, and a party of seventeen from a boy's camp all hefted the two salmon and found themselves in agreement with the others. The lone dissenter sat on a pointed boulder, and when everyone had had his say, he, the dissenter, had his.

"The scales?" he remarked. He remarked it again, in a faint whisper which could be heard as far upriver as Slate Island Rapids. "The scales?"

The assemblage was duly impressed—and the bottle of Hernando's Fiery Dagger duly unscathed, until rather late on the morrow. The two competing fish, meanwhile, were drawn—or "drawed," as it is best pronounced. This simply means they were slit open and the entrails and gills removed, so that they wouldn't spoil.

Uncle Jeff slept with his salmon that night. Well, why not? It was a beautiful fish.

The ultimate and official weighing took place in Room Number One in the Queen Hotel in Fredericton. There were, in truth, seven or eight ultimate weighings, on as many different scales which were loaned by local hardware stores, the hotel management, and some innocent bystanders.

Mr. Coongate's entry was furtively, then openly examined for concealed heavy metals, such as old anvils, or short sections of railroad iron. Mr. Coongate sat idly by, thoughtfully eyeing the bottle of Hernando's Fiery Dagger, which glinted pleasantly on a bureau with a mirror behind it which imparted a happy sense of doubleness to the bottle—in the eyes of the most interested beholder. His—Mr. Coongate's—salmon weighed three ounces more than Beaver Smith's leading candidate on all the scales save one, on which it weighed six pounds more. These scales were destroyed by the manager of The Queen.

"Well," said the genteel Professor Marshall, and added, "Well—"

"Well?" said Uncle Jeff Coongate, faithful to the echo, and daintily wiping the saliva from his mustache with a long, stripping motion.

"Well," said Beaver Smith, "hell. You win, Uncle Jeff."

The old master bowed with superb grace. He went to the bureau and folded in the two outer plates of the mirror. It was one of those triple affairs that ladies use for fixing their hair on all sides at once. The mirror had never, however, been put to better use than at present. From the proper angle—and Uncle Jeff was there—you could see four bottles of Hernando's Fiery Dagger, including the original.

The manager of The Queen produced a bottle of high-priced and very superior Scotch whiskey. He opened it and poured out an appropriate number of liberal drinks, passing the largest to Uncle Jeff.

"Thank you, no," declined the one-eyed poacher, with a graceful arm-gesture, like the boom of a schooner swinging in the wind. "I'll jest have a leetle mite of the other, over there on the dresser. But first, maybe I better ice down them salmon, and pack 'em for shipment. You can have mine, too, Beaver," he added generously.

"Gosh, don't you want it, Uncle Jeff?"

"No, son—no. It wa'n't caught right. If I et it, caught on that fly rod, I'd perish from self-disgust."

The truth was that the salmon—all, or both of them—had begun to smell very much like salmon in the warm summer night, so Uncle Jeff's offer was received at its face value, and he repaired to carry it out.

The party took the night train to Boston, but Uncle Jeff got off in the small hours at a flag station near Mopang, in his own country, where he had honor and prestige. The train, he said, didn't stop at the flag station. He, he also said, didn't mind. It didn't, he said, matter. He had been sitting up alone with the prize for the heaviest salmon, in the express car, and when he smelled the cool wind blowing across the forest from Mopang Lake, he knew he was near home, and jumped.

"Did you break the bottle, Uncle Jeff?" I asked, solicitously.

His eye at once assumed its extreme-scorn look. "'Course not, son. You got to have a powerful bottle to stand up under Hernando's. It'd eat through any ordinary bottle in a few hours. So they make the glass an inch thick. Nope, she didn't even bend when I lit amongst the spruces."

I watched the old man, marveling at his endurance, his pride, and at his magnificent history in the wild lands, law or no law. He was sitting on a splintered post on the lake shore in Privilege when he told me this story, and now, at story's end, he was gazing off across the rippling blue water, dreaming, I suspected, of jacklights, moose meat, and jails. But I was wrong again, for he remarked with seeming irrelevance: "Beaver Smith should have slep' with his salmon, too."

"Why is that, Uncle Jeff?"

"Well, 'cause in the night a thought come to me."

I waited, breathless for the inevitable revelation from the master mind.

"Yes," the old poacher went on, "he should of slep' with his salmon. 'Cause when this thought come, I got up out of my blanket, an' covered up my salmon so's he'd be warm an' cozy, an' I went down by that river, an' set a spell, figurin'. I figured how fishermen allus loaded their fish full of buckshot, an' old scrap iron, an' spark plugs, to win bets. But I figured *they'd* figure I'd do somethin' like that. But not me. It ain't fair, nor honest. So I went over to the li'l shed where Beaver's salmon hung, an' I took my knife that I skin mink with, an' I done some tax—tax—uh-dirmy with it. I peeled in under the skin of that fish, and withdrawed my pound of flesh, an' stuffed back my handkerchief, an' socks, an' the skin folded back jest lovely, an' smooth, an' all."

"My Lord, Uncle Jeff!" I said. "I wonder what Beaver thought, when he cooked that salmon!"

"Dang it, son!" said the one-eyed poacher, irritably. "Didn't I jest tell you how I give him *my* fish? That makes it square, don't it? All square an' fair, all aroun', except—" He brooded for a moment, watching the ends of his mustache, as they streaked out ahead of him in the wind. "Except," he finished, remorsefully, "I stole from them boys. I stole them danged scales an' flang 'em in the river up there. They—they was nice boys, too."

ON DRY-COW FISHING
AS A FINE ART

Rudyard Kipling

IT MUST BE CLEARLY UNDERSTOOD that I am not at all proud of this performance. In Florida men sometimes hook and land, on rod and tackle a little finer than a steam-crane and chain, a mackerel-like fish called "tarpon," which sometime run to 120 pounds. Those men stuff their captures and exhibit them in glass cases and become puffed up. On the Columbia River sturgeon of 150 pounds weight are taken with the line. When the sturgeon is hooked the line is fixed to the nearest pine tree or steamboat-wharf, and after some hours or days the sturgeon surrenders himself, if the pine or the line do not give way. The owner of the line then states on oath that he has caught a sturgeon, and he, too, becomes proud.

These things are mentioned to show how light a creel will fill the soul of a

man with vanity. I am not proud. It is nothing to me that I have hooked and
played seven hundred pounds weight of quarry. All my desire is to place the
little affair on record before the mists of memory breed the miasma of exaggeration.

The minnow cost eighteenpence. It was a beautiful quill minnow, and the
tackle-maker said that it could be thrown as a fly. He guaranteed further in
respect to the triangles—it glittered with triangles—that, if necessary, the minnow would hold a horse. A man who speaks too much truth is just as offensive
as a man who speaks too little. None the less, owing to the defective condition
of the present law of libel, the tackle-maker's name must be withheld.

The minnow and I and a rod went down to a brook to attend to a small
jack who lived between two clumps of flags in the most cramped swim that
he could select. As a proof that my intentions were strictly honourable, I may
mention that I was using a light split-cane rod—very dangerous if the line
runs through weeds, but very satisfactory in clean water, inasmuch as it keeps
a steady strain on the fish and prevents him from taking liberties. I had an
old score against the jack. He owed me two live-bait already, and I had reason
to suspect him of coming up-stream and interfering with a little bleak-pool
under a horse-bridge which lay entirely beyond his sphere of legitimate influence. Observe, therefore, that my tackle and my motives pointed clearly to
jack, and jack alone; though I knew that there were monstrous big perch in
the brook.

The minnow was thrown as a fly several times, and, owing to my peculiar,
and hitherto unpublished, methods of fly throwing, nearly six pennyworth of
the triangles came off, either in my coat-collar, or my thumb, or the back of
my hand. Fly fishing is a very gory amusement.

The jack was not interested in the minnow, but towards twilight a boy
opened a gate of the field and let in some twenty or thirty cows and half-a-
dozen cart-horses, and they were all very much interested. The horses gal-
loped up and down the field and shook the banks, but the cows walked solidly
and breathed heavily, as people breathe who appreciate the Fine Arts.

By this time I had given up all hope of catching my jack fairly, but I wanted
the live-bait and bleak-account settled before I went away, even if I tore up
the bottom of the brook. Just before I had quite made up my mind to borrow
a tin of chloride of lime from the farm-house—another triangle had fixed
itself in my fingers—I made a cast which for pure skill, exact judgement of
distance, and perfect coincidence of hand and eye and brain, would have taken
every prize at a bait-casting tournament. That was the first half of the cast.
The second was postponed because the quill minnow would not return to its
proper place, which was under the lobe of my left ear. It had done thus before,
and I supposed it was in collision with a grass tuft, till I turned round and
saw a large red and white bald faced cow trying to rub what would be withers
in a horse with her nose. She looked at me reproachfully, and her look said
as plainly as words: "The season is too far advanced for gadflies. What is this
strange disease?"

I replied, "Madam, I must apologize for an unwarrantable liberty on the part of my minnow, but if you will have the goodness to keep still until I can reel in, we will adjust this little difficulty."

I reeled in very swiftly and cautiously, but she would not wait. She put her tail in the air and ran away. It was a purely involuntary motion on my part: I struck. Other anglers may contradict me, but I firmly believe that if a man had foul-hooked his best friend through the nose, and that friend ran, the man would strike by instinct. I struck, therefore, and the reel began to sing just as merrily as though I had caught my jack. But had it been a jack, the minnow would have come away. I told the tackle-maker this much afterwards, and he laughed and made allusions to the guarantee about holding a horse.

Because it was a fat innocent she-cow that had done me no harm the minnow held—held like an anchor-fluke in coral moorings—and I was forced to dance up and down an interminable field very largely used by cattle. It was like salmon fishing in a nightmare. I took gigantic strides, and every stride found me up to my knees in marsh. But the cow seemed to skate along the squashy green by the brook, to skim over the miry backwaters, and to float like a mist through the patches of rush that squirted black filth over my face. Sometimes we whirled through a mob of her friends—there were no friends to help me—and they looked scandalized; and sometimes a young and frivolous cart-horse would join in the chase for a few miles, and kick solid pieces of mud into my eyes; and through all the mud, the milky smell of kine, the rush and the smother, I was aware of my own voice crying: "Pussy, pussy, pussy! Pretty pussy! Come along then, puss-cat!" You see it is so hard to speak to a cow properly, and she would not listen—no, she would not listen.

Then she stopped, and the moon got up behind the pollards to tell the cows to lie down; but they were all on their feet, and they came trooping to see. And she said, "I haven't had my supper, and I want to go to bed, and please don't worry me." And I said, "The matter has passed beyond any apology. There are three courses open to you, my dear lady. If you'll have the common sense to walk up to my creel I'll get my knife and you shall have all the minnow. Or, again, if you'll let me move across to your near side, instead of keeping me so coldly on your off side, the thing will come away in one tweak. I can't pull it out over your withers. Better still, go to a post and rub it out, dear. It won't hurt much, but if you think I'm going to lose my rod to please you, you are mistaken." And she said, "I don't understand what you are saying. I am very, very unhappy." And I said, "It's all your fault for trying to fish. Do go to the nearest gate-post, you nice fat thing, and rub it out."

For a moment I fancied she was taking my advice. She ran away and I followed. But all the other cows came with us in a bunch, and I thought of Phaeton trying to drive the Chariot of the Sun, and Texan cowboys killed by stampeding cattle, and *Green Grow the Rushes, O!*" and Solomon and Job, and "loosing the bands of Orion," and hooking Behemoth, and Wordsworth who talks about whirling round with stones and rocks and trees, and "Here we go round the Mulberry Bush," and "Pippin Hill," and "Hey Diddle

Diddle," and most especially the top joint of my rod. Again she stopped—but nowhere in the neighborhood of my knife—and her sisters stood moonfaced round her. It seemed that she might, now, run towards me, and I looked for a tree, because cows are very different from salmon, who only jump against the line, and never molest the fisherman. What followed was worse than any direct attack. She began to buck-jump, to stand on her head and her tail alternately, to leap into the sky, all four feet together, and to dance on her hind legs. It was so violent and improper, so desperately unladylike, that I was inclined to blush, as one would blush at the sight of a prominent statesman sliding down a fire escape, or a duchess chasing her cook with a skillet. That flopsome *abandon* might go on all night in the lonely meadow among the mists, and if it went on all night—this was pure inspiration—I might be able to worry through the fishing line with my teeth.

Those who desire an entirely new sensation should chew with all their teeth, and against time, through a best waterproofed silk line, one end of which belongs to a mad cow dancing fairy rings in the moonlight; at the same time keeping one eye on the cow and the other on the top joint of a split-cane rod. She buck-jumped and I bit on the slack just in front of the reel; and I am in a position to state that that line was cored with steel wire throughout the particular section which I attacked. This has been formally denied by the tacklemaker, who is not to be believed.

The *wheep* of the broken line running through the rings told me that henceforth the cow and I might be strangers. I had already bidden good-bye to some tooth or teeth; but no price is too great for freedom of the soul.

"Madam," I said, "the minnow and twenty feet of very superior line are your alimony without reservation. For the wrong I have unwittingly done to you I express my sincere regret. At the same time, may I hope that Nature, the kindest of nurses, will in due season——"

She or one of her companions must have stepped on her spare end of the line in the dark, for she bellowed wildly and ran away, followed by all the cows. I hoped the minnow was disengaged at last; and before I went away looked at my watch, fearing to find it nearly midnight. My last cast for the jack was made at 6.23 p.m. There lacked still three and a-half minutes of the half-hour; and I would have sworn that the moon was paling before the dawn!

"Simminly someone were chasing they cows down to bottom o' Ten Acre," said the farmer that evening. " 'Twasn't you, sir?"

"Now under what earthly circumstances do you suppose I should chase your cows? I wasn't fishing for them, was I?"

Then all the farmer's family gave themselves up to jam-smeared laughter for the rest of the evening, because that was a rare and precious jest, and it was repeated for months, and the fame of it spread from that farm to another, and yet another at least three miles away, and it will be used again for the benefit of visitors when the freshets come down in spring.

But to the greater establishment of my honour and glory I submit in print this bald statement of fact, that I may not, through forgetfulness, be tempted later to tell how I hooked a bull on a Marlow Buzz, how he ran up a tree and took to water, and how I played him along the London-road for thirty miles, and gaffed him at Smithfield. Errors of this kind may creep in with the lapse of years, and it is my ambition ever to be a worthy member of that fraternity who pride themselves on never deviating by one hair's breadth from the absolute and literal truth.

A DAY'S FISHING, 1948

Ed Zern

I HAD BEEN THREE JULY days on the West Branch of the Ausable in the Adirondacks and had seen few trout moving and brought fewer to the fly; in the evening there would be fifteen minutes of lackadaisical rising to a small sulfury mayfly, perhaps a *dorothea*, and while that was going on a trout or two might suck in a sparsely tied Light Cahill, but the bigger fish weren't having any, thank you. In the daytime the river was dead, and there are few things deader than a dead brown trout stream. Then I recalled that Wendle Collins had told me of a bigger river ninety miles to the north, and had praised it, and I thought it might not be as slow as the West Branch. The next morning I got up early and drove to the town Wendle had mentioned, and looked up the doctor who had been his companion when he fished there. "Ah, yes," said the doctor, "but the river's in terrible shape. Low and warm. There's another, though, that you might try since you've come so far. Small, but at least it has water. Here it is on the map—a rainbow river, with a few natives in the slow runs, and once in a while a two-pounder. The best stretch runs through the place of a man named Thompson—drive down this dirt road and his is the first farmhouse after you pass a white church.

"This Thompson," said the doctor, "is a queer bird. A widower, in his seventies. If he likes your looks he may let you go through his place to get to the river, and if he doesn't he won't, and that's that. You can say I sent you—I've treated his arthritis for a long time—but if he doesn't like the way your chin dimples it won't do any good at all. He owns three miles of the river—in fact, he owns a good chunk of that township—and he turns away a lot of people for no reason, since he doesn't fish and has no stock on the place nor land in cultivation. If there's ever an unpopularity contest in this county he'll win it hands down."

I drove out the highway to the dirt turn-off, and after passing a white church came to a large frame farmhouse beside the road; the mailbox was marked "Thompson." I parked the car in the driveway to the barn, across the road from the house, and walked across the road and up onto the front porch. When nobody answered my knock on the door I walked around to the back, where I found the door open to the kitchen but could see no one. I tried several out-buildings behind the house, then went back to the front porch and knocked again, louder. When it occurred to me that I'd forgot about the barn I turned and saw a man leaning back against it, blending his weatheredness into the barn's and watching me without much interest. He was six feet and a few inches tall, in soiled, faded overalls and shirt and badly needing a shave and haircut. He's the hired man, I thought, but as I walked closer and saw him more clearly I changed my mind. "I'm looking for Mr. Thompson," I said. He looked at me for four or five seconds, still without interest, and then said, "You've found him." "I'm a friend of Dr. Summers," I said. "He told me if you liked my looks you'd let me go through your place to the river, and if you didn't you wouldn't."

He looked at me some more while he mulled this over, then unfolded his arms and shifted onto his own frame the weight the building had supported. "I'll show you the way to the river," he said. I got into my waders, took my rod in sections and followed him across the road and over several fallow fields. Walking beside him I said, "Do you eat trout? I don't keep them, usually, but I'll bring some back if you'd like."

A hundred paces later, when I was sure he hadn't heard me, he said, "I guess I could use some. If they're cleaned." We had come to the edge of a field and the remnants of a stone fence, and down the slope from it through a sprawl of alders I could see the sparkle of water. "There it is," he said, and turned and walked back across the field. I went down through the blackberry tangle on the slope and through the alders to the stream; it was a fast, pretty river, only slightly swamp-stained and with good pocket-water where trout can lie and rest while the current brings manna, and where a nymph or wetfly on a long, light leader will linger a second or two—long enough for a fish to seize it before the rush of water whirls it on downstream.

It was noon then, and I fished half a mile down the river and took two ten-inch rainbows before eating the sandwich I'd packed in my vest the night before. Both trout had taken a small wet leadwing coachman, but when I came to a beautiful deep pool with a foot-high falls at the head I changed to a tiny red-and-white maribou streamer and struck a fourteen-inch rainbow under the falls and a thirteen-inch brook trout in the tail of the pool. Then I changed reels to have a floating line and fished a dry fly back to where I'd entered the river, picking up three more nine- and ten-inch fish and losing a sixteen- or seventeen-inch rainbow that caught me with my rod-tip down and broke the 4X gut on his first wild jump.

It was almost seven o'clock when I got back to the farmhouse, and as I came up to the kitchen door I could see that Thompson had just finished putting away his supper dishes. The white-enamelled sink was just inside the door, and so I stepped inside and slid the seven cleaned and still beautiful trout out of my grass-mat creel onto the sink top. "I'll trade you these for a glass of cold water," I said. The old man came across the kitchen and peered down at the fish. Then he picked up a pail that was three-quarters full, poured it into the sink and started out the door; "I'll get some fresh," he said.

I followed him outside and around the back of the house to an uncovered dug well with a wooden windlass; he hooked the bucket onto the rope and let it drop into the water, then reeled it back up. It was the first time I'd seen a wooden windlass since my boyhood in West Virginia, and I said, remembering that the doctor had said he was well-to-do, "Why don't you get a pump for this?" He finished winding in the bucket; when it rested on the edge of the well-wall he said, "Had a pump once. It froze. This don't freeze." We went back to the kitchen, and he got a glass from the shelf, filled it from the bucket and handed it to me. While I was drinking it he wrapped the trout in waxed paper and put them in the ice-box. Then he took a chocolate layer cake from a cupboard and set it on the kitchen table. "There's cake," he said, in the way he might have said it was raining. I waited to see if he meant to pursue the subject, and then asked if I could have a piece of it. He seemed relieved, and took a knife from the table drawer. While he was cutting a slab from the cake I said it looked home-made, and he said it was.

"A neighbor?" I said. He looked at me in genuine surprise, and when he saw I was serious he said, "I do my own cooking." It was good cake. I stepped outside and sat on the bench beside the kitchen door while I ate it, so as not to get crumbs on the floor, and when he'd put the cake back in the cupboard he came out and sat down on the other end of the bench. Through a mouthful of cake I asked him if he fished the river much.

"Don't fish it a-tall," he said. "Don't see the sense on it." "Trout are pretty good eating," I said. "Not that good," he said. "Not good enough to go traipsing up and down a river all day getting bit by black flies."

I finished the cake, and asked if I could come back sometime and fish the upstream water, and he said, "I guess so. But don't bring nobody with you. I don't want all creation tramping across them fields." I said I'd come alone, and asked if he had any help around the place. "Don't need none," he said. "Used to have a man for the milking, but I don't have cows now. You ever milk a cow?" I said I had, but that I wasn't very good at it, and he said he had known. "I can tell a man that's milked cows," he said. "Never missed a one." I asked him how he could tell, and he thought for a minute and said, "I couldn't rightly say. But I can tell, all right."

I said it was nearly nine o'clock and I had to drive ninety miles back to the motel, and had better be going, and the old man was silent while I gathered up my creel and rod and vest. I thanked him for the fishing and the cake, and he said, "This is the first time I been up after eight o'clock for a long time. Maybe ten years." He followed me across the road and watched while I stowed the rod and gear in the station wagon. I got in and started the motor and said so-long and was turning out of the driveway onto the road when I heard him call. I stopped, thinking I'd left some gear on the ground, and he walked across the barnyard and stooped to put his head in the opposite window.

"You can bring somebody, if you want," he said. I said thanks, I'd be back the first chance I got, and would only bring someone who had milked a cow. I meant to go back, of course, but I never did.

THE INTRUDER

Robert Traver

IT WAS ABOUT NOON WHEN I put down my fly rod and sculled the little cedar boat with one hand and ate a sandwich and drank a can of beer with the other, just floating and enjoying the ride down the beautiful broad main Escanaba River. Between times I watched the merest speck of an eagle tacking and endlessly wheeling far up in the cloudless sky. Perhaps he was stalking my sandwich or even, dark thought, stalking me. . . . The fishing so far had been poor; the good trout simply weren't rising. I rounded a slow double bend, with high gravel banks on either side, and there stood a lone fisherman—the first person I had seen in hours. He was standing astride a little feeder creek on a gravel point on the left downstream side, fast to a good fish, his glistening rod hooped and straining, the line taut, the leader vibrating and sawing the water, the fish itself boring far down out of sight.

Since I was curious to watch a good battle and anxious not to interfere, I eased the claw anchor over the stern—plop—and the little boat hung there, gurgling and swaying from side to side in the slow deep current. The young fisherman either did not hear me or, hearing, and being a good one, kept his mind on his work. As I sat watching he shifted the rod to his left hand, shaking out his right wrist as though it were asleep, so I knew then that the fight had been a long one and that this fish was no midget. The young fisherman fumbled in his shirt and produced a cigarette and lighter and lit up, a real cool character. The fish made a sudden long downstream run and the fisherman raced after him, prancing through the water like a yearling buck, gradually coaxing and working him back up to the deeper slow water across from the gravel bar. It was a nice job of handling and I wanted to cheer. Instead I coughed discreetly and he glanced quickly upstream and saw me.

"Hi," he said pleasantly, turning his attention back to his fish.

"Hi," I answered.

"How's luck?" he said, still concentrating.

"Fairish," I said. "But I haven't anything quite like you seem to be on to. How you been doin'—otherwise, I mean?"

"Fairish," he said. "This is the third good trout in this same stretch—all about the same size."

"My, my," I murmured, thinking ruefully of the half-dozen-odd barely legal brook trout frying away in my sun-baked creel. "Guess I've just been out floating over the good spots."

"Pleasant day for a ride, though," he said, frowning intently at his fish.

"Delightful," I said wryly, taking a slow swallow of beer.

"Yep," the assured young fisherman went on, expertly feeding out line as his fish made another downstream sashay. "Yep," he repeated, nicely taking up slack on the retrieve, "that's why I gave up floating this lovely river. Nearly ten years ago, just a kid. Decided then 'twas a hell of a lot more fun fishing a hundred yards of her carefully than taking off on these all-day floating picnics."

I was silent for a while. Then: "I think you've got something there," I said, and I meant it. Of course he was right, and I was simply out joy-riding past the good fishing. I should have brought along a girl or a camera. On this beautiful river if there was no rise a float was simply an enforced if lovely scenic tour. If there was a rise, no decent fisherman ever needed to float. Presto, I now had it all figured out. . . .

"Wanna get by?" the poised young fisherman said, flipping his cigarette into the water.

"I'll wait," I said. "I got all day. My pal isn't meeting me till dark—'way down at the old burned logging bridge."

"Hm . . . trust you brought your passport—you really are out on a voyage," he said. "Perhaps you'd better slip by, fella—by the feel of this customer it'll be at least ten-twenty minutes more. Like a smart woman in the mood for play, these big trout don't like to be rushed. C'mon, just bear in sort of close to me, over here, right under London Bridge. It won't bother us at all."

My easy young philosopher evidently didn't want me to see how really big his fish was. But being a fisherman myself I knew, I knew. "All right," I said, lifting the anchor and sculling down over his way and under his throbbing line. "Thanks and good luck."

"Thanks, chum," he said, grinning at me. "Have a nice ride and good luck to you."

"Looks like I'll need it," I said, looking enviously back over my shoulder at his trembling rod tip. "Hey," I said, belatedly remembering my company manners, "want a nice warm can of beer?"

Smiling: "Despite your glowing testimonial, no thanks."

"You're welcome," I said, realizing we were carrying on like a pair of strange diplomats.

"And one more thing, please," he said, raising his voice a little to be heard over the burbling water, still smiling intently at his straining fish. "If you don't mind, please keep this little stretch under your hat—it's been all mine for nearly ten years. It's really something special. No use kidding you—I see you've spotted my bulging creel and I guess by now you've got a fair idea of what I'm on to. And anyway I've got to take a little trip. But I'll be back—soon I hope. In the meantime try to be good to the place. I know it will be good to you."

"Right!" I shouted, for by then I had floated nearly around the downstream bend. "Mum's the word." He waved his free hand and then was blotted from view by a tall doomed spruce leannig far down out across the river from a crumbling water-blasted bank. The last thing I saw was the gleaming flash of his rod, the long taut line, the strumming leader. It made a picture I've never forgotten.

That was the last time ever that I floated the Big Escanaba River. I had learned my lesson well. Always after that when I visited this fabled new spot I hiked in, packing my gear, threading my way down river through a pungent needled maze of ancient deer trails, like a fleeing felon keeping always slyly away from the broad winding river itself. My strategy was twofold: to prevent other sly fishermen from finding and deflowering the place, and to save myself an extra mile of walking.

Despite the grand fishing I discovered there, I did not go back too often. It was a place to hoard and save, being indeed most good to me, as advertised. And always I fished it alone, for a fisherman's pact had been made, a pact that became increasingly hard to keep as the weeks rolled into months, the seasons into years, during which I never again encountered my poised young fisherman. In the morbid pathology of trout fishermen such a phenomenon is mightily disturbing. What had become of my fisherman? Hadn't he ever got back from his trip? Was he sick or had he moved away? Worse yet, had he died? How could such a consummate young artist have possibly given up fishing such an enchanted spot? Was he one of that entirely mad race of eccentric fishermen who cannot abide the thought of sharing a place, however fabulous, with even one other fisherman?

By and by, with the innocent selfishness possessed by all fishermen, I dwelt less and less upon the probable fate of my young fisherman and instead came smugly to think it was I who had craftily discovered the place. Nearly twenty fishing seasons slipped by on golden wings, as fishing seasons do, during which time I, fast getting no sprightlier, at last found it expedient to locate and hack out a series of abandoned old logging roads to let me drive within easier walking distance of my secret spot. The low cunning of middle age was replacing the hot stamina of youth. . . . As a road my new trail was strictly a spring-breaking bronco-buster, but at least I was able to sit and ride, after a fashion, thus saving my aging legs for the real labor of love to follow.

Another fishing season was nearly done when, one afternoon, brooding over that gloomy fact, I suddenly tore off my lawyer-mask and fled my office, heading for the Big Escanaba, bouncing and bucking my way in, finally hitting the Glide—as I had come to call the place—about sundown. For a long time I just stood there on the high bank, drinking in the sights and pungent river smells. No fish were rising, and slowly, lovingly, I went through the familiar ritual of rigging up; scrubbing out a fine new leader, dressing the tapered line, jointing the rod and threading the line, pulling on the tall patched waders, anointing myself with fly dope. No woman dressing for a ball was more fussy. . . . Then I composed myself on my favorite fallen log and waited. I smoked a slow pipe and sipped a can of beer, cold this time, thanks to the marvels of dry ice and my new road. My watching spot overlooked a wide bend and commanded a grand double view: above, the deep slow velvet glide with its little feeder stream where I first met my young fisherman; below a sporty and productive broken run of white water stretching nearly a half-mile. The old leaning spruce that used to be there below me had long since bowed in surrender and been swept away by some forgotten spring torrent. As I sat waiting the wind had died, the shadowing waters had taken on the brooding blue hush of evening, the dying embers of sundown suddenly lit a great blazing forest fire in the tops of the tall spruces across river from me, and an unknown bird that I have always called simply the "lonely" bird sang timidly its ancient haunting plaintive song. I arose and took a deep breath like a soldier advancing upon the enemy.

The fisherman's mystic hour was at hand.

First I heard and then saw a young buck in late velvet slowly, tentatively splashing his way across to my side, above me and beyond the feeder creek, ears twitching and tall tail nervously wigwagging. Then he winded me, freezing in midstream, giving me a still and liquid stare for a poised instant; then came charging on across in great pawing incredibly graceful leaps, lacquered flanks quivering, white flag up and waving, bounding up the bank and into the anonymous woods, the sounds of his excited blowing fading and growing fainter and then dying away.

In the meantime four fair trout had begun rising in the smooth tail of the glide just below me. I selected and tied on a favorite small dry fly and got down below the lowest riser and managed to take him on the first cast, a short dainty float. Without moving I stood and lengthened line and took all four risers, all nice firm brook trout upwards of a foot, all the time purring and smirking with increasing complacency. The omens were good. As I relit my pipe and waited for new worlds to conquer I heard a mighty splash above me and wheeled gaping at the spreading magic ring of a really good trout, carefully marking the spot. Oddly enough he had risen just above where the young buck had just crossed, a little above the feeder creek. Perhaps, I thought extravagantly, perhaps he was after the deer. . . . I waited, tense and watchful, but he did not rise again.

I left the river and scrambled up the steep gravelly bank and made my way through the tall dense spruces up to the little feeder creek. I slipped down the bank like a footpad, stealthily inching my way out to the river in the silted creek itself, so as not to scare the big one, *my* big one. I could feel the familiar shock of icy cold water suddenly clutching at my ankles as I stood waiting at the spot where I had first run across my lost fisherman. I quickly changed to a fresh fly in the same pattern, carefully snubbing the knot. Then the fish obediently rose again, a savage easy engulfing roll, again the undulant outgoing ring, just where I had marked him, not more than thirty feet from me and a little beyond the middle and obliquely upstream. Here was, I saw, a cagey selective riser, lord of his pool, and one who would not suffer fools gladly. So I commanded myself to rest him before casting. "Twenty-one, twenty-two, twenty-three . . ." I counted.

The cast itself was indecently easy and, finally releasing it, the little Adams sped out on its quest, hung poised in midair for an instant, and then settled sleepily upon the water like a thistle, uncurling before the leader like the languid outward folding of a ballerina's arm. The fly circled a moment, uncertainly, then was caught by the current. Down, down it rode, closer, closer, then—*clap!*—the fish rose and kissed it, I flicked my wrist and he was on, and then away he went roaring off downstream, past feeder creek and happy fisherman, the latter hot after him.

During the next mad half-hour I fought this explosive creature up and down the broad stream, up and down, ranging at least a hundred feet each way, or so it seemed, without ever once seeing him. This meant, I figured, that he was either a big brown or a brook. A rainbow would surely have leapt a dozen times by now. Finally I worked him into the deep safe water off the feeder creek where he sulked nicely while I panted and rested my benumbed rod arm. As twilight receded into dusk with no sign of his tiring I began vaguely to wonder just who had latched on to whom. For the fifth or sixth time I rested my aching arm by transferring the rod to my left hand, professionally shaking out my tired wrist just as I had once seen a young fisherman do.

Nonchalantly I reached in my jacket and got out and tried to light one of my rigidly abominable Italian cigars. My fish, unimpressed by my show of aplomb, shot suddenly away on a powerful zigzag exploratory tour upstream, the fisherman nearly swallowing his unlit cigar as he scrambled up after him. It was then that I saw a lone man sitting quietly in a canoe, anchored in midstream above me. The tip of his fly rod showed over the stern. My heart sank: after all these years my hallowed spot was at last discovered.

"Hi," I said, trying to convert a grimace of pain into an amiable grin, all the while keeping my eye on my sulking fish. The show must go on.

"Hi," he said.

"How you doin'?" I said, trying to make a brave show of casual fish talk.

"Fairish," he said, "but nothing like you seem to be on to."

"Oh, he isn't so much," I said, lying automatically if not too well. "I'm working a fine leader and don't dare to bull him." At least that was the truth.

The stranger laughed briefly and glanced at his wrist watch. "You've been on to him that I know of for over forty minutes—and I didn't see you make the strike. Let's not try to kid the Marines. I just moved down a bit closer to be in on the finish. I'll shove away if you think I'm too close."

"Nope," I answered generously, delicately snubbing my fish away from a partly submerged windfall. "But about floating this lovely river," I pontificated, "there's nothing in it, my friend. Absolutely nothing. Gave it up myself eighteen-twenty years ago. Figured out it was better working one stretch carefully than shoving off on those floating picnics. Recommend it to you, comrade."

The man in the canoe was silent. I could see the little red moon of his cigarette glowing and fading in the gathering gloom. Perhaps my gratuitous pedagogical ruminations had offended him; after all, trout fishermen are a queer proud race. Perhaps I should try diversionary tactics. "Wanna get by?" I inquired silkily. Maybe I could get him to go away before I tried landing this unwilling porpoise. He still remained silent. "Wanna get by?" I repeated. "It's perfectly O.K. by me. As you see—it's a big roomy river."

"No," he said dryly. "No thanks." There was another long pause. Then: "If you wouldn't mind too much I think I'll put in here for the night. It's getting pretty late—and somehow I've come to like the looks of this spot."

"Oh," I said in a small voice—just "Oh"—as I disconsolately watched him lift his anchor and expertly push his canoe in to the near gravelly shore, above me, where it grated halfway in and scraped to rest. He sat there quietly, his little neon cigarette moon glowing, and I felt I just had to say something more. After all I didn't *own* the river. "Why sure, of course, it's a beautiful place to camp, plenty of pine knots for fuel, a spring-fed creek for drinking water and cooling your beer," I ran on gaily, rattling away like an hysterical realtor trying to sell the place. Then I began wondering how I would ever spirit my noisy fish car out of the woods without the whole greedy world of fishermen learning about my new secret road to this old secret spot. Maybe I'd even have to abandon it for the night and hike out. . . . Then I remembered there was an uncooperative fish to be landed, so I turned my full attention to the unfinished and uncertain business at hand. "Make yourself at home," I lied softly.

"Thanks," the voice again answered dryly, and again I heard the soft chuckle in the semidarkness.

My fish had stopped his mad rushes now and was busily boring the bottom, the long leader vibrating like the plucked string of a harp. For the first time I found I was able gently to pump him up for a cautious look. And again I almost swallowed my still unlit stump of cigar as I beheld his dorsal fin cleaving the water nearly a foot back from the fly. He wallowed and shook like a dog and then rolled on his side, then recovered and fought his way back down and away on another run, but shorter this time. With a little pang I knew then that my fish was a done, but the pang quickly passed—it always did—and again I gently, relentlessly pumped him up, shortening line, drawing him in to the familiar daisy hoop of landing range, kneeling and stretching and straining out my opposing aching arms like those of an extravagant archer. The net slipped fairly under him on the first try and, clenching my cigar, I made my pass and lo! lifted him free and dripping from the water. "Ah-h-h . . ." He was a glowing superb spaniel-sized brown. I staggered drunkenly away from the water and sank anywhere to the ground, panting like a winded miler.

"Beautiful, *beautiful*," I heard my forgotten and unwelcome visitor saying like a prayer. "I've dreamed all this—over a thousand times I've dreamed it."

I tore my feasting eyes away from my fish and glowered up at the intruder. He was half standing in the beached canoe now, one hand on the side, trying vainly to wrest the cap from a bottle, of all things, seeming in the dusk to smile uncertainly. I felt a sudden chill sense of concern, of vague nameless alarm.

"Look, chum," I said, speaking lightly, very casually, "is everything all O.K.?"

"Yes, yes, of course," he said shortly, still plucking away at his bottle. "There . . . I—I'm coming now."

Bottle in hand he stood up and took a resolute broad step out of the canoe, then suddenly, clumsily he lurched and pitched forward, falling heavily, cruelly, half in the beached canoe and half out upon the rocky wet shore. For a moment I sat staring ruefully, then I scrambled up and started running toward him, still holding my rod and the netted fish, thinking this fisherman was indubitably potted. "No, no, no!" he shouted at me, struggling and scrambling to his feet in a kind of wild urgent frenzy. I halted, frozen, holding my sagging dead fish as the intruder limped toward me, in a curious sort of creaking stiffly mechanical limp, the uncorked but still intact bottle held triumphantly aloft in one muddy wet hand, the other hand reaching gladly toward me.

"Guess I'll never get properly used to this particular battle stripe," he said, slapping his thudding and unyielding right leg. "But how are you, stranger?" he went on, his wet eyes glistening, his bruised face smiling. "How about our having a drink to your glorious trout—and still another to reunion at our old secret fishing spot?"

A FATAL SUCCESS

Henry van Dyke

BEEKMAN DE PEYSTER WAS PROBABLY the most passionate and triumphant fisher-man in the Petrine Club. He angled with the same dash and confidence that he threw into his operations in the stock-market. He was sure to be the first man to get his flies on the water at the opening of the season. And when we came together for our fall meeting, to compare notes of our wanderings on various streams and make up the fish-stories for the year, Beekman was almost always "high hook." We expected, as a matter of course, to hear that he had taken the most and the largest fish.

It was so with everything that he undertook. He was a masterful man. If there was an unusually large trout in a river, Beekman knew about it before any one else, and got there first, and came home with the fish. It did not make him unduly proud, because there was nothing uncommon about it. It was his habit to succeed, and all the rest of us were hardened to it.

When he married Cornelia Cochrane, we were consoled for our partial loss by the apparent fitness and brilliancy of the match. If Beekman was a masterful man, Cornelia was certainly what you might call a mistressful woman. She had been the head of her house since she was eighteen years old. She carried her good looks like the family plate; and when she came into the breakfast-room and said good-morning, it was with an air as if she presented every one with a check for a thousand dollars. Her tastes were accepted as judgments, and her preferences had the force of laws. Wherever she wanted to go in the summer-time, there the finger of household destiny pointed. At Newport, at Bar Harbor, at Lenox, at Southampton, she made a record. When she was joined in holy wedlock to Beekman De Peyster, her father and mother heaved a sigh of satis-faction, and settled down for a quiet vacation in Cherry Valley.

It was in the second summer after the wedding that Beekman admitted to a few of his ancient Petrine cronies, in moments of confidence (unjustifiable, but natural), that his wife had one fault.

"It is not exactly a fault," he said, "not a positive fault, you know. It is just a kind of a defect, due to her education, of course. In everything else she's magnificent. But she doesn't care for fishing. She says it's stupid—can't see why any one should like the woods—calling camping out the lunatic's diversion. It's rather awkward for a man with my habits to have his wife take such a view. But it can be changed by training. I intend to educate her and convert her. I shall make an angler of her yet."

And so he did.

The new education was begun in the Adirondacks, and the first lesson was given at Paul Smith's. It was a complete failure.

Beekman persuaded her to come out with him for a day on Meacham River, and promised to convince her of the charm of angling. She wore a new gown, fawn-colour and violet, with a picture-hat, very taking. But the Meacham River trout was shy that day; not even Beekman could induce him to rise to the fly. What the trout lacked in confidence the mosquitoes more than made up. Mrs. De Peyster came home much sunburned, and expressed a highly unfavorable opinion of fishing as an amusement and of Meacham River as a resort.

"The nice people don't come to the Adirondacks to fish," said she; "they come to talk about the fishing twenty years ago. Besides, what do you want to catch that trout for? If you do, the other men will say you bought it, and the hotel will have to put in another for the rest of the season."

The following year Beekman tried Moosehead Lake. Here he found an atmosphere more favourable to his plan of education. There were a good many people who really fished, and short expeditions in the woods were quite fashionable. Cornelia had a camping-costume of the most approved style made by Dewlap on Fifth Avenue—pearl-gray with linings of rose-silk—and consented to go with her husband on a trip up Moose River. They pitched their tent the first evening at the mouth of Misery Stream, and a storm came on. The rain sifted through the canvas in a fine spray, and Mrs. De Peyster sat up all night in a waterproof cloak, holding an umbrella. The next day they were back at the hotel in time for lunch.

"It was horrid," she told her most intimate friend, "perfectly horrid. The idea of sleeping in a showerbath, and eating your breakfast from a tin plate, just for sake of catching a few silly fish! Why not send your guides out to get them for you?"

But, in spite of this profession of obstinate heresy, Beekman observed with secret joy that there were signs, before the end of the season, that Cornelia was drifting a little, a very little but still perceptibly, in the direction of a change of heart. She began to take an interest, as the big trout came along in September, in the reports of the catches made by the different anglers. She would saunter out with the other people to the corner of the porch to see the fish weighed and spread out on the grass. Several times she went with Beekman in the canoe to Hardscrabble Point, and showed distinct evidences of pleasure when he caught large trout. The last day of the season, when he returned from a successful expedition to Roach River and Lily Bay, she inquired with some particularity about the results of his sport; and in the evening, as the company sat before the great open fire in the hall of the hotel, she was heard to use this information with considerable skill in putting down Mrs. Minot Peabody of Boston, who was recounting the details of her husband's catch at Spencer Pond. Cornelia was not a person to be contented with the back seat, even in fish-stories.

When Beekman observed these indications he was much encouraged, and resolved to push his educational experiment briskly forward to his customary goal of success.

"Some things can be done, as well as others," he said in his masterful way, as three of us were walking home together after the autumnal dinner of the Petrine Club, which he always attended as a graduate member. "A real fisherman never gives up. I told you I'd make an angler out of my wife; and so I will. It has been rather difficult. She is 'dour' in rising. But she's beginning to take notice of the fly now. Give me another season, and I'll have her landed."

Good old Beekman! Little did he think____ But I must not interrupt the story with moral reflections.

The preparations that he made for his final effort at conversion were thorough and prudent. He had a private interview with Dewlap in regard to the construction of a practical fishing-costume for a lady, which resulted in something more reasonable and workmanlike than had ever been turned out by that famous artist. He ordered from Hook & Catchett a lady's angling-outfit of the most enticing description—a split-bamboo rod, light as a girl's wish and strong as a matron's will; an oxidized silver reel, with a monogram on one side, and a sapphire set in the handle for good luck; a book of flies, of all sizes and colours, with the correct names inscribed in gilt letters on each page. He surrounded his favorite sport with an aureole of elegance and beauty. And then he took Cornelia in September to the Upper Dam at Rangeley.

She went reluctant. She arrived disgusted. She stayed incredulous. She returned____ Wait a bit, and you shall hear how she returned.

The Upper Dam at Rangeley is the place, of all others in the world, where the lunacy of angling may be seen in its incurable stage. There is a cosy little inn, called a camp, at the foot of a big lake. In front of the inn is a huge dam of gray stone, over which the river plunges into a great oval pool, where the trout assemble in the early fall to perpetuate their race. From the tenth of September to the thirtieth, there is not an hour of the day or night when there are no boats floating on that pool, and no anglers trailing the fly across its waters. Before the late fishermen are ready to come in at midnight, the early fishermen may be seen creeping down to the shore with lanterns in order to begin before cock-crow. The number of fish taken is not large—perhaps five or six for the whole company on an average day—but the size is sometimes enormous—nothing under three pounds is counted—and they pervade thought and conversation at the Upper Dam to the exclusion of every other subject. There is no driving, no dancing, no golf, no tennis. There is nothing to do but fish or die.

At first, Cornelia thought she would choose the latter alternative. But a remark of that skilful and morose old angler, McTurk, which she overheard on the verandah after supper, changed her mind.

"Women have no sporting instinct," said he. "They only fish because they see men doing it. They are imitative animals."

That same night she told Beekman, in the subdued tone which the architectural construction of the house imposes upon all confidential communications in the bedrooms, but with resolution in every accent, that she proposed to go fishing with him on the morrow.

"But not on that pool, right in front of the house, you understand. There must be some other place, out on the lake, where we can fish for three or four days, until I get the trick of this wobbly rod. Then I'll show that old bear, McTurk, what kind of an animal woman is."

Beekman was simply delighted. Five days of diligent practice at the mouth of Mill Brook brought his pupil to the point where he pronounced her safe.

"Of course," he said patronizingly, "you haven't learned all about it yet. That will take years. But you can get your fly out thirty feet, and you can keep the tip of your rod up. If you do that, the trout will hook himself, in rapid water, eight times out of ten. For playing him, if you follow my directions, you'll be all right. We will try the pool to-night, and hope for a medium-sized fish."

Cornelia said nothing, but smiled and nodded. She had her own thoughts.

At about nine o'clock Saturday night, they anchored their boat on the edge of the shoal where the big eddy swings around, put out the lantern and began to fish. Beekman sat in the bow of the boat, with his rod over the left side; Cornelia in the stern, with her rod over the right side. The night was cloudy and very black. Each of them had put on the largest possible fly, one a "Bee-Pond" and the other a "Dragon"; but even these were invisible. They measured out the right length of line, and let the flies drift back until they hung over the shoal, in the curly water where the two currents meet.

There were three other boats to the left of them. McTurk was their only neighbour in the darkness on the right. Once they heard him swearing softly to himself, and knew that he had hooked and lost a fish.

Away down at the tail of the pool, dimly visible through the gloom, the furtive fisherman, Parsons, had anchored his boat. No noise ever came from that craft. If he wished to change his position, he did not pull up the anchor and let it down again with a bump. He simply lengthened or shortened his anchor rope. There was no click of the reel when he played a fish. He drew in and paid out the line through the rings by hand, without a sound. What he thought when a fish got away, no one knew, for he never said it. He concealed his angling as if it had been a conspiracy. Twice that night they heard a faint splash in the water near his boat, and twice they saw him put his arm over the side in the darkness and bring it back again very quietly.

"That's the second fish for Parsons," whispered Beekman, "what a secretive old Fortunatus he is! He knows more about fishing than any man on the pool, and talks less."

Cornelia did not answer. Her thoughts were all on the tip of her own rod. About eleven o'clock a fine, drizzling rain set in. The fishing was very slack. All the other boats gave it up in despair; but Cornelia said she wanted to stay out a little longer, they might as well finish up the week.

At precisely fifty minutes past eleven, Beekman reeled up his line, and remarked with firmness that the holy Sabbath day was almost at hand and they ought to go in.

"Not till I've landed this trout," said Cornelia.

"What? A trout! Have you got one?"

"Certainly; I've had him on for at least fifteen minutes. I'm playing him Mr. Parsons' way. You might as well light the lantern and get the net ready; he's coming in towards the boat now."

Beekman broke three matches before he made the lantern burn; and when he held it up over the gunwale, there was the trout sure enough, gleaming ghostly pale in the dark water, close to the boat, and quite tired out. He slipped the net over the fish and drew it in—a monster.

"I'll carry that trout, if you please," said Cornelia, as they stepped out of the boat; and she walked into the camp, on the last stroke of midnight, with the fish in her hand, and quietly asked for the steelyard.

Eight pounds and fourteen ounces—that was the weight. Everybody was amazed. It was the "best fish" of the year. Cornelia showed no sign of exultation, until just as John was carrying the trout to the icehouse. Then she flashed out: "Quite a fair imitation, Mr. McTurk—isn't it?"

Now McTurk's best record for the last fifteen years was seven pounds and twelve ounces.

So far as McTurk is concerned, this is the end of the story. But not for the De Peysters. I wish it were. Beekman went to sleep that night with a contented spirit. He felt that his experiment in education had been a success. He had made his wife an angler.

He had indeed, and to an extent which he little suspected. That Upper Dam trout was to her like the first taste of blood to the tiger. It seemed to change, at once, not so much her character as the direction of her vital energy. She yielded to the lunacy of angling, not by slow degrees (as first a transient delusion, then a fixed idea, then a chronic infirmity, finally a mild insanity), but by a sudden plunge into the most violent mania. So far from being ready to die at Upper Dam, her desire now was to live there—and to live solely for the sake of fishing—as long as the season was open.

There were two hundred and forty hours left to midnight on the thirtieth of September. At least two hundred of these she spent on the pool; and when Beekman was too exhausted to manage the boat and the net and the lantern for her, she engaged a trustworthy guide to take Beekman's place while he slept. At the end of the last day her score was twenty-three, with an average of five pounds and a quarter. His score was nine, with an average of four pounds. He had succeeded far beyond his wildest hopes.

The next year his success became even more astonishing. They went to the Titan Club in Canada. The ugliest and most inaccessible sheet of water in that territory is Lake Pharaoh. But it is famous for the extraordinary fishing at a certain spot near the outlet, where there is just room enough for one canoe. They camped on Lake Pharaoh for six weeks, by Mrs. De Peyster's command; and her canoe was always the first to reach the fishing-ground in the morning, and the last to leave it in the evening.

Someone asked him, when he returned to the city, whether he had good luck.

"Quite fair," he tossed off in a careless way; "we took over three hundred pounds."

"To your own rod?" asked the inquirer, in admiration.

"No—o—o," said Beekman, "there were two of us."

There were two of them, also, the following year, when they joined the Nata-sheebo Salmon Club and fished that celebrated river in Labrador. The custom of drawing lots every night for the water that each member was to angle over the next day, seemed to be especially designed to fit the situation. Mrs. De Peyster could fish her own pool and her husband's too. The result of that year's fishing was something phenomenal. She had a score that made a paragraph in the newspapers and called out editorial comment. One editor was so inadequate to the situation as to entitle the article in which he described her triumph "The Equivalence of Woman." It was well-meant, but she was not at all pleased with it.

She was now not merely an angler, but a "record" angler of the most virulent type. Wherever they went, she wanted, and she got, the pick of the water. She seemed to be equally at home on all kinds of streams, large and small. She would pursue the little mountain-brook trout in the early spring, and the Labrador salmon in July, and the huge speckled trout of the northern lakes in September, with the same avidity and resolution. All that she cared for was to get the best and the most of the fishing at each place where she angled. This she always did.

And Beekman—well, for him there were no more long separations from the partner of his life while he went off to fish some favourite stream. There were no more home-comings after a good day's sport to find her clad in cool and dainty raiment on the verandah, ready to welcome him with friendly badinage. There was not even any casting of the fly around Hardscrabble Point while she sat in the canoe reading a novel, looking up with mild and pleasant interest when he caught a larger fish than usual, as an older and wiser person looks at a child playing some innocent game. Those days of a divided interest between man and wife were gone. She was now fully converted, and more. Beekman and Cornelia were one; and she was the one.

The last time I saw the De Peysters he was following her along the Beaverkill, carrying a landing-net and a basket, but no rod. She paused for a moment to exchange greetings, and then strode on down the stream. He lingered for a few minutes longer to light a pipe.

"Well, old man," I said, "you certainly have succeeded in making an angler of Mrs. De Peyster."

"Yes, indeed," he answered—"haven't I?" Then he continued, after a few thoughtful puffs of smoke, "Do you know, I'm not quite so sure as I used to be that fishing is the best of all sports. I sometimes think of giving it up and going in for croquet."

ONCE ON A SUNDAY

Philip Wylie

SOMEWHERE UP THE RIVER a noon whistle blew; quiet came over the boatyard. The band saw stopped screaming first; mallets and hammers fell silent; old man Kane's handsaw was last. Crunch Adams, acting yard superintendent that day, picked up the box of lunch his wife, Sari, had prepared for him and walked over to the lean, gnarled shipwright. Crunch inspected the intricately worked chunk of madeira—looked his thoughts—and the old fellow nodded with satisfaction.

Crunch sat in the shade of a cabbage palm, out of the heat. Kane moved beside him and opened a pasteboard shoebox. The two men began to eat. Multiple riffles moved along the turgid river at their feet.

"Mullet," Crunch said.

"Mullet," the old man agreed.

The backdrop of Miami glittered in the sunlight and murmured with an abnormal springtime industry occasioned by the presence of thousands of soldiers and sailors. By and by Crunch's eyes traveled purposefully to the blue-grey sides of the hauled crash boat on which they were working. "Navy'd like to have her back in the water tomorrow night."

"No doubt," said the skillful old man. "But it's Sunday."

The *Poseidon*'s skipper nodded. "Yeah." He let time pass. They watched a brace of pelicans float up the river on stiff wings. "Enemy works on Sunday, though. Usually attacks then, if possible."

Mr. Kane spat. "Swine."

"Short-handed," Crunch went on. "We are. Everybody is. If we could get that piece fitted tomorrow morning, they could paint it later—"

"I'm a strict Presbyterian," the old man replied firmly. "At eleven tomorrow,

I'll be in church, that's where I'll be."

"I know how it is." Crunch's expression was innocent. "I fished a Presbyterian minister once—on a Sunday."

"You don't *say!*"

Desperate, the *Poseidon*'s mate, was swabbing down. The sun was a red disc—a stagy decoration; it emitted no glare but it dyed the line of boats at the Gulf Stream Dock a faint orange. Soon it would be gone. Crunch and Sari were up on the pier, laughing with the last customer. A tall stranger made his way past them, stared at the boats' names, and walked lithely to the stern of the *Poseidon*.

"Are you Crunch Adams?" he asked. His "r's" burred with a trace of Scotland and the voice that pronounced them had a slow sonority.

"I'm Des, the mate. Crunch is yonder."

The eyes of the stranger were cavernous. His nose was large and beaklike; above the six-foot level of his craggy head was a shock of iron-grey hair. Des wondered what sort of man he was and had a partial answer when the man saw young Bill Adams. Bill was three, then—proudly toting a suitcase for his father. The evening breeze stirred his blond curls. He tugged and grunted—a scale model of Hercules, in a blue sunsuit. A twinkle came in the man's recessed eyes and his broad mouth broke into a smile. "Likely lad!"

"Crunch's. The skipper's."

"I've been told he's the best. It shows—in the offspring."

Des began to like the guy. "Hey, Crunch!" he called.

"My problem," said the man, as he and the two charter-boatmen put their heads together, "is as difficult as it is simple. I'm a minister o' the gospel—a Presbyterian—though I wouldn't like it to be held against me."

Crunch and Des chuckled.

"When I went to school in Edinburgh—which was a considerable long while ago—I used to slip out as often as the opportunity afforded and cast a fly for trout and sometimes for salmon. I haven't wet a line since." He rubbed his chin. "My daughter spends her winters here with her husband, who's a man of means. I've joined them for a few days' vacation and my son-in-law insists I put in a few on the sea. He's footing the bill—and a man ought to keep in good with his son-in-law, don't you think?" He beamed.

"Very sound," Crunch said.

"But there's more to it than that," the man went on. "Do you mind if I light a pipe? It's safe on these gasoline boats?"

Crunch struck the match.

The prospective customer sat down with a sigh of composure. He sniffed the air. "Salty. I like it. Smells as good as the recollection of a frith. Unfortunately, for the past twenty-five years, I've hardly smelled it at all. I've been preaching the gospel inland. Not that it isn't as desperately needed there as on the coasts. I am simply explaining the rest of my predicament—an altogether happy one, as it chances. This vacation I'm on comes between my old church and a new one

I'm to take directly after Christmas. What's that yonder?" He pointed with the stem of his pipe.

Crunch looked in time to see the triangular top of a dark fin ease into the blue water. "Porpoise."

"You don't say! They come here in this Bay?"

"Some of 'em live in here."

"Well!" He watched the big mammal rise and blow. "Fine creature! But to get to the point. Where I'm taking the new pastorate, fishing is partly a business and largely a recreation, besides. It's in New Jersey, at a place called Antasquan— a big town or small city, whichever you will. Some of my new congregation are commercial fishermen, and some of the wealthier ones are boat-owners, like yourselves. They go out for big tunny, I understand. Then, there's something called 'blues' they're partial to—"

"We know a little about it," Crunch said appreciatively. "We've fished a few summers from the Manasquan nearby."

The minister smiled. "Which, no doubt, is one of the reasons my son-in-law stipulated you two! What can a man expect in a corporation lawyer, though, except guile? At any rate, I've got a congregation of fishermen—and golf players, to boot. Being a Scot, I can handle the golf, on week days, though it somewhat drains my congregations on the Sabbath, I hear. As fishing does, to an even greater degree, in the summer. But I like to know something of the pursuits of the men I preach to. So I'm doubly glad to be able to take advantage of this vacation to find out what I can of salt-water fishing. Have I made myself clear?"

"You sure have, Mr.—?"

"McGill. The Reverend Doctor Arthur McGill. And if, in the heat of excitement in the three days I've got to fish, it should become necessary to use a shorter term, you'll find I respond to 'Mac.' "

He shook hands with them to seal the bargain.

When he was gone, Des grinned at the descending twilight. "The trouble is, there aren't enough ministers like that. If there were, I'd go to church oftener, myself."

"Just what I was thinking," his skipper agreed.

The Reverend Doctor Arthur McGill appeared on the Gulf Stream Dock at seven o'clock the following morning—a green-visored hat flopping above his grey mane and a huge hamper carried lightly over his bony arm. He took the gap between dock and stern in an easy stride and deposited the basket.

It was a cool, breezy day—it would be choppy outside—but, if he knew it, he did not seem concerned. "Bracing weather," he said. "I hadn't expected it of the tropics. I rose before the servants and picked my own grapefruit from a tree in the yard. There was something burning out toward the Everglades and it recalled my autumn fire anywhere in the world. But the grapefruit was a distinctly pagan note; it made me understand a little why it is that north country men always have a sense of guilt in the south. It ought to be snowing and blowing—and here you are picking fruit!"

Des was already hanging the bow lines on the dolphins. The *Poseidon* pushed into the ship channel and started east. At the jetty-mouth, the outgoing tide, bulled by the easterly wind, threw up an unpredictable maelstrom of lumpy current; the *Poseidon* tossed, smashed hard and found her sea gait for the day. Three warm December weeks had changed, overnight, into the Floridian equivalent of a winter day—a day with a twelve-mile breeze and a temperature in the shade of sixty—a "cold" day, in the opinion of the natives.

Crunch cut baits. The minister wrapped an elbow around one of the canopy supports and watched, his eyes bright under his tangled brows. Once or twice, the skipper glanced at him covertly; he wasn't going to be seasick. He took in each detail, as the strip was sliced wafer-thin, tapered, pointed, beveled, and pierced for the hook. "It's an art, I can see that."

"The idea is to make it flutter in the water—like a fish with a busy tail." Crunch dropped over a bait on a leader and tested it to make sure it would not spin and wind up—or unwind—the line. He handed the rod to Reverend McGill and, under the same intense scrutiny, he arranged two balao on the outrigger lines. Then, because his passenger looked quizzical, he explained the operation of outriggers.

"You see," said the minister, "I'm a dub and a tyro and I have plenty of need to learn all this. A congregation of fishing enthusiasts will listen with a polite and patronizing interest if their dominie discusses the fine points of netting fishes in the Sea of Galilee two thousand years ago. But if you can bring the matter up to date—put it in terms of outriggers, so to speak—and use it in an illustration, you may even wake up the habitual sleepers."

Crunch laughed. "I get the idea, parson. Now. About 'blues.' Being a part-time Jersey fisherman myself, I understand the Jersey attitude. It's cold today—and we may run along like this for hours without a strike—so I'll explain what they do off the 'Squan Inlet—and why. Their fishing is done this way—and other ways."

"I'd appreciate it." The minister snuggled into the fighting chair and pulled his muffler tighter.

Crunch was deep in a lucid description of the art of chumming for tuna—remembering to cite the fact that Jersey old-timers still call them "horse mackerel" —when there was a splash behind the center bait. Reverend McGill went taut as his reel warbled.

"Bonita!" Crunch said. "Just hang on till he gets that run out of his system."

Reverend McGill hung on—and hung on properly—with his rod high enough so that no sudden bend could snap it over the stern and low enough so that he had room to lift it and take in slack in the event the fish turned suddenly. It did. The rod went higher and the minister began to reel. He brought the bonita to within a few yards of the boat and it sounded a good seventy-five feet. His rod tip shivered with the rapid tail action. He pumped the fish up, under Crunch's instruction. It sounded again—ran again—and came to gaff.

Crunch brought it aboard and the exhilarated minister looked. "Magnificent creature! Herringbone back—and the underside as white and sleek as alabaster!

Funny thing! It's almost as big as any fish I ever caught in my life—and yet it pulled so hard I expected a fish my own size!"

"Bonitas are strong," Crunch said. He resumed his discussion of chumming. His back was turned to the water when Reverend McGill had his second strike. The minister handled the fish with considerable skill. " 'Cuda," Crunch said, after a moment.

It proved to be a barracuda. Crunch flipped it over the gunwale, showed the ferocious teeth by clamping the fish's head under the lid of the box in the stern, and removed the hook with pliers in a gingerly fashion. The *Poseidon* ran steadily for some two hours after that. Then there was a bluish flash under one of the outrigger baits and its line drifted gently down to the water only to spring tight like the wire of a snare. Crunch eyed the line as it cut the surface—pointing, in a curve, to a fish that was barely under water. "Dolphin," he explained. "Get ready for him to jump. And when he does jump—watch him."

When the fish jumped, it was quite a sight. This particular dolphin at the particular instant was green and silver. Sometimes they are luminous cobalt and silver or gold—with pale blue spots. Sometimes they are almost pure gold or silver. Their rainbow patterns cannot be predicted—they change in seconds—and they range through all the natural colors save red and those with red in them, as well as through the spectra of precious metals.

"I know," the minister said quietly and between breaths, when Crunch gaffed the dolphin, "why people write poetry about them." He watched Crunch bait up again and went back to his vigil. "It's amazing," he continued, "what eyes you have. Now, in all three strikes, all I saw was a flicker and a lot of spray. But— each time—you saw the fish and named it correctly."

Crunch laughed. "I didn't see the fish, itself, any time. Except, as you say, an impression of a fish. I could tell what they were by the way your rod tip behaved —by the angle at which the fish fought—by a lot of little things."

"They must be fine points, for fair! I don't suppose you reveal them to the novitiate—the lucky novitiate, I might add?"

"Why not?" Crunch grinned benignly. "Take—the bonita. He was first. He hits hard and fast, usually at a sharp angle to the course of the bait. When he feels the hook he puts on every ounce of power he's got. He goes away, maybe for thirty yards or so, and then, still feeling the hook, he goes down. He'll bore straight down or go down in a spiral, like an auger. Now there's a fish out here that's related to the tuna, called an albacore. He does the same thing. But when the albacore swims, it's like a glide, all power and no wiggle. With a bonita there's the wiggle. A flutter. You see it in the rod tip. You feel it in your arms."

"You do that," the minister agreed.

" 'Cuda's can sound—or run—or jump. In fact, they usually give a jump or two like a pike or a muskie. On the same tackle, they're even stronger, I believe. But they do one thing that's characteristic—they jerk. If you get one near the boat you can see him do it under water. He'll yank his head back and forth trying to get rid of the hook or to break the line, just the way a bulldog yanks."

"And the dolphin?"

"He always skims along at a terrific rate right below the surface. You can tell that because your line, instead of boring down into the sea, will be stretching out over it for a long way. Then the dolphin will circle, first one way and then the other, in big arcs. That is, he will unless he's foul-hooked. Hooked from the outside, in the back, say. Or hooked through the eye. In that case, he's very apt to sound—and if you haven't seen him when he hit, you'll be hard put to guess what you're fighting. Of course, you occasionally do see dolphin before they hit, because they sometimes make several bounds into the air to get the bait, as if they were impatient with the resistance of the water."

"I see." The minister mused, "Funny, that. If you're fishing for salmon—you take salmon. You know what you've got when you have your rise. Trout, too, unless you happen to encounter a chub or dace. Here, though, the possibilities are vast."

"There are hundreds."

The minister thought that over. "And what would a sailfish be like? That is, if we were to have the fantastic good fortune—?"

So Crunch told him about the ways of sailfish. And in the end, he was, as usual, completely at a loss: "What I've said goes for the average sailfish. But you're continually running into the exception. The fellow who just gulps the bait and runs. The one who strikes like a bonita—with only a flash under the bait. And then, when you know it was a sail because you saw its high fin and its bill—and you hook it—it'll possibly turn out to be a white marlin."

"I presume, in the three days I have, there's no chance of that?"

"I dunno," Crunch answered. "There's always some chance. They're tailing today, though. I've seen a couple. They don't strike, as a rule, when they're running south from a cold snap."

The minister nodded. Crunch knew by his attitude during the discussion of sailfish that the Reverend Doctor McGill had a very definite dream about his three days of deep-sea angling and the dream was centered around that particular breed of fish. In his mind's eye, the minister wanted not only what knowledge of marine angling he could glean from the period, but a particular object, a mounted sail, to hang, probably, in his study, where the visiting members of his new congregation could observe it and admire. Reverend McGill did not say so. He was too humble a man. But Crunch knew.

While the skipper was contemplating that matter, the novice in the *Poseidon*'s stern had another strike. The reel sang. The fish ran. Then it went deep. The rod tip fluttered. "A bonita!" the preacher cried with certainty.

"Well—it's not quite like a bonita. A little, just a shade, less powerful. Not quite so vicious. It might be a small bonita, at that. But I think it's a kingfish."

It was a kingfish. The minister chuckled. "You're not giving away all your trade secrets in one day!"

"Well, that one wasn't easy. I couldn't be sure myself. If we call three quarters of them correctly we're doing fine."

"I won't be so rash and conceited on the next," the minister promised. But there wasn't any "next." They ate the excellent lunch in the big hamper. They trolled the length of the island that is Miami Beach. Then they turned south and went as far as the old lighthouse. But there were no more strikes upon which the minister could test his fresh knowledge.

That evening the *Poseidon* came in as late as the winter sun would allow. "I've had a wonderful day," the minister said. "I've thought of at least six new sermons. I've settled in my head a minute point of ethics brought to me by one of my former flock which stuck me for a long time. I've caught four prime fish—whoppers, all—and two of 'em, you say, are superb eating. There's a good fifteen pounds of meat for the larders of myself and the friends of my son-in-law. And I'll never be able to thank you enough. The best part of it all is," his eyes crinkled, "we'll be at it again in the morning—and the day after, also. That's what they mean when they call this place a paradise on earth!"

Crunch stopped the recital and carefully poured a cup of coffee from his thermos. He raised his eyebrows enquiringly at old man Kane. The shipwright nodded and held out a cup from which he had been drinking milk. "Thanks, Crunch. So—what happened? Did he get a sail?"

"No," Crunch said. He peered reminiscently at the murky river and tossed a coral pebble to break the immaculate surface. "No. Doctor McGill never caught a sail, so far as I am aware."

"I'm disappointed."

"Maybe he wasn't! Des and I got fond of that gent. Whatever a good man is, he's it. And by that I mean he was both a man, and good. We fished Friday, from seven till dark, and got skunked. It was raw and windy with low clouds. Not a strike. But the old boy saw a whale, a fine-back, that came up close to the *Poseidon* and cruised along, blowing—and he insisted it made the day worth while.

"Then—Saturday came. His last day. He was going home Monday and he was planning to take in a couple of Miami preachers Sunday and Sunday night. So we started at six, in the dark, and we dragged a bait till night. He caught one grouper over the reef, and a rock hind, and he had one sailfish rise. I swear the old boy's hair stood on end. The sail came like an upside-down yacht with her keel out, and it followed the bait for a mile, but it never hit. Old Mac McGill stood up the whole time, muttering. First I thought he was praying and then I had a kind of shock because I thought he was swearing, but he wasn't doing either—he was just coaching the fish—like a quarterback on the bench when his team's in a spot. The fish never did hit, just eyed that bait, wallowed behind it, and finally swam away. And then it got dark and we came in and the dominie's vacation was over. He said he'd be back some day when his pocketbook could stand it and he said he'd had more fun than ever before in his life. His eyes shot sparks and he meant every word of it. He was disappointed, I am certain, but not as much disappointed as pleased. Des and I, of course, tried to make up for the thin fishing by telling him as many stories as we could—and by giving him as much dope as we knew how."

"A good sport," Kane nodded.

"The real thing. Well, he shook our hands and thanked us and went away. Mr. Williams, the dock manager, had us down Sunday for a party—we didn't know the people—and we sat around Saturday evening feeling pretty low about the preacher. Sunday, we got down about seven and our party hadn't shown up. So we just sat around some more. Lots of people get a special kick out of deep-sea fishing for the main and simple reason that you don't have to get out at the crack of dawn. I mean, they'll hit at noon just as often as they'll hit at daybreak, which isn't like freshwater stuff. Anyway_____"

During the night the wind had hauled. The norther had blown itself out and the Trade Wind, dawdling back from the southeast, had taken its place, pushing the cold air aside, dissipating the lowering clouds, and substituting the regimented wool-balls of Caribbean cumulus. The thermometer, between midnight and sunrise, had gone up fifteen degrees and a balminess characteristic of Florida had supplanted the sharp chill. Even the first level bars of sunshine were warm and it was certain that by noon the temperature in the shade would be eighty. On such days, after a cold-weather famine, the sailfish are likely to be ravenous. Crunch knew it, and Des, and they wondered in their separate silences what Reverend McGill would think about it. Because he knew, too. They'd told him how, as a rule, the sailfish would come up fighting on these days when the weather broke.

By nine o'clock, they were getting restless. Their party hadn't appeared. All the other boats were out, with the exception of one, engine parts of which were strewn over its stern cockpit for repair. Des was commenting on the laggardliness of some people when Crunch said, "Look. There's Reverend McGill."

The minister stepped from a car. He was wearing a neat serge suit and a high, starched collar. He walked down the dock with a sheepish expression and said, "That was my son-in-law. Off to play golf—like too many in my own congregations! I went along with him this far—I can walk the balance of the way to the kirk." Then he realized that the boats had gone. "How does it happen you're still hanging to the pilings?"

"We were chartered," Des said bitterly, "by some slug-a-bed named Ellsworth Coates."

The minister turned pale. He swallowed. "That," he finally murmured, "is the name of my son-in-law—the heathen tempter!"

Crunch merely glanced up at the tall man on the dock. Then he squinted across the Bay. He neither smiled nor frowned—just squinted. I guess he must have seen the weather prediction—and realized what it would probably be like out there today."

Reverend McGill sat down shakily. "It's like him! The lawyer's guile! Dropping me here to walk to church! And with you two boys waiting, steam up and bait in the box! What does he take me for—a weakling? Is some crafty second-rate, amoral attorney to be the first to make me break the Sabbath? Not that, in the proper cause, I mightn't! I'm none of your hardshell preachers! I've been known far and wide as a liberal man, these long years! But a precedent is a precedent and I've kept the Lord's day, in my own fashion, as an example. Fie to Ellsworth —the wretch!"

"This might turn out to be a good cause," Des said. "After all, it's a day in a hundred, and you wanted your future parish to feel you were one of them."

"It could be a day in a million!" the minister said scornfully.

Time passed—a good deal of time. Crunch began to repair a light rod which had lost a guide in an encounter with a wahoo. Up where the Gulf Stream Dock joined the Florida shore a school of big jack got under a walloping school of small mullet. The result was aquatic chaos: fish showered into the air as if they were being tossed up in barrelfuls by Davy Jones himself. The minister watched, goggle-eyed, and said something that Crunch thought was, "It's more than flesh can withstand!" But Crunch wasn't certain.

And then the *Clarissa B.* came in. She came in because one of her four passengers, a novice, had been taken ill—although the sea was smooth: only a vague ground swell kept it from being as calm as pavement. The *Clarissa,* as she approached, throwing two smart wings of water from her bows, was flying four sailfish flags.

"Four of them!" Reverend McGill whispered disconsolately. "I could have stood two—or possibly three—!"

The boat turned, backed in smartly, and deposited her shaky passenger with little ceremony: the other anglers were manifestly annoyed at the interruption and anxious to get back on the Gulf Stream. She pulled away from her slip again —showing four forked tails above her gunwales.

"Good fishing, eh?" Crunch called to the skipper.

"They'll jump in the boat!" he yelled back. "It's red-hot! We've already had a triple and two doubleheaders and a single!" He turned his wheel and purred into the blue distance.

Reverend McGill sighed and stood up. He shook out his full length of supple anatomy. He brushed back his iron-grey hair. "In any event," he said, grinning, "I'll not rationalize. I had it on the tip of my tongue to say that the Reverend Doctor Stone, whom I had intended to hear this morning, isn't so much of a preacher-man. We'll agree that he's the finest preacher in the south—and that by going fishing, I'm committing a mortal sin of the first magnitude. But—boys— let's get a lunch on board and make all the haste we can to violate the canon that has to do with this precious and altogether magnificent day!" He took off his collar as he came aboard.

By four o'clock in the afternoon, the lone passenger was stunned. In the interim, no less than seven sailfish had come up from the purple depths and done their best to be caught by the cleric. But in each instance that gentleman, through bad luck and inexperience, had failed to bring his fish to boat. In testament of his effort there was a broken rod. There were blisters on his fingers. There was a burn on his left arm where the running line had cut him. There was an empty reel from which the line had been stripped. And there was on the deck, a leader to which was still attached the upper half of a broken hook. But no sailfish flag flew from the *Poseidon*'s outrigger.

The loquacious Reverend McGill was dour, and his accent had become more Scottish. "I will nae say it's injustice," he proclaimed morosely, "an' a' would not ha' missed this day for the worrld—but it's a sterrn way to remind a mon of his evil intent!"

Crunch and Des exchanged glances. "There'll be more of 'em, parson," Des said encouragingly. "Just—take it easy."

And, even while he spoke, the outrigger line on the port side fell again and a big boil of water showed briefly where the bait had been. The line came tight and the minister struck to set the hook. The fish ran off rapidly for about forty yards and sounded. "It's no sailfish this time," he cried. "A bonita, I think. At least, perhaps we'll ha' one small fishie to show for our sins!"

Crunch looked critically at the bend in the rod. "If it's a bonita, it's the father of all bonitas," he said quietly.

"Very unlikely," Reverend McGill replied as he jockeyed to get in a few feet of slack. "Nothing sensational. The last two hours, I've realized I was predestined to have misfortune to the end of the day. But at least my face will be saved. I'll never have to exhibit a sailfish I caught on Sunday and acknowledge my guilt. The deed will be a secret between the two of us—and my son-in-law—who will use it, no doubt, for some blackmailing tomfoolery, one day. Now—he's coming toward us nicely!"

The fish swam toward the *Poseidon* for several yards. Then it turned, still deep under the water, and ran three hundred yards with the speed of an express train. The reel screamed. Crunch yelled. Des brought the *Poseidon* around in a fast arc. They chased the fish at full throttle for five hundred yards more before the minister stopped losing line from a spool that was by then no thicker than his thumb.

"It must be a sailfish, after all," Reverend McGill murmured.

"It's no sailfish," Crunch replied. His mouth was tight and he shot an enquiring glance at Des.

"What then?"

"I dunno. I dunno, Reverend. Maybe a marlin—"

"A marlin! It isn't possible—!"

"I think," Des called, "it's an Allison tuna. Better take it easy, Mac. You've got a long fight on your hands if it is."

"I'll gentle it like a baby," the angler promised. "I'm getting a bit of line, now." He tried tentatively and then with fury. "He's running to us—*to* us—faster than I can reel!"

Crunch waved—and waved again. The *Poseidon* leaped away from the fish but even at full gun she barely made enough speed so that the man on the rod could keep his line taut. Presently Crunch signalled again and the boat stood still. "Mac," as Des had called him in the stress of excitement, began to horse his fish toward the boat, lifting slowly until his bowed rod came high, dropping the tip swiftly, and winding in the slack thus gained. Two feet at a time, he brought the fish toward the place where the two guides leaned in tense concentration and where he labored sweatily. When the reel-spool was well filled with line, the fish turned and raced away again—a hundred yards, two, three. The process was repeated. The fish ran.

On the fifth struggle to the boat Reverend McGill gasped, "It's a new tribulation! I've hung a whale! Every joint in me is protesting—!"

"Stay with it," Crunch breathed fervently.

"Mon—I'm a *Scot*."

He stayed with it. Stayed with it until it tired and until, an hour and three quarters after he had hooked it, a head and jaws rolled out of water not forty feet from the *Poseidon*. Crunch felt himself grow weak. He just stood there. Des said in a small voice, "You see it?"

"Yeah."

"What is it?"

"I dunno." Crunch repeated the words as if they angered him. "I dunno. It was red—wasn't it?"

"Yeah. It was red."

"But it wasn't a snapper," Crunch continued. "Not a snapper—not a monster mangrove snapper. I never saw it before. Mac—take it mighty easy, now. It's something new you've got there."

"I couldn't put any strength on it if I had to," the minister said grittily. Then he did put on strength. The fish made a last flurry—a rush, a mighty splash—and Crunch got the leader in his gloved hand. Swiftly, skillfully, he rammed home the gaff. The tail hammered on the boat's hull like a piston. Des jumped clear down from the canopy without hanging and made a noose around the leader. He dropped the rope into the sea. The two men pulled, and the fish came aboard tail first.

It was red, scarlet, from mouth to caudal. Its underside was greenish-white. It had big fins and a square tail. It was toothed. Its eyes were green. It gasped like a grouper and flopped heavily. They guessed it weighed about a hundred and eighty.

The minister flexed his raging arms slowly, caught some of his wind, stirred his back a little as if he were afraid any further motion would shatter it, and he looked and looked at the fish. "You mean—this is one you boys can't give a name to?"

Crunch said slowly, "No, Mac. And I don't think anybody—any taxidermist, any ichthyologist—can give it a name, either. I think it's a new one. Somebody comes in with a brand-new one every year or so, around these parts. Tonight you're gonna, Mac."

"Whatever the name is," Des said with the voice of a man who had seen a miracle, "part of it will probably be McGill—forever."

Crunch walked stiffly to the radio telephone. He put in a call for Hal—and for Bob Breastedt—the two foremost piscatorial authorities on the coast. "It's built like an amberjack—something," he said into the transmitter. "Fought like one—

more or less. But it has scales like a tarpon, almost, and fins like a bass, and the darned thing's red all over!"

The experts came to the dock to meet the *Poseidon*—and so did the reporters.

It was a new one. Part of its long scientific name eventually became McGillia.

Many weeks later, Crunch had a letter from the minister. It was postmarked "Antasquan, N.J." It said, in part:

". . . and the celebrated catch we made that memorable day has become a not unmixed blessing. It served the purpose of giving my new flock an advance notice that I'm a fisherman of distinction. Indeed, the reputation carried ahead of me by the national publicity was so great that I'm alarmed whenever I remember that next summer I'll have to go out and show my lack of proficiency on the blues and the school tuna—not to mention the great horse mackerel. However, I'll take my chances on that.

"The point is, the fact that I caught the fish on the Sabbath was one which the press associations did not glaze over. On the contrary, they prominently noted it, and my congregation here was quick to make the discovery. Some of them chided me. And all of those who fish, and those who play golf, are smugly planning to be absent from their pews as soon as the spring weather breaks. After all, their dominie fishes on Sunday! This, however, has set me thinking—this—and the lesson in wiliness I learned from my son-in-law.

"Even now, war work is engaging the daytime hours of some of my people on Sunday—so I have stressed the evening service. It is already a feature in this city and the kirk is full every Sunday night though it was formerly sparsely attended at that hour. Come spring, my friends, and I expect to have most of the golfers and anglers in the evening habit and it'll be another bit of triumph I can credit to you and your fine ship! In short, I'm punished by the richly deserved lampoons of a fine group of people—and rewarded with an evening attendance that beats the old morning service average!

"The fish itself arrived in due course—splendidly mounted and a thing of wonder. In that, I lost out, also—because I still have no symbol of my dubious skill to hang on my study wall. One of my parishioners is on the board of the American Museum of Natural History—and there the creature hangs. Still—I think the day was well spent—for myself and my fellow men—don't you?"

Crunch rose and stretched. He looked at his watch. One o'clock. Presently, the sound of the band saw rent the air. The boatyard resumed work for the U.S. Navy. Crunch had been reading the letter—having taken it from his hip pocket at the proper moment. He handed it, now, to the old shipwright, who stared blankly.

"You mean—you brought this thing here this morning?"

"Sure," Crunch said.

"You knew I was going to tell you I wouldn't work tomorrow?"

Crunch nodded. "Yep. But we need you—if we're going to get that job back in the water on time for Uncle Sam."

Kane glanced down at the name of the church on the letterhead. He sucked his teeth. "Well," he said slowly, "if that preacher can go fishing—and have it turn out all right—I guess I can work."

"It was for a cause. So's this."

"I still don't get it! You planned to tell me this story—and brought the letter to prove it was the truth—"

"I'm like the preacher's son-in-law," Crunch said as he walked away. "Guileful."

STRIPED BASS AND SOUTHERN SOLITUDE

Ellington White

THE BEST WAY TO FISH is alone. The best time to fish is the fall. Believing these simple truths to be self-evident, I set out alone each fall to fish the rivers and creeks that flow out of Virginia into the Chesapeake Bay. It is a good time of year all around. Everybody else in the world is watching a football game. Leaves cover the roadside beer cans, and the traffic is light. Whenever a car appears pulling a boat, I know it is bound for the city, not the sea, for the water skiers have beached their skis and skin divers have taken up bowling. Praise the fall.

In truth, fishermen should do as fish do in the summer—lie low. We should give the beaches to the sunbathers and admit that during this idle season, when the great fiber-glass fleet rules the waterways, the thing to do is haul in our lines and run for cover. Of course, we will never do this. We aren't as smart as fish. We persist in thinking that the summer is big enough for all of us—fishermen, skin divers, water skiers, the whole shebang. What a delusion.

But now it is the fall, and I am driving east on Route 33. Pine trees crowd the shoulders, and the morning sun is hot. In the Tidewater, summer and fall merge with each other so quietly that for a few weeks you need a calendar to tell where you are. Straddling two seasons, one foot in each, you feel both seasons at once.

At West Point, under a cloud of pulpmill smoke, I cross the Pamunkey and Mattaponi rivers, tributaries of the York River, which enters the bay just north of the James. All of these rivers belong to the fall in my mind, the James especially, where I once saw the fall arrive.

I had taken a boat up the river to fish for bass in the mouth of a small creek near Presque Isle Swamp, about twelve miles below Richmond. Here the James takes its time, dawdling along between odorous mud flats, mesmerizing fish and fishermen alike. It just about put me to sleep that day, I recall. After several hours I had had enough, and started back, half paddling, half drifting down the river on the outgoing tide, drowsing among the slumberous sounds of wallowing carp and turtles dropping off logs.

It was a warm day in early October. Most of the clothing I had started out in lay heaped in the bottom of the boat. I was glad the tide and I were going the same way. Farther down the river a handful of gulls was circling a row of stakes that had once supported fish-nets. The shoreline slid past, marshy and still. I drifted by a small bay and across a gravel bar. By this time the gulls were wheeling overhead. The fog lifted just enough for me to catch the glimmerings of an idea, something about gulls following stripers. . . . Oh, nonsense, I thought. Nevertheless, there was the rod resting against the middle seat. All I had to do was pick it up. Why not? I cast into the shore. It was an idle cast and went farther than I had intended it to, landing among a drift of leaves and pine needles. The surface plug bobbed a few times. The leaves bulged and then blew open. It was an astonishing moment. I had often driven hundreds of miles chasing stripers up and down the eastern seaboard, and here I had *drifted* into a school of them. Later I visualized our paths as two crooked lines, wobbling all over the river, and somehow miraculously bisecting under a flock of gulls. In ten minutes it was all over. We had drifted apart, and without a motor I had no way of following them. It didn't matter, though. I had four of them, all about six pounds, flopping on top of my clothes.

I don't know of any fish that gives as much pleasure to as many fishermen as the ubiquitous striper. He may not be as dazzling as a bonefish or as much a roughneck as a snook, but he covers more ground than these fish do and so comes into contact with more people. There is nothing provincial about him, either. He can get along in fresh water just as well as he can in salt water, river water as well as ocean water, shallow water or deep water—it's all the same to him. People fish for him in boats, on banks, in the surf or by wading. They use trolling rods, boat rods, casting rods, spinning rods, fly rods and every kind of bait made—wood, plastic, feathered and live. And he survives them all. Praise the striper, I thought, looking at my four, the most democratic fish that swims.

By the time I reached the landing, the temperature had dropped sharply. A chill wind swept across the river. I climbed back into my clothes and walked home smelling of fish. That was six years ago. The sweater is still with me, as is the scent. Maybe nobody else can smell it, after tons of mothballs and innumerable dry cleanings, but I was putting the sweater in the car this morning, prior to setting off down Route 33, and caught a whiff of it again, every bit as strong as that day I passed through a school of stripers.

Stutts Creek, my destination, is one of many tidal creeks found along the Virginia side of the Chesapeake Bay. Itself a branch of the bay, it sprouts still other branches and ends up looking on a map like a tree that has fallen into the bay's marshy fringes. Once a waterway for crabbers and oystermen, it has become in recent years something of a playground as well, conveying many more svelte Chris-Crafts than lumbering workboats. But like playgrounds everywhere, it is crowded in the summer and all but empty during the winter.

When I fish Stutts Creek I always stay with a man who was raised on it, Norris Richardson, who runs Pine Hall, an inn for fishermen and exhausted city dwellers who drive down on the weekends from Richmond. Pine Hall is a large white house overlooking the creek from a summit of green grass. Norris runs the place as though he were not really trying to, and as a result it is one of the best-run places I know of. You have the comfortable feeling that everyone is there to relax, even the help. Norris is a small, distracted man with an inexhaustible supply of country stories, little pastoral romances about coons and possums and what happened to old Uncle So-and-so when a pail of crabs turned over in his kitchen. Listen to enough of these tales and you forget all about Vietnam and overpopulation. I always like to hear one or two before setting off up the creek. They are like steppingstones to another world.

Stutts Creek enters the bay between two islands lying just off the mainland. One of these, Gwynn Island, is a well-known vacation spot, but the other, Rigby Island, is little more than an exposed sandbar. There is a channel between the islands, but elsewhere the water is shallow and marshy.

Stripers seem to regard the bay as a school they have to complete before graduating into the Atlantic Ocean. The school lasts four years. A few dropouts may tackle the ocean sooner than that, but the majority are content to wait until graduation day. Then they are ready to join the big ocean community on the outside. At least, this is what a tagging program instigated by the Atlantic States Marine Fisheries Commission indicates. The young striper just out of school tends to stay pretty close to home for the first year or so, but as his size increases so does his boldness, and off he goes to prowl the New England coast 700 miles away. In the fall he frequently returns, packing weights of twenty and thirty pounds. It is a curious fact that stripers reach the bay about the same time that alumni are arriving in Charlottesville, Virginia, to watch Mr. Jefferson's eleven take another licking, but if you think *that* homecoming is worth watching you ought to see what happens when the Old Boys get together in the bay. It's an alumni secretary's dream. Gulls throw up tents all over the place, covering the big feeds, and the campus becomes one huge thrashing contest. Before long the racket reaches the shore, and here comes a fleet of fishermen pounding out to join in the fun.

It's great sport if you like that sort of thing, and most striper fishermen do, but not caring for homecomings myself, in Charlottesville or the bay, I cut the motor and drift into the shallows behind Rigby Island. It's quieter there. You can hear the tide running through the grass. I toss out the anchor, rig up a rod, stuff my pockets with flies, climb into a pair of boots and wade off in search of a few first-graders.

Cold nights have distilled the water. Croakers, spot, crabs, nettles—all of sum-

mer's impedimenta—have been frozen out, and the once-green marsh is now the color of bronze. A line of pine trees stands on the far shore; nearer, dead limbs mark an oyster bed. Where the bay has breached Rigby Island slightly left of center, the tide crosses a sandbar and then spreads out over the marsh, dividing it into a number of small grassy clumps. The water is a hard, glinty, blue.

I have never yet caught a fish on a first cast, nor have I ever made a first cast without thinking I would catch a fish. My heart pounds, my hands shake. I tie on a white streamer, wet it with saliva so that it will sink fast, and drop it at the edge of the marsh. It crosses the tide on a series of swift jerks and returns to my feet untouched. I pick it up and cast again. By the fifteenth cast my hands are steady and my heart has resumed its normal tempo. Now begins the long haul.

Stripers like moving water, and when the tide is slack so are they. I walk along casting. Hours pass. I switch to a popping bug and try that until the marsh is brimful of water and a gold chain leads across it to where the sun is settling into a thicket of trees. Lights appear on shore. Gulls are coming in to roost on the channel markers. Soon it will be dark. I want a fish to whack the popper right out of the water, and I hold onto this hope as long as there is light. Then, when there is no more light, I return to Pine Hall.

So begins the first of many fall weekends on Stutts Creek. As the days shorten, my clothes increase. Sweaters pile up. By December I look like a woolen balloon with legs. Norris Richardson's dogs jump aside when they see me coming. Some mornings dawn fair, others overcast and wet. The best mornings are those when frost covers the ground and a brittle stillness films the creek. Coming up, the sun looks like a forest fire. The worst mornings come out of Canada on a northwest wind that wants to shred you alive, and you need more than sweaters to keep warm. Some fishermen use insulated underwear, some carry bottles, some turn on the furnace words of the English language. I resort to fantasy myself. As soon as numbness reaches the top of my waders, I wrap myself in the vision of a big striper who has gotten tired of homecoming and returned to the shallows of his youth. I see him passing through the inlet just as I am rounding the marsh directly in front of him. There was a time when he would not enter the shallows without company, but now that he has grown up the rewards of fellowship have diminished and he finds that the marsh is something of a relief after the tumult of the bay. So here he is enjoying the freedom of being alone, and here I am doing the same—smothered in wool, walking toward him. I see him nudge the grass. His tail lifts a cloud of sand, then carries him into the mouth of a small feeder creek. (In actual fact, there is such a creek, though it lies closer to Pine Hall than it does in my fantasy. I never pass it without thinking what a wonderful place it would be to catch a striper—smooth sandy bottom, tufts of grass choking the mouth, a line of pine trees to break the wind.) Once he is in the creek, however, the striper finds that the water is not as deep as it appeared to be on the outside and he starts back, cruising like a porpoise. By then I have planted a popper squarely in the middle of the opening, and when he is within sight of it I twitch the line and the popper jumps forward. You can guess the rest.

It is astonishing how much heat a scene like that can generate.

For a moment last Thanksgiving Day I thought I had caught this fish. I went out early in the morning and fished straight through until dusk. It was a cold, blustery day. The wind piled up big waves and hurled them at the shore. Casting a heavy saltwater fly rod is hard work in itself, but casting it in the wind for seven or eight hours is pure torture. In the middle of the afternoon I found three small fish, two- and three-pounders, huddled up in a pocket of deep water, but catching them had rekindled no fires, and by evening I was numb and sore all over.

Even my fantasy had quit working. The tide had just about run itself out, and so had I. I switched to a spinning rod, a less taxing instrument than a fly rod, and waded out along a point of land for a few final casts. I tossed the lure, a weighted jig, into a trench the tide had dug between two sandbars. It was an ordinary sort of place, a place you fish because you know you should rather than because it appeals to you. I had fished the place many times before, ever since Brook Jones, a fine fisherman from Richmond, had pointed it out to me. Brook takes fish out of it all the time, but I had never had much luck with it. Today was different. The lure bounced down one wall of the trench, disappeared in deep water, then climbed up the other wall. It had just reached the top when a shadow rose off the bottom and pulled it back down. I knew it was a big fish by the size of the shadow. He lunged around in the depths for a while, then plowed off across the shallows with a second fish right behind him. Why the second fish, I don't know. Perhaps the two of them had been lying in the trench getting fat together. In any case, the follower soon veered off in the direction of the channel while my fish bore straight ahead. There is nothing spectacular about the way stripers behave after they are hooked. A heavy fish simply lays into a line and bulls his way along. He's a plodder. I could have let this striper run a mile before he reached anything to break off on, but it had been a long cold day and I was taking no chances. I could plod, too. So I set a hard drag and in time wore him down the way you break horses—with sheer force.

One thing he had done was thaw me out. I could feel again. He would go eight or nine pounds, I supposed. Holding him up against the horizon, I found there was more light left in him than was left in all the sky—no fantasy fish, but a good solid striper, all the same.

THE 'LUNGE

Stewart Edward White

DICK AND I TRAVELED IN a fifteen-foot wooden canoe, with grub, duffel, tent, and Deuce, the black-and-white setter dog. As a consequence we were pretty well down toward the water line, for we had not realized that a wooden canoe would carry so little weight for its length in comparison with a birchbark. A good heavy sea we could ride—with proper management and a little bailing; but sloppy waves kept us busy.

Deuce did not like it at all. He was a dog old in the wisdom of experience. It had taken him just twenty minutes to learn all about canoes. After a single tentative trial he jumped lightly to the very centre of his place, with the lithe caution of a cat. Then if the water happened to be smooth, he would sit gravely on his haunches, or would rest his chin on the gunwale to contemplate the passing landscape. But in rough weather he crouched directly over the keel, his nose between his paws, and tried not to dodge when the cold water dashed in on him. Deuce was a true woodsman in that respect. Discomfort he always bore with equanimity, and he must often have been very cold and very cramped.

For just over a week we had been traveling in open water, and the elements had not been kind to us at all. We had crept up under rock-cliff points; had weathered the rips of white water to shelter on the other side, had struggled across open spaces where each wave was singly a problem to fail in whose solution meant instant swamping; had bailed, and schemed, and figured, and carried, and sworn, and tried again, and succeeded with about two cupfuls to spare, until we as well as Deuce had grown a little tired of it. For the lust of travel was on us.

The lust of travel is a very real disease. It usually takes you when you have made up your mind that there is no hurry. Its predisposing cause is a chart or map, and its main symptom is the feverish delight with which you check off the landmarks of your journey. A fair wind of some force is absolutely fatal.

With that at your back you cannot stop. Good fishing, fine scenery, interesting bays, reputed game, even camps where friends might be visited—all pass swiftly astern. Hardly do you pause for lunch at noon. The mad joy of putting country behind you eats all other interests. You recover only when you have come to your journey's end a week too early, and you must then search out new voyages to fill in the time.

All this morning we had been bucking a strong north wind. Fortunately, the shelter of a string of islands had given us smooth water enough, but the heavy gusts sometimes stopped us as effectively as though we had butted solid land. Now about noon we came to the last island, and looked out on a five-mile stretch of tumbling seas. We landed the canoe and mounted a high rock.

"Can't make it like this," said I. "I'll take the outfit over and land it, and come back for you and the dog. Let's see that chart."

We hid behind the rock and spread out the map.

"Four miles," measured Dick. "It's going to be a terror."

We looked at each other vaguely, suddenly tired.

"We can't camp here—at this time of day," objected Dick, to our unspoken thoughts.

And then the map gave him an inspiration. "Here's a little river," ruminated Dick, "that goes to a little lake, and then there's another little river that flows from the lake, and comes out about ten miles above here."

"It's a good thirty miles," I objected.

"What of it?" asked Dick, calmly.

So the fever-lust of travel broke. We turned to the right behind the last island, searched out the reed-grown opening to the stream, and paddled serenely and philosophically against the current. Deuce sat up and yawned with a mighty satisfaction.

We had been bending our heads to the demon of wind; our ears had been filled with his shoutings, our eyes blinded with tears, our breath caught away from us, our muscles strung to the fiercest endeavor. Suddenly we found ourselves between the ranks of tall forest trees, bathed in a warm sunlight, gliding like a feather from one grassy bend to another of the laziest little stream that ever hesitated as to which way the grasses of its bed should float. As for the wind, it was lost somewhere away up high, where we could hear it muttering to itself about something.

The woods leaned over the fringe of bushes cool and green and silent. Occasionally through tiny openings we caught instant impressions of straight column-trunks and transparent shadows. Miniature grass marshes jutted out from the bends of the little river. We idled along as with a homely rustic companion through the aloofness of patrician multitudes.

Every bend offered us charming surprises. Sometimes a muskrat swam hastily in a pointed furrow of ripple; vanishing wings, barely sensed in the flash, left us staring; stealthy withdrawals of creatures, whose presence we realized only in the fact of those withdrawals, snared our eager interest; porcupines rattled

and rustled importantly and regally from the water's edge to the woods; herons, ravens, an occasional duck, croaked away at our approach; thrice we surprised eagles, once a tassel-eared Canada lynx. Or, if ll else lacked, we still experienced the little thrill of pleased novelty over the disclosure of a group of silvery birches on a knoll; a magnificent white pine towering over the beech and maple forest; the unexpected aisle of a long, straight stretch of the little river.

Deuce approved thoroughly. He stretched himself and yawned and shook off the water, and glanced at me open-mouthed with doggy good-nature, and set himself to acquiring a conscientious olfactory knowledge of both banks of the river. I do not doubt he knew a great deal more about it than we did. Porcupines aroused his especial enthusiasm. Incidentally, two days later he returned to camp after an expedition of his own, bristling as to the face with that animal's barbed weapons. Thenceforward his interest waned.

We ascended the charming little river two or three miles. At a sharp bend to the east a huge sheet of rock sloped from a round grass knoll sparsely planted with birches directly down into a pool. Two or three tree-trunks jammed directly opposite had formed a sort of half dam under which the water lay dark. A tiny grass meadow forty feet in diameter narrowed the stream to half its width.

We landed. Dick seated himself on the shelving rock. I put my fish-rod together. Deuce disappeared.

Deuce always disappeared whenever we landed. With nose down, hindquarters well tucked under him, ears flying, he quartered the forest at high speed, investigating every nook and cranny of it for the radius of a quarter of a mile. When he had quite satisfied himself that we were safe for the moment, he would return to the fire, where he would lie, six inches of pink tongue vibrating with breathlessness, beautiful in the consciousness of virtue. Dick generally sat on a rock and thought. I generally fished.

After a time Deuce returned. I gave up flies, spoons, phantom minnows, artificial frogs, and cray-fish. As Dick continued to sit on the rock and think, we both joined him. The sun was very warm and grateful, and I am sure we both acquired an added respect for Dick's judgment.

Just when it hapened neither of us was afterwards able to decide. Perhaps Deuce knew. But suddenly, as often a figure appears in a cinematograph, the diminutive meadow thirty feet away contained two deer. They stood knee deep in the grass, wagging their little tails in impatience of the flies.

"Look a' there!" stammered Dick aloud.

Deuce sat up on his haunches.

I started for my camera.

The deer did not seem to be in the slightest degree alarmed. They pointed four big ears in our direction, ate a few leisurely mouthfuls of grass, sauntered to the stream for a drink of water, wagged their little tails some more, and quietly faded into the cool shadows of the forest.

An hour later we ran out into reeds, and so to the lake. It was a pretty lake, forest-girt. Across the distance we made out a moving object which shortly resolved itself into a birch canoe. The canoe proved to contain an Indian, an Indian boy of about ten years, a black dog, and a bundle. When within a few rods of each other we ceased paddling and drifted by with the momentum. The Indian was a fine-looking man of about forty, his hair bound with a red fillet, his feet incased in silk-worked moccasins, but otherwise dressed in white men's garments. He smoked a short pipe, and contemplated us gravely.

"Bo' jou', bo' jou'," we called in the usual double-barreled North Country salutation.

"Bo' jou', bo' jou'," he replied.

"Kée-gons?" we inquired as to the fishing in the lake.

"Áh-hah," he assented.

We drifted by each other without further speech. When the decent distance of etiquette separated us, we resumed our paddles.

I produced a young cable terminated by a tremendous spoon and a solid brass snell as thick as a telegraph wire. We had laid in this formidable implement in hopes of a big muscallunge. It had been trailed for days at a time. We had become used to its vibration, which actually seemed to communicate itself to every fiber of the light canoe. Every once in a while we would stop with a jerk that would nearly snap our heads off. Then we would know we had hooked the American continent. We had become used to that also. It generally happened when we attempted a little burst of speed. So when the canoe brought up so violently that all our tinware rolled on Deuce, Dick was merely disgusted.

"There she goes again," he grumbled. "You've hooked Canada."

Canada held quiescent for about three seconds. Then it started due south.

"Suffering serpents!" shrieked Dick.

"Paddle, you sulphurated idiot!" yelled I.

It was most interesting. All I had to do was to hang on and try to stay in the boat. Dick paddled and fumed and splashed water and got more excited. Canada dragged us bodily backward.

Then Canada changed his mind and started in our direction. I was plenty busy taking in slack, so I did not notice Dick. Dick was absolutely demented. His mind automatically reacted in the direction of paddling. He paddled, blindly, frantically. Canada came surging in, his mouth open, his wicked eyes flaming, a tremendous indistinct body lashing foam. Dick glanced once over his shoulder, and let out a frantic howl.

"You've got the sea serpent!" he shrieked.

I turned to fumble for the pistol. We were headed directly for a log stranded on shore, and about ten feet from it.

"Dick!" I yelled in warning.

He thrust his paddle out forward just in time. The stout maple bent and cracked. The canoe hit with a bump that threw us forward. I returned to the young cable. It came in limp and slack.

We looked at each other sadly.

"No use," sighed Dick at last. "They've never invented the words, and we'd upset if we kicked the dog."

I had the end of the line in my hands.

"Look here!" I cried. That thick brass wire had been as cleanly bitten through as though it had been cut with clippers. "He must have caught sight of you," said I.

Dick lifted up his voice in lamentation. "You had four feet of him out of water," he wailed, "and there was a lot more."

"If you had kept cool," said I, severely, "we shouldn't have lost him. You don't want to get rattled in an emergency. There's no sense in it."

"What were you going to do with that?" asked Dick, pointing to where I had laid the pistol.

"I was going to shoot him in the head," I replied, with dignity. "It's the best way to land them."

Dick laughed disagreeably. I looked down. At my side lay our largest iron spoon.

We skirted the left-hand side of the lake in silence. Far out from shore the water was ruffled where the wind swept down, but with us it was as still and calm as the forest trees that looked over into it. After a time we turned short to the left through a very narrow passage between two marshy shores, and so, after a sharp bend of but a few hundred feet, came into the other river.

This was a wide stream, smoothly hurrying, without rapids or tumult. The forest had drawn to either side to let us pass. Here were the wilder reaches after the intimacies of the little river. Across stretches of marsh we could see an occasional great blue heron standing mid-leg deep. Long strings of ducks struggled quacking from invisible pools. The faint marsh odor saluted our nostrils from the point where the lily-pads flashed broadly, ruffling in the wind. We dropped out the smaller spoon and masterfully landed a five-pound pickerel. Even Deuce brightened. He cared nothing for raw fish, but he knew their possibilities. Towards evening we entered the hilly country, and so at the last turned to the left into a sand cove where grew maples and birches in beautiful park order under a hill. There we pitched camp, and, as the flies slacked, built a friendship-fire about which to foregather when the day was done.

Dick still vocally regretted the muscallunge as the largest fish since Jonah. So I told him of my big bear.

One day, late in the summer, I was engaged in packing some supplies along an old fur trail north of Lake Superior. I had accomplished one back-load, and with empty straps was returning to the cache for another. The trail at one point emerged into and crossed an open park some hundreds of feet in diameter, in which the grass grew to the height of the knee. When I was about halfway across, a black bear arose to his hind legs not ten feet from me and remarked *Woof!* in a loud tone of voice. Now, if a man were to say *woof!*

to you unexpectedly, even in the formality of an Italian garden or the accustomedness of a city street, you would be somewhat startled. So I went to camp. There I told them about the bear. I tried to be conservative in my description, because I did not wish to be accused of exaggeration. My impression of the animal was that he and a spruce-tree that grew near enough for ready comparison were approximately of the same stature. We returned to the grass park. After some difficulty we found a clear footprint. It was a little larger than that made by a good-sized coon.

"So, you see," I admonished, didactically, "that 'lunge probably was not quite so large as you thought."

"It may have been a Chinese bear," said Dick, dreamily—"a Chinese lady bear, of high degree."

I gave him up.

FISH ARE SUCH LIARS!

Roland Pertwee

THERE HAD BEEN A FUSS in the pool beneath the alders, and the small rainbow trout, with a skitter of his tail, flashed upstream, a hurt and angry fish. For three consecutive mornings he had taken the rise in that pool, and it injured his pride to be jostled from his drift just when the May fly was coming up in numbers. If his opponent had been a half-pounder like himself, he would have stayed and fought, but when an old hen fish, weighing fully three pounds, with a mouth like a rat hole and a carnivorous, cannibalistic eye rises from the reed beds and occupies the place, flight is the only effective argument.

But Rainbow was very much provoked. He had chosen his place with care. Now the May fly was up, the little French chalk stream was full of rising fish, and he knew by experience that strangers are unpopular in that season. To do one's self justice during a hatch, one must find a place where the fly drifts nicely overhead with the run of the stream, and natural drifts are scarce even in a chalk stream. He was not content to leap at the fly like a hysterical youngster who measured his weight in ounces and his wits in milligrams. He had reached that time of life which demanded that he should feed off the surface by suction rather than exertion. No living thing is more particular about his table manners than a trout, and Rainbow was no exception.

"It's a sickening thing," he said to himself, "and a hard shame." He added: "Get out of my way," to a couple of fat young chub with negroid mouths who were bubbling the surface in the silly, senseless fashion of their kind.

"Chub indeed!"

But even the chub had a home and he had none—and the life of a homeless river dweller is precarious.

"I will not and shall not be forced back to midstream," he said.

For, save at eventide or in very special circumstances, trout of personality do not frequent open water where they must compete for every insect with the wind, the lightning-swift sweep of swallows and martins, and even the laborious pursuit of predatory dragon-flies with their bronze wings and bodies like rods of colored glass. Even as he spoke he saw a three-ouncer leap at a dapping May fly which was scooped out of his jaws by a passing swallow. Rainbow heard the tiny click as the May fly's body cracked against the bird's beak. A single wing of yellowy gossamer floated downward and settled upon the water. Under the shelving banks to right and left, where the fly, discarding its nymph and still too damp for its virgin flight, drifted downstream, a dozen heavy trout were feeding thoughtfully and selectively.

"If only some angler would catch one of them, I might slip in and occupy the place before it gets known there's a vacancy."

But this uncharitable hope was not fulfilled, and with another whisk of his tail he propelled himself into the unknown waters upstream. A couple of strands of rusty barbed wire, relic of the war, spanned the shallows from bank to bank. Passing beneath them he came to a narrow reach shaded by willows, to the first of which was nailed a board bearing the words Pêche Réservée. He had passed out of the communal into private water—water running languidly over manes of emerald weed between clumps of alder, willow herb, tall crimson sorrel and masses of yellow iris. Ahead, like an apple-green rampart, rose the wooded heights of a forest; on either side were flat meadows of yellowing hay. Overhead, the vast expanse of blue June sky was tufted with rambling clouds. "My scales!" said Rainbow. "Here's water!"

But it was vain to expect any of the best places in such a reach would be vacant, and to avoid a recurrence of his unhappy encounter earlier in the morning, Rainbow continued his journey until he came to a spot where the river took one of those unaccountable right-angle bends which result in a pool, shallow on the one side, but slanting into deeps on the other. Above it was a water break, a swirl, smoothing, as it reached the pool, into a sleek, swift run, with an eddy which bore all the lighter floating things of the river over the calm surface of the little backwater, sheltered from above by a high shelving bank and a tangle of bramble and herb. Here in this backwater the twig, the broken reed, the leaf, the cork, the fly floated in suspended activity for a few instants until drawn back by invisible magnetism to the main current.

Rainbow paused in admiration. At the tail of the pool two sound fish were rising with regularity, but in the backwater beyond the eddy the surface was still and unbroken. Watching open-eyed, Rainbow saw not one but a dozen May flies, fat, juicy, and damp from the nymph, drift in, pause, and carried away untouched. It was beyond the bounds of possibility that such a place could be vacant, but there was the evidence of his eyes to prove it; and nothing if not a tryer, Rainbow darted across the stream and parked himself six inches below the water to await events.

It so happened that at the time of his arrival the hatch of fly was temporarily suspended, which gave Rainbow leisure to make a survey of his new abode. Beyond the eddy was a submerged snag—the branch of an apple tree borne there by heavy rains, water-logged, anchored, and intricate—an excellent place to break an angler's line. The river bank on his right was riddled under water with old rat holes, than which there is no better sanctuary. Below him and to the left was a dense bed of weeds brushed flat by the flow of the stream.

"If it comes to the worst," said Rainbow, "a smart fish could do a get-away here with very little ingenuity, even from a cannibalistic old hen like—hullo!"

The exclamation was excited by the apparition of a gauzy shadow on the water, which is what a May fly seen from below looks like. Resisting a vulgar inclination to leap at it with the violence of a youngster, Rainbow backed into the correct position which would allow the stream to present the morsel, so to speak, upon a tray. Which it did—and scarcely a dimple on the surface to tell what had happened.

"Very nicely taken, if you will accept the praise of a complete stranger," said a low, soft voice, one inch behind his line of sight.

Without turning to see by whom he had been addressed, Rainbow flicked a yard upstream and came back with the current four feet away. In the spot he had occupied an instant before lay a great old trout of the most benign aspect, who could not have weighed less than four pounds.

"I beg your pardon," said Rainbow, "but I had no idea that any one—that is, I just dropped in *en passant,* and finding an empty house, I made so bold_____"

"There is no occasion to apologize," said Old Trout seductively. "I did not come up from the bottom as early to-day as is my usual habit at this season. Yesterday's hatch was singularly bountiful and it is possible I did myself too liberally."

"Yes, but a gentleman of your weight and seniority can hardly fail to be offended at finding_____"

"Not at all," Old Trout broke in. "I perceive you are a well-conducted fish who does not advertise his appetite in a loud and splashing fashion."

Overcome by the charm of Old Trout's manner and address, Rainbow reduced the distance separating them to a matter of inches.

"Then you do not want me to go?" he asked.

"On the contrary, dear young sir, stay by all means and take the rise. You are, I perceive, of the rainbow or, as they say here in France, of the Arc-en-ciel family. As a youngster I had the impression that I should turn out a rainbow, but events proved it was no more than the bloom, the natural sheen of youth."

"To speak the truth, sir," said Rainbow, "unless you had told me to the contrary, I would surely have thought you one of us."

Old Trout shook his tail. "You are wrong," he said. "I am from Dulverton, an English trout farm on the Exe, of which you will have heard. You are doubtless surprised to find an English fish in French waters."

"I am indeed," Rainbow replied, sucking in a passing May fly with such excellent good manners that it was hard to believe he was feeding. "Then you, sir," he added, "must know all about the habits of men."

"I may justly admit that I do," Old Trout agreed. "Apart from being hand-reared, I have in my twelve years of life studied the species in moods of activity, passivity, duplicity, and violence."

Rainbow remarked that such must doubtless have proved of invaluable service. It did not, however, explain the mystery of his presence on a French river.

"For, sir," he added, "Dulverton, as once I heard when enjoying 'A Chat about Rivers,' delivered by a much-traveled sea trout, is situated in the west of England, and without crossing the Channel I am unable to explain how you arrived here. Had you belonged to the salmon family, with which, sir, it is evident you have no connection, the explanation would be simple, but in the circumstances it baffles my understanding."

Old Trout waved one of his fins airily. "Yet cross the Channel I certainly did," said he, "and at a period in history which I venture to state will not readily be forgotten. It was during the war, my dear young friend, and I was brought in a can, in company with a hundred yearlings, to this river, or rather the upper reaches of this river, by a young officer who wished to further an entente between English and French fish even as the war was doing with the mankind of these two nations."

Old Trout sighed a couple of bubbles and arched his body this way and that.

"There was a gentleman and a sportsman," he said. "A man who was acquainted with our people as I dare to say very few are acquainted. Had it ever been my lot to fall victim to a lover of the rod, I could have done so without regret to his. If you will take a look at my tail, you will observe that the letter W is perforated on the upper side. He presented me with this distinguishing mark before committing me, with his blessing, to the water."

"I have seldom seen a tail more becomingly decorated," said Rainbow. "But what happened to your benefactor?"

Old Trout's expression became infinitely sad. "If I could answer that," said he, "I were indeed a happy trout. For many weeks after he put me into the river I used to watch him in what little spare time he was able to obtain, casting a dry fly with the exquisite precision and likeness to nature in all the likely pools and runs and eddies near his battery position. Oh, minnows! It was a pleasure to watch that man, even as it was his pleasure to watch us. His bravery too! I call to mind a dozen times when he fished unmoved and unstartled while bullets from machine guns were pecking at the water like herons and thudding into the mud banks upon which he stood."

"An angler!" remarked Rainbow. "It would be no lie to say I like him the less on that account."

Old Trout became unexpectedly stern.

"Why so?" he retorted severely. "Have I not said he was also a gentleman and a sportsman? My officer was neither a pot-hunter nor a beast of prey. He was a purist—a man who took delight in pitting his knowledge of nature against the subtlest and most suspicious intellectual forces of the wild. Are you so young as not yet to have learned the exquisite enjoyment of escaping disaster and avoiding error by the exercise of personal ingenuity? Pray, do not reply, for I would hate to think so hard a thing of any trout. We as a race exist by virtue of our brilliant intellectuality and hypersensitive selectivity. In waters where there are no pike and only an occasional otter, but for the machinations of men, where should we turn to school our wits? Danger is our mainstay, for I tell you, Rainbow, that trout are composed of two senses—appetite, which makes of us fools, and suspicion, which teaches us to be wise."

Greatly chastened not alone by what Old Trout had said but by the forensic quality of his speech, Rainbow rose short and put a promising May fly onto the wing.

"I am glad to observe," said Old Trout, "that you are not without conscience."

"To tell the truth, sir," Rainbow replied apologetically, "my nerve this morning has been rudely shaken, but for which I should not have shown such want of good sportsmanship."

And with becoming brevity he told the tale of his eviction from the pool downstream. Old Trout listened gravely, only once moving, and that to absorb a small blue dun, an insect which he keenly relished.

"A regrettable affair," he admitted, "but as I have often observed, women, who are the gentlest creatures under water in adversity, are a thought lacking in moderation in times of abundance. They are apt to snatch."

"But for a turn of speed, she would certainly have snatched me," said Rainbow.

"Very shocking," said Old Trout. "Cannibals are disgusting. They destroy the social amenities of the river. We fish have but little family life and should therefore aim to cultivate a freemasonry of good-fellowship among ourselves. For my part, I am happy to line up with other well-conducted trout and content myself with what happens along with my own particular drift. Pardon me!" he added, breasting Rainbow to one side. "I invited you to take the rise of May fly, but I must ask you to leave the duns alone." Then, fearing this remark might be construed to reflect adversely upon his hospitality, he proceeded: "I have a reason which I will explain later. For the moment we are discussing the circumstances that led to my presence in this river."

"To be sure—your officer. He never succeeded in deluding you with his skill?"

"That would have been impossible," said Old Trout, "for I had taken up a position under the far bank where he could only have reached me with a fly by wading in a part of the river which was in view of a German sniper."

"Wily!" Rainbow chuckled. "Cunning work, sir."

"Perhaps," Old Trout admitted, "although I have since reproached myself with cowardice. However, I was at the time a very small fish and a certain amount of nervousness is forgivable in the young."

At this gracious acknowledgment the rose-colored hue in Rainbow's rainbow increased noticeably—in short, he blushed.

"From where I lay," Old Trout went on, "I was able to observe the maneuvers of my officer and greatly profit thereby."

"But excuse me, sir," said Rainbow, "I have heard it said that an angler of the first class is invisible from the river."

"He is invisible to the fish he is trying to catch," Old Trout admitted, "but it must be obvious that he is not invisible to the fish who lie beside or below him. I would also remind you that during the war every tree, every scrap of vegetation, and every vestige of natural cover had been torn up, trampled down, razed. The river banks were as smooth as the top of your head. Even the buttercup, that very humorous flower that tangles up the back cast of so many industrious anglers, was absent. Those who fished on the Western Front had little help from nature."

Young Rainbow sighed, for, only a few days before, his tongue had been badly scratched by an artificial alder which had every appearance of reality.

"It would seem," he said, "that this war had its merits."

"My young friend," said Old Trout, "you never made a greater mistake. A desire on the part of our soldiery to vary a monotonous diet of bully beef and biscuit often drove them to resort to villainous methods of assault against our kind."

"Nets?" gasped Rainbow in horror.

"Worse than nets—bombs," Old Trout replied. "A small oval black thing called a Mills bomb, which the shameless fellows flung into deep pools."

"But surely the chances of being hit by such a_____"

"You reveal a pathetic ignorance," said Old Trout. "There is no question of being hit. The wretched machine exploded under water and burst our people's insides or stunned us so that we floated dead to the surface. I well remember my officer coming upon such a group of marauders one evening—yes, and laying about him with his fists in defiance of King's Regulations and the Manual of Military Law. Two of them he seized by the collar and the pants and flung into the river. Spinning minnows, that was a sight worth seeing! 'You low swine,' I heard him say; 'you trash, you muck! Isn't there enough carnage without this sort of thing?' Afterward he sat on the bank with the two dripping men and talked to them for their souls' sake.

" 'Look ahead, boys. Ask yourselves what are we fighting for? Decent homes to live in at peace with one another, fields to till and forests and rivers to give us a day's sport and fun. It's our rotten job to massacre each other, but, by gosh, don't let's massacre the harmless rest of nature as well. At least, let's give 'em a running chance. Boys, in the years ahead, when all the mess is cleared up, I look forward to coming back to this old spot, when there is alder growing by the banks, and willow herb and tall reeds and the drone of insects instead of the rumble of those guns. I don't want to come back to a dead river that I helped to kill, but to a river ringed with rising fish—some of whom were old comrades of the war.' He went on to tell of us hundred Dulverton trout that he had marked with the letter *W*. 'Give 'em their chance,' he said, 'and in the years to come those beggars will reward us a hundred times over. They'll give us a finer thrill and put up a cleaner fight than old Jerry ever contrived.' Those were emotional times, and though you may be reluctant to believe me, one of those two very wet men dripped water from his eyes as well as his clothing.

" 'Many's the 'appy afternoon I've 'ad with a roach pole on Brentford Canal,' he sniffed, 'though I've never yet tried m' hand against a trout.' 'You shall do it now,' said my officer, and during the half-hour that was left of daylight that dripping soldier had his first lesson in the most delicate art in the world. I can see them now—the clumsy, wet fellow and my officer timing him, timing him— "one and two, and one and two, and____' The action of my officer's wrist with its persuasive flick was the prettiest thing I have ever seen."

"Did he carry out his intention and come back after the war?" Rainbow asked.

"I shall never know," Old Trout replied. "I do not even know if he survived it. There was a great battle—a German drive. For hours they shelled the river front, and many falling short exploded in our midst with terrible results. My own bank was torn to shreds and our people suffered. How they suffered! About noon the infantry came over—hordes in field gray. There were pontoons, rope bridges and hand-to-hand fights on both banks and even in the stream itself."

"And your officer?"

"I saw him once, before the water was stamped dense into liquid mud and dyed by the blood of men. He was in the thick of it, unarmed, and a German officer called on him to surrender. For answer he struck him in the face with a light cane. Ah, that wrist action! Then a shell burst, smothering the water with clods of fallen earth and other things."

"Then you never knew?"

"I never knew, although that night I searched among the dead. Next day I went downstream, for the water in that place was polluted with death. The bottom of the pool in which I had my place was choked with strange and mangled tenants that were not good to look upon. We trout are a clean people that will not readily abide in dirty houses. I am a Dulverton trout, where the water is filtered by the hills and runs cool over stones."

"And you have stayed here ever since?"

Old Trout shrugged a fin. "I have moved with the times. Choosing a place according to the needs of my weight."

"And you have never been caught, sir, by any other angler?"

"Am I not here?" Old Trout answered with dignity.

"Oh, quite, sir. I had only thought, perhaps, as a younger fish enthusiasm might have resulted to your disadvantage, but that, nevertheless, you had been returned."

"Returned! Returned!" echoed Old Trout. "Returned to the frying-pan! Where on earth did you pick up that expression? We are in France, my young friend; we are not on the Test, the Itchen, or the Kennet. In this country it is not the practice of anglers to return anything, however miserable in size."

"But nowadays," Rainbow protested, "there are Englishmen and Americans on the river who show us more consideration."

"They may show you consideration," said Old Trout, "but I am of an importance that neither asks for nor expects it. Oblige me by being a little more discreet with your plurals. In the impossible event of my being deceived and caught, I should be introduced to a glass case with an appropriate background of rocks and reeds."

"But, sir, with respect, how can you be so confident of your unassailability?" Rainbow demanded, edging into position to accept an attractive May fly with yellow wings that was drifting downstream toward him.

"How?" Old Trout responded. "Because_____" Then suddenly: "Leave it, you fool!"

Rainbow had just broken the surface when the warning came. The yellow-winged May fly was wrenched off the water with a wet squeak. A tangle of limp cast lapped itself round the upper branches of a willow far upstream and a raw voice exclaimed something venomous in French. By common consent the two fish went down.

"Well, really," expostulated Old Trout, "I hoped you were above that kind of thing! Nearly to fall victim to a downstream angler. It's a little too much! And think of the effect it will have on my prestige. Why, that incompetent fool will go about boasting that he rose me. Me!"

For some minutes Rainbow was too crestfallen even to apologize. At last: "I am afraid," he said, "I was paying more heed to what you were saying than to my own conduct. I never expected to be fished from above. The fly was an uncommonly good imitation and it is a rare thing for a Frenchman to use Four-X gut."

"Rubbish," said Old Trout testily. "These are mere half-pound arguments. Four-X gut, when associated with a fourteen-stone shadow, should deceive nothing over two ounces. I saved your life, but it is all very provoking. If that is a sample of your general demeanor, it is improbable that you will ever reach a pound."

"At this season we are apt to be careless," Rainbow wailed. "And nowadays it is so hard, sir, to distinguish the artificial fly from the real."

"No one expects you to do so," was the answer, "but common prudence demands that you should pay some attention to the manner in which it is presented. A May fly does not hit the water with a splash, neither is it able to sustain itself in midstream against the current. Have you ever seen a natural insect leave a broadening wake of cutwater behind its tail? Never mind the fly, my dear boy, but watch the manner of its presentation. Failure to do that has cost many of our people their lives."

"You speak," said Rainbow, a shade sulkily, "as though it were a disgrace for a trout ever to suffer defeat at the hands of an angler."

"Which indeed it is, save in exceptional circumstances," Old Trout answered. "I do not say that a perfect upstream cast from a well-concealed angler, when the fly alights dry and cocked and dances at even speed with the current, may not deceive us to our fall. And I would be the last to say that a grasshopper skillfully dapped on the surface through the branches of an overhanging tree will not inevitably bring about our destruction. But I do most emphatically say that in such a spot as this, where the slightest defect in presentation is multiplied a hundred-fold by the varying water speeds, a careless rise is unpardonable. There is only one spot—and that a matter of twelve yards downstream—from which a fly can be drifted over me with any semblance to nature. Even so, there is not one angler in a thousand who can make that cast with success, by reason of a willow which cramps the back cast and the manner in which these alders on our left sprawl across the pool."

Rainbow did not turn about to verify these statements because it is bad form for a trout to face downstream. He contented himself by replying, with a touch of acerbity: "I should have thought, sir, with the feelings you expressed regarding sportsmanship, you would have found such a sanctuary too dull for your entertainment."

"Every remark you make serves to aggravate the impression of your ignorance," Old Trout replied. "Would you expect a trout of my intelligence to put myself in some place where I am exposed to the vulgar assaults of every amateur upon the bank? Of the green boy who lashes the water into foam, of the purblind peasant who slings his fly at me with a clod of earth or a tail of weed attached to the hook? In this place I invite attention from none but the best people—the expert, the purist."

"I understood you to say that there were none such in these parts," grumbled Rainbow.

"There are none who have succeeded in deceiving me," was the answer. "As a fact, for the last few days I have been vastly entranced by an angler who, by any standard, is deserving of praise. His presentation is flawless and the only fault I can detect in him is a tendency to overlook piscine psychology. He will be with us in a few minutes, since he knows it is my habit to lunch at noon."

"Pardon the interruption," said Rainbow, "but there is a gallant hatch of fly going down. I can hear your two neighbors at the tail of the pool rising steadily."

Old Trout assumed an indulgent air. "We will go up if you wish," said he, "but you will be well advised to observe my counsel before taking the rise, because if my angler keeps his appointment you will most assuredly be *meunièred* before nightfall."

At this unpleasant prophecy Rainbow shivered. "Let us keep to weed," he suggested.

But Old Trout only laughed, so that bubbles from the river bed rose and burst upon the surface.

"Courage," said he; "it will be an opportunity for you to learn the finer points of the game. If you are nervous, lie nearer to the bank. The natural fly does not drift there so abundantly, but you will be secure from the artificial. Presently I will treat you to an exhibition of playing with death you will not fail to appreciate." He broke off and pointed with his eyes. "Over you and to the left."

Rainbow made a neat double rise and drifted back into line. "Very mellow," he said—"very mellow and choice. Never tasted better. May I ask, sir, what you meant by piscine psychology?"

"I imply that my angler does not appreciate the subtle possibilities of our intellect. Now, my officer concerned himself as vitally with what we were thinking as with what we were feeding upon. This fellow, secure in the knowledge that his presentation is well-nigh perfect, is content to offer me the same variety of flies day after day, irrespective of the fact that I have learned them all by heart. I have, however, adopted the practice of rising every now and then to encourage him."

"Rising? At an artificial fly? I never heard such temerity in all my life," gasped Rainbow.

Old Trout moved his body luxuriously. "I should have said, appearing to rise," he amended. "You may have noticed that I have exhibited a predilection for small duns in preference to the larger *Ephemeridae*. My procedure is as follows: I wait until a natural dun and his artificial May fly are drifting downstream with the smallest possible distance separating them. Then I rise and take the dun. Assuming I have risen to him, he strikes, misses, and is at once greatly flattered and greatly provoked. By this device I sometimes occupy his attention for over an hour and thus render a substantial service to others of my kind who would certainly have fallen victim to his skill."

"The river is greatly in your debt, sir," said Young Rainbow, with deliberate satire.

He knew by experience that fish as well as anglers are notorious liars, but the exploit his host recounted was a trifle too strong. Taking a sidelong glance, he was surprised to see that Old Trout did not appear to have appreciated the subtle ridicule of his remark. The long, lithe body had become almost rigid and the great round eyes were focused upon the surface with an expression of fixed concentration.

Looking up, Rainbow saw a small white-winged May fly with red legs and a body the color of straw swing out from the main stream and describe a slow circle over the calm surface above Old Trout's head. Scarcely an inch away a tiny blue dun, its wings folded as closely as the pages of a book, floated attendant. An upward rush, a sucking kerr-rop, and when the broken water had calmed, the dun had disappeared and the May fly was dancing away downstream.

"Well," said Old Trout, "how's that, my youthful skeptic? Pretty work, eh?"

"I saw nothing in it," was the impertinent reply. "There is not a trout on the river who could not have done likewise."

"Even when one of those two flies was artificial?" Old Trout queried tolerantly.

"But neither of them was artificial," Rainbow retorted. "Had it been so, the angler would have struck. They always do."

"Of course he struck," Old Trout replied.

"But he didn't," Rainbow protested. "I saw the May fly go down with the current."

"My poor fish!" Old Trout replied. "Do you presume to suggest that I am unable to distinguish an artificial from a natural fly? Are you so blind that you failed to see the prismatic colors in the water from the paraffin in which the fly had been dipped? Here you are! Here it is again!"

Once more the white-winged insect drifted across the backwater, but this time there was no attendant dun.

"If that's a fake I'll eat my tail," said Rainbow.

"If you question my judgment," Old Trout answered, "you are at liberty to rise. I dare say, in spite of a shortage of brain, that you would eat comparatively well."

But Rainbow, in common with his kind, was not disposed to take chances.

"We may expect two or three more casts from this fly and then he will change it for a bigger. It is the same programme every day without a variation. How differently my officer would have acted. By now he would have discovered my little joke and turned the tables against me. Aye me, but some men will never learn! Your mental outfit, dear Rainbow, is singularly like a man's," he added. "It lacks elasticity."

Rainbow made no retort and was glad of his forbearance, for every word Old Trout had spoken was borne out by subsequent events. Four times the white-winged May fly described an arc over the backwater, but in the absence of duns Old Trout did not rise again. Then came a pause, during which, through a lull in the hatch, even the natural insect was absent from the river.

"He is changing his fly," said Old Trout, "but he will not float it until the hatch starts again. He is casting beautifully this morning and I hope circumstances will permit me to give him another rise."

"But suppose," said Rainbow breathlessly, "you played this game once too often and were foul hooked as a result?"

Old Trout expanded his gills broadly. "Why, then," he replied, "I should break him. Once round a limb of that submerged apple bough and the thing would be done. I should never allow myself to be caught and no angler could gather up the slack and haul me into midstream in time to prevent me reaching the bough. Stand by."

The shadow of a large, dark May fly floated cockily over the backwater and had almost returned to the main stream when a small iron-blue dun settled like a puff of thistledown in its wake.

The two insects were a foot nearer the fast water than the spot where Old Trout was accustomed to take the rise. But for the presence of a spectator, it is doubtful whether he would have done so, but Young Rainbow's want of appreciation had excited his vanity, and with a rolling swoop he swallowed the dun and bore it downward.

And then an amazing thing happened. Instead of drifting back to his place as was expected, Old Trout's head was jerked sideways by an invisible force. A thin translucent thread upcut the water's surface and tightened irresistibly. A second later Old Trout was fighting, fighting, fighting to reach the submerged apple bough with the full weight of the running water and the full strength of the finest Japanese gut strained against him.

Watching, wide-eyed and aghast, from one of the underwater rat holes into which he had hastily withdrawn, Rainbow saw the figure of a man rise out of a bed of irises downstream and scramble upon the bank. In his right hand, with the wrist well back, he held a light split-cane rod whose upper joint was curved to a half-circle. The man's left hand was detaching a collapsible landing net from the ring of his belt. Every attitude and movement was expressive of perfectly organized activity. His mouth was shut as tightly as a steel trap, but a light of happy excitement danced in his eyes.

"No, you don't, my fellar," Rainbow heard him say. "No, you don't. I knew all about that apple bough before ever I put a fly over your pool. And the weed bed on the right," he added, as Old Trout made a sudden swerve half down and half across stream.

Tucking the net under his arm the man whipped up the slack with a lightning-like action. The maneuver cost Old Trout dear, for when, despairing of reaching the weed and burrowing into it, he tried to regain his old position, he found himself six feet farther away from the apple bough than when the battle began.

Instinctively Old Trout knew it was useless to dash downstream, for a man who could take up slack with the speed his adversary had shown would profit by the expedient to come more quickly to terms with him. Besides, lower down there was broken water to knock the breath out of his lungs. Even where he lay straining and slugging this way and that, the water was pouring so fast into his open mouth as nearly to drown him. His only chance of effecting a smash was by a series of jumps, followed by quick dives. Once before, although he had not confessed it to Rainbow, Old Trout had saved his life by resorting to this expedient. It takes the strain off the line and returns it so quickly that even the finest gut is apt to sunder.

Meanwhile the man was slowly approaching, winding up as he came. Old Trout, boring in the depths, could hear the click of the check reel with increasing distinctness. Looking up, he saw that the cast was almost vertical above his head, which meant that the moment to make the attempt was at hand. The tension was appalling, for ever since the fight began his adversary had given him the butt unremittingly. Aware of his own weight and power, Old Trout was amazed that any tackle could stand the strain.

"Now's my time," he thought, and jumped.

It was no ordinary jump, but an aerial rush three feet out of the water, with a twist at its apex and a cutting lash of the tail designed to break the cast. But his adversary was no ordinary angler, and at the first hint of what was happening he dropped the point of the rod flush with the surface.

Once and once more Old Trout flung himself into the air, but after each attempt he found himself with diminishing strength and with less line to play with.

"It looks to me," said Rainbow mournfully, "as if my unhappy host will lose this battle and finish up in that glass case to which he was referring a few minutes ago." And greatly affected, he burrowed his nose in the mud and wondered, in the event of this dismal prophecy coming true, whether he would be able to take possession of the pool without molestation.

In consequence of these reflections he failed to witness the last phase of the battle, when, as will sometimes happen with big fish, all the fight went out of Old Trout, and rolling wearily over and over, he abandoned himself to the clinging embraces of the net. He never saw the big man proudly carry Old Trout back into the hayfield, where, before proceeding to remove the fly, he sat down beside a shallow dike and lit a cigarette and smiled largely. Then, with an affectionate and professional touch, he picked up Old Trout by the back of the neck, his forefinger and thumb sunk firmly in the gills.

"You're a fine fellar," he said, extracting the fly; "a good sportsman and a funny fish. You fooled me properly for three days, but I think you'll own I outwitted you in the end."

Rummaging in his creel for a small rod of hard wood that he carried for the purpose of administering the quietus, he became aware of something that arrested the action. Leaning forward, he stared with open eyes at a tiny *W* perforated in the upper part of Old Trout's tail.

"Shades of the war! Dulverton!" he exclaimed. Then with a sudden warmth: "Old chap, old chap, is it really you? This is red-letter stuff. If you're not too far gone to take another lease of life, have it with me."

And with the tenderness of a woman, he slipped Old Trout into the dike and in a tremble of excitement hurried off to the *auberge* where the fishermen lodged, to tell a tale no one even pretended to believe.

For the best part of an hour Old Trout lay in the shallow waters of the dike before slowly cruising back to his own place beneath the overhanging bank. The alarming experience through which he had passed had made him a shade forgetful, and he was not prepared for the sight of Young Rainbow rising steadily at the hatch of fly.

"Pardon me, but a little more to your right," he said, with heavy courtesy.

"Diving otters!" cried Young Rainbow, leaping a foot clear of the water. "You, sir! You!"

"And why not?" Old Trout replied. "Your memory must be short if you have already forgotten that this is my place."

"Yes, but____" Rainbow began and stopped.

"You are referring to that little circus of a few minutes ago," said Old Trout. "Is it possible you failed to appreciate the significance of the affair? I knew at once it was my dear officer when he dropped the artificial dun behind the natural May fly. In the circumstances I could hardly do less than accept his invitation. Nothing is more delightful than a reunion of comrades of the war." He paused and added: "We had a charming talk, he and I, and I do not know which of us was the more affected. It is a tragedy that such friendship and such intellect as we share cannot exist in common element."

And so great was his emotion that Old Trout dived and buried his head in the weeds. Whereby Rainbow did uncommonly well during the midday hatch.

5

MORE THAN TO FISH

"... 'tis not all of fishing to fish"
—IZAAK WALTON

SONG OF THE ANGLER

A. J. McClane

PEOPLE OFTEN ASK ME why I enjoy fishing, and I cannot explain it to them because there is no reason in the way they want meanings described. They are asking a man why he enjoys breathing when he really has no choice but to wonder at its truth. Psychologists such as Dr. Ronald Ley have tried to explain its mystique in terms of behavioral conditioning, but this is as oddly misleading as his comparison of angling to golf. There are also pundits who believe that the rod provides an outlet for our hostilities, our frustrated egos, or our competitive instincts, or that it symbolizes the primitive feelings of man in his search for food, ergo the need to kill. To a degree I believe all these qualities exist in every participant in any sport, and if so, healthfully so, as it is far more harmless to vent one's spleen on a trout stream or a golf course than on one's fellow man. However, if this assumption is logical, then the rationale of *angling* is still without explanation.

The chirping plague of analysts who have invaded every chamber of the mind from the bedroom to the tackle room has missed one thing—angling is a robe that a man wears proudly. It is tightly woven in a fabric of moral, social, and philosophical threads which are not easily rent by the violent climate of our times. It is foolish to think, as it has been said, that all men who fish are good men, as evil exists on all of life's paths; but to join Walton's "company of honest men" requires first the ability to accept a natural tempo of misfortune not only in the allegory where failure is represented by the loss of a fish (or success by its capture) but in life itself. In the lockstep slogan of young radicals thumbing their noses at their world, reality is no longer realistic; but I would argue that life is a greater challenge than death, and that reality is as close as the nearest river. Perhaps an exceptional angler doesn't prove the rule, but then anglers are exceptional people.

Lord Fraser of Lonsdale is not only a peer, but he wears the robe of an angler as well. He is a skilled fly-fisherman, and when last we visited together, he caught a 35-pound salmon which was the biggest in the camp for many weeks. What's more, he could charm the socks off Willie Sutton, and I have heard him spell-bind a roomful of strangers with tales of his life in South Africa, while sipping rare wines, naming each chateau and its vintage. This introduction would be fatuous were it not for the fact that Lord Fraser is totally blind. Both his eyes were shot out in the First World War. A profoundly intellectual man, Fraser has developed his other senses to a point that most of the people who sat with him that night had no idea that he was unable to see them; yet later he could sum-marize the physical characteristics of each person as though he was describing a rare burgundy.

I don't know if you have ever tried wading (unaided) and fly-fishing a stream while blindfolded. I cannot do it, and I would probably lack the guts if I *had* to do it. Fraser's explanation for his ability to do this is that he can hear all things around him: the changing tempo of deep and shallow water, the curling smack of a rapid against a boulder, even the roll or rise of a fish. His ear for the music of angling is incredibly keen. Is this Dr. Ley's behavioral conditioning? In terms of a compensatory development of the senses, perhaps, but it does not explain *why* a man, even a blind man, enjoys angling.

The music of angling is more compelling to me than anything contrived in the greatest symphony hall. What could be more thrilling than the ghostly basso note of a channel buoy over a grumbling surf as the herring gulls screech at a school of stripers on a foggy summer morning? Or an organ chorus of red howler monkeys swinging over a jungle stream as the tarpon roll and splash in counter-point? I have heard them all—the youthful voice of the little Beaverkill, the growling of the Colorado as it leaps from its den, the kettledrum pounding of the Rogue, the hiss of the Yellowstone's riffles, the sad sound of the Orinoco, as mournful as a G chord held on a guitar. These are more familiar to me than Bach, Beethoven, and Brahms, and for my part more beautiful. If there are three "B's" in angling, they are probably the Beaverkill, the Broadhead, and the Big Hole.

Big-game angling has quite another music. The hull creaks and the outriggers clap as the ship comes into the wind while the sea increases the tempo as she turns from stern to bow. Then the frigate birds scream at a ball of bait and you know the marlin are below. As the ship lurches over the chop her screws bite air in a discordant whine and the mullet trails *skitter flap skitter flap* until the pitching hull sounds like the soft rolling of drums.

At last one note assails the ears, the *snap* of white linen pulled from the out-rigger. Now the water explodes in a crescendo of hot engines roaring into life before you lean into a quarter ton of shoulder-rocking fury. And in that ageless walking leap which follows no path in the ocean the angler hears the most ex-citing sound of all—the wailing of a reel as stark and as lonely as a Basin Street clarinet.

But my protracted maundering leads us away from Dr. Ley's hypothesis which he reinforced with the learned E. L. Thorndike's thesis of punishments and rewards. What *are* the rewards of angling? A dead fish? A trophy? At some point perhaps, but then it takes years to become an angler.

There are tidal marks in our development. In the beginning, when one is very young and inexperienced, fish are measured in quantity. Then, only quality becomes important. Eventually even record fish lose their significance unless they are of a particular species, and ultimately the size doesn't matter provided they are difficult to catch.

The latter condition is fairly easy to find in these days of declining resources. Trout in the upper Beaverkill average about a half pound in weight, but they can be the most demanding kind. The water is diamond clear and at the shadow of a passing bird or the glint of sun against rod they instantly vanish under the nearest boulder. You must work with a leader of cobweb diameter and have enough control to drop your fly in a teacup target through a maze of overhanging limbs. There are large trout in the stream, of course, wise old browns which you might catch a glimpse of once in a while, usually in a pool that everybody believes has been emptied.

Recalling the years when anglers gathered at the old Gould cottage on the Beaverkill—a temple now fallen to death and taxes—which Arnold Gingrich described in his wonderful book, *The Well-Tempered Angler* (you can even smell the waders drying in the rafters)—one man comes to mind who knew perhaps a bit more about the rewards of angling than most of us.

Ellis Newman could cast a fly line to 90 feet with his bare hands. I saw him make three measured casts with tournament tackle, each of which fell short of 200 feet by inches. I doubt if a more polished caster ever lived. He had neither the time nor the inclination to compete in games (except for the pigeon shooting circuit which he did for money). We often fished along opposite banks of the Beaverkill, or alternated pools, just for the pleasure of each other's company.

One day, when the mayflies were on the water, Ellis caught and released several good browns below the dam, one going about three pounds. At the top of the next run we met a young boy who proudly displayed a nine-inch brook trout. Ellis admired it so much that I thought we were looking at the biggest squaretail captured since Cook hit the jackpot on the Nipigon in 1914. When the lad asked Ellis if he had any luck, he looked very serious; "Oh, I caught a few, but none were as *pretty* as yours."

Ellis worked with underprivileged children and handicapped people at his own expense. And the expense was appreciable. He designed Rube Goldberg wheelchairs and tractor-driven bucket seats for fishing and for hunting as well, and he even developed a method of running steel cable through a string of boulders to build "necklace" dams on his eroding Beaverkill. Ellis never waited for the fulmination of a new idea to die down before putting it into practice, and the people who loved him may be consoled with the reflection that angling would have suffered a greater blow had he regarded each new venture carefully.

Arnold Gingrich became, as Charley Ritz once called him, "that terrible fishing machine" in the sense that he was on a first-name basis with every trout in the stream. He would appear with smaller and smaller fly rods, considering any stick over two ounces as heavy tackle, and any leader above 7X suitable only for salmon. But the publisher of *Esquire* magazine is a tremendously energetic individual and the pistonlike style of casting with flea rods was duck soup for him.

Arnold earned his robe in my eyes the first time we angled together; in releasing a tired trout he held the fish underwater gently, almost lovingly, stroking its belly and talking to it. He is a master of conversation and, so help me, at times the fish swim away with an impossible but perceptible grin on their faces. Arnold has that passionate blood fire, typical of anglers, which no psychologist (nor wife who hears her husband stumbling out into an April blizzard at 4 A.M.) has satisfactorily explained.

One morning I was crossing the Swinging Bridge Pool and happened to look down; there stood Arnold in an icy torrent banging away with a little dry fly. Something was protruding from his mouth. I didn't recall that Arnold smoked cigars.

"When did you start smoking cigars?" I called. He pulled the bulbous object from his mouth and examined it as though he didn't know it was there.

"Oh. That's my stream thermometer."

"Your *what?*"

"I'm sick. I have a fever."

"Then what are you doing in the river?"

"Oh hell, it's only 99.8. If I break 100, I'll go to bed."

Whenever somebody asks me why I enjoy fishing another thing that comes to mind is what it means in terms of friendships. General Charles Lindeman was always impeccably dressed, cologne lashed, and wearing his stiff upper lip as Counsel to the British Ambassador in Washington. During the years we fished together he had a running verbal duel with Charles Ritz for reasons which only an Englishman would feel about a Frenchman and vice-versa. There was no evil lurking beneath this play of wit; it had the woolly camaraderie of barracks talk. When Lindeman stepped into the river, Ritz would ask him, "Where is your gaff, old boy? All Englishmen carry gaffs." Although a stranger would think that the General meant to hang Ritz with his old school tie, they were really fond of each other.

This good-natured combativeness continued until we stopped to lunch on the bank of the Stamp River one noon. A sudden change came over the General. For a moment he became misty-eyed. He told us that he had sat in this very spot with his young wife a half-century before and made his life's plans. Now she was buried in France, a geographical anomaly which he made no attempt to explain except to refer to a war-time plane crash. Later that day, while I was beaching a steelhead, I saw Ritz crawling along the bank picking wild flowers. Swearing me to silence he carefully packed a bouquet in his duffle bag. "I know the cemetery outside of Paris. I will take these to her. She would like that."

Lindeman didn't know what he had done, and despite my old friend's deserved reputation as one of the world's great anglers, I would embarrass him now by saying that Charles Ritz wears his robe because he is a truly kind and loving man. The General is gone, and it wasn't until his death a few years ago that a certain irony became apparent in our secret when we learned that General Lindeman had been Chief of the British Secret Service.

The only psychologist I have ever met, who knew anything about anglers, was Dr. J. H. Cooper of Kansas City, Missouri. He made sense because he invented the marabou bone-fish jig, which reveals him as a practical man. We met, as anglers so often do, through his giving me a duplicate of his lure at a time when I was having lousy fishing at Andros Island.

Have you ever noticed how often anglers tend to share their good fortune? I have seen this happen many times among perfect strangers who simply meet on a stream. I remember a man, who, after landing a beautiful rainbow trout below the Fair Ground Bridge on the East Branch of the Delaware, turned to a bug-eyed kid holding a 98-cent telescopic fly rod, and snipping the March Brown pattern off his leader gave it to the boy. "See what you can do with it, son." That's all he said. I was that boy and I can't tie a March Brown on my leader today without blessing my Good Samaritan.

Before you conclude that the author has broken loose from his moorings and is bobbing impotently on a sea of virtue, let me reassure you that the world is full of narrowly shrewd self-seeking people, blind to God and goodness, and for all I know, Dame Juliana Berners could have been some piscatorial Mary Poppins or a grosser wart on the face of society than Polly Adler. But I would be untrue to my craft if I did not add that although we live in a curiously touchy age when Mom's apple pie, the flag, and the Boy Scouts oath are losing currency, these still make a better frame of reference than Harvard's pellet fed rats or Pavlov's dogs.

Psychologists tell us that one reason why we enjoy fishing is because it is an escape. This is meaningless. True, a man who works in the city wants to "escape" to the country, but the clinical implication is that (no matter where a man lives), he seeks to avoid reality. This is as obtuse as the philosophical doctrine which holds that no reality exists outside the mind.

Perhaps it's the farm boy in me, but I would apply Aristotelian logic—the chicken came before the egg because it is real and the egg is only potential. By the same reasoning the fluid content of a stream is nothing but water when it erupts from a city faucet but given shores it becomes a river, and as a river it is perfectly capable of creating life, and therefore it is real. It is not a sewer, nor a conveyor of barges and lumber, although it can be pressed to these burdens and, indeed, as a living thing it can also become lost in its responsibilities.

So if escapism is a reason for angling—then the escape is *to* reality. The sense of freedom that we enjoy in the outdoors is, after all, a normal reaction to a more rational environment.

Who but an angler knows that magic hour when the red lamp of summer drops behind blackening hemlocks and the mayflies emerge from the dull folds of their nymphal robes to dance in ritual as old as the river itself? Trout appear one by one and the angler begins his game in movements as stylized as Japanese poetry. Perhaps he will hook that wonder-spotted rogue, or maybe he will remain in silent pantomime long into the night with no visible reward.

And that, Professor, is why anglers *really* angle.

THE FISH

Elizabeth Bishop

I caught a tremendous fish
and held him beside the boat
half out of water, with my hook
fast in a corner of his mouth.
He didn't fight.
He hadn't fought at all.
He hung a grunting weight,
battered and venerable
and homely. Here and there
his brown skin hung in strips
like ancient wallpaper,
and its pattern of darker brown
was like wallpaper:
shapes like full-blown roses
stained and lost through age.
He was speckled with barnacles,
fine rosettes of lime,
and infested
with tiny white sea-lice,
and underneath two or three
rags of green weed hung down.
While his gills were breathing in
the terrible oxygen
—the frightening gills,
fresh and crisp with blood,

that can cut so badly—
I thought of the coarse white flesh
packed in like feathers,
the big bones and the little bones,
the dramatic reds and blacks
of his shiny entrails,
and the pink swim-bladder
like a big peony.
I looked into his eyes
which were far larger than mine
but shallower, and yellowed,
the irises backed and packed
with tarnished tinfoil
seen through the lenses
of old scratched isinglass.
They shifted a little, but not
to return my stare.
—It was more like the tipping
of an object toward the light.
I admired his sullen face,
the mechanism of his jaw,
and then I saw
that from his lower lip
—if you could call it a lip—
grim, wet, and weaponlike,
hung five old pieces of fish-line,
or four and a wire leader
with the swivel still attached,
with all their five big hooks
grown firmly in his mouth.
A green line, frayed at the end
where he broke it, two heavier lines,
and a fine black thread
still crimped from the strain and snap
when it broke and he got away.
Like medals with their ribbons
frayed and wavering,
a five-haired beard of wisdom
trailing from his aching jaw.
I stared and stared
and victory filled up
the little rented boat,
from the pool of bilge
where oil had spread a rainbow

around the rusted engine
to the bailer rusted orange,
the sun-cracked thwarts,
the oarlocks on their strings,
the gunnels—until everything
was rainbow, rainbow, rainbow!
And I let the fish go.

"KTAADN TROUT" and "THE PONDS"
(Selections)

Henry David Thoreau

"KTAADN TROUT"

THE LAST HALF MILE carried us to the Sowadnehunk dead-water, so called from the stream of the same name, signifying "running between mountains," an important tributary which comes in a mile above. Here we decided to camp, about twenty miles from the Dam, at the mouth of Murch Brook and the Aboljack-nagesic, mountain streams, broad off from Ktaadn, and about a dozen miles from its summit, having made fifteen miles this day.

We had been told by McCauslin that we should here find trout enough; so, while some prepared the camp, the rest fell to fishing. Seizing the birch poles which some party of Indians, or white hunters, had left on the shore, and baiting our hooks with pork, and with trout, as soon as they were caught we cast our lines into the mouth of the Aboljacknagesic, a clear, swift, shallow stream, which came in from Ktaadn. Instantly a shoal of white chivin (*Leucisci pulchelli*), silvery roaches, cousin-trout, or what not, large and small, prowling thereabocts, fell upon our bait, and one after another were landed amidst the bushes. Anon their cousins, the true trout, took their turn, and alternately the speckled trout, and the silvery roaches, swallowed the bait as fast as we could throw in; and the finest specimens of both that I have ever seen, the largest one weighing three pounds, were heaved upon the shore, though at first in vain, to wriggle down into the water again, for we stood in the boat; but soon we learned to remedy this evil; for one, who had lost his hook, stood on shore to catch them as they fell in a perfect shower around him—sometimes, wet and slippery, full in his face and bosom, as his arms were outstretched to receive them. While yet alive, before their tints had faded, they glistened like the fairest flowers, the product of primitive rivers; and he could hardly trust his senses, as he stood over them, that these jewels should have swam away in that Aboljacknagesic water for so long, so many dark ages—these bright fluviatile flowers, seen of Indians only, made beautiful, the Lord only knows why, to swim there! I could understand better for this, the truth of mythology, the fables of Proteus, and all those beautiful sea-monsters—how all history, indeed, put to a terrestrial use, is mere history; but put to a celestial, is mythology always.

But there is the rough voice of Uncle George, who commands at the frying-pan, to send over what you've got, and then you may stay till morning. The pork sizzles and cries for fish. Luckily for the foolish race, and this particularly foolish generation of trout, the night shut down at last, not a little deepened by the dark side of Ktaadn, which, like a permanent shadow, reared itself from the eastern bank. Lescarbot, writing in 1609, tells us that the Sieur Champdoré, who, with one of the people of the Sieur de Monts, ascended some fifty leagues up the St. John in 1608, found the fish so plenty, *"qu'en mettant la chaudière sur le feu ils en avoient pris suffisamment pour eux disner avant que l'eau fust chaude."* Their descendants here are no less numerous. So we accompanied Tom into the woods to cut cedar-twigs for our bed. While he went ahead with the axe and lopped off the smallest twigs of the flat-leaved cedar, the arbor-vitae of the gardens, we gathered them up, and returned with them to the boat, until it was loaded. Our bed was made with as much care and skill as a roof is shingled; beginning at the foot, and laying the twig end of the cedar upward, we advanced to the head, a course at a time, thus successively covering the stub-ends, and producing a soft and level bed. For us six it was about ten feet long by six in breadth. This time we lay under our tent, having pitched it more prudently with reference to the wind and the flame, and the usual huge fire blazed in front. Supper was eaten off a large log, which some freshet had thrown up. This night we had a dish of arbor-vitae, or cedar-tea, which the lumberer sometimes uses when other herbs fail,

A quart of arbor-vitae,
To make him strong and mighty,

but I had no wish to repeat the experiment. It had too medicinal a taste for my palate. There was the skeleton of a moose here, whose bones some Indian hunters had picked on this very spot.

In the night I dreamed of trout-fishing; and, when at length I awoke, it seemed a fable that this painted fish swam there so near my couch, and rose to our hooks the last evening, and I doubted if I had not dreamed it all. So I arose before dawn to test its truth, while my companions were still sleeping. There stood

Ktaadn with distinct and cloudless outline in the moonlight; and the rippling
of the rapids was the only sound to break the stillness. Standing on the shore,
I once more cast my line into the stream, and found the dream to be real and
the fable true. The speckled trout and silvery roach, like flying-fish, sped swiftly
through the moonlight air, describing bright arcs on the dark side of Ktaadn,
until moonlight, now fading into daylight, brought satiety to my mind, and the
minds of my companions, who had joined me.

*

''THE PONDS''
(From *Walden*)

OCCASIONALLY, after my hoeing was done for the day, I joined some impatient
companion who had been fishing on the pond since morning, as silent and motionless as a duck or a floating leaf, and, after practising various kinds of philosophy, had concluded commonly, by the time I arrived, that he belonged to
the ancient sect of Coenobites. There was one older man, an excellent fisher and
skilled in all kinds of woodcraft, who was pleased to look upon my house as a
building erected for the convenience of fishermen; and I was equally pleased
when he sat in my doorway to arrange his lines. Once in a while we sat together
on the pond, he at one end of the boat, and I at the other; but not many words
passed between us, for he had grown deaf in his later years, but he occasionally
hummed a psalm, which harmonized well enough with my philosophy. Our in-
tercourse was thus altogether one of unbroken harmony, far more pleasing to
remember than if it had been carried on by speech. When, as was commonly
the case, I had none to commune with, I used to raise the echoes by striking with
a paddle on the side of my boat, filling the surrounding woods with circling and
dilating sound, stirring them up as the keeper of a menagerie his wild beasts,
until I elicited a growl from every wooded vale and hill-side.

In warm evenings I frequently sat in the boat playing the flute, and saw the
perch, which I seem to have charmed, hovering around me, and the moon travelling over the ribbed bottom, which was strewed with the wrecks of the forest.
Formerly I had come to this pond adventurously, from time to time, in dark summer nights, with a companion, and making a fire close to the water's edge, which
we thought attracted the fishes, we caught pouts with a bunch of worms strung
on a thread, and when we had done, far in the night, threw the burning brands
high into the air like skyrockets, which, coming down into the pond, were
quenched with a loud hissing, and we were suddenly groping in total darkness.
Through this, whistling a tune, we took our way to the haunts of men again.
But now I had made my home by the shore.

Sometimes, after staying in a village parlor till the family had all retired, I
have returned to the woods, and, partly with a view to the next day's dinner,

spent the hours of midnight fishing from a boat by moonlight, serenaded by owls and foxes, and hearing, from time to time, the creaking note of some unknown bird close at hand. These experiences were very memorable and valuable to me —anchored in forty feet of water, and twenty or thirty rods from the shore, surrounded sometimes by thousands of small perch and shiners, dimpling the surface with their tails in the moonlight, and communicating by a long flaxen line with mysterious nocturnal fishes which had their dwelling forty feet below, or sometimes dragging sixty feet of line about the pond as I drifted in the gentle night breeze, now and then feeling a slight vibration along it, indicative of some life prowling about its extremity, of dull uncertain blundering purpose there, and slow to make up its mind. At length you slowly raise, pulling hand over hand, some horned pout squeaking and squirming to the upper air. It was very queer, especially in dark nights, when your thoughts had wandered to vast and cosmogonal themes in other spheres, to feel this faint jerk, which came to interrupt your dreams and link you to Nature again. It seemed as if I might next cast my line upward into the air, as well as downward into this element, which was scarcely more dense. Thus I caught two fishes as it were with one hook.

The scenery of Walden is on a humble scale, and, though very beautiful, does not approach to grandeur, nor can it much concern one who has not long frequented it or lived by its shore; yet this pond is so remarkable for its depth and purity as to merit a particular description. It is a clear and deep green well, half a mile long and a mile and three quarters in circumference, and contains about sixty-one and a half acres; a perennial spring in the midst of pine and oak woods, without any visible inlet or outlet except by the clouds and evaporation. The surrounding hills rise abruptly from the water to the height of forty to eighty feet, though on the south-east and east they attain to about one hundred and one hundred and fifty feet respectively, within a quarter and a third of a mile. They are exclusively woodland. All our Concord waters have two colors at least; one when viewed at a distance, and another, more proper, close at hand. The first depends more on the light, and follows the sky. In clear weather, in summer, they appear blue at a little distance, especially if agitated, and at a great distance all appear alike. In stormy weather they are sometimes of a dark slate color. The sea, however, is said to be blue one day and green another without any perceptible change in the atmosphere. I have seen our river, when, the landscape being covered with snow, both water and ice were almost as green as grass. Some consider blue "to be the color of pure water, whether liquid or solid." But, looking directly down into our waters from a boat, they are seen to be of very different colors. Walden is blue at one time and green at another, even from the same point of view. Lying between the earth and the heavens, it partakes of the color of both. Viewed from a hill-top it reflects the color of the sky; but near at hand it is of a yellowish tint next the shore where you can see the sand, then a light green, which gradually deepens to a uniform dark green in the body of the pond. In some lights, viewed even from a hill-top, it is of a vivid green next the shore.

Some have referred this to the reflection of the verdure; but it is equally green there against the railroad sand-bank, and in the spring, before the leaves are expanded, and it may be simply the result of the prevailing blue mixed with the yellow of the sand. Such is the color of its iris. This is that portion, also, where in the spring, the ice being warmed by the heat of the sun reflected from the bottom, and also transmitted through the earth, melts first and forms a narrow canal about the still frozen middle. Like the rest of our waters, when much agitated, in clear weather, so that the surface of the waves may reflect the sky at the right angle, or because there is more light mixed with it, it appears at a little distance of a darker blue than the sky itself; and at such a time, being on its surface, and looking with divided vision, so as to see the reflection, I have discerned a matchless and indescribable light blue, such as watered or changeable silks and sword blades suggest, more cerulean than the sky itself, alternating with the original dark green on the opposite sides of the waves, which last appeared but muddy in comparison. It is a vitreous greenish blue, as I remember it, like those patches of the winter sky seen through cloud vistas in the west before sundown. Yet a single glass of its water held up to the light is as colorless as an equal quantity of air. It is well known that a large plate of glass will have a green tint, owing, as the makers say, to its "body," but a small piece of the same will be colorless. How large a body of Walden water would be required to reflect a green tint I have never proved. The water of our river is black or a very dark brown to one looking directly down on it, and, like that of most ponds, imparts to the body of one bathing in it a yellowish tinge; but this water is of such crystalline purity that the body of the bather appears of an alabaster whiteness, still more unnatural, which, as the limbs are magnified and distorted withal, produces a monstrous effect, making fit studies for a Michael Angelo.

The water is so transparent that the bottom can easily be discerned at the depth of twenty-five or thirty feet. Paddling over it, you may see many feet beneath the surface the schools of perch and shiners, perhaps only an inch long, yet the former easily distinguished by their transverse bars, and you think that they must be ascetic fish that find a subsistence there. Once, in the winter, many years ago, when I had been cutting holes through the ice in order to catch pickerel, as I stepped ashore I tossed my axe back on to the ice, but, as if some evil genius had directed it, it slid four or five rods directly into one of the holes, where the water was twenty-five feet deep. Out of curiosity, I lay down on the ice and looked through the hole, until I saw the axe a little on one side, standing on its head, with its helve erect and gently swaying to and fro with the pulse of the pond; and there it might have stood erect and swaying till in the course of time the handle rotted off, if I had not disturbed it. Making another hole directly over it with an ice chisel which I had, and cutting down the longest birch which I could find in the neighborhood with my knife, I made a slip-noose, which I attached to its end, and, letting it down carefully, passed it over the knob of the handle, and drew it by a line along the birch, and so pulled the axe out again.

The shore is composed of a belt of smooth rounded white stones like paving-stones, excepting one or two short sand beaches, and is so steep that in many places a single leap will carry you into water over your head; and were it not for its remarkable transparency, that would be the last to be seen of its bottom till it rose on the opposite side. Some think it is bottomless. It is nowhere muddy, and a casual observer would say that there were no weeds at all in it; and of notice-able plants, except in the little meadows recently overflowed, which do not properly belong to it, a closer scrutiny does not detect a flag nor a bulrush, nor even a lily, yellow or white, but only a few small heart-leaves and potamogetons, and perhaps a water-target or two; all which however a bather might not perceive; and these plants are clean and bright like the element they grow in. The stones extend a rod or two into the water, and then the bottom is pure sand, except in the deepest parts, where there is usually a little sediment, probably from the decay of the leaves which have been wafted on to it so many successive falls, and a bright green weed is brought up on anchors even in midwinter.

We have one other pond just like this, White Pond, in Nine Acre Corner, about two and a half miles westerly; but though I am acquainted with most of the ponds within a dozen miles of this centre, I do not know a third of this pure and well-like character. Successive nations perchance have drank at, admired, and fathomed it, and passed away, and still its water is green and pellucid as ever. Not an intermitting spring! Perhaps on that spring morning when Adam and Eve were driven out of Eden Walden Pond was already in existence, and even then breaking up in a gentle spring rain accompanied with mist and a southerly wind, and covered with myriads of ducks and geese, which had not heard of the fall, when still pure lakes sufficed them. Even then it had com-menced to rise and fall, and had clarified its waters and colored them of the hue they now wear, and obtained a patent of Heaven to be the only Walden Pond in the world and distiller of celestial dews. Who knows in how many unremem-bered nations' literatures this has been the Castalian Fountain? or what nymphs presided over it in the Golden Age? It is a gem of the first water which Concord wears in her coronet.

Yet perchance the first who came to this well have left some trace of their footsteps. I have been surprised to detect encircling the pond, even where a thick wood has just been cut down on the shore, a narrow shelf-like path in the steep hill-side, alternately rising and falling, approaching and receding from the water's edge, as old probably as the race of man here, worn by the feet of aboriginal hunters, and still from time to time unwittingly trodden by the present occupants of the land. This is particularly distinct to one standing on the mid-dle of the pond in winter, just after a light snow has fallen, appearing as a clear undulating white line, unobscured by weeds and twigs, and very obvious a quarter of a mile off in many places where in summer it is hardly distinguishable close at hand. The snow reprints it, as it were, in clear white type alto-relievo. The ornamented grounds of villas which will one day be built here may still pre-serve some trace of this.

The pond rises and falls, but whether regularly or not, and within what period, nobody knows, though, as usual, many pretend to know. It is commonly higher in the winter and lower in the summer, though not corresponding to the general wet and dryness. I can remember when it was a foot or two lower, and also when it was at least five feet higher, than when I lived by it. There is a narrow sand-bar running into it, with very deep water on one side, on which I helped boil a kettle of chowder, some six rods from the main shore, about the year 1824, which it has not been possible to do for twenty-five years; and, on the other hand, my friends used to listen with incredulity when I told them that a few years later I was accustomed to fish from a boat in a secluded cove in the woods, fifteen rods from the only shore they knew, which place was long since converted into a meadow. But the pond has risen steadily for two years, and now, in the summer of '52, is just five feet higher than when I lived there, or as high as it was thirty years ago, and fishing goes on again in the meadow. This makes a difference of level, at the outside, of six or seven feet; and yet the water shed by the surrounding hills is insignificant in amount, and this overflow must be referred to causes which affect the deep springs. This same summer the pond has begun to fall again. It is remarkable that this fluctuation, whether periodical or not, appears thus to require many years for its accomplishment. I have observed one rise and a part of two falls, and I expect that a dozen or fifteen years hence the water will again be as low as I have ever known it. Flints' Pond, a mile eastward, allowing for the disturbance occasioned by its inlets and outlets, and the smaller intermediate ponds also, sympathize with Walden, and recently attained their greatest height at the same time with the latter. The same is true, as far as my observation goes, of White Pond.

This rise and fall of Walden at long intervals serves this use at least; the water standing at this great height for a year or more, though it makes it difficult to walk round it, kills the shrubs and trees which have sprung up about its edge since the last rise—pitch-pines, birches, alders, aspens, and others—and, falling again, leaves an unobstructed shore; for, unlike many ponds and all waters which are subject to a daily tide, its shore is cleanest when the water is lowest. On the side of the pond next my house a row of pitch-pines, fifteen feet high, has been killed and tipped over as if by a lever, and thus a stop put to their encroachments; and their size indicates how many years have elapsed since the last rise to this height. By this fluctuation the pond asserts its title to a shore, and thus the *shore* is *shorn,* and the trees cannot hold it by right of possession. These are the lips of the lake on which no beard grows. It licks its chaps from time to time. When the water is at its height, the alders, willows, and maples send forth a mass of fibrous red roots several feet long from all sides of their stems in the water, and to the height of three or four feet from the ground, in the effort to maintain themselves; and I have known the high-blueberry bushes about the shore, which commonly produce no fruit, bear an abundant crop under these circumstances.

Some have been puzzled to tell how the shore became so regularly paved. My townsmen have all heard the tradition, the oldest people tell me that they heard it in their youth, that anciently the Indians were holding a pow-wow upon a hill here, which rose as high into the heavens as the pond now sinks deep into the earth, and they used much profanity, as the story goes, though this vice is one of which the Indians were never guilty, and while they were thus engaged the hill shook and suddenly sank, and only one old squaw, named Walden, escaped, and from her the pond was named. It has been conjectured that when the hill shook these stones rolled down its side and became the present shore. It is very certain, at any rate, that once there was no pond here, and now there is one; and this Indian fable does not in any respect conflict with the account of that ancient settler whom I have mentioned, who remembers so well when he first came here with his divining rod, saw a thin vapor rising from the sward, and the hazel pointed steadily downward, and he concluded to dig a well here. As for the stones, many still think that they are hardly to be accounted for by the action of the waves on these hills; but I observe that the surrounding hills are remarkably full of the same kind of stones, so that they have been obliged to pile them up in walls on both sides of the railroad cut nearest the pond; and, moreover, there are most stones where the shore is most abrupt; so that, unfortunately, it is no longer a mystery to me. I detect the paver. If the name was not derived from that of some English locality—Saffron Walden, for instance—one might suppose that it was called originally *Walled-in* Pond.

The pond was my well ready dug. For four months in the year its water is as cold as it is pure at all times; and I think that it is then as good as any, if not the best, in the town. In the winter, all water which is exposed to the air is colder than springs and wells which are protected from it. The temperature of the pond water which had stood in the room where I sat from five o'clock in the afternoon till noon the next day, the sixth of March, 1846, the thermometer having been up to 65° or 70° some of the time, owing partly to the sun on the roof, was 42°, or one degree colder than the water of one of the coldest wells in the village just drawn. The temperature of the Boiling Spring the same day was 45°, or the warmest of any water tried, though it is the coldest that I know of in summer, when, beside, shallow and stagnant surface water is not mingled with it. Moreover, in summer, Walden never becomes so warm as most water which is exposed to the sun, on account of its depth. In the warmest weather I usually placed a pailful in my cellar, where it became cool in the night, and remained so during the day; though I also resorted to a spring in the neighborhood. It was as good when a week old as the day it was dipped, and had no taste of the pump. Whoever camps for a week in summer by the shore of a pond, needs only bury a pail of water a few feet deep in the shade of his camp to be independent of the luxury of ice.

There have been caught in Walden pickerel, one weighing seven pounds,—to say nothing of another which carried off a reel with great velocity, which the fisherman safely set down at eight pounds because he did not see him—perch and pouts, some of each weighing over two pounds, shiners, chivins or roach (*Leuciscus pulchellus*), a very few breams, and a couple of eels, one weighing four pounds—I am thus particular because the weight of a fish is commonly its only title to fame, and these are the only eels I have heard of here; also, I have a faint recollection of a little fish some five inches long, with silvery sides and a greenish back, somewhat dace-like in its character, which I mention here chiefly to link my facts to fable. Nevertheless, this pond is not very fertile in fish. Its pickerel, though not abundant, are its chief boast. I have seen at one time lying on the ice pickerel of at least three different kinds: a long and shallow one, steel-colored, most like those caught in the river; a bright golden kind, with greenish reflections and remarkably deep, which is the most common here; and another, golden-colored, and shaped like the last, but peppered on the sides with small dark brown or black spots, intermixed with a few faint blood-red ones, very much like a trout. The specific name *reticulatus* would not apply to this; it should be *guttatus* rather. These are all very firm fish, and weigh more than their size promises. The shiners, pouts, and perch also, and indeed all the fishes which inhabit this pond, are much cleaner, handsomer, and firmer fleshed than those in the river and most other ponds, as the water is purer, and they can easily be distinguished from them. Probably many ichthyologists would make new varieties of some of them. There are also a clean race of frogs and tortoises, and a few muscles in it; muskrats and minks leave their traces about it, and occasionally a travelling mud-turtle visits it. Sometimes, when I pushed off my boat in the morning, I disturbed a great mud-turtle which had secreted himself under the boat in the night. Ducks and geese frequent it in the spring and fall, the white-bellied swallows (*Hirundo bicolor*) skim over it, and the peet-weets (*Totanus macularius*) "teter" along its stony shores all summer. I have sometimes disturbed a fish-hawk sitting on a white-pine over the water; but I doubt if it is ever profaned by the wing of a gull, like Fair Haven. At most, it tolerates one annual loon. These are all the animals of consequence which frequent it now.

You may see from a boat, in calm weather, near the sandy eastern shore, where the water is eight or ten feet deep, and also in some other parts of the pond, some circular heaps half a dozen feet in diameter by a foot in height, consisting of small stones less than a hen's egg in size, where all around is bare sand. At first you wonder if the Indians could have formed them on the ice for any purpose, and so, when the ice melted, they sank to the bottom; but they are too regular and some of them plainly too fresh for that. They are similar to those found in rivers; but as there are no suckers nor lampreys here, I know not by what fish they could be made. Perhaps they are the nests of the chivin. These lend a pleasing mystery to the bottom.

The shore is irregular enough not to be monotonous. I have in my mind's eye the western indented with deep bays, the bolder northern, and the beautifully scolloped southern shore, where successive capes overlap each other and suggest unexplored coves between. The forest has never so good a setting, nor is so distinctly beautiful, as when seen from the middle of a small lake amid hills which rise from the water's edge; for the water in which it is reflected not only makes the best foreground in such a case, but, with its winding shore, the most natural and agreeable boundary to it. There is no rawness nor imperfection in its edge there, as where the axe has cleared a part, or a cultivated field abuts on it. The trees have ample room to expand on the water side, and each sends forth its most vigorous branch in that direction. There Nature has woven a natural selvage, and the eye rises by just gradations from the low shrubs of the shore to the highest trees. There are few traces of man's hand to be seen. The water laves the shore as it did a thousand years ago.

A lake is the landscape's most beautiful and expressive feature. It is earth's eye; looking into which the beholder measures the depth of his own nature.

THE FISHERMAN

W. B. Yeats

Although I can see him still,
The freckled man who goes
To a grey place on a hill
In grey Connemara clothes
At dawn to cast his flies,
It's long since I began
To call up to the eyes
This wise and simple man.
All day I'd looked in the face
What I had hoped 'twould be
To write for my own race
And the reality;
The living men that I hate,
The dead man that I loved,
The craven man in his seat,
The insolent unreproved,
And no knave brought to book
Who has won a drunken cheer,
The witty man and his joke
Aimed at the commonest ear,

The clever man who cries
The catch-cries of the clown,
The beating down of the wise
And great Art beaten down.

Maybe a twelvemonth since
Suddenly I began,
In scorn of this audience,
Imagining a man,
And his sun-freckled face,
And grey Connemara cloth,
Climbing up to a place
Where stone is dark under froth,
And the down-turn of his wrist
When the flies drop in the stream;
A man who does not exist,
A man who is but a dream;
And cried, "Before I am old
I shall have written him one
Poem maybe as cold
And passionate as the dawn."

BLUE DUN

Frank Mele

IT IS NATURAL, I think, for beginnings to be arbitrary. Even human lives, it seems, can begin somewhat capriciously. Any account of inceptions is therefore apt to be treacherous, or at best, unreliable—especially so, if one seeks for causes to satisfy the human prerequisite to Effect. How to enter into even the merest thumbnail history of an attitude compounded from flowing waters, bankside dawdlers, bamboo, cock's hackles, and a certain color of indeterminate hue, and to give some intimation of their genesis, is a task for wiser heads than mine.

I suppose I could say, for example, that the glowing vision of a Blue Dun cape materialized one night as my pregnant mother knelt at prayer before her little Madonna. But this would be sheer fabrication, and even worse, an affront to the quality of her fervor, for she wanted her unborn son to be a violinist. In her frame of mind, the Blue Dun cape would have been taken for some harping angel in miniature, or a biblical dove with Blue Dun feathers appropriate to the sky of Heaven.

Now, all this might ingratiate me to the good folks of the world, but I would be answerable to the few who know that it is from just such compromises that many a potent myth has had its start. Caught thus, between the half-truths of our salty worthies and the gem-hard unpleasantries of the few, I could try to salvage some of my peace of mind by affirming that since myths appear to be as necessary as breathing to the run-of-the-mill of the species, I shall not try to discredit them, since, by acquiescing to that grand old custom, there is the chance of an absolution of anglers. In other words, if what is sauce for the goose, et cetera, there is no longer ground for casting aspersions on anglers. And no need to take their redemption any farther. For all that anglers' myths tend to fragility, they are still a good deal less vulnerable than the contrivances of ordinary men. I trust that now I can get on with the narrative without ransacking my racial memory for some specious cause—say, an angling ancestor who might justify the events to follow.

There was little in my childhood that might have cast any significant shadows before, unless it was a predilection for puddles. Later, in boyhood, when great and sudden rainstorms magically transformed the city streets into brooks, an unexplainable ecstasy would drive me out of doors to hover dreamy-eyed about the curbstone banks of the new rivulets. To this day, when a muskrat clambers out to some riverbank, I am reminded of the rats that scrambled out of the flooded sewer drains and went scurrying over the great cobblestones of the street.

Some years later, done with early studies, well past the intermediate stage, and reeking with the faint, musty odor of the mud, weeds, and pickerel of the farmland streams near my native Rochester, I went to Syracuse to find new ways for scaling the higher reaches of violin playing. That I had already been one of the youngest members of the Rochester Philharmonic Orchestra did not seem to me as impressive, honorable, or profitable as to have the inner beauty of a musical phrase revealed to me by a gaunt and profane master, Andre Polah, my teacher, an artist of stature—one of the elect, whose career had been stifled by an ironic accident.

An ominous silence had settled over the nation. And when in its deepest recesses, a cataclysmic bomb exploded, shattering the national economy, the country reeled and staggered in a state of shock. Life went on, but with empty pockets and, quite often, an empty belly—that is, among the laboring classes and those of us in the arts. And when, against the protestations and vilifications of outraged Pilgrims, who had acquired affluence presumably without the help of

God, a crippled and compassionate President decreed the Work Projects, we musicians filed due notice of bona fide indigence, cut the fringes from our trouser cuffs, and began to use our professional skills as members of the new symphony orchestra. It was held to be one of the more contemptible projects, in that men were getting paid, however minimally, for merely making great music.

Andre was a gifted conductor as well, and when he was appointed director of the orchestra he set about reconciling his passion for a high standard of performance, as much as his choleric nature would permit, with the inevitable quota of mediocrities that were better suited to vaudeville than to Mozart, Brahms, Debussy, and yes, even Stravinsky. There was now relief from want, but not from the humiliation that attended its formalities; and what shreds of dignity had survived the stigma attached to the projects were annihilated by a jibing press and the indignation of the good burghers of upper New York State. Those were gloomy days, scarcely relieved by the pall of grime that hung over the scabrous public buildings. The drabness of that city was exceeded only by a pervasive meanness of spirit. But redemption could be found in the beauty of its countryside. Out beyond the green drumlins, among the valleys to the northeast and south, beautiful streams with Indian names beckoned, inviting heavy hearts to lightness, and corroded hopes to a good burnishing at the hands of waterside alders.

Andre was a fly-fisher, and when this mad Dutchman adopted me as his fishing companion, my hopes began to soar as an early zeal for bait casting got transposed to the fly rod. As in violin playing, I sought out the masters, ransacking the shelves of the university and public libraries for books on flyfishing. In the stacks I found Emlyn Gill, Bergman, Hewitt, Southard, Lord Grey. I saved enough to send to Paul Young for his *Making and Using the Fly and Leader*. And then I began to tie flies, buying hooks by the dozen when I could afford them. Certain exotic materials could only be purchased. Others I begged. And many I borrowed from an environment that had taken on a new depth. A rich world of texture and color had opened to me. For the first time I saw the extraordinary range of color in dogs, cats, pet and wild rabbits, monkeys, mice, squirrels, ducks, geese, and fowl of all kinds. My visits to the zoo now had a vibrant urgency that gave pause to children and made the keepers nervous. And when the orchestra played at a county fair that was famous for its yearly exhibit of rare fowl, and I found the attendant away for lunch, my head swam. In the operation that followed, a dizziness nearly overcame me, fearing that at any moment the uproar would fetch a guard.

One morning at rehearsal a new man came in dragging a cello by the scruff of the neck. Andre had briefed me about him over the previous day's intermission coffee. In the excitement Andre's English, normally unpredictable, had slipped a few cogs and was being ground up by Dutch, French, and German accents. Under those great eyebrows of Holland straw his blue eyes were gleaming wolfishly. In a gravelly bass he told me the news. "This man is un maker of rodts!

Un goddamt specialiste von fly rodts! Dry-fly rodts!" I could not have been more impressed had Andre announced the entry of Pablo Casals into our ranks. Our rods were of poor quality, soft as willow. Andre's treasured rods and reels by Hardy had been stolen from his car years ago.

Andre's words were still reverberating in my ear as Brenan took his place at the rear of the cello section. As he began to tune his cello he looked so unprofessional that. I began to get faintly sick. But shortly I saw something that made me close my eyes in blessed relief. There would not be, could not be, any repercussion from the podium. Hopelessly out of practice after years of rodmaking, Brenan had sacked valor for a plausible discretion. It would have been difficult for him to have made an audible mistake. He was bowing away impassively, in step with the others, the bow hair hovering over the treacherous rapids then settling down agreeably in the more navigable runs, glides, and pools. It was a stroke of true wisdom, appreciated none the less by Andre than by me. One day, Brenan invited me to his shop.

Coming in to the warmth of a little world of bamboo out of the whiplashing snows and icy sidewalks of Syracuse was no less than a bit of parochial magic, bringing easement and balm to a troubled soul. The shop's mood was a mélange of violinmaker's shop and tackle store, sources both for repose and wonder. There I saw and fondled my first dry-fly rods. Had Brenan had an apprenticeship or a family tradition there would not have been any flaw of workmanship. If imperfect, they were superb in action; I have had a few in hand since then that were comparable to his best rods, and many that were inferior. However prudent a cellist, Dan was an adventurous rodmaker; and in the matter of rod design for the dry fly he was ahead of his time.

A blackboard with the chalked heading, "Days to Opening Day" read "63," awaiting the first of the coterie to come in to roost out of the waning afternoon, leaving the gloom, chill, and snow to the defeated day. By five-thirty the blackboard read "62." I basked in the warmth of talk that diverted the winter stream to its summer course on the shop's floor. Rods sprang to life. Lines darted and looped under the soiled sky of the ceiling. At a bench to one side sat Bill, Dan's son, at his afterwork vise, contriving a better bivisible fly than the last. Flies whisked about. A great trout rose to McBride's fly of last summer, then plunged downward to sulk in the depths of the floor below. It was the rite of the Waiting Men enduring their season of work with invocations to a reluctant spring—not a whit less primitive than the crude and basic formalities of their remote ancestors. From a judicial chamber, from a locomotive's cab, from symphony hall, office, machine shop, barroom, laboratory, they had come to improvise upon their truth, which was the Dry Fly.

Later, at a nearby tavern, Dan, mellowing in whisky, would hold forth for the hardier few. A gifted writer on many aspects of the sport, Dan had an extensive correspondence with leading figures in the field. His knowledge of angling history of the Catskill and Adirondack mountains was imposing and intimate; and the names I culled out of those benign extemporizations sounded like a roll call of latter-day saints: Theodore Gordon, La Branche, Hewitt, Holden, of the "Idyll of the Split Bamboo," Izaak Walton (no less a figure than Dante), Halford, the English Prince of the True Faith, and then the glorious school of Catskill fly-tyers who had received Gordon's afflatus at death: Rueben Cross, Herman Christian, the Darbees, Walt Dette. By now Dan had become for me the arbiter of all things piscatorial, and an inexhaustible source of fishing lore.

One afternoon at the tavern Dan had soared to really admirable form, and was weaving in and out of the key of Dry Fly Major with the skill of an Irish Bach when, at once, he struck an arresting chord. "The Quill Gordon fly," said Dan, "was the great turning point in American dry-fly fishing. Gordon's creativity in his choice of materials and his ingenuity in determining a just style for our waters set the pattern that was to become our tradition. After an extensive correspondence with the mighty Halford, and a cordial exchange of flies, he departed once and for all from the English tradition, retaining only that which could be adapted to his concept of a fly that could dance on our broken waters, and which, on our long glides and pools, looked like a newly hatched dun. It is therefore *de rigueur,* mandatory, that this fly be tied with the natural Blue Dun hackle! Else it is not a true Quill Gordon fly!" By now Dan's voice had the ring of One Hundred Proof. "For that matter," he added, "no fly could rightfully bear the name Dun unless it was tied in the natural color!"

There it was. With four words Dan had wakened me out of a deep sleep, only to plunge me into a nightmare of frustration at the thought of all those Quill Gordon flies I had tied from a very well dyed cock's neck of excellent quality. I had traded a pernambuco violin bow for it to a greedy dealer in fly-tying materials. The fact that the bow was not a true pernambuco was small consolation. The neck was not a true Blune Dun. Dan's words resolved all doubts that I had had from time to time about those flies. Their color was inert. They reminded me of ash. Dan's incantation had at once set me before the Veil that concealed a great Mystery. What the revelation could conceivably be was as yet only a strange stirring of blood in my head. This color, Blue Dun, would I know it were I to come suddenly face to face with it? What could there be about it which had set it apart so remotely yet compellingly on a mountain peak in my mind?

"Well, Frankie," said Dan. "I can only say that there is nothing quite like it. I don't know how to describe it. One simply has to see the natural Blue Dun for himself, with his own eyes. Only then can he understand. It is one of Nature's rare moods. It is color and light making their ways out of chaos and darkness." For the moment I had to content myself with this Hibernian tune from the Prophet. Had Dan had access then to Gordon's letters to the great English angler, G. E. M. Skues, he would have quoted:

"My farmer friend and I have been trying to breed good dun hackles, but the cocks are turning out poorly."

Later: "I found a blue cock of the year yesterday and hope that I will succeed in buying the bird—the neck is of such a lovely color—"

And six years later: "It seems too bad when we consider how rarely one finds a cock with blue dun hackles." Even then, it seems, the natural color was painfully scarce.

Dan, I am sure, was not aware of what was happening to me, else he would have modified his dictum from unalterable law to permissible deviation. He had a deep respect for my skill as a violinist, and a personal liking that probably set me only a cut or two below Theodore Gordon, for Dan adored great music. But I do believe that had he altered his pronunciamento out of care for my peace of mind, and that of my family's, I doubt that it would have greatly diverted the course of the future. Blue Dun was now a fever in my brain.

The violence of my reaction and its later consequences cannot be entirely ascribed to Dan, with all due respect to his eloquence and imagery. Later events tend to suggest that the occasion triggered something deep within, well beyond normal reach, well to the other side of any intimation, even, of its existence; for I had yet to see a single feather of natural Blue Dun.

Then, streambound early one Sunday morning, as the car was hurtling over the road, the irascible Marcel gave me what appears now to be the first lucid description of the color Blue Dun. This taut but amiable Frenchman, a hairdresser, was a passionate angler whose fly casting was a model of elegance and precision. He was singing obscene French songs, by way, I thought, of exorcising the previous day's ordeal with fat and fretful matrons. When he had finished still another classic of the latrine I put the question to him. He was a knowledgeable and meticulous fly-tyer.

"Marcel. What is the real Blue Dun like? The natural—you know—"

"Ah, mon cher," he replied. "That? What can I say? It is like nothing else, and everything. It is not blue, like the flag blue. It is something that is always— How shall I say? Becoming?"

Late that afternoon at Marcel's home I saw my first natural Blue Dun neck. I was silent a long time. It was real, and it was there. But it was unreal; and it was somewhere else. Marcel was right. It was in the act of becoming. I raised my eyes at last and spoke.

"Marcel. Where is Blue Dun?"

"Ah." Marcel canted his head a bit to one side. "That is a difficult question. How shall I tell you? That it is where you find it? Yes. To find it. Until then it is like the— Like the smoke—"

"In search of the sky."

"Yes! Exactly!" Marcel nodded sharply, then suddenly fixed me with a curious look followed by an expression of bewilderment, as of a spirit scurrying through the ages.

"But how did you know?" he asked, from a great distance.

"I'm not sure," I said, my words sounding from afar. "You may have said it once before, and I remembered it."

Hairdressers, I believe, are masters of applied psychology. Marcel had read something in my face that was unintentional, of which I was not aware.

"What size do you tie the Quill Gordon?" he asked.

"Twelve."

He riffled affectionately through the quivering hackles, then carefully plucked out two and gave them to me. It was an act of superlative generosity, well beyond friendship. I had heard it said that the French were stingy. I say that they are selectively extravagant. On that occasion it was nothing less than a minor sacrifice, which only a cynic can make without pomp. "Bon!" concluded Marcel. "You are now fit to enter the Beaverkill. You are going next week with Dan?"

"Yes. Dan is taking three of us. It will be my very first time. I have never seen it, except in dreams."

"Ah," sighed Marcel. "It is a dream within a dream."

On a fresh summer morning a week later, as Blue Dun was rising in the east, a Ford went wheezing toward the valleys where the sacred rivers ran. Under the wise and gentle guidance of Dan, the Prophet, three of us were to have our baptism at last in the Beaverkill River.

Hours later, when the southern hills had greatened to Catskill massiveness, we descended a long, winding grade and the Ford stopped, heaving and burbling in exhaustion at the bank of a majestic pool. We alighted. The Prophet turned to us, intoned the keynote and conducted an impromptu cantata, the hymn, "Praise God from Whom All Blessings Flow." It was an unlikely chorus: a nominal Protestant, a fled Catholic, a remoted Jew, and an atheist. But it was in tune, and fervent. In a many-celled fly box, squatting in its own special compartment, the fly with the mystical color listened, awaiting its first flight over the holy waters.

If memory serves me, and often it doesn't, we camped near to the Mountain Pool. Darkness was nigh, and wood was fetched at Dan's request for a fire big enough to conjure up the Spirits of the River, that he might transpose the secrets that passed back and forth from the distant rapids to the crackling flames. As the night deepened, the thin, reedy chords of a harmonica floated in and out of the conversational murmur. It was a nostalgic whimper before the fact of smallness beneath a firmament of stars—the Aeolian harp of the Catskills singing of humility and peace, and gratitude to the great Unknown.

Later, two figures materialized from the outer world of darkness and entered the glow of the fire to bring their hands to Dan's. Gladness and surprise were in the Prophet's greetings, and through their fullness there ran a finely gleaming thread of respect. One of them was Reuben Cross, the greathearted and improvident master of fly-making who was already a legend, and with him was Alfred W. Miller, the Sparse Grey Hackle of the genial writings that were enriching Beaverkill lore.

In the early morning I entered the waters, rod in hand. I do not remember how many trout rose to my fly—or whether, indeed, any did. But I shall not forget that I moved as in a dream, hearing the voices of the river rising and falling with mysterious clarity through the hovering mists. And I remember the crystalline water that seemed to magnify the purity of the rocks, and the cool green darkness of the ferns, a profusion of frail, lush arches in the shadowed banks; and as the mist began to rise, a doe and her fawn crossed the pool below.

In the ensuing years, my work as a symphonist took me to various parts of the country for the fall, winter, and spring months. As each music season rounded its peak, and spring was faintly visible in the distant valley, the voice of a wakened obsession would begin loudening to a command to action. The trail was faint, often washed out. But, like a stubborn hound, I would return to certain crossways, hoping for a cold scent that would lead miraculously to a Blue Dun cape of quality that had fallen asleep in mid-flight. When the orchestra played *The Moldau*, a tone poem which the Bohemian Smetana had distilled from the sounds of a great river, my left-hand fingers would scurry agreeably with the riffles at its headwaters, but the bow had become a fly rod in the other hand. The fly was, appropriately, a Blue Dun, since I had long ago formulated the theory that the natural Dun-hackled fly would take trout anywhere in the world at one time or another.

On nights off, a few of us would meet to play chamber music. The music we made, mostly for ourselves, was the most rewarding of all in terms of personal fulfillment. And if a pianist and a bassist were present, no great persuasion was needed for them to join us in a reading of Schubert's "Trout" Quintet, a tribute to that noble fish by the Austrian genius. As in the song that had inspired the Quintet, the measured, buoyant cheer of its theme would have been perfect incidental music to the ballet of a stately brown swirling at his feast of mayfly nymphs aspiring to dunhood. Later, in the quiet of the Pittsburgh night, I would write another of those ritual letters—this time to a house in England: "Gentlemen, would you by chance have a cock's cape of natural Blue Dun of good quality to offer? I am aware of the rarity of this colour and am, accordingly, prepared to consider the payment of a premium. I would be most grateful—"

I suppose it was inevitable that I should one day settle in the Catskills. I had had as much as I wanted of the unquiet life, and one year I returned, not merely for the summer, but to stay, in a village within twenty minutes' drive of the Esopus, a river proud and mighty still, its spirit unbroken after years of torment by water-greedy Manhattan. My community had a rich and highly respected tradition of the arts, offering scope for playing in a summer series of distinction and a likely potential for students of the violin and viola. Then, within one to two hours' reach there flowed the great rivers of angling history, allegedly tired, but still alluring and productive in their classically temperamental fashion. These were the Schoharie, the Delawares, East and West, the Willowemoc, and the Neversink and Beaverkill rivers.

My decision, however, had come at a time when, for perhaps too many reasons, mind and body had wandered off into a twilight world. There is a withering hostility in the winter Catskills, a taut suspension of life outdoors that can drive men's backs against their own walls. There is beauty, too; and joy may be found or contrived. But the gnawings of a marginal life can dispose a man toward the consolations of the jug. The cheapness and goodness of native apple-jack made it possible to appease a growing congenital thirst, transporting me to an inner island so beguiling that I did not want to leave. I was unable to. Years drifted by. Then, shambling one day through the familiar vapors, I stumbled over my persistent little man again, the one I had ignored and even insulted so often in the past. This time I heard him out; I believed him, and together we managed to stop it once and for all. I did not know it then, but he was congenital, too.

As I improved I began reconstituting the sport, and shortly began to hear the distant crowing of Blue Dun roosters again. The awakening was owing in part to the interest and kindness of Preston Jennings, who had recently retired to nearby Bearsville. His classic *A Book of Trout Flies* was, for me, the first truly significant work on angling entomology and dry-fly design for Eastern streams. It brought order to the chaos of a still rather wayward tradition of American dry-fly fishing and carried it to solid ground. It was issued in a limited edition by a private press in elegant format and was, ironically, re-maindered. Its cost at the time was one factor. The other may have been the cool objectivity of a style uninviting to those American anglers who were still disposed toward boyish writings on fishing. However, by now the book had reemerged as a rare find, commanding premium prices—and it was very scarce. All told, it amounted very nearly to a conspiracy. Accordingly, Jennings was not awarded the honor due him in his lifetime. His genius is reflected in an-other work, the *Streamside Guide*, by Arthur Flick; and Jennings may be said to have been godfather to this indispensable little book.

Curiously, I found that Jennings' passion for the stream had also entered a state of suspension, although unlike mine, his was marked by sobriety, tinged however, with disillusion. Some causes for the latter have been implied. Then, too, Bobby was a man of sensibility, intelligence, and aesthetic awareness, all of which together can incline one to vulnerability. Such persons must stand on reserve or perish, at risk of incurring a judgment of pride. But such was not the case, and I like to think that I may have played a small part in his rec-onciliation to the Catskill streams, for which I think he was glad, or so it seemed as I watched him flexing his beloved Payne rod over a rifflehead, proving the potency of his Blue Dun Variant in conjuring a fifteen-inch brown out of its depths.

At his home one evening, Bobby brought out a small box and opened it with a reverence suggestive of a collector opening to some fabulous diamond. In it were dry flies which had been tied by Herman Christian and Theodore Gordon. I could not imagine them more perfect had they been tied that morning. One of the original models for the Quill Gordon fly was among them. Its form and color engraved themselves in my mind and thereafter became the model for my own imitations. I have since seen other flies allegedly by Gordon, but none had the finesse or the buoyant elegance.

As a tyer, Bobby was a superior artist, and his materials were the finest I had ever seen, or have ever seen since. Among his necks were Blue Duns as fine as I ever hope to see. Jennings was also inclined to the artist's brush and palette, and I believe that this, together with a related color-study, in which he had been absorbed for some time, had drawn him and his gracious wife to an artistic environment. His experience with salmon flies while fishing the great coastal rivers of the East had led to an inquiry into the reasons for the effectiveness of the many-hued salmon fly; and that to a study of the prismatic effect given off by the tiny bubbles of air formed about the microscopic filaments or hairs on the body of a rising nymph. Further inquiry had suggested that the salmon's memory held an indelible association of these colors with the food nymphs of its grilsehood. All told, his efforts had begun to yield up a logical case for the salmon fly and its seemingly irrational gaudiness.

I felt pleased, even honored by Jennings' friendship, but in a rather vague, disembodied way. For those were difficult days—days in which the slow withdrawal of the alcohol had brought to view the shambles of a once productive life, and of a collective fruitfulness reduced to abject singleness. Vaguely aware of trudging forward, I was mostly conscious of a mouthful of ashes, of a battered spirit which had barely averted bankruptcy. But, as I have since gathered, my outer aspect was one of calm bordering on indifference, occasionally rising to arrogance. How far this was from the actual inward state would be a volume in itself, a compact little book, some of whose contents Bobby may have discerned; for one evening, in his studio, as he was delving into a drawer, he turned suddenly to me with a smile. In his outstretched hand was a superb cape of natural Blue Dun. For reasons that have never been clear, I declined it, with a thick murmur of thanks. I doubt whether I could have offended him more. I had virtually spit into the face of a noble gesture, one prompted by the purest motive of intuitive sensibility. Apparently, my reconstruction still had a long way to go. It is not surprising then, that after an unfortunate misunderstanding, we never saw each other again.

An offer came from an orchestra in Texas. Glad for the opportunity of relief from the aftermath of recent history, I accepted. Far from the Catskills, far from trout, my bewildered fly rods huddling in a friend's closet, I entered into the symphonic world again under the benevolent auspices of a mild Texas winter. But when the last Norther had subsided to spring, the old song of the quest began humming in my head again—and the voices of the rivers that flowed under the distant silhouettes of my mountains. I began to write letters that were utterly incongruous with that flat and surly land: "Gentlemen, would you by chance— Blue Dun? I would be most grateful—"

Returned to a comparatively tranquil and ordered life in the Catskills, I found it necessary from time to time to suspend the attrition of the long, bitter winters with occasional jaunts to Jerusalem. Together with my angling companions of some years we found respite from the winter jitters by observing, from time to time, one of a number of what may be called "Darbee Days." I suppose that, given other circumstances, they may have been called "Walt Dette," "Bill Kelly," or "Roy Steenrod" Days, for they, too, were a part of the angling-conservation custodianship at the banks of the great tradition. They were the Keepers of the Gate. But the Darbees were friends of long standing; and then—well, yes, there was also the little matter of their Blue Dun fowl, a strain of their own breeding that glared peevishly out the many cages in the back yard. Inside, we basked in the homemade sunlight of hackles, hooks, furs, rods, reels, lines, leaders, nets, selecting materials with which to tie flies at home later, by way of preserving our sanities during the deserted time of the year. There was talk of flies, of streams, of the men who lived for them, of books in which the waters ran, and where now and then one found a superior music which had been inspired by the trout, a simple vertebrate, but with this difference: That it stirred a mystery in the deepest recess of our beings, a primal nostalgia that quickened in the sight of its brilliant spots and bands of iridescence where gulps of moonlight had congealed to color. Padding in with feminine unobtrusiveness, the First Lady of American fly-tying gave greeting and passed to some other phase of sorting. Held by some to be, craftwise, the better half of the Darbee legend, Elsie would have disdained and Harry confirmed it. Actually, the difference, if any, was beyond the ken of niggling amateurs. Above the genial drone of Harry's voice on the trail of a point of conservation there sounded the faint, rhythmical fanfare of Blue Dun cocks, proud in their little beaked trumpets.

Later, on the long drive home, fly life hatched and surfaced in the murmuring car, and the unheard litanies to a reluctant spring that sang under our words must surely have been noted under the thick ice of Pepacton Reservoir and commented upon with frigid bubbles by the huge trout which had greatened in it within a few miles of its source, the self-renouncing Delaware.

Came the fall of another year, and Fate took one of us for a disastrous ride. For two weeks Jim Mulligan lay in a coma. Waking, he was to lie for two years in a veterans hospital bed until the one half of his body could support the paralyzed half. How many connivances and fabrications that Joe Nazzaro and I dreamed up en route to the hospital I cannot remember; nor how many precious days of liberty that Joe, and I, too, gave up that we might bring the stream to the distant bedside where our shattered friend lay.

But mercy, however capricious, will also have its say; and in having regained the use of one half of his body, Jim, a distinguished cartoonist, set himself the formidable task of transferring the skill of a now inert hand to the strong but untrained one. There came a winter's day at last when the inroads of "cabin fever" decreed a Darbee Day. Once again, with our valiant but unsteady Jim, we set off on wings of Blue Dun.

At Margaretville we crossed the upper Delaware and shortly were following the shoreline road of the severely beautiful Pepacton. Later, turning away from the reservoir, we began the long ascent, then down to Roscoe; and when we crossed the upper Beaverkill I doffed the only hat for the three of us. Shortly beyond the village, on the Manor road, we skirted the Willowemoc, green-bubbling at its icy lips and winter-dark in the upper pool. In the riffles above, a cold fire flared under a shaft of brilliant sunlight from a rift in the gray clouds.

Time has not perceptibly dimmed my memory of Darbee's greeting to the man whom destiny had banged on the brain; nor the implication that it had done so ineffectively. Out the candor of his blue eyes, out the heart of a rich experience, came the blessing of man's humanity to man: a beckoning to Jim to search and find a wholeness of his own. Before we left he gave Jim the token that would articulate his wish for many a year. It was in a paper sack.

As the car was cantering home along the Pepacton road Jim opened the paper sack with his good hand. In the waning light of the afternoon we saw the Blue Dun cape glowing. As he turned it we saw the component glints in the light from the reflecting whiteness of the reservoir. Visibly moved by his great good fortune, Jim's speech, till now painfully laborious, made a curious modulation and he said, slowly but clearly, "It seems to have other meanings."

In my cabinet of fly materials there is a special drawer. Lying in it is a small number of Blue Dun capes of varying shades nestling about each other in all the glory of their muted iridescence. They were all acquired more or less honorably: that is, in the sense that legitimacy and honesty are terms subject to parochial rules, and that it takes a good deal of imagination to transcend our little moral geographies.

I will not say how many there are, because I want to be surprised each time I count them. And when I do so, it is less to affirm my possessiveness than the privilege of their custody. That they are only a small part of countless numbers of shades and attitudes of color piques me, but it does not disturb me, for the ones allotted to me all have their special meaning. Each is a memento of a particular quest. They invite, of course, to other quests, but I really need not undertake them, because each day the colors are a little bit different, as each day is different; and thus they multiply in my mind's eye. Through their difference, as in the multicolored variants of Bach's great "Chaconne," there runs the somber strain of the fact that I grow older, and soon the fiddle strings will fray out and their sound must fade. But the colors will not, for Blue Dun waits upon other questions, whose answers, even more than mine, will disavow finality. As for instance, "Why is Blue Dun?"

One could as well ask: "Why is Love?" Or, indeed, "Why is Life?"

TO KNOW A RIVER...

Roderick L. Haig-Brown

I HAVE WRITTEN in this book nearly always of rivers—occasionally of lakes or the salt water, but nearly always of rivers and river fishing. A river is water in its loveliest form; rivers have life and sound and movement and infinity of variation, rivers are veins of the earth through which the life blood returns to the heart. Rivers can attain overwhelming grandeur, as the Columbia does in the reaches all the way from Pasco to the sea; they may slide softly through flat meadows or batter their way down mountain slopes and through narrow canyons; they may be heavy, almost dark, with history, as the Thames is from its mouth at least up to Richmond; or they may be sparkling fresh on mountain slopes through virgin forest and alpine meadows.

Lakes and the sea have great secret depths quite hidden from man and often almost barren of life. A river too may have its deep and secret places, may be so large that one can never know it properly; but most rivers that give sport to fly-fishermen are comparatively small, and one feels that it is within the range of the mind to know them intimately—intimately as to their changes through the seasons, as to the shifts and quirks of current, the sharp runs, the slow glides, the eddies and bars and crossing places, the very rocks of the bottom. And in knowing a river intimately is a very large part of the joy of fly-fishing.

One may love a river as soon as one sets eyes upon it; it may have certain features that fit instantly with one's conception of beauty, or it may recall the qualities of some other river, well known and deeply loved. One may feel in the same way an instant affinity for a man or a woman and know that here is pleasure and warmth and the foundation of deep friendship. In either case the full riches of the discovery are not immediately released—they cannot be; only knowledge and close experience can release them. Rivers, I suppose, are not at all like human beings, but it is still possible to make apt comparisons; and this is one: understanding, whether instinctive and immediate or developing naturally through time or grown by conscious effort, is a necessary preliminary to love.

Understanding of another human being can never be complete, but as it grows toward completeness, it becomes love almost inevitably. One cannot know intimately all the ways and movements of a river without growing into love of it. And there is no exhaustion to the growth of love through knowledge, whether the love be for a person or a river, because the knowledge can never become complete. One can come to feel in time that the whole is within one's compass, not yet wholly and intimately known, but there for the knowing, within the last little move of reaching; but there will always be something ahead, something more to know.

I have known very few rivers thoroughly and intimately. There is not time to know many, and one can know only certain chosen lengths of the few. I know some miles of the Dorsetshire Frome and of the little river Wrackle that cuts away from the Frome by Stratton Mill and rejoins it farther down, because I grew up with them and had all the quick instinctive learning power of the very young when I fished there. It was a happy and proud thing to know those streams, and the knowing paid great dividends in fish; it paid even greater dividends in something that I can still recapture—sheer happiness in remembering a bend or a run or the spread below a bridge as I saw them best, perhaps open in sunlight with the green weeds trailing and a good fish rising steadily, or perhaps pitted by rain under a gray sky, or white and black and golden, opaque in the long slant of the twilight. I knew those streams through fishing them, through cutting the weeds in them, through shooting ducks and snipe all along them, through setting night lines in them, through exploring them when the hatches were down and the water was very low. I carry them with me wherever I go and can fish them almost as well sitting here as I could were I walking the meadow grass along their banks six thousand miles from here.

I learned other waters almost as easily, though more superficially, when I was very young. The lower reaches of the Frome, between Wool and Wareham, where we used to fish for salmon, were harder to know than the best of the trout water because the river was deeper and darker and slower down there, more secret within itself. But I fished with a man who knew all the secrets, and we used the prawn a lot, fishing it deep down and slow, close to bottom and close under the banks. Fish lay where he said they should lie and took hold as he said they would take, and one remembered and fished it that way for oneself until the knowledge was properly one's own. I think I could still start at Bindon Mill and work on all the way down to the Salmon Water without missing so very many of the good places. And then, perhaps, I could walk back along the railroad track toward evening with a decent weight of salmon on my back.

I knew the little length of narrow carrier in Lewington's field by the bakery at Headbourne Worthy; it was so small and clear that one couldn't help knowing it and so difficult that one had to know it. I knew where each fish lay and why, how he would rise and when, what chance of ground would hide me during the cast, what tuft of grass would probably catch my fly on each attempted recovery. And Denis and I knew the narrow part of Avington Lake where the great pike lay under the shadow of the rank weeds; we knew the schools of roach and rudd and the few solitary trout; we had seen the big carp and the slow black tench; we knew, almost, where each little one- or two-pound pike had his hunting ground.

The winter days at Avington, under the tall bare beeches and ashes and sycamores, were very good. There were always mallard to be seen in hundreds, always herons, sometimes a peregrine falcon chasing the mallards; the cock pheasants were richer, burnished gold against the gold of fallen beech leaves, and rabbits sometimes rustled the leaves softly, unaware that we were fishing near them. The rank thick weed banks of the bottom showed clearly, green through the shallow water of the narrow part of the lake. We cast our big spoons and phantoms and wagtails far out, letting them into the unrippled water as gently as we could, then brought them twinkling back over the dark mystery of the weed beds. Sometimes a big pike was lying out over the weeds, and we tried and tried to tempt him. Sometimes one appeared suddenly behind the spoon, followed it and took or turned away. Sometimes—and this was the best and surest of all—there was a heavy flash and a swirl as the spoon passed over a known lie, then the pull and the lunging fight.

The first western river I learned was the Nimpkish, the seven twisting miles of it that lie between the lake and the sea. I learned the best of the trout pools first, wading the round and slippery rocks in an old pair of calked shoes, letting the swift water climb up to the pockets of my shirt and sometimes letting it knock me down and carry me half the length of a pool before I could find a way out of it. Then I learned the tyee pools and the cutthroat trout runs of the tidal reaches. Taking the canoe up to go over the traps, lining the big skiff through to the lake, fishing for steelhead, watching the salmon runs, I learned more of it and felt it my own. But I never really knew the river as one can know a river. I don't know, even today, just how and when the steelhead run there, nor more than a fraction of their lying places. And I never could solve the secrets of Ned's Canyon and Wright's Canyon or that third one of the long, slow, deep pools on the river; they were so big, and I knew so many other places to catch fish that it was hard to give them time. But I once wrote a book that had the Nimpkish for a heroine and I saw and learned so much of her for myself through five or six years that I feel my faulty knowledge has given me a full love of her. Whenever I think of a western fishing river, one typical of all the best things that western fishing can offer, I think of the Nimpkish; and I expect I always shall.

The Campbell I know almost as a man should know a river. I don't know the whole story, or anything like the whole story; but the outlines of plot and characterization are clear and definite, much of the detail is filled in and each new detail fits neatly into an appointed place as I learn it. The Campbell is a little like the Nimpkish, yet most unlike it. Both rivers are broad and clear and swift, with broken, white water, rare, smooth pools and rocky beds. But the Campbell runs only three or four miles to salt water from the foot of its great

Elk Falls, beyond which salmon and steelhead and cutthroat trout from the sea cannot pass. The Nimpkish is a highway to all the miles of Nimpkish Lake and the Kla-anche River and Woss Lake, to the Hustan River and the chain of lakes beyond that, and to all the tributary streams of the watershed. The Campbell draws to itself a noble run of winter steelhead, a run of fine cutthroats, a queer little run of small summer steelheads; it has its great tyees, its dying run of humpbacks, a fair run of cohos and dogs in some years, but no more than an occasional sockeye, probably a stray from some other parent stream. The Nimpkish has all the runs that the Campbell has in fullest strength and adds to them a fine run of true summer steelheads, a wonderful sockeye run and a fabulous dog-salmon run. The Campbell is the simpler river of the two, easier to know and understand for all those reasons. Nimpkish is more wonderful, more impressive, more beautiful; but Campbell—and not simply because I live within sight and sound of her—is the better of the two to love.

I can mark the months on the Campbell and tell myself, at least to my own satisfaction, what will be happening in the river during each one of them: In January the steelhead are running well; in February the cutthroats are spawning; in March and April the winter steelheads spawn; in May the little summer steelhead should be in the Island Pools, most of the humpback fry will already have found their way to the sea and the flying ants will hatch out; in August it is time to go to the Canyon Pool and look for the big cutthroats; in September the tyees are in the river; during October the cohos will come; in December the steelhead again. I know the May-fly and stone-fly nymphs that I will find under the rocks and the caddises that will crawl over the bottom in the different months; I know the rocks that the net-winged midges will blacken with their tiny cases, the places where the bright-green cladophora will grow richly, and where and when the rocks will be slippery with brown diatom growth. Some of these things, perhaps, are not important to know if one only wishes to catch fish; but they have their part in the pleasure of fishing.

I find I am quite often wrong about the Campbell even now. I may say that it is too early for the fish to be in, then go up and find them there. I can't always judge when the freshets are coming, but that, perhaps, is no more than saying I'm not an infallible weather prophet. Perhaps it is truer to say that I often find new things about the river than I am often wrong about her; and sometimes I suddenly realize things that I have known for quite a long time almost unconsciously. It is years, for instance, since I first knew that I could kill fish well in August with the fly I call the "Silver Brown." I tied the fly to imitate coho fry, which are the only numerous salmon fry in that month. In spring, when the river is full of many kinds of fry, the Silver Brown does not do so well for me, and I use the Silver Lady, which has a paler wing and a more complicated tying. I changed over with comparatively little thought, and the true inference of the change only came to me this year—trout may at times feed rather selectively on fry of different species.

Apart from bullheads and sticklebacks, one can expect some five or six different species of fry in the Campbell. Cutthroat fry and coho fry are so much alike that no sensible fish would bother to distinguish between them; it is reasonable to use the Silver Brown as an imitation of both. But humpback fry are like no other fry, trout, or salmon; they are, for instance, quite without parr marks, their bellies are brightest silver, their backs generally bluish. I remember that I have fished a fly with long blue hackles for wings and often killed well with it during the humpback run. From there it is only a step to the making of a special humpback imitation; I think I shall start with something of this sort: tail—green swan, body—flat silver tinsel, hackle—scarlet and quite small, wing—blue hackles, back to back, enclosing a white strip and perhaps a strand or two of blue herl, cheeks—pale-blue chatterer. When I fish the river again in spring-time, I shall use that fly.

If a coho-cutthroat imitation and a humpback imitation, why not imitations of the others in their days and seasons? The Silver Lady, perhaps, is sufficiently like spring salmon and steelhead fry. Yet the spring salmon fry has a light brown in his back and an impression of palest pink about him which the steelhead fry has not. It might make all the difference one day. So I shall build a fly with a tail of pink swan, a silver body and wings of barred summer duck enclosing yellow swan; and if that isn't good, I shall try grizzled hackles, preferably from a Plymouth cock with a touch of Red Game in him, set back to back with light-red hackles between them.

None of that is desperately important or highly significant, and I suppose I should feel ashamed of having waited ten or fifteen years to think of it. What I really feel is a good measure of gratitude to the Campbell for having at last brought home to me the rather obvious point that, if it is worth trying for exact imitation of sedges and May flies, it is worth trying for reasonably exact imitations of salmon and trout fry. In time I shall think of dressings for the green color that is dominant in the backs of dog-salmon fry and the olive-grass green of the young sockeye's back. I may catch very few more fish through my efforts than I should have caught without them, but it's going to be fun.

I fish the Campbell with a sense of ownership fully as strong as that of any legitimate owner of fishing rights in the world, not because I do own any part of the river, nor even because I should like to keep other people away from it; I should not care to do either of these things. The sense of ownership grows simply from knowing the river. I know the easiest ways along the banks and the best ways down to the pools. I know where to start in at a pool, where to look for the fish in it, how and where I can wade, what point I can reach with an easy cast, what lie I can barely cover with my strongest effort. This is comfortable and pleasant and might well begin to seem monotonous sooner or later were it not something of an illusion. I have a fair idea of what to expect from the river, and usually, because I fish it that way, the river gives me approximately what I expect of it. But sooner or later something always comes up to change the set of my ways. Perhaps one day, waiting for a friend to fish down a pool, I start in a little farther up than usual and immediately hook a fish where I had never been able to hook one before. A little more of the river becomes mine, alive and productive to me. Or perhaps I notice in some unusual slant of light what looks to be a glide of water along the edge of a rapid; I go down to it and work my fly through, and whether or not a fish comes to it, more of the river is known and mine.

For years I have promised myself to fish through the sort of half pool below the Sandy Pool. It starts almost opposite my own line fence and is little more than a smoothing off of the long rapid that runs right down to the Highway Bridge; but there are many big rocks in it and—I can say this now—some obvious holding water. I fished it twice this spring. On the first evening I caught two or three fair-sized cutthroats, and once a really good fish broke water at the fly. I went down earlier on the second evening. A three-pound cutthroat came to my first cast. There was a slow silver gleam as the fly came around on the second cast, a solid heavy pull and the 2X gut was broken. I put up heavier gut and hooked a clean steelhead that ran me almost to the end of the backing. I hooked two others along the pool that evening, both of them too close to their spawning; but the pool is the Line Fence Pool now, something so close to home and so obvious that I took ten years to learn about it, a discovery as well worth while as any I have ever made.

One discovers other things than new pools and new fish lies in old pools. One learns to mark one's casts by such things as the kidney stones and the flat rock in General Money's Pool in the Stamp, one learns to hope for the sight of a pileated woodpecker crossing the river in swooping flight at this place, a flock of mergansers at that place, a dipper against black rocks and rippled water somewhere else, deer coming down to eat the moss on the rocks at the water's edge in hard weather. All these things are precious in repetition and, repeated or no, they build the river for one. They are part of the background of knowing and loving it, as is every fish hooked, every cast fished through, every rock trodden. And men and women come strongly into it. Here, I can remind myself, was where Ann sat that first day we came up the river together, and here it was that she loved the September sun the year before Valerie was born. Here we stopped and Letcher made us an old-fashioned before we went on to the Canyon Pool that day. Here Buckie brought his first fish to the bank, here I gaffed Sandy's first steelhead for him, here Tommy hooked one last winter, there it was that the big fish took Reg's line across the roots of the cedar tree. . . .

I still don't know why I fish or why other men fish, except that we like it and it makes us think and feel. But I do know that if it were not for the strong, quick life of rivers, for their sparkle in the sunshine, for the cold grayness of them under rain and the feel of them about my legs as I set my feet hard down on rocks or sand or gravel, I should fish less often. A river is never quite silent; it can never, of its very nature, be quite still; it is never quite the same from one day to the next. It has its own life and its own beauty, and the creatures it nourishes are alive and beautiful also. Perhaps fishing is, for me, only an excuse to be near rivers. If so, I'm glad I thought of it.